THE WRATH TO COME

SARAH CHURCHWELL is Professorial Fellow in American Literature and Chair of Public Understanding of the Humanities at the School of Advanced Study, University of London. An American living in London, she is the author of *Behold, America: A History of America First and the American Dream*, *Careless People: Murder, Mayhem and The Invention of The Great Gatsby*, and *The Many Lives of Marilyn Monroe*. Her journalism has been published widely, including in the *New York Review of Books*, *Guardian*, *New Statesman* and *Financial Times*, and she contributes frequently to broadcast media on both sides of the Atlantic. She was co-winner of the 2015 Eccles British Library Writer's Award and longlisted for the 2021 Orwell Prize for Journalism.

Also by Sarah Churchwell

*Behold America: A History of America First
and the American Dream*

*Careless People: Murder, Mayhem
and the Invention of The Great Gatsby*

The Many Lives of Marilyn Monroe

SARAH CHURCHWELL

THE WRATH TO COME

GONE WITH THE WIND AND THE LIES AMERICA TELLS

HEAD
of ZEUS

An Apollo Book

Head of Zeus Ltd
First Floor East
5–8 Hardwick Street
London EC1R 4RG

WWW.HEADOFZEUS.COM

To WJA _____

Contents

'It is terrible to watch people cling to their captivity and insist on their own destruction. I think black people have always felt this about America, and Americans, and have always seen, spinning above the thoughtless American head, the shape of the wrath to come.'

James Baldwin, *No Name in the Street*[1]

Prologue

On 6 January 2021, as the rancorous presidency of Donald Trump came to an anarchic end, the Confederate Battle Flag flew in the United States Capitol for the first time in American history.

It was also the first time an American election loss was greeted with utter pandemonium. Many of those watching would have expected a cold day in hell to come first, but it was just a cold day in 2021.

A mob of around 9,000 people had journeyed to Washington, DC from around the country to support Trump as he repeated the lie that he had won the 2020 election. As they gathered to defy Trump's defeat (confirmed by multiple state and federal courts, state legislatures, and independent election watchers), they shouted, 'Stop the Steal.' Inflamed by speeches telling them what they already believed, they charged the Capitol building, where lawmakers had gathered to certify the fact that Trump had lost.

What appeared at the time to be Trump's last-ditch effort (until he dug further ditches) to stop Biden's election came at a 'Save America' rally, held as Congress was voting to certify Biden's win on 6 January 2021. Describing his loss as 'a comprehensive assault on our democracy', Trump told the crowd: 'We fight. We fight like hell and if you don't fight like hell you're not going to have a country anymore.' He also informed his overwhelmingly white crowd, 'You are allowed to go by very different rules'.[1]

Inflamed by his lies, exceptionalism, and thinly veiled white nationalism, they charged the Capitol. Waving flags with Trump's name, they chanted 'Hang Mike Pence!' and demanded that the Capitol police reveal Speaker Nancy Pelosi's whereabouts. 'Execute the traitors!' one man shouted through a megaphone, 'I want to see executions!'[2] They raised effigies with the word 'traitor' emblazoned on their chests, carried truncheons, nooses and zip ties, and had concealed guns and pipe bombs nearby. They sent social media messages telling each other that Congress 'members are in the tunnels under capital seal them in. Turn on gas'.[3] They built makeshift gallows with a dangling noose on the Mall.

Rioters swarmed up the sides of the Capitol building, dangling from balustrades and windowsills as if it were a medieval siege, rather than electoral politics in one of the world's most developed democracies. They attacked police officers who tried to preserve order, some of whom later died, one of whom demanded to know what the fuck they thought they were doing. They used flagpoles wrapped in the stars and stripes as weapons to bash through windows and doors, shouting violent bullhorned threats against American politicians. They smashed and grabbed, screaming their intention to seize the government by force. There were reports that they smeared the hallways of the Capitol with shit.[4]

One of them, wearing a cowboy hat and holding aloft a Confederate flag, clambered onto the memorial to Ulysses S. Grant, who led the Union forces during the American Civil War before becoming the nation's eighteenth president. Grant's army defeated the white supremacist slavocracy that was the Confederate States of America, holding the nation together by sheer force as it moved painfully, with great reluctance, toward the eradication of the slave economy. On 6 January, the insurrectionist perched astride a bronze charger, grinning, as he waved the Southern Cross. It was a windy day, and videos caught the sound of the Confederate flag whipping hard over the head of the great Union general, an eerie, dark portent of battle, as if the moral victory Grant had won was suddenly, shockingly, obliterated.

Many who fly the Confederate flag today insist it has been rehabilitated, having shrugged off its unfortunate origins as the actual standard for human enslavement, and has evolved into an inoffensive symbol of Southern heritage and culture. But symbols are not changed so easily. The Southern Cross was created to signal offence: it was the battle flag Confederates flew as they charged into war, ready to die to preserve what they called 'African slavery'; eventually it was adopted as the favourite flag of Confederate memory.[5] A good clue that the Southern Cross hasn't become innocent is that it keeps emerging in the context of violent white nationalism.

When it was created in 1861, the flag's originators dreamed of its red-backed, white-starred diagonal blue cross inspiring white supremacists until it flew from the nation's Capitol. They never achieved that dream.

The South had seceded from the United States in armed revolt against the idea that the federal government might (someday) unilaterally outlaw slavery in the so-called land of the free. The North fought for five bloody years to hold the Union together, to create a country that was not, as Abraham Lincoln famously said, half-slave and half-free. An estimated 600,000 Americans and more died on the battlefields of that war, from the green farmlands of Pennsylvania to the red clay of Georgia. Abraham Lincoln had his head blown off by John Wilkes Booth, a white supremacist actor who shouted *sic semper tyrannis* as he fired – 'thus always to tyrants', calling Lincoln a tyrant for ending the legal entitlements of some people to enslave other people. It was not the last time an American president would be accused of tyranny for thwarting American citizens in the exercise of their will to power.

3

Booth and his co-conspirators were executed for their crimes. Confederate leaders were jailed (briefly), barred (temporarily) from holding further political office, and gradually died off, believing they had failed. They were fighting to preserve human bondage: they should have failed.

But exactly 160 years after it was created, the Southern Cross was paraded through the corridors of American government. It was unfurled over the marble steps of the Capitol and hung from the balcony. It bobbed amid a sea of other flags in the Rotunda; a man in combat fatigues and a red Trump hat shouldered it as he stood on a balustrade. But the most widely circulated image was of an insurrectionist who casually strolled with the Southern Cross outside the Senate Chamber, beneath the nose of the fierce abolitionist Charles Sumner, who adamantly opposed slavery and was nearly beaten to death on the floor of the Senate by a South Carolina slavocrat.

To anyone who knows the history – the real history – of what that flag meant, who these people were and what they fought for, it was a terrible, sickening sight. But as America has spent the last century and a half trying to obliterate that real history, only a tiny minority fully grasped the reckoning at hand.

Instead, as lawmakers cowered in fear from the rampaging mob, the world watched in mostly uncomprehending horror, wondering what had happened to America.

*

What has happened to America?

As an American who lives abroad and writes about modern American culture and history, I have been asked this question many times since 2016, when the election of a property developer turned reality television star, who was bankrupt morally and probably fiscally, dumbfounded most of the watching world. Was this choice to elevate a braggart and blowhard of staggering ignorance provoked by economic anxiety, people wondered, or racial animus? Was it the culture wars, or the reverberations of the collapsing neoliberal market order in 2008? Was it the proof of a new populist politics, an organic expression of nationalist identity in the wake of globalization? Was it the death clutch of the old order, the last gasp of white male oligarchy – or the tightening of its grip?

During Trump's administration, the world kept watching as self-proclaimed white nationalists churned violence across the United States, slaughtering peaceful people gathered in churches and synagogues and shopping malls and nail spas and night clubs and movie theatres. They targeted African Americans, Jewish Americans, Asian Americans, gay Americans. Some waved the Confederate flag as they planned their rampages; others expressed their hatred of the groups they targeted in words as explicit as their violence. Most of these killers had a history of violence against women. But when they were arrested, they were treated gently by white police officers, who stopped and bought one mass murderer a hamburger from Burger King on the way to the police station. They were defended, excused, rationalized. Meanwhile police officers on the same forces were murdering unarmed Black American citizens day after day after day – Black people who were routinely criminalized in the same media accounts that so relentlessly normalized white nationalist killers.

This had not started with the inauguration of Donald Trump – far from it. But from the day in August 2017 when Trump responded to a far-right rally in Charlottesville against the removal of a statue of Robert E. Lee by calling the neo-Nazis and white supremacists who were shouting blood-and-soil slogans 'very fine people', licence had been given to Americans who were nursing rage. They heard the call, and unleashed it.

What is happening to America? The questions intensified as squadrons of militarized police aimed guns at suburban mothers wearing Black Lives Matter T-shirts in the streets of Portland, Oregon during the outbreaks of violence after the filmed murder of George Floyd further shocked the world in the summer of 2020. As far-right militias occupied the government buildings of the state of Michigan and plotted to abduct the governor for being more liberal and female than they were, the questions got louder.

When Trump mustered a private militia and prepared to deploy it against the nation's citizens; as he threatened liberal cities with occupation in the run-up to an election; when he said he wouldn't promise to concede if he lost that election, and began firing the nation's top legal and military officials in search of people whose loyalty to him, or his party, superseded their loyalty to American democracy: these stopped being questions, and started looking like answers.

After the 2020 election, when Trump did just as he'd said he would and refused to concede, the world kept trying to understand. Tensions mounted while America's much-vaunted democratic checks and balances were stretched to breaking point during his protracted, embattled, and fraudulent campaign to challenge the results of the election he lost.

And then came the events of 6 January 2021, and the sacking of the US Capitol. The insurrectionists failed, but most of the Republican leadership refused to repudiate their efforts. Several had actively incited the insurrection; the rest, with only two or three exceptions, turned a blind eye, excused, or flatly denied it. Some observers concluded that the country had been tested, but its safeguards had held. Others argued the guardrails were collapsing before our eyes, and predicted that at America's next national elections, the midterms in 2022 and the presidential contest of 2024, they are likely to give way all together, as the country moves from outright, legalized voter suppression to state legislatures that are creating the conditions for overturning election results they oppose.

*

What the hell happened to America?

There are many ways of answering that question. One is that when a nation's myths no longer make sense of its reality, violence erupts. That is one of the many things that has happened to America, and it's the subject of this book.

As someone who studies American mythologies, I have also been trying to make sense of what is happening to my country. Mythmaking and misinformation have been spinning wildly through American political discourse, but they can be hard to capture as they float, disembodied, across our conversations. We don't have many Homers and Ovids anymore, locating our epic myths about ourselves in one handy place.

But eventually I realized I was just looking in the wrong direction – and that misdirection is part of what mythmaking does. Like a carnival magician, mythmaking points at something with its right hand while picking our pockets with its left. If we stop looking where it's pointing, we might just manage to protect our valuables – in this case, a republic if we can keep it, as Ben Franklin said.[6] (Franklin also warned America that although 'the first man put at the helm will be a good one', because it was going to be George Washington, 'nobody knows what sort may come afterwards'.[7])

Looking at what the story doesn't want us to see reveals its magician's tricks, its mythic elements. These always include the tragic failure of hubris, the pride going before any epic fall. If we don't understand the myth, we will never understand what is happening in America today, and we will never keep our democracy.

So this book goes to the source. Because it turns out that the heart of the myth, as well as its mind and its nervous system, most of its arguments and beliefs, its loves and hates, its lies and confusions and defence mechanisms and wish fulfilments, are all captured (for the most part inadvertently) in America's most famous epic romance: *Gone with the Wind*.

Gone with the Wind provides a kind of skeleton key, unlocking America's illusions about itself. When we understand the dark truths of American experience that have been veiled by one of the nation's favourite fantasies, we can see how the country travelled from the start of the Civil War in 1861 to parading the flag of the side that lost that war through the US Capitol in 2021. That journey was erratic and unpremeditated, but America ended up there all the same.

When we know the full history, we know what happened to America.

*

Margaret Mitchell always said she wrote it backwards. In the final scene of *Gone with the Wind,* Rhett Butler walks out on Scarlett O'Hara, declaring he no longer gives a damn where she goes or what she does. This ending gave the idea with which Mitchell started; the rest unspooled retrospectively, to make sense of that outcome. What is probably the most famous love story of the twentieth century thus ends not (like most love stories) on reconciliation, but on rupture.

Gone with the Wind is not merely a romance between Rhett and Scarlett, however. It is also the world's most popular romance with the American Civil War and its aftermath. Its version of American history, known in shorthand as the Lost Cause, was also written backwards to account for a break-up.

A mythical version of Southern history, the Lost Cause claims that the Confederacy fought the Civil War (1861–65) as a principled defence of a noble civilization (the Old South) and its democratic rights, rather than as an unprincipled defence of the white supremacist system of chattel slavery. An information war followed the Civil War, during the period of Reconstruction (1865–77): what became known as the Lost Cause was pure propaganda, a self-justifying counterfactual history circulated by Confederate leaders and their legal and spiritual heirs. Claiming that defeat 'was but apparent', the Lost Cause encouraged Americans to reject the apparent, to deny the moral and political realities of the war they had just fought and the society it helped engender.[8]

When Scarlett loses her battle to keep Rhett, she also rejects reality, announcing her intention to carry on without learning any lessons at all. She doesn't ask herself what she has done wrong, what she might do better, how she and Rhett might forge a new path together. Instead, she declares her determination to maintain the same 'insane obstinacy' he's just informed her is driving him away. 'She could get Rhett back. She knew she could. There had never been a man she couldn't get, once she set her mind upon him.'[9] Defeat was but apparent.

The myth of the Lost Cause was predicated on two staggeringly shameless denials about chattel slavery: that the Civil War was caused by it, and that there was anything wrong with it. Southerners said it was a war fought over Northern aggression, illegitimate federal expansion, and states' rights. The specific rights in question were individual states' rights to keep and trade enslaved people, but the Lost Cause skipped that part, insisting secession was caused by anything except the horrors of plantation slavery.

By 1900, the idea of the Lost Cause had hardened into an article of faith for most Southerners, and was accepted by the white North in the interests of reconciliation – moving on after the divisiveness of the war to reunify the nation. That reconciliation was secured by a shared national popular culture, even as the racial hierarchies of slavery were simply transposed as nearly as possible into Jim Crow segregation, with its systems of sharecropping, debt peonage, mass incarceration, summary violence, and voter disfranchisement. Most of these systems, too, were absorbed by the North. National mythologies began to develop about the Civil War that flattered the South and abused the North, because, as the historian W. E. B. Du Bois trenchantly put it, the South was determined to rewrite the history of slavery, and the North was not interested in history but in wealth.

The South was also interested in wealth, of course: chattel slavery was above all a racial economy. When that form of it was dismantled, they rebuilt it in the shape of Jim Crow. Just as Scarlett O'Hara would find some way, any way, to get the man she wanted, so would America find some way, any way, to keep the systems of white wealth in place. This story connects the dots between the Civil War era of the 1860s that *Gone with the Wind* chronicles, the interwar era of the 1930s into which it exploded, and the United States today.

In the wake of the 2020 US election, when Trump refused to concede, he also claimed that his defeat was but apparent. Suddenly, the Lost Cause came roaring back into America's political story, a point made by many historians and commentators. *Gone with the Wind* came along with it, as a kind of fictional afterthought, a shorthand for explaining to readers unfamiliar with the Lost Cause what it means: 'You know, the world of *Gone with the Wind.*'

But these stories used *Gone with the Wind* only gesturally, to help describe the basics of the Lost Cause myth. *Gone with the Wind* has a great deal more to teach us about how American mythmaking works, however: it shows how turning wish fulfilment into popular stories helped create the conditions that could bring the United States to the point of an insurrection on 6 January 2021.

Individually, many of these factors, including the rise of the modern American right under Donald Trump, are well re-searched, while slavery and the Civil War are easily the most dominant topics in American history today. The Jim Crow era of the 1930s is also widely studied, although the native fascism of the interwar period was almost entirely neglected until the Trump administration brought it alarmingly back into view. The truth about the Civil War and its aftermath is not the only truth that American history long suppressed: we also tried, with even more success, to erase the histories of American fascism. This book brings all these histories together in one place and weighs them against some of our most popular national myths, to try to make sense of what has appeared so senseless.

Whether the word fascism accurately describes what is happening in America today has been fiercely debated. Finding the right word matters, but it matters less than admitting the family resemblance: autocrats and authoritarians suggest only power is at stake; kleptocrats are in it for the money; oligarchs and monarchists are classists who support the monied elite; white nationalists believe in a racist-defined state. For many, 'fascist' was a bridge too far to describe Trump, a word they reserved for Hitler and his followers. Some might reserve it instead for Mussolini, who after all invented the modern meaning of the term, and whose fascism was distinct in important ways from Nazism (it did not institutionalize anti-Semitic genocide, for starters, although it did pursue racial genocide in Ethiopia). In fact, fascism was not unique to Europe during the interwar period, as we shall see. Nor are such labels mutually exclusive: in the end, they name different ways of construing power. The best answer to the question of which description best fits Trumpism is 'whatever works', or 'all of the above'.

Whatever we call these ruthless forces, their dark anti-democratic heart is the same: small groups of people prepared to impose their beliefs by force, and immolate the rest of the human race on the altar of their own power. In the 1930s, when *Gone with the Wind* appeared, they called these antidemocratic forces fascism, and so that's mostly what they will be called here.

The American political and cultural situation in the early decades of the twenty-first century has come as an enormous shock to people around the world largely because America has successfully mystified so much of its history. The past has consequences in the present regardless of whether we know what happened in it; learning the history makes those consequences intelligible. *Gone with the Wind* is history as sleight of hand: it urges us to look away (look away!) from what really happened, using mythmaking and romance as techniques of distraction. And so we must refuse to look where it points and turn our attention to what it would keep us from noticing: the enduring results of an economy built on human property.

Anyone who's even heard of *Gone with the Wind* knows that its depiction of slavery is inaccurate, and its portraits of Black characters are racist. But the scale of its distortions of American history is vastly underestimated, even by people broadly familiar with that history. That mythmaking remains so serviceable, so gratifying, to globally popular ideas about America that it continues to shape the world's understanding of United States history to a gratuitous degree.

The cultural script must be judged against the historical reality, in all its (often malign) complexity, to be adequately understood, which means going far beyond recognizing that Mammy is a minstrel caricature, or that Black people were not, as *Gone with the Wind* fatuously claims, 'far better off under slavery than they were now under freedom'. As early as 1811, a Southern historian acknowledged that because Black people 'could not be supposed to be content in slavery', they would naturally make even the 'most desperate attempts which promised freedom'.[10] By the late 1930s that obvious truth had been so shamelessly denied that a story celebrating the contented cheer of enslavement (for some people), while swearing fierce vengeance against any limitations on freedom (for other people), was embraced the world over.

The 1811 historian who knew that enslavement would make anyone desperate for freedom was writing about the state of Georgia, where all the action of *Gone with the Wind* takes place, and where Margaret Mitchell lived all her life. Georgia also played a pivotal role in the 2020 election – which is not a coincidence. Nothing in this story is a coincidence, because it offers a genealogy of how mythmaking helped get us where we are, unravelling consequences back to at least some of their origins.

Because Lost Cause history is predicated on denial, facts are needed to chart the extent of those denials. But how that denial *works* – the emotional, psychological, and political effects on the people who believe its denials – is captured better in popular stories than in documentary history. *Gone with the Wind* offers as complete a record of one key version of mythical American popular memory as one could hope to find. Romance gives cover to political mythmaking: *Gone with the Wind* is romantic propaganda, peddling a worldview, and peddling it hard. Therefore we need to understand both, how fact and fiction work together. This book pits the popular story against the documentary facts, because only in their conflict can we begin to apprehend the contradictory, dissonant American experience that together they created.

The problem goes beyond the falsification of history. Millions of Americans have, for more than a century, formed real beliefs and deep convictions around that fabricated history. When such convictions are challenged, whether by other beliefs, or by the obdurate limits of reality – when stories are no longer sufficient to reconcile severe cognitive dissonance – violence enflames. That's where America is today.

A master plot has emerged to justify and sustain the violence of modern American politics, taking us from military civil war then, to our uncivil culture wars today. That plot is imprinted in *Gone with the Wind*, which records the creation myth of white victimhood in America.

*

Like many Americans of my generation, most of what I knew about the Civil War as a child I first gleaned from *Gone with the Wind*. It premiered on network television in 1977, when I was just old enough to watch it, several years before I was reading even children's books about the war. Its world soon became part of my imaginative inheritance: its charismatic stars, its lurid

Technicolor glories, the flaming skies and lush, romantic music, the elaborate dresses, the sweep of its emotions, from humour to romance to grievous loss to the vast carnage of war, the excitement of Atlanta burning, the terror of Scarlett's flight home to Tara, and the galvanizing energy of her refusal to accept defeat.

When I was older, I read the novel, and found Scarlett's stupidity irritating – Vivien Leigh brought her to life with an intelligence that Mitchell specifically denies her. Although the Scarlett of the novel is shrewd about business, she has the emotional intelligence of a gnat, and her inability to figure out that Rhett is in love with her, and she with him, was exasperating even to a fifteen-year-old.

I also believed that the story's portrayal of the Civil War and its aftermath was basically accurate, that Mitchell's characters were fictional but that they lived, loved, and struggled against a realistic historical background. It turns out Margaret Mitchell believed that, too. But in fact *Gone with the Wind* is not merely (or arbitrarily) inaccurate: it precisely and compulsively inverts historical actuality.

By the time I read it I was old enough to reject some of its more asinine ideas, not least that the enslaved were contented under slavery because Black people don't know any better. The novel's racism is much more extreme than the film's – which is saying something. The film mitigated the novel's racism in various ways, as we shall see, which included casting skilled Black actors who could humanize Mitchell's one-dimensional caricatures. This book isn't about catching racism out, however. Instead, it tries to think harder about what debates about racism can sometimes obscure, which is how racism works, and what it's for.

It took me longer to recognize how many other aspects of American history *Gone with the Wind* encourages us to disregard. We could start with the fact that the protagonists of the most popular American story of the twentieth century burn with hatred for the United States, and despise its government.

Although there is not a direct line of descent from this loathing of American government to the twenty-first-century Trumpian politics that sought to dismantle it a century later, they certainly grew on the same family tree.

Even more fundamentally, it's a globally influential tale about the American Civil War that manages to miss the entire point of that war. The simple fact, explicitly stated by the story on multiple occasions, is that Scarlett O'Hara and Rhett Butler are both homicidal white supremacists with profoundly fascistic worldviews. It's a thousand-page novel about enslavers busily pretending that slavery doesn't matter — which is pretty much the story of American history.

Part of what kept me from recognising this for so long was my assumption that the story's racism belonged to the past – that although slavery had been terrible, it was long gone, and Americans could congratulate ourselves on our moral progress. The story's racism seemed so obsolete as to be ludicrous, the legacy of a brutal system that my (virtuous) side of the country had fought a war to extinguish, which we had repudiated and largely overcome thanks to the efforts of the civil rights movement and its great leaders like Dr Martin Luther King, Jr.

The United States decided to honour Dr King with a national holiday around the time I was first encountering *Gone with the Wind*, before I understood that this was a way for white America to pretend that paying lip service to King's legacy would suffice, and save us the hard work of actually living up to it. Forty years later, in 2021, the United States declared Juneteenth, originally an African American folk celebration of emancipation, a national holiday, even as many Southern school boards were mandating that the history of slavery cannot be described accurately in textbooks. We still tell ourselves that lip service can be enough.

In the meantime came the sequential elections of Barack Obama, Donald Trump and Joseph Biden, and the defeat of Hillary Clinton, along with all the political and social turmoil that accompanied them. As debates mounted about white women and Black voters, Confederate monuments and white supremacism, so, too, did the death toll from the violence of white terrorists and police officers, and the resulting protests and riots. It became ever clearer to me that *Gone with the Wind* explained far more of what was happening – albeit mostly backwards – than most people seemed to recognize.

When the US Capitol insurrection elevated Lost Cause history back into clear view, it confirmed my sense that *Gone with the Wind* is the story we need to think harder about – not despite its flaws, but because of them. The explosion of racism in the United States around these elections was a phenomenon for which I, like so many white Americans, was frankly unprepared. I had never believed for a moment that Obama's presidency would usher in a post-racial America, and I publicly argued against that fantasy. But the scale of the backlash, the vitriol of it, the explicitness of it, still came as a shock, as did the degree to which racial progress in America is consistently met with an ever-deeper retrenchment of the myth of white victimhood. *Gone with the Wind* had been explaining it to me for decades. I just hadn't paid attention.

It turns out that disregarding was the point. That was what my society had trained me to do – disregard the misogyny in classic literature and read it for its great human wisdom (Saul Bellow, for example, won the Nobel Prize for his 'humanism', despite being an unadulterated jackass about half the human race). And don't worry about the racism in *Gone with the Wind*; it's a historical relic, nothing to do with life in America now. But such wilful blindness has everything to do with life in America now.

When we examine it closely, the wilfulness comes through: the need to deny what we do not want to see. Negations and disavowals work like Freudian slips, as what has been suppressed emerges by being actively repudiated. 'I don't know what that dream was about, but it wasn't about my father' means you were dreaming about your father, but you don't want to admit it. *Gone with the Wind* is riddled with negation: it keeps revealing what America is dreaming about but actively doesn't want to know. When a country becomes so lost in dreams of itself that it can no longer see reality, it loses its moral sanity.

As Toni Morrison observed thirty years ago, the issue in American life was never merely that Black people had a particular skin colour, but 'that this color "meant" something' – legally and politically, but also psychologically and symbolically.[11] The interpretation of race is at the heart of the American experience. Once we understand not *what* race means, but *that* race means, interpretation becomes not a choice, but an imperative. And it means we cannot foreclose that conversation – which is why I believe that returning to *Gone with the Wind* can take us somewhere new. And it is why I do not believe that we should 'cancel' *Gone with the Wind*, censor it, or cast it on the ash heaps. Far more meaning is to be found in thinking about what its story makes possible, what it helped imagine into existence – and what it tried to obliterate. It is a story that offers, among many other pleasures, a way of not thinking about justice.

Gone with the Wind marks a cultural breakdown, the point where mythology triumphed over history. It helped derail our understanding of America's past, and urging the erasure of *Gone with the Wind* would simply reinforce that failure, even as the American right is currently engaged in a mighty effort to create another fraudulent history around its new lost cause.

This book follows American history back down into the myth, to excavate what's been buried – not just the facts that historians have long been carefully bringing to light (and upon whose vast scholarship this book depends), but also suppressed psycho-political realities. The lies, the distortions, the justifications, the half-truths, the rampant projections, the cognitive dissonances, the negations, the flat denials – all the stinging truths Americans don't want to admit about ourselves that *Gone with the Wind* caught like flypaper.

The many slips of the tongue in *Gone with the Wind* would matter far less if they were just one writer's unconscious associations. But they were taken up by audiences at a mass scale. It is because the story remains so phenomenally popular that these slips become significant – because they mark losses of control not only in Mitchell's individual narrative, but in the American master narrative it captures so fully. *Gone with the Wind* shows what white America has believed – and wanted to believe – about its own history; it curates and cultivates America's great white myths about itself.

James Baldwin shouted the truth at us half a century ago: 'White man, hear me! History, as nearly no one seems to know, is not merely something to be read. And it does not refer merely, or even principally, to the past. On the contrary, the great force of history comes from the fact that we carry it within us, are unconsciously controlled by it in many ways, and history is literally *present* in all that we do.'[12] It was in an essay called 'The White Man's Guilt', part of Baldwin's long, frustrating project to try to persuade America to face the dark realities of its history and the legacies of enslavement and segregation. *Gone with the Wind* captures that great force of history we carry within us: history is *present* in all it does – controlling it, but unconsciously.

There is a reckoning in the distance, rolling ever nearer – the reckoning of which Baldwin and others have been warning America for a century and more. It is past time for us to confront what Baldwin said Black Americans have 'always seen, spinning above the thoughtless American head, the shape of the wrath to come.'[13]

This book is part of my effort to look up and see what was always there, spinning above my thoughtless American head.

A Note on Language and Violence

merica's most notorious racial slur occurs throughout the history this book relates. The issue of whether to quote this word in a work of historical nonfiction is complex, as the history recounted here concerns the consequences of sanitizing brutal realities. It is also about the power of language and storytelling, and the ways in which a logic of exceptionalism can unravel our own moral and political positions. Racist abuse, in all its vicious casualness, was never an exception in American life – it was the rule, and it reflected a commonplace reality of hate and violence that needs to be recognized in full.

There is also a history of debates over the redaction of the word, as we shall see. It matters that in the 1930s a wealthy white Atlantan like Margaret Mitchell repeatedly used the full word over one hundred times in the novel, and then angrily defended her right to do so, even as the film's producers were negotiating with the NAACP and their own Black cast about whether they could (or should) say the word on film. They were also negotiating with Hollywood's censorship bureau, whose production rules, known as the Hays Code, determined from the 1930s to the 1960s what would and would not appear in American film. Meanwhile some, but not all, Black American writers were objecting to the use of the word, redacting the term when they used it themselves in print, whether typographically (with asterisks or dashes) or euphemistically ('the n-word' was already in use as a phrase). But many of them also printed the word in full – a choice that seems, in an important sense, worth respecting.

Most of the import of that debate would be lost if Mitchell and her contemporaries' use of the full word were invisibly redacted on their behalf. Moreover, our standard redactions and euphemisms were also used at that time, so that employing them now would confuse how and to what degree Black audiences then were rebuking or resisting the word's use. The forms that hate took is the point; so is the forms taken by resistance to hate. American cultural discourse is highly coded – if not 'exceptionally' so – in part because its self-deceptions have required a substitute language that can deflect attention from its lies. Codes are linguistic veils, there to keep everything safe, to stop us from seeing the violence behind the screen of words.

Printing the word where it is fully spelled out in source documents, however, would put me in the same position as Margaret Mitchell, a white woman defending her use of the term in the name of historical accuracy, ignoring the many voices insisting that the word continues to do real harm. The best people to judge whether something is harmful are those who are most vulnerable to it. Eliminating the word at a minimum removes a major obstacle from people's ability, or willingness, to encounter a book today in which some version of racial invective needs to appear in the historical realities it is discussing.

Therefore: where the word was historically redacted, this book reproduces that redaction exactly, whether with asterisks, dashes, euphemism, or in some other form. Where it was spelled in full, I substitute the word 'nxxxxr' to indicate that the entire word appears in the original source, using 'x's to imply a strikethrough, so that the word might register, but in abeyance. In the authorial language of this book, it is referred to generically as the racial slur, insult, or invective. There are other racially offensive words that do appear in full in quotations, so that some of the historical casual racism comes through. This decision was reached after consultation with several readers, including African Americans with different areas of expertise and perspectives. I hope that the choices in this book honour those conversations.

There is also an important discussion about how best to render racial identities within the history of enslavement. Language is fluid and these uses are changing, but there are obvious reasons for rejecting the language of the enslaver, which used words to naturalize the relationship of 'master' to 'slave', so that the word 'slaveowner', for example, implicitly affirms the claim of ownership. Increasingly the custom is to use 'enslaved' and 'enslaver', which is the standard formulation here.

The dehumanization of the enslaved included the stripping of African tribal, ethnic or national identities that people with European heritage can claim, identities that are customarily capitalized. This is one reason for arguing that Black should be capitalized whereas white should not (as it can be differentiated with capitalized national and ethnic identities). When the *New York Times* adopted the standard capitalization of Black in 2020, following the murder of George Floyd, it explained its reasons including a pithy quotation from its national editor: 'It seems like such a minor change, black versus Black,' the editor said. 'But for many people the capitalization of that one letter is the difference between a color and a culture.'[1] And so in this book Black is capitalized and white is not, but ethnic and national identities associated with whiteness, such as Irish–American, are capitalized in the customary way. The spelling in quotations has not been altered.

Finally, there is significantly graphic violence in the history that follows. The ways in which that savagery has been sanitized by American historiography is again part of the point. The violence of the historical record has thus not been alleviated in the language of this book; such language is only ever quoted from primary documents but has not been redacted. There is also one photograph of a lynching victim, because the obscenity of this practice can only be apprehended visually.[2] Readers should understand that some of what follows depicts physical atrocities in detail and be prepared for its gravity. These examples are here to demonstrate the range, and depth, of the brutality that has shaped American history; they are, sadly, all too typical.

Historical Timeline

1861	The Civil War begins.
1863	The Emancipation Proclamation frees enslaved people in the United States, but only in areas still in open rebellion.
1865	Robert E. Lee surrenders to Ulysses S. Grant at Appomattox, ending the Civil War.
1865	Lincoln is assassinated by white supremacist John Wilkes Booth. Andrew Johnson becomes president.
1865	The Thirteenth Amendment is ratified, formally abolishing slavery.
1865	The first Black Codes are passed in the South, restricting the rights of newly freed African Americans.
1866	The Civil Rights Act of 1866 confers citizenship upon African Americans.
1866	The Ku Klux Klan is founded in Pulaski, Tennessee.
1868	President Johnson is impeached, partly because of his pardoning of former Confederates. He avoids conviction and removal from office by one Senate vote.
1868	The Fourteenth Amendment is ratified, guaranteeing birthright citizenship, due process, and equal rights under the law to all Americans.
1869	Tennessee and Georgia 'redeem' their local governments from multiracial representatives and begin restoring white supremacist rule.
1870	The Fifteenth Amendment is ratified, extending the franchise to all American men regardless of race, colour,

or previous condition of servitude. It explicitly excludes women.

1870   North Carolina and Virginia vote in 'redeemer' white supremacist state governments.

1870   Congress passes the first Enforcement Act to enforce the Reconstruction amendments and protect the rights of African Americans.

187   The Ku Klux Klan Act gives federal government the right and duty to oversee elections and to enforce civil and electoral rights.

1871–3   The Klan is effectively eradicated, and many of its leaders jailed.

1873–4   The White League attempts several armed rebellions to overthrow the elected Republican state government of Louisiana.

1876   Republicans challenge the validity of election results in the South.

1877   The Compromise of 1877 makes Republican Rutherford B. Hayes president in exchange for withdrawing federal troops from the South and ending Reconstruction.

1881   The first Jim Crow segregation laws are passed.

1896   The Supreme Court issues the doctrine of 'separate but equal' in *Plessy* v. *Ferguson*, legalizing Jim Crow segregation for the next sixty years.

1899   Sam Hose is lynched about forty miles from Atlanta, Georgia.

1900   Margaret Mitchell is born in Atlanta, Georgia.

1905   Thomas Dixon, Jr publishes *The Clansman*, popularizing legends about the first Ku Klux Klan.

1915   *The Birth of a Nation*, the first full-length narrative feature film, is adapted from *The Clansman* and becomes the most popular silent movie of all time.

1915   Leo Frank is abducted from an Atlanta jail and lynched in Marietta, Georgia.

1915   The Ku Klux Klan is declared reborn outside of Atlanta,

Georgia. The second Klan flourishes across the United States for the next decade.

1918   Mary Turner and at least twelve others are lynched in southern Georgia.

1922   Mussolini's fascists take power in Italy.

1926   Margaret Mitchell begins *Gone with the Wind* in Atlanta, Georgia.

1929   Martin Luther King, Jr is born in Atlanta, Georgia.

1933   Hitler becomes German Chancellor.

1935   Germany passes the Nuremberg race laws, partly modelled on Jim Crow laws.

1936   *Gone with the Wind* is published, set in and around Atlanta, Georgia.

1939   The Second World War begins.

1939   The film *Gone with the Wind* premieres in Atlanta, Georgia. Its Black cast is not invited.

1940   Hattie McDaniel becomes the first African American to win an Academy Award for her portrayal of Mammy in *Gone with the Wind*, at a racially segregated ceremony in Los Angeles.

1940   The America First Committee is formed to keep the United States out of the Second World War.

1941   Charles Lindbergh becomes the spokesman for the America First Committee. Some of his speeches are written by Lawrence Dennis, the 'most famous fascist in America'.

1941   The United States enters the Second World War.

1945   The Second World War ends.

1946   Donald Trump is born in New York.

1954   The Supreme Court rules in *Brown* v. *Board of Education*, overturning the doctrine of 'separate but equal' and declaring Jim Crow segregation unconstitutional.

1961   Barack Obama is born in Hawaii, the son of a white American mother and Black Kenyan father, making him legally American.

1965   The Voting Rights Act is passed, prohibiting racial discrimination in voting.

1968   Martin Luther King, Jr is assassinated.

1968   Republican candidate Richard M. Nixon endorses Johnson's 'war on crime', and in 1971, as president, calls for a 'war on drugs'. Both lead to the vastly disproportionate incarceration of Black Americans.

1981   Republican operative Lee Atwater admits that the Republicans' 'Southern Strategy' relied upon deliberately whitewashing and encoding racism.

1994   Nixon's advisor John Ehrlichman admits that the 'war on drugs' was racially and politically motivated.

2001   The attacks on the World Trade Center provoke an Islamophobic backlash.

2008   Barack Obama is elected, becoming the first Black US president.

2013   In *Shelby County* v. *Holder* the Supreme Court reverses key provisions of the Voting Rights Act, enabling renewed voter suppression. Certain states, mostly in the former Confederacy, begin instantly and demonstrably targeting Black voters.

2016   Donald Trump is elected US president, defeating Hillary R. Clinton, the first female nominee, having come to political prominence by supporting a conspiracy that Barack Obama was not an American citizen, and therefore not legitimately president.

2019   More than two dozen Trump judicial nominees refuse to state their support for the landmark *Brown* v. *Board of Education* ruling against racial segregation.

2020   Joe Biden is elected president but Trump refuses to concede, the first time in US history a president has not cooperated with the peaceful transfer of power.

2021   Thousands of Trump supporters violently sack the US Capitol, trying to overturn Biden's election. Biden is inaugurated as president two weeks later.

The Plot of *Gone with the Wind*

S poiled, wilful and headstrong, Scarlett O'Hara lives at her father's idyllic plantation, Tara, where she reigns as an archetypal Southern belle in the closing days before the Civil War, in the spring of 1861. Scarlett believes she is in love with Ashley Wilkes, who lives at neighbouring Twelve Oaks and is engaged to his gentle cousin Melanie Hamilton. The honourable Ashley refuses Scarlett's overtures, although he desires her physically; their encounter is overseen by the wealthy, charming rogue Rhett Butler, who recognizes in Scarlett a kindred renegade spirit (even their names are twinned).

When war is declared, Ashley and Melanie hasten their wedding and Scarlett marries Melanie's brother Charles out of spite and to keep Ashley close, while all the men but Rhett Butler volunteer for the Confederate army. Charles soon dies of an unheroic case of measles followed by pneumonia, and Scarlett moves to Atlanta to wait out the war. There she again encounters Rhett, who, refusing to join what he regards as a hopeless cause, runs blockades and flirts with Scarlett. She is too obsessed with Ashley to realize that Rhett is in love with her and trying to liberate her from the constraints of old Southern femininity into modern independent womanhood.

As Sherman's conquering army marches to the sea and burns

Atlanta, Melanie goes into labour; Scarlett, honouring a promise to Ashley, stays by her side and delivers the baby, with notably little help from the enslaved Prissy, who had promised she was experienced at childbirth. Terrified of the coming Yankee army, Scarlett demands that Rhett help her and the household escape home to Tara. Halfway there, ashamed by the wounded and defeated soldiers he sees on the road, Rhett abandons them to join the Confederate army at its last stand. Scarlett and Melanie return to find Twelve Oaks razed, Tara's farms ruined, Scarlett's mother dead, her father half-mad with grief, and everyone destitute. Scarlett vows that she will never be hungry or frightened again, and that she will save Tara.

Taking responsibility for a large extended family at the age of nineteen hardens Scarlett's heart and her conscience (never very robust), although nothing can erode her stubborn love for Ashley. After the war, to avoid foreclosure on Tara, Scarlett returns to Atlanta to try to seduce Rhett, who made a fortune war profiteering, into giving her the money she needs for property taxes. In jail for murdering a Black man who was 'uppity' to a lady, Rhett sees through Scarlett's deception, so she marries her sister's fiancé, Frank Kennedy, instead, and takes the money from his small store. Her mercenary instincts turn Frank's store into a success; she borrows money from Rhett to buy a sawmill, hiring convicts as cheap labour to capitalize on the rebuilding of Atlanta.

One day when out driving alone she is assaulted by two vagrants, and only saved from rape by a loyal former slave. When Frank and Ashley Wilkes muster the local Klan to lynch her assailants, Frank is killed. On the day of Frank's funeral Rhett proposes to Scarlett, and she agrees to marry him for his money. Scarlett continues to believe that she loves Ashley, although Rhett is the only one who understands her. They have a daughter, Bonnie, whom Rhett adores and spoils, and live in wealthy, vulgar splendour amid the gossip of the genteel Old Guard. Realizing that, because Melanie is too frail to bear more children, she and

Ashley now have a celibate marriage, Scarlett decides that it will be romantic to be faithful to Ashley and turns Rhett out of their bedroom; he knows she still loves Ashley but is too self-possessed to reveal his bitterness.

During an encounter when they are reminiscing about the old days, Scarlett and Ashley embrace innocently, but are overseen by Ashley's sister, India, who has always suspected Scarlett's true feelings. She spitefully tells Melanie and rumours rapidly spread, precipitating a confrontation between Scarlett and a drunken Rhett. Overcome with frustration at her obtuseness, he finally admits his love.

Rhett sweeps Scarlett up the stairs over her protests into a vague but 'wild night', after which she awakens blushing to remember the 'rapture' and 'ecstasy', in which she had 'gloried'. Rhett disappears for a while; when he returns, he apologizes for his behaviour that night and offers a divorce, but Scarlett tells him she is pregnant again. When Rhett taunts her about the paternity of the baby, she falls down the stairs and miscarries, almost dying. Distraught, Rhett hopes that she will call for him; in her delirium she wants Rhett to come but fears his rejection and never asks.

Not long after Scarlett's recovery, their daughter Bonnie is killed falling off her horse, which further devastates Rhett. When Melanie Wilkes dies in childbirth, freeing Ashley, Scarlett suddenly sees the true Ashley, realizing she loves not Ashley but Rhett. She rushes home to declare her feelings, only for Rhett to inform her that she wore out his love with her stubborn refusal to see him, or herself, clearly, and he is leaving; he may go to Europe, he may return to Charleston. Calling her immature, headstrong, and insensitive, saying he doesn't give a damn what she does, he walks out. Scarlett ends the story determined to get him back, and decides to return to Tara, where she can face the future knowing that tomorrow is another day.

PART ONE

I'LL THINK ABOUT THAT TOMORROW

1

Look Away, Look Away

'For her, for the whole South, the war would never end. The bitterest fighting, the most brutal retaliations, were just beginning.' So thinks Scarlett O'Hara during the moment of her greatest moral crisis, when she decides that she will do whatever is necessary to retain her land and regain her power after the South has lost the Civil War.

The American Civil War never really ended: it continues to be waged in proxy battles and brutal retaliations, of which the sacking of the Capitol on 6 January 2021 was the latest iteration. The United States has never been united for long.

To understand the full implications of this shattering moment in American politics, and why the events of 6 January were at once unprecedented and archetypal, requires considerable explanation. A complex history has, for a century and a half, been whitewashed, rewritten and distorted, in part so that insurrectionists could be reconciled with the government they tried to overthrow, without morally conceding defeat. That was how the country learned to reabsorb insurrectionists, and it does not appear to have changed its tactics in 160 years.

Trump's followers were not only carrying Confederate flags as they stormed the US Capitol: far from it. There were flags everywhere: American flags, pro-gun flags (often emblazoned on the Southern Cross), all sorts of Trump flags, America First flags, 'Blue Lives Matter' flags (professing support for the police they were about to attack), and flags from the American Revolution, including the colonial Gadsden flag, which warns 'Don't Tread on Me'. Some waved the flag of QAnon, which claimed that Democrat leaders, Jewish financiers, wealthy philanthropists, and well-known liberal celebrities were members of a satanic cult of sex trafficking, blood-drinking paedophiles who rule the world. During the 2020 coronavirus lockdown, QAnon had spread as virally online as the pandemic was spreading physically; in early 2022, the *New York Times* reported that 41 million Americans believed in QAnon – equivalent to the entire population of Ukraine at the moment it was being invaded by Russia.[1]

The people who proved most susceptible to the QAnon conspiracy were white women. By appropriating the hashtag 'Save the Children' (a legitimate charity fighting actual child sex trafficking), QAnon helped convince millions of American women that a cabal of liberals and Black Lives Matter supporters were illegitimately overturning Trump's 2020 electoral win. Only Trump himself could defeat this plot with his secret plan, sometimes called 'The Great Awakening', sometimes 'The Storm', as the history of American evangelical millenarianism was mashed up with Nazi imagery. 'Trust the Plan', read QAnon T-shirts.

Others waved the lime-green flag of an imaginary nation called 'Kekistan', which originated in gaming culture and had become a far-right symbol. Displaying four Ks in the form of a square, it is derived from the Nazi swastika, while clearly also invoking the Ks of the Ku Klux Klan. As the Trump administration's actions increasingly elicited accusations that it was fascist, or at least fascistic, many argued that American white supremacism and European fascism were distinct phenomena, and that those distinctions must be upheld when trying to understand modern American politics.

Trump's followers, as the Kekistan flag makes clear, did not always respect such fine distinctions. Although they claimed that their invocation of the swastika was an ironic provocation, irony is the first stop of plausible deniability. People who oppose fascism tend not to find its symbols amusing.

If it seems strange that the white supremacist flag of an imaginary country or the paranoid flags of a farrago of conspiratorial nonsense were carried in a real insurrection, it shouldn't. The country represented by the Confederate Battle Flag – the Old South of *Gone with the Wind* – is almost as mythical as Kekistan and QAnon. This is a story of how violence can make myths come true.

*

The assault on the US Capitol took place the same day that the state of Georgia, once a white supremacist stronghold, confirmed the election of a Black man and a Jewish man to the Senate. It was also the first time the state returned a non-white majority in its electorate. The global uproar about the Capitol sacking effectively distracted from the significance of the timing for most observers, but it was in no way a coincidence.

Nor is it a coincidence that Georgia is also the place where the imaginary Old South of *Gone with the Wind* is located. To make the symbolism about progressive civil rights all the clearer, Georgia's first Black senator, Rev. Raphael Warnock, was the senior pastor of the Ebenezer Baptist Church, where a young Martin Luther King, Jr had sung in the choir, which he was leading when he was assassinated in 1968 – and Warnock is only the second Black senator from a former Confederate state to be elected since Reconstruction ended in 1877.

Trump's supporters were waving an incoherent jumble of white nationalist symbols as they screamed their determination to 'reclaim' 'their' nation by lynching, raping, and torturing members of Congress, especially women and people of colour.

They shouted racist slurs at officers of colour, and assaulted several. Officer Brian Sicknick died of multiple strokes within hours of the insurrection. Two officers, Jeffrey Smith and Henry Liebengood, took their own lives within days of the attack; two more took their own lives that summer.

Four rioters also died, including an Air Force veteran named Ashli Babbitt and a woman from Georgia named Rosanne Boyland, both of whom were said by relatives to have been radicalized by QAnon. Babbitt, reportedly 'deep into QAnon', tweeted 'the storm is here and it is descending upon DC', hours before she was gunned down by police officers as she tried to break into the Speaker's Lobby, wearing a Trump flag like a superhero cape.[2]

Democrat Jim McGovern, who briefly took over proceedings while Speaker of the House Nancy Pelosi was taken to safety, told reporters that the insurrection was not a protest. It was, he said, 'basically home-grown fascism, out of control'.[3] Trump had first started invoking tropes of interwar fascism, not only from Europe, but from the history of native American fascism as well, during his 2015 campaign; on election night in 2016, the word 'fascism' was the most searched term on the Merriam-Webster online dictionary, followed closely by 'bigot'.[4] (Six years later, searches for 'insurrection' spiked 34,450 per cent.[5])

But if the insurrection looked and sounded alarmingly like American fascism, it also sounded like the Civil War all over again, as if the Confederate anthem 'Dixie' ('Look away, look away, look away, Dixie Land') had been remixed to a twenty-first century beat.

The photograph of the Confederate Battle Flag outside the Senate Chamber became one of the most iconic images from a visually chaotic scene, a still image in the midst of so much noise, as a white American man waved his pro-slavery symbol in 2021 before portraits of two Civil War figures: the anti-slavery Charles Sumner on the right, who criticized Lincoln for appeasing the

South, and the pro-slavery John C. Calhoun on the left, who called institutional slavery 'a positive good'. The image, as many observed at the time, powerfully encapsulated an explosively volatile history.[6]

But few remarked upon the fact that this corner of the US Capitol was already shared by two such bitter foes. We might question especially why Calhoun, whose arguments later helped inspire the Confederacy to declare a treasonous war on the United States government, should be honoured with a portrait inside that government's Capitol building. Even without the Confederate flag waving under Calhoun's nose, the corner already symbolized America's profound divisions, the nation's dark unresolved background coming suddenly into focus.

The chimes of history were ringing madly but most people could only hear the noise around the insurrection itself, which was part of its objective. The rioters screaming that only their candidate could win were also making a symbolic point: the US Capitol belonged to them, not to the Black and Jewish people represented by the senators who won Georgia that day. They were there to suck up the oxygen and assert their pre-eminence, to shift attention from America's slow, grinding, gradual progress toward representative multiracial democracy.

The United States is, one might argue, especially prone to cognitive dissonance as a society, because the brutal realities of American life are so perpetually in conflict with its exalted ideals. Its very name suggests cognitive dissonance: any country that calls itself the United States is protesting too much.

The severity of that cognitive dissonance has frequently erupted in violence. 'In America violence is idiomatic,' the novelist Nathanael West declared in 1932, four years before *Gone with the Wind* appeared.[7] Nearly a century later, American violence has become axiomatic. Tragedy inheres in our politics, the systemic roots from which violence across the country keeps blooming. West was writing as the kidnapping and murder of

Charles Lindbergh's infant son filled the headlines, while popular movies like *Scarface* and *The Public Enemy* glamorized organized crime and the rise of the mob. After Al Capone's arrest his place in the headlines was taken by Dutch Schultz and Lucky Luciano, while Bonnie and Clyde, John Dillinger, and Baby Face Nelson became folk heroes whose crime sprees were daily reading material. Meanwhile Mussolini was drawing more praise from the United States than from any other democratic nation.[8] 'If this country ever needed a Mussolini, it needs one now,' declared Senator David A. Reed in 1932, a decade after sponsoring the most restrictionist immigration legislation in American history.[9] In the spring of 1933 Hollywood released *Mussolini Speaks,* a propaganda puff-piece trumpeting 'Italy's man of the hour who is making history', to rapturous domestic applause: Mussolini was 'revealed in all his greatness – truly a modern Caesar', a Brooklyn critic gushed, even as audiences were watching *Little Caesar* help invent the modern gangster film.[10]

Three years later, *Gone with the Wind*, romanticizing blood-and-soil white nationalists, would become the most popular American novel of the century. A nation so ready to glorify white supremacists, fascists, and thugs should probably have been less surprised by their appearance at the US Capitol a century later. The American story keeps seeking a modern Caesar, and finding only gangsters.

*

Within hours of the 2021 insurrection the nation's lawmakers were calling for unity, encouraging everyone to hasten past its violence, to avoid a reckoning that would be 'divisive'. (Americans have frequently decided that justice will be more divisive than injustice.) Maintaining a false appearance of unity requires mythmaking, so they immediately started erasing the conspicuous divisiveness of a huge mob of Americans charging the Capitol to overturn an election. The pledge of allegiance teaches every American schoolchild to intone that we are one nation, 'indivisible'. We should start noticing how often the figure of division hovers in the background.

Republican leaders and conservative pundits declared that calling the rampage an 'insurrection' was overblown and hysterical, brazenly denying the savagery of the video footage and the testimony of police offers who nearly died at the scene, as well as the brutal evidence of their colleagues and the rioters who had died. A congressman from Georgia said it was just 'a normal tourist visit': 'To call it an insurrection, in my opinion, is a bold-faced lie.'[11]

As it happens, some of the insurrectionists disagreed: 'We weren't there to do damage,' one helpfully explained. 'We were just there to overthrow the government.'[12]

Calls for unity also drove the logic of the Lost Cause, which was just as shameless in its denials that the Civil War had been an insurrection fought to defend slavery. Having brought the Confederacy by brute force back into a Union it was trying to leave, the nation then rushed past the consequences of the Civil War, refused to discuss slavery and race again, and enacted a hasty and superficial reconciliation. That tactic worked no better than it would with any other divorce.

A flagrantly artificial power structure requires a fabricated history to buttress it: 'From the totalitarian point of view', as George Orwell noted, 'history is something to be created rather than learned.'[13] In 2022 an authoritarian Republican party is working to create such a history in real time. This in part reflects a leadership coterie that has spent decades building deep partisan loyalty to itself, rather than to specific policies or values it might uphold: Republicanism in America today has become its own ideology. But it also reflects deeply held convictions about the meanings of whiteness and power in America – and their persistence.

The first rule of survivalism, as taught to Scarlett O'Hara, is to bide her time. 'If we folks have a motto, it's this: "Don't holler

– smile and bide your time." We've survived a passel of things that way, smiling and biding our time, and we've gotten to be experts at surviving.' The woman who says this is a white matriarch of the plantation class, an enslaver deprived of her human property – but not of her land – after the war. She tells Scarlett to bide her time, a phrase repeated several times by other characters, including the novel's moral touchstone, Rhett Butler.

Seventy-five years after the end of the Civil War, when *Gone with the Wind* was published, the Old South was still biding its time, waiting it out. They were 'those whose motto was "No surrender"', Mitchell wrote, knowing full well that decades after the war had ended, they were still determined to make a comeback.

In the context of the Capitol insurrection the vow of No Surrender becomes sinister rather than stalwart. It is the poison in the well of the nation, cultivated by the embittered who refused to concede that they had lost – not only the war, but the proposition they had fought to defend. That proposition was the structure of white governance and its concomitant refusal of multiracial democracy, what *Gone with the Wind* describes as the horrors of 'negro rule'. Calling their grievance heroic martyrdom, they told each other to bide their time. This is how Ashley Wilkes and Rhett Butler, the story's two heroes, persuade the members of the Atlanta Klan to disband: 'We convinced the hot heads that watching, waiting and working would get us further than nightshirts and fiery crosses.'

Wait long enough, and you can bring the nightshirts and fiery crosses to the American Capitol.

2

Don't Look Back!

News reports around the world used *Gone with the Wind* as a shorthand to explain the significance of the Confederate flag flying in the US Capitol during the insurrection, from Kolkata's *Indian Express* to Tallahassee's *Florida Phoenix*. *Gone with the Wind* kept arising because it symbolizes, more completely than any other single story, the fraught afterlife of plantation politics in America.

From the 'incredible brutality' of plantation slavery, as James Baldwin once observed, 'we get the myth of the happy darky and *Gone with the Wind*. And the North Americans appear to believe these legends, which they have created and which absolutely nothing in reality corroborates, until today. And when the legends are attacked, as is happening now – all over a globe which has never been and never will be White – my countrymen become childishly vindictive and unutterably dangerous.'[1] Forty years after Baldwin wrote these words, the Capitol insurrection proved their enduring truth once more.

One of the rioters, a white Pennsylvania woman named Rachel Powell, who became known as 'the bullhorn lady' for her role in the riots, was profiled in the *New Yorker*, which reported she had tweeted in 2013, 'what's up, my nxxxas?' and then defended her use of the slur by explaining: 'My favorite book is "Gone with the Wind", and it uses that term freely.'[2]

People take licence from words and stories, as Powell's defence makes clear. 'Make America Great Again' is not only nostalgic, it is imperative, demanding action of its believers. And it is regressive, holding the present hostage to an imaginary past. The problem is compounded when believers are prepared to use violence to bring this imaginary past to life, because it never existed. First come the hazy invocations of a racially harmonious history, along with simultaneous, contradictory assurances that all racism is behind us – which together serve to erase the reality of racial inequality. The master narrative legitimates this worldview, but only violence can bring it about.

In the midst of the Black Lives Matter protests sparked in the summer of 2020 by the murder of George Floyd, HBO Max announced that it was temporarily withdrawing *Gone with the Wind* from its streaming service, in order to reframe it with context that clarified some of the story's historical and political distortions. The film's removal provoked furious charges of censorship, despite HBO's reiteration that it was temporary. Six months earlier Donald Trump had invoked *Gone with the Wind* to complain about *Parasite,* the first South Korean film to win an Oscar for Best Picture, saying he wished America would 'bring back' films like *Gone with the Wind.* That he preferred a film about American white supremacists to a subtitled film by and about Asians did not go unremarked.

Gone with the Wind offers a glorious vision of white America rising from the ashes (of its own self-immolation, but that's part of what we ignore). It's the nation's favourite alibi: plausible deniability for assertions of white supremacy, letting us pretend we're talking about something else – nostalgia, pastoral legends, old movies from a vaguely better time, or a more graceful world, as Rhett tells Scarlett when he walks out. But what Rhett leaves out of that description is precisely the point: his graceful world was purchased at the cost of a brutalizing system that afforded him the ultimate luxury of pretending it didn't even exist.

The Lost Cause also tries to redeem a vicious past, a revisionist history that denies the foundational truths of slavery and its consequences. Glorifying those realities as 'noble' is not merely a lie, it is a poison. With 'all the grandeur of Hollywood', a Black journalist named Ben Davis, Jr wrote in 1940, *Gone with the Wind* sanitized the brutal truths of American history, making it 'even more dangerous, because it is calculated to deceive the public'.[3] *Gone with the Wind*, perhaps more than any other single narrative work, continues to deceive the public, shaping global perceptions of American history and racial culture. The Old South as chronicled by *Gone with the Wind* remains relevant because this is what unresolved history feels like, spinning us vertiginously around.

*

Published on 30 June 1936, *Gone with the Wind* offered America a Homeric epic, part Iliad, part Odyssey, as Scarlett O'Hara's world is destroyed by war and she tries to journey back to the home she's lost. It depicts the fall of an old order and its replacement by the new. The story's immediate, blazing popularity has become legendary: it sold a million copies in less than six months, and within a few years surpassed *Uncle Tom's Cabin* - its political antithesis - as the bestselling American novel of all time.[4] It won the 1937 Pulitzer Prize and has been translated into at least twenty-seven languages; some 300,000 copies are sold each year, with total sales exceeding 30 million.

The film smashed all records upon its release in 1939. It was breathlessly awaited, with three years of publicity about David O. Selznick's 'Search for Scarlett', even before its extravagant premiere surpassed all the expectations Selznick had so audaciously stoked, as nostalgic ideas of aristorcracy in the Old South converged with the power of modern American aristocracy in the form of celebrity culture.

A Gallup poll in 1939 reported that 56.5 million people planned to attend the film's release, or about 65 per cent of the nation's moviegoing population, while more than 14 million had already read the novel.[5] It remains, when adjusted for inflation, the highest-grossing film of all time. Rhett Butler's departing shot – 'Frankly, my dear, I don't give a damn' – still tops the American Film Institute's list of most famous movie lines ever. Reviews of the film were ecstatic, the *New York Times* calling it 'the greatest motion mural we have seen and the most ambitious film-making venture in Hollywood's spectacular history'.[6] It was an international hit as well, triumphantly exporting its version of the American Civil War around the world, through war-torn Europe and beyond.

The film's phenomenal success helped make the story of its production legendary in its own right: the huge list of directors and writers (including F. Scott Fitzgerald, Ben Hecht, and the credited writer, Sidney Howard) who were roped in to work on it, only to be removed (Fitzgerald only lasted about ten days), as well as the 'Search for Scarlett', as the most famous actresses of the day including Joan Crawford, Bette Davis, Katharine Hepburn, Irene Dunne, Paulette Goddard, Miriam Hopkins, Tallulah Bankhead, Joan Bennett, Norma Shearer, Lana Turner and Loretta Young all vied for the part, before it was finally given to the unknown British actress Vivien Leigh. Gary Cooper, Errol Flynn and even Basil Rathbone were considered for Rhett Butler, before Selznick's personal first choice, Clark Gable, was finally secured on loan from MGM.

Selznick struggled with the story's racial depictions from the start. Some Black activists objected to filming the novel at all, while others, including the cast, saw professional opportunity for Black performers, so often kept from American screens altogether in the 1930s. Hattie McDaniel, whose parents had both been enslaved, became the first Black actor to win an Oscar for her performance as Mammy; she famously retorted to critics that she had chosen between $700 a week to play a maid, or $7 a week to be a maid.[7]

Selznick eventually agreed to eliminate the novel's casual racial slurs from the film, a decision lobbied for by his Black actors. But the movie also maintains the 'heroic' racism of its protagonists Rhett Butler and Ashley Wilkes, euphemizing Ashley's membership in the Ku Klux Klan as a 'social club' and sympathizing with vigilante violence that supposedly defends white heroines from sexual violence.

Meanwhile the Black cast was being forced to pay the price of systemic racism even as they performed in a story that insisted slavery had inflicted no costs upon American society at all. They were not invited to the film's world premiere in segregated Atlanta in December 1939; they could not attend the gala dinners, or the Junior League Ball at which the Ebenezer Baptist Church choir sang. The premiere, like the story itself, was strictly for whites. But the 'colour line' was not merely drawn across the South. When McDaniel became the first African American actor to win an Oscar, she was initially barred from the ceremony because the Cocoanut Grove in Los Angeles was also only for whites. Selznick pulled strings to get her into the club, but she was forced to sit at a separate table from the rest of the cast, against a wall by herself.

Racial segregation ran right across the United States, creating economic and political benefits for white people and then rewarding them further for disregarding it. If Southerners in 1936 didn't want to admit that their grandparents had fought a war to defend an indefensible way of life, Northerners didn't want to admit they benefited from the failure of Reconstruction and the imposition of Jim Crow segregation.

The myth of the Lost Cause, which turned seventy the year the novel came out, hugely strengthened that psychological investment. *Gone with the Wind* perpetuated the nation's lingering myths about the Old South, created to justify the injustices of plantation slavery. The plantation legend endures, despite its travestied history of life in the antebellum South – or rather, because of it.

Glorifying the Old South as a noble and chivalric but doomed civilization was more than a vast project in collective face-saving, although the psychological pressure to vindicate the Confederacy after its catastrophic loss was profound. But after the Civil War finally ended, the white South needed emotional and economic redemption, and the Union needed to find a way to welcome the rebels back into the reunited states, to recreate national unity – or at least its semblance.

Avoiding the humiliation of defeat was as important as evading its consequences, which would have been the loss of absolute white power: the two motivations worked together to produce the story of the Lost Cause, which created an imaginary past and convinced everyone – first Southerners, then Northerners, then people beyond the United States – to accept unthinkingly a series of barefaced lies.

It created a vast alternative historical reality, one in which millions of Americans still believe. The myth of Southern exceptionalism spread by the Lost Cause echoed and reinforced older myths of American exceptionalism, which regard America as perennially innocent, as if it were exempt from history. It became a cliché that Donald Trump's politics had created an alternate reality during his administration, but alternate realities are nothing new in America.[8]

Part of what *Gone with the Wind*'s popularity reflects is how deeply dependent American culture was on its myth of a racial equipoise founded on individual choice, a state of racial neutrality that is only imbalanced by bad actors who out of malice or greed or instinctive brutality create 'race problems'. Generally the people blamed for creating race problems have been Black people pointing them out, just as lawmakers insisted that discussing an insurrection would be more divisive than holding one. The myth of racial neutrality includes rewriting enslavement as voluntary servitude – because without that myth, the whole edifice of righteous America comes tumbling down. Plantation politics, the entire social order of patriarchal white supremacy, with its brutally enforced racial and gender hierarchies, depended upon the ruthless maintenance of lies about Black contentment as well as a Black inferiority that upheld Southern white aristocracy.

These politics constructed social identities across America and justified white male power through the Jim Crow period and beyond. 'Naturally the British aristocracy sympathized with the Confederacy,' Mitchell's narrator declares, 'as one aristocrat with another, against a race of dollar lovers like the Yankees.' This was the favourite legend of both the antebellum and the postbellum South: the abolition of slavery as a financially motivated incursion by Yankee opportunists who cared only for making a buck – as if slave plantations were charitable institutions. From the beginning of Donald Trump's campaign to the turbulent end of his presidency, debates raged about whether his supporters were motivated by economic anxiety or racial animus. But in America the two are intertwined in a system of racial capitalism. *Gone with the Wind* doesn't just romanticize that system – it eroticizes it.

The Lost Cause provided a genesis myth for modern America's racialized economics and paramilitary white nationalism, in which racial segregation was the supposedly logical outcome of a fight over states' rights. But the most vicious fights over these supposedly principled stances on states' rights have always, consistently, been over racial power. In fact, states' rights are almost never invoked in a context that is distinct from race. States' rights created a fig leaf, an alibi from which white America benefited so deeply that the denials continue to this day.

Southern exceptionalism served as a palliative fantasy at a time of great social and political unrest, reassuring white Americans on either side of the Mason–Dixon line that one day they could recover 'the calm dignity life can have when it's lived by gentle folks, the genial grace of days that are gone', as Rhett tells Scarlett when he leaves her at novel's end. *Gone with the Wind* pretends that modernity is the wind that blew the romantic feudal idyll away, but despite itself keeps revealing that racial injustice was what was stirring the air.

Scarlett's modernity means that she contemptuously dismisses the sentimentality of the Lost Cause, more than once: she 'wasn't like these people who had gambled everything on a Cause that was gone and were content to be proud of having lost that Cause, because it was worth any sacrifice. They drew their courage from the past. She was drawing hers from the future.' None of this implies there was anything objectionable about the Cause, merely that it leaves Scarlett unmoved. The rhetoric of lost or noble causes misdirects from the real cause of the war, which was slavery.

Mitchell herself claimed to despise the glamorizing of the Old South;[9] and yet she ties Scarlett's indomitable courage explicitly to the Lost Cause in the novel's uplifting closing words: 'With the spirit of her people who would not know defeat, even when it stared them in the face, she raised her chin. She could get Rhett back. She knew she could.' Scarlett's postwar defiance is where the mood of the Lost Cause meets the mood of the Great Depression, into which the book exploded with such startling popularity.

Despite the famously sad ending of its central romance, the story's fundamental message is not tragic. Scarlett does survive, she does not accept defeat, and she can keep going. It is not a love-affirming ending, but it is life-affirming. *Gone with the Wind* insists that history is a nightmare from which we can escape, while also maintaining that history can never be forgotten – one of the many things about which it is deeply, and characteristically, inconsistent.

*

After almost a century, *Gone with the Wind* now works as a code even for those who have neither read nor watched it. It has become part of our lingua franca, one of those stories of which most people become aware as part of our cultural inheritance, its characters and setting ambiently familiar from the fusion of novel and film into a dominant cultural story.

Art, as Henry James once remarked, is nothing if not exemplary, meaning that any story puts before us an example that we must judge for ourselves – not only how it makes us feel, but also what we think. The values a story expresses or enacts can be quite distinct from the values its characters hold. When Huck Finn decides he'll go to hell rather than betray his enslaved friend Jim, he does so in a novel that depicts a racist slaveholding society that taught him slavery is good, Black people are inferior, and he will go to hell if he helps them. But Huck, the voice of the novel, rejects that society, choosing to suffer eternal damnation rather than uphold those values: 'All right then, I'll *go* to hell.' He runs away, lighting out for the territory where he will be free to live according to his conscience. *The Adventures of Huckleberry Finn* is exemplary in the sense James meant – a novel offering an example of a society that is deeply wrong. By marked contrast, *Gone with the Wind* offers a justification of slavery and white governance from start to finish. It sustains a self-deluding account of American history, a story told in deeply bad faith.

Most bestselling stories are unstable emotionally, so their audiences can have it both ways: that is their pleasure and their consolation. *Gone with the Wind* offers a version of American history that its (presumptively white) audiences would find emotionally satisfying and historically plausible – while letting them profoundly, and permanently, off the hook.

'"Gone with the Wind" does such violence to American history that it practically lynches it,' Ben Davis, Jr rightly declared.[10] The ferocity of that violence – to humans, as to history – has to be seen to be believed.

3

Why Can't They Forget?

one with the Wind is a story about delusions, from first line to last. 'Scarlett O'Hara was not beautiful, but men seldom realized it,' the novel begins. (Popular memory of Scarlett O'Hara also seldom realizes that she wasn't beautiful, because she would soon be immortalized on film by the egregiously beautiful Vivien Leigh.) Mitchell was explicit about Scarlett's shortcomings; she is very much an anti-heroine. She had 'set out to depict a far-from-admirable woman', Mitchell wrote in an exasperated letter after publication: 'I have not found it wryly amusing when Miss O'Hara became somewhat of a national heroine and I have thought it looked bad for the moral and mental attitude of a nation.'[1]

The story begins and ends in the same place: Scarlett O'Hara is in love with a man she cannot have. The only thing that changes is the man. Born in 1845, she is sixteen as both the tale, and the Civil War, begin in 1861; it takes her from the Old South of the antebellum period to the New South that emerged after Reconstruction. Mitchell stresses that Scarlett and Atlanta were christened in the same year, making her an explicitly representative character. This was deliberate, Mitchell said, telling an interviewer that she had planned to 'write a story of a girl who was somewhat like Atlanta – part of the Old South;

part of the New South; she rose with Atlanta and fell with it and how she rose again. What Atlanta did to her; what she did to Atlanta.'[2] It was a city, she adds in the novel, of Scarlett's 'own generation': 'crude with the crudities of youth and as headstrong and impetuous as herself'.

As *Gone with the Wind* closes Scarlett O'Hara is twenty-eight, a survivor of civil war, three marriages, the loss of most of the people she cares about, and also one of her children. Through twelve years of war, turmoil and tragedy, Scarlett emerges indomitable, a defiant, hard-nosed pragmatist who survives whatever life throws at her. But she is also a fantasist, so blinded by her dreams of love that she constantly misreads the world, putting her in flight from reality. Her dreams are self-destructive, but the story presents escapist fantasies as a survival strategy, pretending that consequences can always be outrun. Scarlett bides her time, like her society, certain that if she outwaits them all she will get what she wants. Her persistence is self-defeating, destroying the love she desires, while she never admits that there are things she wants even more than love, things she can and does retain – namely, land, wealth, and power.

Gone with the Wind is essentially a Cinderella story, in which our heroine is degraded from wealth and comfort to poverty and servitude, but has no fairy godmother and so must pursue the restoration of her elite status by herself, working her way to the top like a good modern American. Because she's a particularly pig-headed Cinderella, Scarlett chases the wrong prince for most of the tale; and because it's a modern fairy tale, the right prince rejects her at the end.

The decision to end a popular historical romance with the hero walking out on the heroine was a remarkable choice in 1936, as indeed it would be today. Mitchell shared much of her heroine's hard-headedness, and there is real bitterness in the central love story. If it is a 'tragic' romance, the tragedy is the weariness of disillusionment and misunderstanding, not the broken hearts or star-crossed deaths of adolescent infatuation. It is about what happens when delusion destroys love.

Over the twelve years of her story Scarlett acquires almost no wisdom whatsoever, learning the price of everything and the value of nothing. The only thing she learns, apart from how to run a business, is that she loved Rhett, rather than Ashley – which took her over a decade to figure out. In another story, she would be a stalker, fixated on her first passion, fantasizing about the death of his wife and refusing to sleep with her own husband out of an imaginary pact with the object of her affections, who physically desires her but never returns her love. (American literature is filled with stalkers, from Roger Chillingworth to Captain Ahab to Jay Gatsby; Scarlett O'Hara fits right in.) Scarlett is impatient with her sister Careen for 'mooning about a silly boy who probably never gave her a serious thought', when she ruins her life by doing exactly the same.

Scarlett's imperceptiveness is also a refusal to see. She is deeply insensitive, as Rhett charges when he leaves her, remaining blinded from the truths of her own reality, wrapped up in her own narcissistic illusions – as does the book she dominates. Her feelings for Ashley are primarily projection; she dimly recognizes that he constitutes the best of the Old South, to which she aspires, without understanding that it is alien to her modern, grasping nature. 'You aren't a speck smart about folks,' Grandma Fontaine informs her point blank. Scarlett, characteristically, isn't paying attention.

As a narrator, Mitchell is both intrusive and instructive, constantly intervening to remind the reader of historical facts and Scarlett's failings. Scarlett herself is either bewildered or bored by references to anything beyond the material conditions of her existence, her unremitting selfishness making her indifferent to everything but her own simple desires, while the narrator judges Scarlett and finds her wanting: 'Scarlett had not a subtle bone in her body'; 'to the end of her days she would never be able to understand a complexity'; 'quick though her brain was, it was not made for analysis'; 'insensitive though she was'; 'unanalytical, she struggled with the complex thought'.

These descriptions equally apply to the collective character of Scarlett's society: impatient, calculating but not astute, shrewd about business but foolish about people. Uncurious and acquisitive, self-deceiving and vain, Scarlett shares the failings of both the Old South and modern America. She is also courageous, obstinate and forceful, facing what reality she can see without flinching, and profoundly loyal. She is ashamed of cowardice, squaring her shoulders to many hard realities. There is a lot to like about Scarlett O'Hara, despite her folly.

But Mitchell was far more able to confront Scarlett's failures of character than those of the society she typifies. While mocking Scarlett's ignorance, her novel offers American history lessons that are variously travestied, erroneous, or unconscionable. For all its ostensible interest in history – and for the mental and moral attitude of a nation – the story keeps a tight focus on Scarlett, never cutting away from her to show soldiers fighting in the battlefields, or slaves working in the cotton fields. It cares about the domestic costs of war, the suffering of white civilians, especially women – and much of its message to its first audiences as they watched fascism rising in Europe was, if not pacifist, then certainly anti-war. Scarlett deplores the senseless violence of war, but mostly because it is senseless, not because it is violent. She tends to condone other forms of violence, as long as it is disorganized and visited upon those she resents.

The story is cloaked in self-delusion far worse than Scarlett's, and the film – which recognized the novel's flaws more clearly – perpetuated those delusions out of commercial interests. This modern myth affirmed all the nation's favourite illusions about itself, up to and including its faith in its own innocence – and then sold that bill of goods to all and sundry, making a fortune in the process.

Scarlett's blinkers are typical, too – the wilful ignorance in which American popular memory likes to trade. What she couldn't, or wouldn't, see, is the subject of the rest of this book.

PART TWO

I'LL NEVER BE HUNGRY AGAIN

4

I Won't Think of It Now

In black silhouette against a smoldering orange sky, Scarlett O'Hara slowly raises her fist in defiance. 'As God is my witness – as God is my witness, they're not going to lick me. I'm going to live through this and when it's all over, I'll never be hungry again. No, nor any of my folks. If I have to lie, cheat, steal or kill, as God is my witness, I'll never be hungry again!'

As the music soars, the camera slowly pulls back, emphasizing the smallness of her figure as she stands between a tumbled fence and the charred remains of a tree, against the immensity of the burning, choking clouds. It's one of *Gone with the Wind*'s most iconic scenes, ending the first act with a speech lifted almost verbatim from the novel (as was most of the screenplay), a stirring testament to human resilience and resolve. Scarlett will indeed lie, cheat, steal and kill before story's end, but she also keeps her promise to feed and protect her family.

Placing Scarlett in the desolate remains of what was once a prosperous farm, the film invokes a scene that had become all too familiar to Depression-era audiences by 1939: desperate figures staring through clouds and dust, disappearing into a scorched world. *Gone with the Wind* transforms the swirling dust of Depression-era drought into the smoke and ashes left by Sherman's march across Georgia. The grinding poverty of the

Deep South under Jim Crow was echoed by Scarlett's scrabbling for food in dead earth and the story's evocation of a ravaged land.

When *Gone with the Wind* appeared in 1936, black winds were literally blowing across the United States. The economic crisis of the Great Depression was exacerbated by environmental disaster, as the summer brought the most calamitous heat wave in the recorded history of the continent to the Americas. Created by decades of over-farming, the drought left thousands dead and crops failing, as the once Great Plains desiccated and shriveled. Dust swirled in windstorms they called 'black blizzards', typhoons of dirt, thousands of feet high, blowing devastation across the land.[1] The famous Dust Bowl was not merely the collapsing heartland, but also an immense black cumulus that engulfed the skies. Eventually scientists would prove that this was the latest stage in a much longer history of growing climate crisis – only for many Americans to respond to that truth with yet more denial.

Although they didn't yet know the drought was an early symptom of climate breakdown, its reality was harder to deny in 1936, when black turbulence carried topsoil at speeds of 100 miles an hour, depositing silt like filthy snow on city after city, a blanket of grime eclipsing the sun on bright spring days.[2] Not for nothing was the cyclone that swept Dorothy to the land of Oz finally filmed in 1939, the same year as *Gone with the Wind*, while the novel emerged in 1936 into a season of deadly tornadoes, several in Georgia itself.

The black blizzards were unaffected by temperature, blasting hot or cold indifferently. People disappeared in the filthy fog, pedestrians walked with their eyes closed to keep from being blinded; animals choked to death on it, children suffocated. Dirt was everywhere, inescapably symbolic, besmirching the White House and shrouding the Statue of Liberty. Prosperity, security, fertility – all seemed gone with the wind.

These apocalyptic scenes were the backdrop for intense social and political upheaval at home and abroad. Dorothea Lange's famous 'Migrant Mother' photograph had been published in March, becoming instantly iconic in its summation of the desolate endurance of ruined workers across the country. Membership in the Communist Party soared in 1935 and 1936, and outlaws were capturing the American imagination, as Bonnie and Clyde and John Dillinger robbed banks and died in hails of bullets while Lucky Luciano's luck finally ran out when he was jailed on multiple racketeering charges.

In the summer of 1936 the Scottsboro Nine, a group of young African American men wrongfully accused of rape in a blatant, and protracted, miscarriage of justice, had just lost another retrial; more than one commentator could see in their persecution a cautionary lesson about the perils of 'anti-Negro fascism'.[3] When the Spanish Civil War erupted that summer, Americans joined the 30,000 anti-fascists from around the world volunteering to fight against Franco, while for months Black Americans had been organizing mass protests against Mussolini's invasion of Ethiopia. It was the year that European fascism finally consolidated; that summer both Hitler and Mussolini began assisting Franco in Spain, and a few months later Mussolini declared the formation of an Axis of fascist power.

While Hitler marched through the Rhineland, Americans flocked to newsreels that showed the young British king abdicating to marry a divorcée from Baltimore. Not long after the German-American Bund formed from the remnants of the Friends of New Germany (formerly the Friends of the Hitler Movement) in the United States, Berlin hosted the Olympic Games. They had just passed the Nuremberg race laws, explicitly modelled on American race laws, as stories of terror, violence, and pogrom began to circulate. African American Jesse Owens's medal haul at Berlin that August was widely viewed as a joke against Hitler's bigotry, but also as a rebuke against American hypocrisy about the injustice of Jim Crow segregation.

On the same newspaper page one could read a comment urging 'intelligent Germans, free from race prejudice', to study the happy 'results of tolerance in the United States',[4] and in the next column of Selznick's search for an actress to play Scarlett O'Hara, a profoundly racist enslaver who 'hated the impudent free negroes as much as anyone'.

A growing number of Americans viewed the emergence of fascism in Europe with approval, not alarm – many of them claiming that European fascism had learned everything it needed to know from the United States. It was frequently observed at the time, by critics and enthusiasts alike, that Hitler's policies seemed straight out of the playbook of the Ku Klux Klan.

*

Just as a person's true identity is said to be revealed in a crisis, so is a nation's – but it is also the case that identities are forged through crisis. America in 1936 felt unmoored, a country that had lost its bearings. From President Roosevelt, who promised the country it was emerging from 'a great national crisis with flying colors',[5] to high-school valedictorians giving speeches to banish fears 'that "the great American experiment has failed"',[6] Americans across the country told each other not to worry, the United States was holding together. Now it sounds like they were trying to convince themselves as much as each other: failure and experiment were the watchwords, not success and certainty.

It has often been noted that the grim realities of the Depression spurred American culture into producing some of the most appealing escapist fantasies ever created: the bleaker the facts, the more deluxe the offering. Sorely needing wisdom, the nation flocked to see the *Ziegfeld Follies,* the highest-grossing film of 1936. And historical novels soared in popularity, as audiences escaped into a heroic past that helped restore a shaken national self-confidence.

Seeking solace, Americans found endless reassuring messages about their plucky resilience and stoic endurance, about cheer in the face of adversity. In the hit film *Swing Time,* Ginger Rogers told Fred Astaire to pick himself up and start all over again – and to remember to dust himself off, because dust was everywhere. 'I'll get some self-assurance,' Astaire responds, 'If your endurance is great.' The rhyming of assurance and endurance sums up the mood of the nation, trying to remember the famous men who had to fall to rise again.

Fables of endurance bloomed in the dust. Pearl S. Buck's *The Good Earth,* a story of Chinese peasants working the land, may seem an unlikely bestseller alongside *Gone with the Wind* in an isolationist, xenophobic country, but it, too, was championing the resilience of poor farmers fighting drought and starvation – as was Walter D. Edmonds's bestselling *Drums Along the Mohawk,* set during the American Revolution but focused on the travails of farmers against the backdrop of war. The need for reassurance overflowed into visions of a pastoral America of small towns, rolling farms, and kindly neighbours. 'Brother, Can You Spare a Dime?' the nation asked, and answered with 'Pennies from Heaven', the most popular song of the year, soothingly crooned by Bing Crosby.

And the savage viciousness of Jim Crow produced the consoling legend of a noble land of cavaliers and ladies who presided over loyal servants with gentle benevolence, which would become Americans' favourite story for decades to come. Listen closely to what a culture keeps telling itself, and you'll know not only what's on its mind, but what it needs to hear.

Gone with the Wind told Americans that they could survive anything, especially if they ignored it. Avoidance is Scarlett O'Hara's specialty, 'I won't think of that now – I'll think of it tomorrow' her perpetual charm to ward off repercussions. Scarlett's wilful blindness gives voice to the denialism of American culture, in its refusal to face facts, to recognize that what it tells itself simply isn't true.

Throughout the twelve years of her story, Scarlett compulsively, and consciously, avoids uncomfortable facts that she can't reconcile with her desires. 'I won't think of that now,' she tells herself as the story starts: planning to convince engaged Ashley to run away with her, she suddenly realizes 'it might not turn out this way', only to reject that thought. 'If I think of it now, it will upset me.' During the war, Scarlett becomes

> adept at putting unpleasant thoughts out of her mind... She had learned to say, 'I won't think of this or that bothersome thought now. I'll think about it tomorrow.' Generally when tomorrow came, the thought either did not occur at all or it was so attenuated by the delay it was not very troublesome.

Stunned by the destruction of Ashley's plantation Twelve Oaks during the war, Scarlett says aloud: 'I won't think of it now. I can't stand it now. I'll think of it later.'

'I won't think of it now' is Scarlett's verbatim response to finding her father driven mad by grief, not being able to pay property taxes, killing a Yankee, her decision to marry Rhett to save Tara, the realization she may have to settle for being Rhett's mistress, and the scandal caused when she is found in Ashley's embrace. Leaving Atlanta after her miscarriage, Scarlett musters once more 'her old defense against the world: "I won't think of it now. I can't stand it if I do. I'll think of it tomorrow at Tara. Tomorrow's another day."'

This repetition sets up Mitchell's ending, when Rhett leaves Scarlett and she musters her magic formula a final time:

> 'I won't think of it now,' she thought grimly, summoning up her old charm. 'I'll go crazy if I think about losing him now. I'll think of it tomorrow'... 'I won't think of it now,' she said again, aloud, trying to push her misery to the back of her mind, trying to find some bulwark against the rising tide of pain. 'I'll – why, I'll go home to Tara tomorrow,' and her spirits lifted faintly...

The 'old charm' returns in the novel's famous closing words: 'I'll think of it all tomorrow, at Tara. I can stand it then. Tomorrow, I'll think of some way to get him back. After all, tomorrow is another day.'

Defiance energizes Scarlett's endless forward motion, but denial enables it. Her refusal to submit to reality is both admirable and destructive, not only for herself, but for those around her, who constantly warn that her will to power is endangering everything she claims to love most. Scarlett tells herself she doesn't have the luxury of being polite or compassionate, but in truth would be just as implacably selfish no matter how easy her circumstances. She will never worry about what she did yesterday because she will worry about it tomorrow, thus endlessly deferring the question of morality.

The problem with that strategy, for individuals as for society, is that by the time you can no longer avoid thinking about your history, it has become so complex and confusing that you can no longer think about it clearly, and your morality is what is gone with the wind. Mitchell is clear-sighted about this aspect of her story, at least, having Rhett lecture Scarlett about the fact that she will not be able to reclaim her morality once it is gone. Mitchell is considerably less clear, however, about the morality of the history that Scarlett is trying to disregard, as she keeps being struck by its consequences while looking the other way.

When she decides to prostitute herself to Rhett Butler to save Tara, she consciously suppresses the thought that she could no longer 'feel superior and virtuous' in comparison to Belle Watling, the prostitute with a heart of gold who consoles Rhett, because 'the matter in its true light discomfited her'. Mitchell knows that Scarlett is turning away from 'the matter in its true light', and then proceeds to turn her own face away from the truth of the society she is depicting.

Scarlett just keeps blindly moving forward, rushing past defeat and failure, trusting that tomorrow the storm will have passed.

Scarlett's incantatory denial, 'I won't think of it now', the magic charm of deferred reckonings from the definite past to the indefinite future, is the strategy of America's most representative figures from fiction and history alike, from the 'redemption' of the Lost Cause to the calls for unity from Republican leaders after the 2021 insurrection, urging the country to 'just move on'.

The past doesn't change, but our view of it should: like Scarlett O'Hara, American history is not beautiful, but our myths have seldom realized it. Scarlett lives among the wreckage of her hopes, blaming others for the ruins and carnage while building something new by exploiting those around her. What could be more American?

5

An Ideal Plantation

I n Margaret Mitchell's mind, she was writing anything but a consoling fiction. She intended to create a realistic story about the Old South, repudiating the idealized characters of the 'moonlight and magnolia' stories of the plantation fiction she read as a girl. Her understanding of blackbelt Georgia plantations was, from the vantage-point of the white South at least, minute, and the novel is quite careful in its delineation of the rigid intricacies of the white caste system. She wanted her history to be 'radical, revisionary, and rebellious', in one biographer's words.[1]

As far as she was concerned, it was Hollywood that was guilty of nostalgic hokum, as she told a Virginia paper after the film came out:

> We Southerners could write the truth about the antebellum South, its few slaveholders, its yeomen farmers, its rambling, comfortable houses just fifty years away from log cabins, until Gabriel blows his trump – and everyone would go on believing in the Hollywood version.

'People believe what they like to believe,' she added, 'and the mythical Old South has too strong a hold on their imaginations to be altered by the mere reading of a 1,037 page book.'[2] This is perfectly true – but Mitchell was profoundly oblivious to how much that same mythical version had shaped her own understanding, how many delusions she shared with her far-from-admirable heroine.

Trying to reject the mythical Old South and the sentimental tropes of plantation fiction, Mitchell centred her tale on modern realists who symbolize the coming of the New South in their unashamed laissez-faire self-centredness and reckless determination to succeed at any cost, while her large cast of white Georgians is far more socio-economically diverse than the film suggests.

But *Gone with the Wind* has its share of stock characters from plantation fiction, including its Black minstrel cartoons and the sentimental archetypes Ashley and Melanie Wilkes. Mitchell explicitly linked Ashley with moonlight and magnolias to suggest his unreality, when he writes to Melanie during the war: 'I see Twelve Oaks and remember how the moonlight slants across the white columns, and the unearthly way the magnolias look, opening under the moon.' Etiolated and fragile, clinging desperately to an obsolete world, Ashley and Melanie are too inbred and feeble to endure the New South. Ultimately Melanie will die from the same infirmity as many a nineteenth-century heroine before her: too pure to survive this corrupt world, she dies along with the Old South, the noble civilization she embodies.

Both Rhett and Scarlett are exasperated by nineteenth-century pieties and loyalty to the Cause. They regard illusions as a luxury survivors can't afford, and pride themselves on rising above nostalgia – although Rhett succumbs to both, first when he joins the army at its last stand, and then when he leaves Scarlett in search of 'the old towns and old countries where some of the old times must still linger'. Scarlett's childish self-centredness often blinds her to the realities of her world, as she struggles against a value system she doesn't know how to reject, while Rhett is a cynical truth-teller. Scarlett and Rhett are spirits of modernity striding through antebellum America – but parachuting more realistic characters into a romantic antebellum setting also helps detract from the obvious unreality of that background. This is part of the book's machinery of misdirection, an authorial sleight of hand.

It worked. Mitchell's faith in her revisionist realism was validated by many of the novel's first readers, who registered the story as daring, rather than reactionary. 'There is to her story a certain "vigor" and modernity; she allows her characters to vomit, utter oaths and allude to bodily functions. Scarlett, the heroine, is a vixen and a baggage; Rhett, the hero, is alternately a bounder and a gentleman. Such people are not commonly discovered in romantic stories,'[3] wrote the *New York Times,* while Stephen Vincent Benét praised the novel's 'rather more realistic treatment' of the antebellum South as 'a decided relief' for those readers 'surfeited with wistful reminiscence'.

Although a few more caustic voices noted, with Malcolm Cowley, that *Gone with the Wind* was a veritable 'encyclopedia of the plantation legend',[4] many more praised its 'faithful presentation' of Civil War history,[5] validating the 'photographic faithfulness' of its depiction.[6] One thought its history impressive enough 'to put it on required reading lists in schools'.[7] The *Atlanta Constitution* went so far as crediting *Gone with the Wind* with singlehandedly reuniting the country after the Civil War: 'by the simple expedient of telling the truth', it had done 'more than any other single influence in the last 75 years to erase sectional lines and make us one nation'.[8]

Gone with the Wind 'is better than objective history', said another review, 'for it has a reality that history can never achieve'.[9] This is the problem: it successfully adopts the tone of objective history to pass off what is in fact a wildly fallacious and biased account. 'How accurate this history is is for the expert to tell, but no reader can come away without a sense of the tragedy that overcame the planting families in 1865 and without a better understanding of the background of present-day Southern life,' wrote the *New York Times*.[10]

Eleanor Roosevelt agreed when she wrote later that summer that the novel made the lingering enmity of the South 'easy to understand... even to those who haven't understood it before'. She now sympathized, she said, with the women of the South, whose 'bitterness persisted so long' against the 'northern invaders'. 'It seems only natural,' Roosevelt concluded.[11]

Those relatable Southern women hated their compatriots for forcing them to stop enslaving Black people, but even a white liberal like Eleanor Roosevelt sympathized after reading the novel not with enslaved people but with the women fighting to keep them in chains. This is what it means to naturalize a value system: *Gone with the Wind* took a series of historical falsehoods and made them seem only natural.

*

Publicity for the novel emphasized Mitchell's meticulous research; she later claimed to have spent a decade 'reading thousands of books, documents, letters, diaries, old newspapers', along with the interviews of survivors.[12] A few months before publication, the *Atlanta Constitution* promised that *Gone with the Wind* would offer 'a realistic picture', and that Mitchell had 'verified her facts through extensive research and study'.[13] A 1991 biography affirmed the 'vast amount of time' Mitchell spent 'verifying historical facts', because 'the fear of missing something or getting something wrong drove her to distraction'[14] – long after we might expect a biographer to notice that *Gone with the Wind* gets a few things, such as the entirety of chattel slavery, the history of the Ku Klux Klan, and the politics of Reconstruction, very wrong indeed.

Mitchell herself was always persuaded of her story's historical accuracy ('the book is as true as documentation and years of research could make it'[15]), convinced it offered a realistic portrait of the Atlanta region during the Civil War era. But her blind spots were absolutely colossal, not least because her research consulted only the deeply biased perspective of enslavers. In the end, *Gone with the Wind* gives the impression of respecting fact without giving a Rhett Butler's damn about truth.

Since the moment of publication, its mix of fact and fiction has worked to deceive, which was not Mitchell's intention – but only because she earnestly believed the lies. Not only was its story 'not idealized', declared one critic, it was 'often almost too realistic'. Without 'weeping and wailing after the Lost Cause', the novel was also to be commended for showing 'no disloyalty to the ideals of the old south',[16] although the ideals of the Old South were founded upon human enslavement. By 1936, America had shrugged off this discomfiting truth.

Gone with the Wind's realistic, non-idealized portrait of plantation slavery includes 'devoted' slaves like Mammy and Uncle Peter; the constant description of enslaved labourers as 'willing' 'servants'; and Ellen O'Hara's lessons in benevolent maternalism ('you are responsible for the moral as well as the physical welfare of the darkies God has intrusted to your care. You must realize that they are like children and must be guarded from themselves like children').

Tara is a plantation upon which enslaved people are never beaten – which they intuit thanks to 'African instinct', rather than concluding it rationally from the evidence that they are never beaten ('with unerring African instinct, the negroes had all discovered that Gerald had a loud bark and no bite at all, and they took shameless advantage of him. The air was always thick with threats of selling slaves south and of direful whippings, but there never had been a slave sold from Tara and only one whipping'). There is not a racist trope that *Gone with the Wind* doesn't endorse, including here the 'instinctive' African as mystical, animalistic savage. The O'Haras' neighbours the Tarletons similarly do not permit anyone 'to whip a horse or a slave', because they, too, are kind to all dumb creatures.

No one in *Gone with the Wind* is hurt by slavery, in short, least of all the enslaved, and the profits of the plantation class are earned by their own labour. America's need to maintain the moral high ground is so profound that it ended up insisting even its system of human enslavement was innocent. While allowing by implication that the enslaved might occasionally be slightly maltreated (elsewhere), *Gone with the Wind* dwells upon the benevolent paternalism of the O'Haras and their neighbours. This is the sheerest disavowal of the injustice of slavery, as if the fact that some enslavers were less abusive than others to the people who were sold against their will into a lifetime of forced labour mitigates the crime of enslavement at large. The focus on the comparative abuse of slaves is another sleight of hand, distracting attention from the fundamental abuse that is enslavement itself.

William Faulkner called the Old South 'a makebelieve region of swords and magnolias and mockingbirds which perhaps never existed anywhere', while Malcolm Cowley accurately observed when the novel was published that the plantation legend is 'false in part and silly in part and vicious in its general effect on Southern life today'.[17] When she overturned *Gone with the Wind* in her 2001 novel *The Wind Done Gone*, Alice T. Randall was less qualified, noting that its setting was 'a South without miscegenation, a South without whippings, a South without families sold apart, a South without free blacks striving for their education, a South without Booker T. Washington and Frederick Douglass. [It] depicts a South that never, ever existed.'[18]

As the African American *Chicago Defender* rightly noted back in 1937, *Gone with the Wind* never represents slave labour, only the white wealth it created, while also treating violence against Black Americans as necessary for the creation of that wealth: Mitchell refuses to consider 'how wealth was gotten *before* the war... Not one example of the mistreatment of slaves is shown: not one example of a slave, proud and wise, who wanted to be free.'[19]

After the war, once freedom is a fait accompli, the story holds that emancipation is 'criminal' for ruining most Black people, while 'the better class' of Black Americans are those who 'scorn freedom'. That's quite a price to pay to gain the approbation of white people, but it's precisely what it means to know your place. The story's sympathetic Black characters reject freedom, choosing to stay with their enslavers and agreeing that slavery's supposed horrors are just ignorant Northern propaganda.

When Yankee women insult the 'devoted retainer' Uncle Peter after the war with the racist epithet, he starts crying and tells Scarlett no white person has ever used that word to his face before – as if white supremacists were delicate about protecting the feelings of the people they'd enslaved. Scarlett responds that 'Uncle Peter is one of our family', confusing the racist Yankee women ('You don't suppose she meant a relative? He's exceedingly black'). Uncle Peter blames Scarlett for talking to Yankees at all, thereby putting him in a position where he could be treated 'lak a mule or a Affikun'. When Scarlett protests that she said he was one of the family, he responds that isn't a defence, it's just a fact, affirming that the feeling is mutual, and that the Yankees are the real racists, for treating him like an 'African'.

Outraged on his behalf, Scarlett thinks 'of the faithful few who remained at Tara in the face of Yankee invasion when they could have fled or joined the troops for lives of leisure'. The logic of this is eye-popping: becoming a soldier in the midst of a bloody civil war constitutes a 'life of leisure' and shirking one's duty as an enslaved labourer? In fact, approximately 200,000 Black soldiers served in the Civil War, helping to effect their own emancipation and hold the Union together. The accusation is incriminating if taken at its word: even Margaret Mitchell dimly realized that Black people probably preferred going to war over being enslaved. Words in *Gone with the Wind* have a way of stumbling like this into revealing more than they clearly intend.

At the same time Scarlett's affection for the 'faithful few' recycles the myth that 'superior' house slaves were more likely to stay with the families who held them in bondage than field hands. In fact, plantation enslavers like the O'Haras were deeply hurt when their most 'faithful retainers' were the first to leave. Having convinced themselves of their own propaganda about 'willing slaves', they were bewildered and betrayed by what they viewed as inexplicable ingratitude.[20] 'Those we loved best, and who loved us best – as we thought – were the first to leave us', a Virginia enslaver wrote.[21] Field workers had fewer transferable skills and were more dependent on working the land, and so many were forced back into sharecropping. This is what white landowners chose to construe as 'loyalty'.

Not incidentally, the Yankee women also want to know about 'the bloodhounds which every Southerner kept to track down runaway slaves', and don't believe Scarlett when she says they didn't have bloodhounds at Tara, a dodge that enables Mitchell to evade the question of whether Scarlett knows about runaways. This is the novel's sole mention of fugitive slaves, because where the enslaved are willing they do not flee. In reality, it is estimated that hundreds of thousands of the enslaved escaped to freedom, in all cardinal directions.[22]

The insulting of Uncle Peter is one of endless passages in *Gone with the Wind* affirming that slavery was benevolent, reciprocally welcomed by the enslaved, and its horrors exaggerated by Northerners, who are the real racists. It is precisely emblematic of how much American popular memory treats both slavery and racism – as an unpleasant interlude that is best forgotten, in bad taste to bring up, and has little or nothing to do with American life after the Civil War brought it to an end. Those reversals continue through 2022, as teaching students about histories of entrenched racism is held to be a racist act, imposing racism upon young Americans who would otherwise be entirely innocent of its existence.[23]

And just in case any distress slipped through all the contra-dictions, *Gone with the Wind* placated white Americans by assuring them that slave plantations were idyllic anyway. This is how disavowal manages cognitive dissonance: it means conceding the existence of slavery, while erasing its pain and its profits. It means wilfully pushing slavery to the periphery of popular consciousness and being saved by the logic of exception. The whole point of the way the slave economy developed in the late eighteenth and nineteenth centuries was to make it possible for those profiting from slavery to disavow their active role in it. Few if any of the most powerful figures in American history before 1865 can be understood apart from it, and yet we continually tell stories in which slavery functions as something that happens offstage, instead of one of the primary engines driving the plot of American history.

That *Gone with the Wind* offers an apologia for slavery, from start to finish, is well known, but it's still worth pausing and thinking about. By 1936, seventy years after fighting a bloody war to end slavery, Americans had comfortably convinced themselves that there was nothing very wrong with slavery in the first place. They might have been forgiven for wondering why it was worth fighting a civil war over, in that case.

*

It is true that Mitchell was of her time and place. But it is also true that some of her more acute white Southern contemporaries looked at racial violence and white power in the 1930s with a clearer eye. William Faulkner is an obvious example, with his Civil War masterpiece, *Absalom, Absalom!,* published the same year as *Gone with the Wind.* But there are also writers like Lillian Smith, who lived in Georgia too, and fought against segregation and racial taboos including miscegenation. She disliked Mitchell and dismissed *Gone with the Wind* as 'One More Sigh for the Good Old South' in a 1936 review.[24] It was a trivial 'puffball compounded of printer's ink and bated breath, rolled in sugary sentimentality, stuck full of spicy Southern taboos', she wrote, recognizing its 'limited historical perspective' and naive allegiance to 'the terms of nostalgic old Planter-ideology'. But even Smith considered the novel 'harmless enough'.[25] The harm was still, perhaps, difficult for even the best-intentioned white people to discern in 1936.

Most white Americans evinced a strong need to maintain the ideal of plantation life, as *Gone with the Wind*'s first audiences kept almost admitting: 'Why can't you believe that plantation life was an ideal existence?'[26] demanded a little old white lady in Atlanta who was interviewed about her memories of the Civil War when the film came out. When the interviewer asked if plantation life could really have been 'that perfect' – surely at least some 'rough edges' had been softened by 'nostalgia for what, at its best, was an enviable state'? – the little old lady retorted: 'You moderns are too realistic.'[27]

This conscious refusal to be realistic about chattel slavery played out in responses to *Gone with the Wind* from the moment of its publication, a kind of collective Freudian slip in which Americans kept accidentally exposing what they were trying to deny: namely that a great many white people still viewed institutional Black slavery as, 'at its best, an enviable state'. At its best for white people, it may have been an enviable state – but even this fails to recognize the many ways, explored by historians, that enslavers were themselves brutalized by the systems of chattel slavery; or to acknowledge the overwhelming economic disadvantages faced by the non-enslaving white majority; or to consider the plight of the white underclass, whose degradation, humiliation, and intimidation were systematically enforced by the minority slavocracy.[28]

The story's first white audiences indulged in what they considered nostalgia but was in fact a fantasy quest for the ideal version of human subjugation. 'Where are the great cotton plantations of the South worked by thousands of black slaves?'[29]

asked a review in the summer of 1936. 'Where are the courtly aristocrats, the mint juleps, and the leisure life of long ago? Where are the dainty ladies trained from girlhood in all the arts to enchant and charm their gallants? ... Gone with the wind comes the sighing answer, gone with the wind.' That's one answer, but a more accurate one is that, apart from the mint juleps and the thousands of enslaved people, none of them ever existed, as the little old lady who objected to being 'too realistic' about slavery almost admitted. Even as white Americans were sharply censuring the rise of fascism in Europe, travelling to Spain to volunteer against Franco's army, they were also longing for the good old days when the United States had enslaved millions of non-white Americans.

In what moral universe could one even speak of an 'ideal' slave plantation? The fact that by 1936 such a phrase was an unthinking cliché, rather than self-evidently revolting, bespeaks the depths of delusion into which American history had fallen. As Hannah Arendt observed more than once, clichés protect us from reality, and especially from the political effort of having to think.[30] Cliché lets you talk about slavery without thinking about enslavement.

One might expect these defences of idealized slavery to emerge only from deep within the self-justifying South, but they came from all over the country. A critic in Oakland, California wrote that because Mitchell 'justly resent[ed] the absurd picture of slavery in "Uncle Tom's Cabin"' and other abolitionist 'propaganda', she had chosen instead to write about 'an ideal plantation before the war, with happy Negroes cherished by their white owners, not simply as valuable property, but as human beings', overseen by 'the mistress of the plantation[,] ... sincerely concerned in their wellbeing'.[31] Here is a presumably white journalist in California, in 1936, regurgitating antebellum pro-slavery disinformation wholesale, to the point of describing an antislavery novel as 'propaganda', and sympathizing with the 'just resentment' of readers almost a century later who still hated an

1851 novel for controversially suggesting that chattel slavery was not an ideal social order.

The truth is that mistresses of slave plantations, like their masters, were not sincerely concerned for slaves' wellbeing, or they wouldn't have enslaved them. By 1936 this self-evident fact had not percolated through to the *Oakland Tribune,* a California paper that was printing recruitment advertisements for the Ku Klux Klan just a few years before it published this review.[32] The nation's system of white dominance was justifying itself, producing its origin myth over and over, while applauding itself for its honesty and truthfulness. Its supposed accuracy is part of the mythmaking, its claims to truth-telling at the heart of the legend. White America kept insisting that bad slave plantations were the exception, rather than the definition of slave plantations.

In 1937 the African American historian Lawrence D. Reddick warned that a great many readers were likely to believe that *Gone with the Wind* 'represent[s] the true account in fictionalized form of what actually happened'[33] during the Civil War era, a prediction that proved all too correct. The fury of historic fact was all but obliterated first by aggressive denial, and then by soothing fables.

By 2021, white Americans who may have never set foot in the Deep South were proudly flying the Confederate flag in the US Capitol – while some of those whose grandparents had fought in the Second World War were asking if fascism was really that bad. Newly elected Senator Tommy Tuberville, from Alabama, declared a week after winning the 2020 election that his father, a decorated Second World War veteran who fought at the Battle of the Bulge, had gone to Europe so that he could aid in 'liberating Paris from socialism and communism', as history became whatever Americans wished it to be.[34]

6

Magnolia-white Skin

During the war, Scarlett asks Rhett: 'Is the army so short of men they've got to use darkies?' After the war, during Reconstruction, she is horrified to find that 'men were insulted on the streets by drunken blacks'. When she is assaulted near a shantytown, her two attackers are described as 'that thar nxxxxr and that thar white man'. Across its thousand and more pages, *Gone with the Wind* never once refers to Black people as people or human beings – not a single time. They are only dehumanized and generic racial categories. Black people are either (various) animals, especially all sorts of apes; or they are savages, just out of the jungle; or they are 'slaves', 'blacks', 'darkies', 'pickaninnies', 'negroes', 'mulattos', or 'nxxxxrs' – categories that the novel consistently contrasts with humans.

The novel's racism is far more extreme than those who haven't read it probably imagine. Tara's field hands have 'huge black paws' and 'caper with delight' at encountering Scarlett, while freed slaves run wild 'like monkeys or small children' after emancipation, 'as creatures of small intelligence might naturally be expected to do'. When Big Sam greets Scarlett 'his watermelon-pink tongue lapped out, his whole body wiggled, and his joyful contortions were as ludicrous as the gambolings of a mastiff'; after Gerald's death Pork looks like a 'masterless hound'. The Black man who assaults Scarlett is 'like a gorilla' and a 'black baboon', while Mammy's expression shows 'the uncomprehending sadness of a monkey's face'.

Mitchell was reportedly surprised when a reader for her New York publishers asked her to 'keep out her own feelings in one or two places where she talks about negro rule', and suggested rethinking references to 'Mammy's ape face' and 'black paws'. Mitchell responded that she had 'tried to keep out venom, bias and bitterness as much as possible' when writing about multiracial democracy, which the Confederate South vilified as 'negro rule' over whites. As for her descriptions, she intended 'no disrespect to Mammy for I have heard so many negroes refer to their hands as "black paws"'.[1] Furthermore, she added, 'when an old and wrinkled negro woman is sad there is nothing else in the world she looks like except a large ape. But I had not realized how differently this sounded in type,' she concluded, apparently still feeling that it sounded fine untyped.[2] Nor does Mitchell seem to have questioned why it was not possible for her to keep out venom, bias, and bitterness against the idea of Black people participating in democracy, even as she was protesting her benevolence toward them.

In one of *Gone with the Wind*'s many claims to modern realism that veil its mythmaking, Rhett tells Scarlett to reject the Old South's medievalist romantic trappings:

> 'Our Southern way of living is as antiquated as the feudal system of the Middle Ages. The wonder is that it's lasted as long as it has. It had to go and it's going now. And yet you expect me to listen to orators... tell me our Cause is just and holy? And get so excited by the roll of the drums that I'll grab a musket and rush off to Virginia to shed my blood for Marse Robert? What kind of a fool do you think I am? Kissing the rod that chastised me is not in my line.'

And yet that is precisely the kind of fool *Gone with the Wind* thinks its Black characters are – kissing the rod that chastised them out of fealty to the families they serve: Mammy is 'shining black, pure African, devoted to her last drop of blood to the O'Haras'.

All of the novel's sympathetic Black characters – Mammy, Dilcey, Uncle Peter, Pork, and Big Sam – stay with their former masters after emancipation, with what the Black filmmaker Carlton Moss accurately described in an angry open letter to Selznick in January 1940 as a 'radiant acceptance of slavery'.[3] The eminent Black journalist Joel Augustus Rogers agreed: the novel's '"good" Negroes', he pointed out, are 'the door-mats, the lick-spittles, the faithful dogs' who, in Mitchell's words, 'scorned freedom', while the '"bad" negroes are those who refused to let the whites treat them as if they were still slaves'.[4] When Scarlett runs into Big Sam outside of Atlanta during the early months of Reconstruction, he tells her all he wants is to go home to Tara because he has had enough freedom, and misses being told what to do: 'Ah sho be glad ter see Miss Ellen and Mist' Gerald agin. Ah done had nuff freedom. Ah wants somebody ter feed me good vittles reg'lar, and tell me whut ter do an' whut not ter do, an' look affer me w'en Ah gits sick.'

Most defences of *Gone with the Wind* hold that while the novel's racism is objectionable, it is of its time and in the background, of secondary importance to Scarlett's appealing psychological strength. But that defence replicates the novel's politics, in which white women's power is preserved at the cost of Black people's equality. Their own economic and social power was purchased, in a very real sense, at the cost of Black people; that power may have been limited by gender, but it was underwritten by race.

The breathlessly publicized 'Search for Scarlett', begun at the end of 1936 even as most readers were encountering the book for the first time, used Selznick's considerable promotional skills to add the glamour of Hollywood, at the height of its power, to the obsessive focus on a white woman at the heart of the story.

While Clark Gable stood apart, already anointed 'the King of Hollywood' and everyone's first choice for Rhett, the most beautiful and powerful women in film competed to share the screen with him, returning the story to a familiar, conventional dynamic of women as sexual rivals fighting for the attention of the powerful man.

The press reported on Selznick's determination to find an actress with 'magnolia-white skin – that skin so prized by Southern women and so carefully guarded' which Mitchell bestows upon Scarlett.[5] Fetishized whiteness and colourism went far beyond personal vanity and hierarchical status in a society that subjugated people with visibly brown skin. The historical irony is that the actress Selznick eventually cast, magnolia skin and all, was probably of mixed-race Anglo-Indian heritage (a rumour Vivien Leigh herself always denied) – because the racial purity they sought is a fantasy. It was central to the plantation legend at which Malcolm Cowley jeered in his 1936 review: 'Southern female devotion working its lilywhite fingers uncomplaining to the lilywhite bone.'[6] *Gone with the Wind* can only see Black people as the contrasting background against which a lilywhite woman could stand out more effectively.

*

The film's producers knew from the start that they had to tread warily, especially over the most inflammatory word in the book (then and now). Black Americans objected strenuously to its presence, but many white Americans argued that it added verisimilitude and couldn't see what the fuss was about.

The word had been sufficiently normalized in America by the spring of 1937, as Selznick began preparations for the film, that 'nxxxxr brown' was breezily declared a colour of the season, from New Jersey ('light brown sheer wool is the color with nxxxxr brown velvet lapels')[7] to Indiana ('bright cherry is popular… and nxxxxr brown, navy, saddle, tan, rust, cornflower blue and dark green are all quoted as picked to sell'.)[8] Such ambient casual racism may have helped spur African Americans' ferocious objections to the use of the word in Selznick's film; many prominent journalists and leaders urged Black Americans to boycott any work that employed 'the hate word'.

But Selznick and Mitchell both argued the term was realistic. Selznick said he feared the film would lose some of its 'Negro flavor' without the epithet. Mitchell wrote defensively scoffing at the objections, insisting that those protesting were 'Professional Negroes' causing trouble, sending the newspapers into a 'fine frenzy'.[9] She maintained that it was historically accurate to have her characters think and speak in those terms, citing in her letters the fact that Black people used the word about each other.

Mostly Mitchell's (doubtless genuine) bewilderment came from the fact that her Black figures had 'dignity' and far more wisdom and virtue than Scarlett herself. Rejecting charges that it was 'incendiary and negro baiting', Mitchell wrote: 'As far as I can see, most of the negro characters were people of worth, dignity, and rectitude – certainly Mammy and Peter and even the ignorant Sam knew more of decorous behavior and honor than Scarlett did'.[10]

Perhaps African Americans were unconvinced by this argument because of passages such as this, contrasting the innate dignity of mixed-race Dilcey, the only character with Native American heritage, with Mammy's 'acquired' dignity:

Indian blood was plain in her features, overbalancing the negroid characteristics. The red color of her skin, narrow high forehead, prominent cheek bones and the hawk-bridged nose which flattened at the end above thick negro lips, all showed the mixture of two races. She was self-possessed and walked with a dignity that surpassed even Mammy's, for Mammy had acquired her dignity and Dilcey's was in her blood. When she spoke, her voice was not so slurred as most negroes' and she chose her words more carefully.

In her correspondence about the novel and film, Mitchell herself primarily used the words 'Negroes' or 'colored people', both of which were acceptable usage at the time, widely employed in Black newspapers as well as white, although in some of her earlier letters, Mitchell had occasionally referred to 'darkies' as well. As the controversy about the novel's language mounted, she presumably became more careful about her own words, and always protested her care for verisimilitude, for 'the fact that they call each other "Nxxxxr" today and… the fact that nice people in ante bellum days called them "darkies"'.[11] This remains a common justification for white people who choose to use the word, insisting that if Black people use it, so can they – as if there haven't always been different rules for different groups in America.[12] Mitchell understood this perfectly well, of course – it's why Uncle Peter takes offence at the Yankees using the word, because he had never been called that 'by no w'ite folks'. She knew that it was different when white people used it – but then, like many, concluded that equality should be construed as entitlement.

The racist epithet is frequently used as invective in the novel, and not only by Black people speaking to each other. By no coincidence, the novel's use of the word mounts during Reconstruction, as Mitchell accurately captures the way the insult was weaponized by white rage after emancipation. During the novel's depiction of the benevolent days of slavery, the word is primarily used by Black characters speaking to each other, and occasionally by a (presumptively vulgar) poor white, but never by any of the plantation class.

Only after the war do the novel's white protagonists begin using it, almost always in anger. While they are fighting starvation at Tara after surviving the siege of Atlanta, Scarlett directs the word in a temper at Prissy, which proves a turning point for her lexicon. When Prissy protests against milking a cow by declaring: 'Ah ain' no yard nxxxxr. Ah's a house nxxxxr,' Scarlett retorts: 'You're a fool nxxxxr… And if I ever get the use of my arm again,

I'll wear this whip out on you.' Immediately she reflects: 'There… I've said "nxxxxr" and Mother wouldn't like that at all.'

Mitchell is indeed using the insult carefully, to mark Scarlett's gradual degradation from the standards of her caste, as a symptom of the way Reconstruction is dulling what few sensibilities she had (a reversal of the well-documented, myriad ways that institutional slavery corrupted enslavers). But the scene also instinctively registers how racial invective functioned as a proxy for violence. Its use leads Scarlett directly into threatening to whip Prissy: the two go together. Meanwhile it never occurs to Scarlett that Prissy is now free and therefore Scarlett no longer has the licence to whip her. It doesn't cross her mind that the choice might not be hers – much less that her mother might object to the whipping, as well as to the word. It would seem that the very idea of whipping a slave is less alien to the women of Tara than the story likes to pretend.

During Reconstruction, Scarlett's use of the slur increases along with her swearing and drinking. Soon she is thinking in raging terms about being taunted for her poverty by 'damned nxxxxr lovers', and of the 'free nxxxxrs and Yankee riffraff' who populate the woods outside Atlanta. She refers several times to the 'free issue nxxxxrs' who objectionably exert their freedoms after the war, and when she starts her lumber mills she has trouble with 'free nxxxxrs' who won't work for her (because they have the right to quit).

Mitchell insisted that all of this was accurate, and apart from the fatuous claim that the plantation class never used abusive terms against enslaved people in the antebellum period, it is broadly true. Racist invective was certainly unleashed during Reconstruction to meet the rising threat of racial equality, but Mitchell's denial of the word's casual ubiquity in the antebellum South is staggering, as even the most cursory perusal of a few newspapers makes all too clear. (Not only was the racist slur regularly printed in full; it was not uncommon for editors to redact a blasphemous adjective such as 'infernal' or 'blasted' while printing the full racist noun – 'his i--f---l runaway nxxxxr' – showing if nothing else the evolution of American taboos.[13]) But Mitchell also refused to admit how people take permission from words, how even in her own imaginary example the violence of the word unleashes Scarlett's hot desire for physical brutality.

*

Black Americans under Jim Crow, knowing the connection between the word and violence much more experientially, mounted a campaign against the film's use of the slur. Black papers like the *Chicago Defender* protested: 'the hateful word "nxxxxr" is seemingly in the script ten thousand and ninety-nine times.'[14] Earl Morris accused the Black actors who auditioned of betraying their race by reading from a script 'which contains the word "Nxxxxr" several times... while all their years of racial pride were being wafted away on the wings of a gust of "Wind." They forgot all about self-respect, pride, and duty to their race.'[15] The screenwriters, he added, 'must have worn the letter "N" off their typewriters,'[16] as he urged readers to write to the Hays Office demanding that the word be removed from the script, or they would boycott the film.

Morris also wrote in the nationally distributed African American *Pittsburgh Courier* urging again for Black Americans who 'object to the word "n . . . . r"' to demand its removal, along with 'all material that places the Negro in an inferior position'. To apologists claiming that it was intrinsic to the story's history, Morris rightly retorted that the Hays Code had long restricted its use in Hollywood film.[17]

In February 1939, Ruby Berkeley Goodwin wrote in the Black Atlanta *Daily World* reporting that George Cukor, at that point the film's director, had told her they had cut 'the objectionable term "n – – "' and that only 'in a very few instances will the term "darkey" be allowed'.[18] Goodwin was later said to be the writer who helped Hattie McDaniel with her Academy Award acceptance speech, in which McDaniel promised to always try to be a credit to her race, a line that met with a mixed response from the race in question.

The NAACP's Walter White tried to get Selznick to hire a Black advisor for the film, but the producers decided that Susan Myrick, a white reporter from Georgia and good friend of Mitchell's, who was hired as dialect coach, offered sufficient Southern expertise. This left the film's Black actors objecting to the use of the slur on their own behalf. Both Butterfly McQueen and Hattie McDaniel complained about its use, and McDaniel apparently encouraged her fellow Black actors to speak openly about their objections to it.[19]

The Hays Office, which enforced the production code controlling film content, gradually became more opposed as Black protests mounted, citing fears of the kinds of riots provoked by *The Birth of a Nation* twenty years earlier, and also warned Selznick they would not approve its use. Reluctantly, Selznick agreed to stick to 'darkies' – but soon had reconsidered, firing off one of his endless memos to an assistant:

> Increasingly I regret the loss of the better negroes being able to refer to themselves as nxxxxrs, and other uses of the word nxxxxr by one negro talking about another. All the uses that I would have liked to have retained do nothing but glorify the negroes, and I can't believe that we were sound in having a blanket rule of this kind, nor can I believe that we would have offended any negroes if we had used the word 'nxxxxr' with care; such as in references by Mammy, Pork, Big Sam, etc.[20]

Selznick went on to suggest specifically that they discuss 'with important negroes' the 'wonderful use of the term' when the Yankee women insult Uncle Peter, 'which is the most sympathetic and friendly-to-the-negroes piece possible, and which deals with Peter's reaction to the whites calling him a nxxxxr'.[21]

His Black cast was busily telling him otherwise, as were Black journalists around the country, trying to explain that the people who best understand the power of language are those who don't control its terms, but are defined by them.

Ironically, it was not racism that decided the matter, but a negotiation over a different word that had never yet been said on the American screen. Selznick was determined to force Rhett Butler's final 'damn' past the censors, and ultimately he surrendered the racial insult to retain the impact of Rhett's valedictory line. What was said by white people proved much more important, in the end, than what was said about Black people.

Removing the epithet from the film also had the perverse outcome of reinforcing the Lost Cause myth that white Southerners treated Black people courteously. The *New York Age* called the film a '$4,000,000 sugar-coating of Southern mythology' that tried to avoid boycotts by eliminating the most objectionable elements of the history it depicted – an elimination that had the unfortunate effect of persuading many white audiences that nothing objectionable had happened in the first place.[22]

*

The screenplay cut another racial term that Mitchell uses several times, which white Americans in the 1930s were even more confident was perfectly acceptable – 'pickaninny', used to describe Black children. (The word, which travelled widely around the Black Atlantic, probably comes from the Portuguese *pequeno*, for small.) Although the film never uses the word, press reports about it did.

At the Junior League ball held the night before the film's star-studded premiere in Atlanta, the Black Ebenezer Baptist Choir sang for the exclusively white audience in front of a plantation setting, dressed as slaves. One report, syndicated nationally, described the occasion in fulsome detail. When 'the curtain rolled back on a beautiful colonial setting and plantation darkies sang' spirituals, the actress who played Belle Watling, the prostitute with a heart of gold, was observed to shed a tear as the choir of 'shrill voiced little pickaninnies'[23] promised Atlanta's leading citizens 'There's Plenty of Good Room in Heaven'. One of the little Black children dressed as a slave and bringing a sentimental tear to white America's eye was a ten-year-old boy named Martin Luther King, Jr, who would be dead in thirty years for daring to dream of racial equality in America.

PART THREE

LOOK FOR IT
ONLY IN BOOKS

7

A Land of Cavaliers

'There was a land of Cavaliers and Cotton Fields called the Old South,' the Hollywood film begins. 'Here in this pretty world, Gallantry took its last bow. Here was the last ever to be seen of Knights and their Ladies Fair, of Master and of Slave. Look for it only in books, for it is no more than a dream remembered, a Civilization gone with the wind...'

This famous prologue comes not from Margaret Mitchell's novel, but from a cynical Chicago reporter turned satirical playwright named Ben Hecht, who should have known better – but Selznick was paying Hecht to sell the myth, not to question it. Very little is accurate about Hecht's description of the antebellum South, except that it can only be found in books. It was only ever to be found in books because that's where it was created. Both the Old South and the Lost Cause are fictions, and in a very real sense stories like *Gone with the Wind* are necessary to sustain them – without those fictions they cannot exist, because archival history does not support them.

The international version of the film began with a rewritten prologue, which jettisoned the feudalist trappings but found new ways to be wrong.

A Century ago there were two ways of life in the United States of America. The Northern way was that of growing cities and an industrial tomorrow; the Southern way, that of slave-worked cotton plantations and a romantic yesterday. To the North, slave labor was repellent and unnecessary; to the South, the foundation of its social and economic life. In 1860, Abraham Lincoln was elected president on the issue that a nation could not exist half slave and half free. Eleven proud and fiery Southern states refused to abolish slavery and seceded from the Union, making their bid as a new nation – the Confederate States of America.

This opening recycles several aspects of the Southern apologia, affirming that plantation slavery was romantic and nostalgic and flattering the Confederacy for being proud, fiery, and chivalrous, rather than obdurately committed to chattel slavery. It also repeats the common misconception that the North fought the Civil War out of a moral objection to slavery (which is only partially true), selling this mythologized version of American history as it travelled Europe and the Americas in the early 1940s, and made its way to the rest of the world across the next decade.

There were 'two Civil Wars and two kinds of Civil War novels', as Scott Fitzgerald observed after his brief stint working on the screenplay of *Gone with the Wind* in early 1939. The first kind was Lost Cause plantation fiction, what Fitzgerald described as 'the romantic-chivalric-Sir-Walter-Scott story like "Gone with the Wind," "The Birth of a Nation," the books of Thomas Nelson Page'. But there was also what Fitzgerald called the 'realistic type' of Stephen Crane and Ambrose Bierce, which was more historically accurate, less popular – and as of 1939 had yet to be filmed.[1]

The romantic-chivalric-Scott story is a miscellany of myths and legends, blending American history with English cavaliers, medieval knights, and feudal peonage, to glorify a world of 'master and slave'. It got its title ('lost cause'), characters (cavaliers, knights, ladies fair) and tropes (gallantry, chivalry, nobility) from medievalist romances, especially the stories of Sir Walter Scott. And its supposed facts derive from the self-justifying efforts of the direct beneficiaries of chattel slavery to maintain white sovereignty and avoid the worst consequences of the war they'd precipitated.

*

By the early 1860s, the United States held more than 4 million people of African and Caribbean descent in enslavement. Their combined financial value eclipsed the rest of the nation's economies – enslaved Black people were worth more to white people than the banks, railroads, and manufacturing industries combined, which all too easily obliterated their value as human beings.[2] Mid-century Southern slavery was not the pre-industrial, agrarian economy of popular imagination, inevitably defeated by the industrial power and modern financial systems of the North. The two systems were far more interdependent and mutually benefiting than that simplistic picture allows. Nor was the Civil War the product of a conflict between modern and pre-modern economies, although it was a conflict between wage labour and slave labour. Rather, between 1830 and 1860 the slave economy itself became increasingly industrialized, its profits leveraged by economies of scale.

The antebellum cotton economy powered America's rapid expansion in the early nineteenth century, accounting for more than half of the total goods exported from the US between 1820 and 1860, helping to accelerate the nation's industrial development. In the two decades before the Civil War, the American cotton crop increased greatly for several reasons, including improvements in seeds, while the industrial revolution, powered by immigrant labour, was taking hold in the North.

By the middle of the nineteenth century, much of the US economy was entangled in networks of capital that profited from enslaving people. The prosperity created by enslavement extended far beyond cotton, as world capital markets leveraged the collateral held by enslavers, helping fund vast empires of trade and industry, including shipping, railroads, and manufacture. Agrarian slavery was not simply replaced by modern industrialization. On the contrary, it helped shape many of America's economic and social institutions: today's carceral system, property laws, insurance industry, modern finance systems, all have roots in the Southern slave economy.[3]

Meanwhile the value of chattel slaves could also be transferred into mortgages, securities, and bonds, like any other assets. These debts could be hypothecated, with chattel-slave-backed bonds sold to investors nationally and even internationally, who could thus profit from slavery even in countries that had outlawed the international slave trade – as had the United States in 1808, a fact all too frequently forgotten in the popular memory of American slavery. These new financial systems incentivized the further commodification of enslaved people, stimulating the domestic expansion of slavery westward.

As America's bitter fight over slavery escalated in 1858, Abraham Lincoln delivered his famous House Divided speech, which many believe won him the presidency as war loomed. The conflict between the states could only be resolved by a crisis confronted and resolved, Lincoln rightly predicted, because 'a house divided against itself cannot stand'. If the divisions were not overcome, it would collapse:

> I believe this government cannot endure, permanently half slave and half free. I do not expect the Union to be dissolved – do not expect the house to fall – but I do expect it will cease to be divided. It will become all one thing or all the other.

Three years later, Lincoln was president and America was embroiled in a terrible war over the slave states' determination to preserve slavery in the South and expand it into the West. The fight over whether the western territories would enter the Union as slave states or free states is what finally precipitated armed conflict: although it is a truism that the Civil War was fought between North and South, it was fought over the West.

Nor did the North, as is commonly supposed, go to war to end slavery: while many in the North did fiercely oppose it, and the fight certainly came to a head over the issue of slavery, the fact is that Lincoln's government went to war to stop secession, not slavery (this is why they were the Union Army and not, for example, the Abolitionists). Slavery was the casus belli for the South, but not for the North. Although he had come personally to oppose slavery, in 1862 Lincoln wrote to the editor of the *New York Tribune* (Horace Greeley, who famously told all American young men to go west), declaring: 'My paramount object in this struggle is to save the Union, and is not either to save or destroy Slavery. If I could save the Union without freeing any slave, I would do it; and if I could save it by freeing all the slaves, I would do it; and if I could save it by freeing some and leaving others alone, I would also do that.'[4] Although Lincoln had already resolved on emancipation, his voters were by no means all agreed, forcing Lincoln to conciliate those who supported the Unionist cause but not freeing the enslaved.

Four months later, Lincoln issued the Emancipation Proclamation, unilaterally freeing all enslaved people in states in open rebellion – but maintaining slavery in the border states, which had not seceded and thus were still part of the Union. This effectively made abolition a punishment for states that left the Union, and the maintenance of chattel slavery a reward for those who stayed – the emancipation of the humans in captivity was not yet part of the calculus.

Lincoln's reasons for freeing the slaves were pragmatic as much as (if not more than) moral. As the conflict stormed on, it became clear that sheer manpower would be a major factor in its outcome, and Lincoln could see that whoever mustered the enslaved into their armies would have an advantage. He figured that the Union would benefit from getting there first. And so on 1 January 1863, he proclaimed more than 3.5 million Americans of African descent free at last.

This was not a message that was always conveyed to the enslaved, however – as *Gone with the Wind* inadvertently reveals. When Sherman's army invades Atlanta in September 1864, Melanie has just given birth and Scarlett, desperate to evacuate the remnants of their family, sends Prissy to find Rhett Butler to help them flee Sherman's army. When Prissy drags her heels, Scarlett threatens her: 'You go or I'll sell you down the river. You'll never see your mother again or anybody you know and I'll sell you for a field hand too. Hurry!' Obviously we are meant to sympathize with Scarlett's frustration, and realize she has no intention of fulfilling her threat. But the historical fact is that Prissy was emancipated by presidential proclamation on 1 January 1863 – almost two years before this scene takes place. Not only does Scarlett no longer even have the legal (much less moral) right to issue this threat, it strongly implies that Scarlett and her circle are among the many Confederates who accidentally forgot to inform the people they enslaved and kept illiterate that they had been emancipated.

Many of the enslaved were not in fact freed until after the war had ended in April 1865. By that point, Lincoln was dead, more than 600,000 lives had been lost, and more than two centuries of American chattel slavery were finally over.

But the problems of reuniting a divided nation and evolving out of the complex slave economy had only just begun. As Lincoln said, the nation had to embrace freedom fully for such a reconciliation to take place – and that is precisely what did not happen. The white South, and much of the white North, were prepared to accept the end of slavery, but not the start of racial equality. How to restore the former Confederate states to the Union, to overcome the problem of having declared war on the government they were now being forced to comply with, was a question that America never succeeded in answering.

This was not merely a political question, but also a moral and psychological one. To achieve reconciliation, the Confederate states had to do more than concede defeat in battle: they had to repudiate the white supremacy for which they had battled. The majority of them refused, remaining diehard to the very bitter end.

Overcome with resentment, furiously refusing blame, the South started telling a fable about the end of slavery that evolved out of the tales it had long told to justify slavery's existence. That fable did not question white supremacy, or the South's motives. Instead, it questioned the causes and consequences of the war, rewriting the conflict as one of sovereignty and states' rights: the invidious North destroyed the gallant South, who had never fought a war over slavery (and anyway, they'd add, slavery was a benevolent system in which everyone was happy). Although their cause was lost, it was an honourable one, defending a simple agrarian life wiped out by the aggressively industrial North.

The need to save face, on an individual and a collective level, eclipsed all other concerns. Before long the South was even claiming that they had not really been defeated on the battlefield, their surrender at Appomattox notwithstanding. To this day some white Southerners call the Civil War 'The War of Northern Aggression', despite the fact that it began with the Confederate states seceding and firing upon Fort Sumter.

Denial was the fundamental mechanism of American reconciliation, as white America agreed to pretend, in effect, that it had all been a dreadful mistake. Insisting they fought not over slavery, but over principles of sovereignty, Confederate leaders actively rewrote history to suppress the sordid truth of how hard they fought to perpetuate slavery.

This liberated popular memory into believing what it chose, with no accountability, no reckonings. The Lost Cause became a highly accurate name for a conflict whose true cause was almost lost to history, as the South insisted that the false narrative was of Northern victory. The North, they said, were the ones engaged in creating self-justifying propaganda to claim the moral high ground and conceal the truth of Southern innocence, projecting onto their enemies precisely the revisionist history in which they were so busily engaged.

The past is not a prediction – but it is a precedent, creating the possibilities for what the future will tolerate. The American future would, it turns out, tolerate a great deal.

8

A War of Ideas

D riven from their plantations by the devastation of war, Scarlett's circle of plantation aristocrats, also known as the Old Guard, move to Atlanta as Reconstruction begins to try to rebuild their fortunes, or at least make enough money to survive. They hold political meetings, over which Melanie Wilkes, staunchest symbol of the Old South, presides. She is especially popular with Confederate heroes, naturally, including some historical figures whom Mitchell imports into her story. General John Brown Gordon, 'Georgia's great hero', attends with his family, along with 'Father Ryan, the poet-priest of the Confederacy', author of popular sentimental verses eulogizing the Confederate cause, such as 'The Sword of Robert E. Lee'. They are also visited by 'Alex Stephens, late Vice-President of the Confederacy', so familiar that he can be named informally. 'When the word went about that he was at Melanie's, the house was filled and people sat for hours under the spell of the frail invalid with the ringing voice.'

It is the autumn of 1866, about eighteen months after the war ended at Appomattox, and Confederate leaders, who have just lost a treasonous war, are roaming around Atlanta at will, ruining Ashley's surprise party and charming ladies with their ringing voices. Alexander H. Stephens was, in fact, arrested for treason and imprisoned for about six months after the war, but released before the end of 1865. In early 1866, the Georgia legislature elected Stephens as senator, intending to send him to Congress, only for them to decline the honour of being joined by the leader of the late insurrection. Decrying the South's intransigence in attempting to send Confederate leaders to the Capitol, Northern legislators refused to let Stephens take his seat – leaving him free to wander into fiction and enjoy the company of Mitchell's Old Guard.

Alexander Stephens is best remembered today for the infamous speech he gave just weeks before the Civil War began in 1861, declaring that the Confederacy's 'foundations are laid, its cornerstone rests, upon the great truth that the negro is not equal to the white man; that slavery, subordination to the superior race, is his natural and normal condition'. Stephens repudiated the 'old Constitution' of the United States, written by Thomas Jefferson and the framers, as 'wrong in principle, socially, morally and politically' for upholding the equality of all humans. 'Those ideas', said Stephens, 'were fundamentally wrong; they rested upon the assumption of the equality of the races. This was an error.' 'Our new government', he added, 'is founded on exactly opposite ideas.'

The 'great physical, philosophical, and moral truth' preserved by the Confederacy, Stephens insisted, was that 'African slavery as it exists among us' created 'the proper status of the negro in our form of civilization. This', Stephens explained, 'was the immediate cause of the late rupture and present revolution.'[1] It doesn't get much clearer than that.

That the South went to war to defend, and expand, slavery was not initially in doubt: as Stephens's Cornerstone Speech shows, the Confederacy was quite emphatic, at least at first, that it formed in defence of race-based slavery and white supremacy. Stephens was speaking days before the Constitution of the Confederate States was ratified, which actively promoted the enslavement of 'African races', promising to expand race-based slavery both westward and into the future, as it prohibited any law, whether in the present or ex post facto, 'denying or impairing the right of property in negro slaves'.

This was repeatedly asserted, in political addresses, legal debates over the constitutionality of secession, and in countless newspaper accounts. 'The South is defending slavery against actual aggression,' declared a Missouri paper in 1864. 'The rebellion was inaugurated to protect slavery against Northern aggression.'[2] An Alabama columnist agreed in the midst of war: 'In defending slavery we are defending the word of God.'[3] Lincoln was equally clear, telling the nation in his second inaugural address on 4 March 1865: 'Slaves constituted a peculiar and powerful interest. All knew that this interest was somehow the cause of the war. To strengthen, perpetuate, and extend this interest was the object for which the insurgents would rend the Union even by war.'[4]

In laying out its Declaration of Causes for seceding, the state of Georgia mentioned slavery twenty-six times, starting with numerous complaints against 'non-slaveholding' states for their positions on 'the subject of African slavery'. Lincoln's Republican party was, they charged, an 'anti-slavery party': working to prohibit slavery in the West and espousing 'hostility to it everywhere, the equality of the black and white races, and disregard of all constitutional guarantees in its favor', the federal government's anti-slavery policies were, they insisted, unconstitutional, and gave just cause for secession.[5]

While making the constitutional case in defence of slavery, Confederate leaders tended not to mention the economic argument, but the fact was that most Southern wealth was invested in human property, which comprised both asset and security, and was often the basis on which land was mortgaged. There was a reason the South went to war to keep the slave economy intact – and that it was bankrupted by slavery's abolition. Enslavement was not a consequence of racism; white supremacism was invented to justify the prior enslavement of African people.[6]

And so they bitterly opposed emancipation. Robert E. Lee, who would become the idol of the cult of the Lost Cause, called the Emancipation Proclamation 'a savage and brutal policy' that Confederates must oppose with their lives, 'if we would save the honor of our families from pollution, our social system from destruction'.[7] The 'pollution' Lee feared was racial: the term was a popular euphemism for miscegenation, a word that itself was not coined until the end of 1863, in a pamphlet entitled 'Miscegenation: The Theory of the Blending of the Races, Applied to the American White Man and the Negro'. The year was no coincidence: the threat to white supremacism created by the emancipation of Black people immediately conjured a new word to oppose it.[8]

Even as the war was being fought, however, rebel leaders began to claim higher principles than white supremacist economies. Partly this was because they were seeking international alliances, and the pro-slavery argument was not always a winner in countries that had themselves recently abolished the slave trade. Before long they were creating alibis, which were not always even consistent.

Confederate emissaries abroad approached the Vatican for support in their 'holy war' against Northern 'mobocracy', and made clear that they would consider monarchical government, including as a European protectorate.[9] International opponents of democracy took up the message with alacrity, echoing Southern objections to the 'fanatical egalitarianism' of their neighbours, which would lead to revolution and the anarchy of 'mob rule'.[10] A British conservative MP argued that America's 'sudden and extreme collapse' – 'the great Republic had fallen to pieces' – served as proof that the 'extreme democracy' of American society had failed.[11]

But at home, the Confederates had been appealing to revolutionary democratic principles. During the war Confederate president Jefferson Davis met with unofficial emissaries of peace sent by Lincoln, and told them: 'We are not fighting for slavery; we are fighting for independence,'[12] invoking the spirit of America's founding. The specific independence the Confederacy sought was the independence to enslave other people for their own enrichment, but Davis swept past that point, and soon the rest of the white South was following his lead, claiming the Confederates were freedom fighters upholding the principles of the Constitution they had just violently repudiated.

After Robert E. Lee's surrender at Appomattox, Davis insisted that 'African servitude was in no wise the cause of the conflict, but only an incident,' a claim that goes beyond effrontery into brazen (or pathological) denial.[13] Soon Stephens was similarly declaring that the war 'was not a contest between the advocates or opponents of that Peculiar Institution', pretending he had never given the Cornerstone Speech and even shamelessly claiming he'd been misquoted.

A mere four years after declaring the US Constitution 'wrong in principle' and its supporters 'fanatics' who suffered from 'a defect in reasoning... a species of insanity',[14] Stephens claimed that Southerners were motivated by a pure desire 'to maintain and perpetuate the principles of the Constitution, even out of the Union when they could no longer maintain them in it'.[15] The Civil War was fought, he declared, over 'opposing principles' of democracy – 'between the principles of federation, on the one side, and centralism, or consolidation, on the other'.[16] This was pure false equivalence, claiming that fighting for human enslavement was morally comparable to fighting for political equality, as if each were just differing democratically held viewpoints.

*

While insisting on the nobility of its reasons for going to war, the South also doubled down on the nobility of its way of life. These defences were built upon longstanding pro-slavery legends, which claimed that the South was a chivalric land of noble knights and ladies fair, and that what they characterized as the benevolent paternalism of slavery safeguarded the enslaved from the 'wage slavery' of the industrial North. The pro-slavery myth applauded the South's generosity in enslaving Africans for their own good: slavery rescued 'African Savages' from 'the brute liberty of the wild' and delivered them to 'civilization and Christianity', a benefit for which only a fool would think 'the African's savage freedom too precious to exchange'.[17] In 1859, as war loomed closer, the *Richmond Dispatch* scoffed at the 'abolition philanthropists' who were 'making a terrific outcry on the alleged importation of a ship-load of African savages to a country where they will be clothed, fed, civilized, and Christianized'.[18]

These two myths – that slavery was perfectly splendid, and had nothing to do with the war anyway – together laid the groundwork for the myth of the glorious Lost Cause, for which the South had bravely fought and regrettably lost. Both sides of the Civil War were applying the phrase to the Confederacy's support of slavery before the ink at Appomattox was dry. At first it was used as a criticism, to mean 'hopeless cause', as when a French writer had argued in an 1863 essay circulated by the northern press: 'As to the canonization of slavery, that must be left to the Southern preachers; all the intellect in the country cannot revive that lost cause.'[19]

But the meaning of the phrase soon altered. By December 1865, a couple of months after Alexander Stephens was released from prison for leading the treasonous war, the *New York Tribune* promised it would argue for the Southern states' restoration of power and influence, while also urging the North to avoid 'needless infliction of pain or privation on the upholders of the lost cause'.[20] The *Chicago Tribune* wrote at the same time, in equally sympathetic terms, of the South's 'love of a lost cause… its irrepressible devotion to the ideas that ruled the Confederacy'.[21] Soon both South and North were referring to the lost cause of the Confederacy in terms of commiseration, as the North decided to overlook the trivial matter of declaring war to defend slavery. Whether that decision was magnanimous or monstrous would be for history to judge – and it took most American historians the best part of the next century to do so.

On the first anniversary of the Battle of Appomattox, in 1866, the *New York Times* praised Southerners' continued 'defense of their lost cause', avowing its refusal to pity 'the firmest believers and advocates of Secession', who nursed the seed of rebellion, and 'talked treason until they believed it religion'.[22] In the South young women laid floral wreaths on the graves of soldiers as local papers declared: 'We are paying a tribute of affection to those who sacrificed their lives for a lost cause. We mourn the loss of the brave and patriotic',[23] an early instance of what would become a widespread tactic of conflating the sectional patriotism that led to treason with the national patriotism that opposed it.

It was a prominent journalist named Edward A. Pollard who popularized the name (and then claimed it as a trademark)[24] in a book he called 'the official, Southern history of the war: THE LOST CAUSE',[25] published in the summer of 1866. An editor of the pro-slavery *Richmond Examiner*, Pollard had advocated the revival of the international slave trade in an earlier book, *Black Diamonds* (1859); after the war, he felt impelled to justify the 'peculiar and noble type of civilization' developed in the Cavalier South and opposed to the Puritan North, a feudal society he said was based on principles of chivalry, which slavery promoted. Subtitled *A New Southern History of the War of the Confederates*, Pollard's book laid out in undisguisedly partisan terms the Confederate case for the war.

In a previous book, *The Southern History of the War*, first published in the midst of conflict, Pollard's denials had gone beyond claiming the Civil War wasn't fought to preserve slavery, or even that Southern slavery was benign. Pollard claimed slavery was a malicious fantasy invented by the North to discredit the benevolent institution of 'African servitude': it was fake news.

Slavery was a mere pretext for a quarrel the North was determined to pursue, Pollard argued; in fact, the very idea of slavery in the South, he indignantly (and untruthfully) declared, had been thrust upon it by the North. 'We use the term "slavery" in these pages under strong protest,' Pollard wrote in a wildly inaccurate footnote:

> For there is no such thing in the South: it is a term fastened upon us by the exaggeration and conceit of Northern literature, and most improperly acquiesced in by Southern writers. There is a system of African *servitude* in the South; in which the negro, so far from being under the absolute dominion of his master (which is the true meaning of the vile word 'slavery'), has, by *law* of the land, his personal rights recognized and protected, and his comfort and 'right' of 'happiness' consulted, and by the *practice* of the system, has a sum of individual indulgences, which makes him altogether the most striking type in the world of cheerfulness and contentment.[26]

It was only 'the nomenclature of our enemies' that 'designated as "slavery" what is really the most virtuous system of servitude in the world', Pollard added.[27]

His claims were so outrageous that they were challenged even at the time. A London review in 1865 objected to some of the same phrases, demanding:

> What does Mr. Pollard mean by the elevation of the savage, or by free citizenship in reference to the treatment of their negroes by the Southern planters? Is that a 'virtuous system' which separates husband and wife, and tears little children from the arms of their parents? Is the whip to be included in the 'sum of individual indulgences' which render the negro so exceptionally cheerful and contented? ... If Mr. Pollard has no better defenses than this to offer on behalf of the 'peculiar

institution,' he will do well for the future to remain altogether silent.[28]

Sadly for the future, Pollard did not stay silent, nor did he stop with declaring that 'the system of negro servitude in the South was not "Slavery"'. His denials were sweeping and barefaced: John C. Calhoun was not a 'Disunionist', although he was an outspoken proponent of secession. 'The war of 1861, brought on by Northern insurgents against the authority of the Constitution, was not a "Southern rebellion"', although they called themselves the 'rebel armies', their battle cry the 'rebel yell', and the conflict 'the late rebellion'.[29]

Anyone shocked by the blatant denials of reality issuing from the Trump administration, from the size of his inaugural crowds to his failures in handling the coronavirus pandemic of 2020 – and the complacent acceptance of these lies by tens of millions of Americans – had not been studying Lost Cause history.

*

As the Lost Cause took hold in the aftermath of war, it rapidly absorbed this mélange of arguments into one hazy, nostalgic fable. A hodgepodge of Walter Scott's romanticized medievalism, Thomas Jefferson's yeoman pastoralism, and nebulous ideas of revolutionary sentiment were fused onto extremely concrete power structures. A deep sense of bitter injustice took root and bloomed, fed by economic grievances of the white South, which was indeed devastated, financially and physically, by the war.

That sense of injury was legitimated by Andrew Johnson, a Southern Democrat from Tennessee who became president after Lincoln's assassination in 1865, much to the outrage of his abolitionist and unionist Republican Congress. Johnson passed sweeping pardons for the white supremacist South, forgiving them for taking up arms against the federal government and restoring to them former lands and possessions, easing the cost of defeat. Almost no Confederates, including their leaders, were punished after the war; Robert E. Lee, who led the war against the United States, was imprisoned for two years and then released. Soon after Lee was freed, President Johnson issued an amnesty against all who had taken arms against the nation.

An avowed white supremacist, Johnson maintained that 'white men alone must manage the South' (he also believed, relatedly, that upholding white governance would help his re-election chances). Johnson was an emblematic example of someone who opposed slavery while remaining intransigently white supremacist.[30] Growing up 'bound out' in servitude as a poor white, Johnson wanted to smash the planter-class slavocracy: the socio-economic distinctions between poor and rich whites were a crucial factor in the caste system of plantation politics, which played off the white underclass against enslaved Black people.

It was a divide and conquer strategy, what the historian W. E. B. Du Bois famously called the 'public and psychological wage' of whiteness, and others have since called compensatory whiteness, the zero-sum promise that even poor white people were superior to Black people. Any socio-economic advances by Black people by definition, then, took that psychological wage away from poor whites like Johnson, who used the power of the presidency to restore white supremacy, not challenge it. Thanks to Johnson's reneging on the promises of emancipation, Black Americans found themselves free in name only: penniless, unpropertied, with no education, and facing a raft of new laws and widespread racial terrorism that sought to return them de facto to the conditions of slavery.

Slavery was abolished by the war, but white supremacism was not. The problem was that white Americans could abhor slavery, and fight a war to end it, and also abhor Black people. They could believe that slavery was a moral abomination, and also believe in eugenicist racial science that claimed non-white people were biologically inferior to white people and that racism was the natural order of things, even if slavery was not.

Less than two months after the war had ended, the *Cincinnati Enquirer* offered an epitaph. '"Slavery is dead," so they say: but the negro is not; there is the misfortune. For the sake of all parties, we say: Would that he were!'

The Black American, the editorial added, 'has ceased to be a slave, without ceasing to be a disturbing element'.[31] Violence would be necessary, they agreed, to deal with the disturbance they felt – for surely the nearer Black people returned to the 'brute liberty of the wild' from which enslavement had rescued them, the more their innate savagery threatened white civilization.

The white South grabbed the moral high ground and clung on for dear life – while the white North met it more than halfway. 'All that is left to the South is "the war of ideas"', Pollard had announced in *The Lost Cause*; a '"war of ideas" is what the South wants'.[32] By the turn of the century, the South was winning that war of ideas, its big lie accepted across the United States.

9

The Scourge of Reconstruction

'The scourge of war had been followed by the worse scourge of Reconstruction,' muses Scarlett at novel's midpoint. The idea that Reconstruction was worse than war was fundamental to Lost Cause history, which insisted that the brief experiment in multiracial democracy that followed the Civil War was a fiasco. The second half of *Gone with the Wind* is set during Reconstruction, taking as self-evident that the period was a political debacle, a national tragedy – for white people.

Apologists for the Old South framed not only America's official version of the antebellum era and the Civil War, but also the power struggles during Reconstruction that laid the foundations for Jim Crow segregation. For a century after the war, American popular memory insisted that the decade during which the United States struggled to reunite, rebuild the South, and establish the rights of emancipated African Americans, had been a chaotic period marked by misrule and corruption. This was supposedly thanks to the combined failures of lazy and ignorant newly freed slaves, venal opportunists from the North ('carpetbaggers'), and equally venal collaborators in the South ('scalawags'). This frankly biased, and deeply racist, interpretation of American history was the nation's authoritative account for the next century.

As early as 1874, the national magazine *Harper's Weekly*, published in New York, was printing covers with carnivalesque scenes of Black legislators 'disgracing' their race. The caption reads, 'Colored Rule in a Reconstructed(?) State', while the statue of Columbia, representing the United States, chastises them with a racist pun on 'Aping': 'You are Aping the lowest White. If you disgrace your Race in this way you had better take Back Seats.'

By 1901, reviewing a new history called *The Confederacy*, the *New York Times* was declaring it 'a pleasant duty to concede' to the Confederacy 'the highest motives of honor and conscience. Few Northerners question to-day the moral integrity, the nobility even, of the best Southerners.'[1] This reversal went all but unnoticed at the time: instead of the Confederate South conceding that they had fought a dishonourable war in defence of slavery, the US newspaper of record conceded to them. White supremacy was healing the wounds of civil war, as a myth of white innocence and Black misrule suffused the nation, enabling reconciliation and reunification.

The idea that Reconstruction failed because Black people were inferior, rather than because white supremacists were intransigent, was soon legitimated by historiography that was itself white supremacist, including most influentially the scholarship of William A. Dunning, a professor at New York's Columbia University, and his student John W. Burgess. Starting with Dunning's 1907 *Reconstruction, Political and Economic, 1865–1877*, the Dunning School affirmed the Confederates' version of the war and its aftermath, establishing the orthodox historical view of Reconstruction for most of the twentieth century, to the extent that it even adopted the derogatory terms created by the defeated Confederates for those who opposed them: the carpetbaggers and scalawags. These colloquial terms, although entirely pejorative, were normalized by American historiography until only very recently – so much so that there are not yet equivalent neutral terms to replace them.

The Dunning School justified the structures of Jim Crow segregation, insisting that it was white Southerners, not Black, who were treated unfairly after the war, a credo endorsed by the well-read Ashley in *Gone with the Wind*: 'The South was being treated as a conquered province and... vindictiveness was the dominant policy of the conquerors.' That piece of disinformation became the foundation of America's modern myth of white victimhood.

A defeated South kicked while it was down by a vengeful North was also the story told by Claude Bower's enormously popular 1929 *The Tragic Era: The Revolution after Lincoln*, the most widely read book on Reconstruction for decades – and one 'absolutely devoid of historical judgment', as Du Bois noted a few years later. The accuracy of *Gone with the Wind* was vehemently defended on the basis of its conformity with Bowers's account,[2] and Mitchell's account hews closely to it. Bowers, a Northern white liberal who became a personal friend of Franklin D. Roosevelt, nonetheless wrote a history that is markedly sympathetic to white Southern enslavers and reviles Northern abolitionists. Bowers was not a Klansman, but Klan membership during the 1920s was higher in Indiana, Bowers's home state, than anywhere else in the country.

The entirety of Dunning School historiography gives the lie to the North's complacent belief that it went to war to fight slavery. The North took little interest in defining itself around the moral case for abolition the way the South continued to define itself around the supposed moral case for enslavement.

Thus Bowers could explain in a bestselling history that abolitionists and their allies were 'political parasites and looters, scalawags and scavengers, knaves and fools', who took control of Southern state governments 'and entered upon the pillaging of the stricken people' – who had declared war on the United States so they could keep Black people enslaved. Such accounts normalized the South's flat refusal to accept multiracial democracy, its hostility to Americans from the North as 'alien invaders', and its abiding hatred of the US federal government.

Reconciliation meant absorbing ideas that in any other context would have been abhorrent to many Americans, but which the mythmaking saved them the effort of considering. By the time *Gone with the Wind* was sweeping the nation in the late 1930s, for example, American readers accepted without apparent question Scarlett burning with resentment at seeing the American flag in Atlanta ('it had been a gay beautiful place and now – there was a large United States flag floating over it'). The fact that all of its protagonists despise the United States has never impeded the novel's popularity in the United States. During Reconstruction all Scarlett's friends and family refuse to sign the Ironclad Oath of loyalty, which promised to restore former Confederates their rights if they swore loyalty to the United States and said they had not voluntarily taken up arms against it. The mere idea of repudiating the Confederacy is so abhorrent that it leads directly to the death of Scarlett's father, Gerald, who 'died for our Cause, same as the soldiers did', rather than swear loyalty to American democracy.

The 'tragic failure' of Reconstruction gave Jim Crow segregationists in the 1930s the (biased) evidence they sought that the franchise should never have been extended to Black men and justified their violent efforts to deny the exercise of that franchise. Accepting all this unquestioningly, *Gone with the Wind* describes freed people during Reconstruction: 'Like monkeys or small children turned loose among treasured objects whose value is beyond their comprehension, they ran wild – either from perverse pleasure in destruction or simply because of their ignorance.'

In reality the lawlessness – whether from perverse pleasure or ignorance – was primarily among white Southerners, not Black. As a Chicago paper explained in 1868: 'The "military protection" the Union men need is not against negroes, nor Indians, nor Mexicans – but against Democrats – who have organized themselves into Ku Klux Klans and midnight assassins, to murder and intimidate all who do not hold their political views.'[3]

The collapse of Reconstruction they brought about led to white revanchism, as the Black American became 'the scapegoat in the reconciliation of estranged white classes', as white historian C. Vann Woodward observed back in 1955. The importance of this reconciliation in shaping American experience has become axiomatic in historical scholarship of the United States – but it is an idea that American popular memory has yet to accept.[4]

*

Lost Cause history received its first major challenge the year before *Gone with the Wind* was published, in W. E. B. Du Bois's landmark *Black Reconstruction in America* (1935). Where writers like Dunning and Bowers saw Reconstruction as a tragedy for the white South, Du Bois's revisionist history depicted a tragedy for Black Americans and for the nation, with Reconstruction as 'a crash of hell' that brought a 'whirlwind' of backlash violence against the freed slaves.

Du Bois was the first historian to comprehensively argue that white America reconciled over a mutually agreed silence, eliminating questions of race and slavery from official American history, and skipping over Reconstruction 'with a phrase of regret or disgust', in order to exonerate the white South and expiate its guilt.

'Our histories tend to discuss American slavery so impartially,' Du Bois observed with some asperity, 'that in the end nobody seems to have done wrong and everybody was right. Slavery appears to have been thrust upon unwilling helpless America while the South was blameless in becoming its center.'[5] Moral relativism prevailed as white people forgave each other for going to war over slavery and proceeded to ignore the plight of former slaves.

While *Black Reconstruction* received some critical praise by historians, it was greeted mutedly by the white mainstream press. White reviewers were simply not prepared to reconsider received wisdoms, Du Bois's carefully constructed mountain of evidence notwithstanding. More than one reviewer sarcastically derided Du Bois's thesis that the history of Black Americans and the active role they took in emancipation and Reconstruction had been entirely erased from a white mainstream American history, proving Du Bois's point by dismissing the possibility out of hand.[6]

Not until the civil rights movement did institutional American history begin seriously to question the Dunning School, using archival evidence to document slavery's atrocities and confront white Americans with its discomfiting realities and legacies. Margaret Mitchell, who died in 1949, would never have encountered these revisionist truths, and so her story comfortably recycles established fables about the peaceful antebellum years, the injustice of the North, and the anarchy of Reconstruction.

In marked contrast to the Dunning School and broadly in agreement with Du Bois, historians today concur that postbellum Reconstruction was a radical political experiment during which the United States attempted to go from race-based slavery to multiracial democracy in the space of a decade. The Military Reconstruction Act of 1867 required former Confederate states to adopt new constitutions that recognized the citizenship rights of Black Americans. They responded with retaliatory white supremacist violence, including the emergence of the first Ku Klux Klan, which helped restore white governance in the South after the war.

Du Bois confronted the misrepresentations of the Dunning School in his final chapter, 'The Propaganda of History', in which he reclaimed political agency for Black Americans, dismantling claims that they were the only people in history 'to achieve emancipation with no effort on their part', or that their deficiencies as a people led to the collapse of Reconstruction. Focusing on the biased history in school textbooks, Du Bois warned against writing 'history for our pleasure and amusement, for inflating our national ego', or for 'using a version of historic fact in order to influence and educate the new generation along the way we wish'. Such propagandistic history is merely 'lies agreed upon', and had enabled a toxic mixture of 'libel, innuendo and silence' to poison the well of American historiography.

The invention of race, by some 'unjust God', he added (one who laughed as he dropped a Black man into the capitalist adventures of western empires), 'turned democracy back to Roman Imperialism and Fascism; it restored caste and oligarchy; it replaced freedom with slavery and withdrew the name of humanity from the vast majority of human beings'.

For the best part of a century, that argument was dismissed as a polemical flourish by most historians when it was noticed at all. But this is missing Du Bois's point with a vengeance. The 'real plot' of the story of America was the moral error and guilt of creating slavery 'in the midst of a fateful experiment in democracy'. That conflict between freedom and power, democracy and fascism, is at the heart of the plot of America. And it is yet to be resolved.

10

The Embittered State

'I'm proud of the legislature, proud of their gumption!' Uncle Henry shouts during Reconstruction. 'The Yankees can't force it down our throats if we won't have it.' Scarlett's circle is delighted with Georgia for refusing to ratify 'the amendment letting the darkies vote', framing its 'stout refusal' in heroic terms as staunch defiance of a conquering force.

This is the same 'gumption' that Mitchell invites us to admire in Scarlett: her refusal to admit defeat. But what Scarlett's circle so resolutely defends is straight-up white supremacy: Uncle Henry is proud of Georgia for trying to block the Fifteenth Amendment, which extended the franchise to newly freed Black Americans. Their gumption is defending white governance. 'Confronted with the prospect of negro rule' – otherwise known as Black people participating in democratic self-government – the 'embittered state' of Georgia 'smarted and writhed helplessly', Mitchell explains as Reconstruction begins, describing how painful it was for white people to give up absolute power and share it with Black people, the outrage of watching their 'inferiors' be elected to high office: poor whites, scalawags, 'even some negroes'.

Endeavouring to establish the legal status of emancipated African Americans during and after the war, the Republican Congress passed three constitutional amendments widening citizenship protections and establishing what Lincoln had named Reconstruction. After the Emancipation Proclamation freed most of the slaves in 1863, the Thirteenth Amendment wholly abolished slavery two years later. The Fourteenth, ratified in 1868, guaranteed citizenship rights and equal protections under the law; and, in 1870, the Fifteenth enfranchised Black men. The latter also explicitly excluded women from the franchise in the Constitution for the first time, a point that is not incidental. African Americans were not deemed US citizens until the Fourteenth Amendment in 1868 defined 'national citizenship'. Two years later, the Fifteenth prohibited the denial of suffrage because of 'race, color, or previous condition of servitude'.

The amendments failed to prohibit any number of other pretexts for disfranchising voters, however, so the Reconstruction they were supposed to effect soon collapsed. Many Southern states refused to ratify the amendments at all (they came into effect federally regardless of state law once they passed the necessary majority of state legislatures): Tennessee, the last holdout, did not ratify the Fifteenth Amendment until 1997. Those states that did ratify them in 1868 and 1870, including Georgia, refused to be bound by them in practice. Federal enforcement of the amendments was weak or non-existent, while the South subverted the amendments by aggressively suppressing the Black vote with tactics including voter fraud, threats, intimidation, and violence.

They justified these measures with stories of Black incompetence and malfeasance, insisting that they were acting in simple self-defence. 'As for the negroes, their new importance went to their heads,' as Mitchell puts it. 'Realizing that they had the Yankee Army behind them, their outrages increased. No one was safe.' Tony Fontaine, a 'nice boy' from a neighbouring plantation, complains that carpetbaggers and scalawags are keeping 'the darkies stirred up' with promises of the vote, forcing him to hate Black people: 'If anybody had told me I'd ever live to see the day when I'd hate darkies! Damn their black souls, they believe anything those scoundrels tell them and forget every living thing we've done for them,' such as, presumably, going to war to keep them enslaved.

When Scarlett realizes what 'Reconstruction meant' to the South, she thinks its meaning was as clear 'as if the house were ringed about by naked savages, squatting in breech clouts'. Although this image primarily invokes indigenous Americans, Black characters are also described as savages (Mammy sees the world 'with the directness of the savage and the child'). The difference between naked savages in loincloths and African savages becomes moot, as the novel endorses the myth that Reconstruction meant victimized white Southerners were governed by brute primitives.

The Southern press likewise inveighed against multiracial governance as 'negro politics', 'negro supremacy', or 'negro rule' over whites.[1] In 1868, the *Atlanta Constitution* differentiated the 'genuine "carpet-bagger" – the thriftless, characterless, moneyless fellow' who came south after the war to 'speculate in negro politics', from the earlier history of immigrants, arguing that if immigrants had come like carpetbaggers 'to overturn our attractive system of government and to establish negro rule', to alter political practice or 'displace, in one-third of the nation, the white race', then they would have been shut out.[2] They could stay because they supported white governance, too.

The prospect of a single Black legislator sends Mitchell's characters, as it did the Southern press, into hysterical predictions of the collapse of civilization. Outraged at the mere concept of Black enfranchisement in 'our state', Tony Fontaine warns: 'Soon we'll have nxxxxr judges, nxxxxr legislators – black apes out of the jungle.' The racism of this is not merely dehumanizing. *Gone with the Wind* appeared a mere decade after the Scopes Monkey Trial took Darwinism to court to try to deny that humans were related to apes. The immense anxiety sparked by this idea was bound up in older racist tropes which held that Black people were apes and white people were human. Proof that white people were also descended from apes challenged the entire racial hierarchy.

It was Darwin's cousin, Francis Galton, who adapted these ideas into the pseudo-science of eugenics, which allowed that white people might have evolved into a higher species of human. This is why Scarlett thinks about how many generations separate Africans from the jungle when she muses in similar terms to Tony Fontaine: 'Here was the astonishing spectacle of half a nation attempting, at the point of bayonet, to force upon the other half the rule of negroes, many of them scarcely one generation out of the African jungles.' Once white people were forced to concede that they might have come out of jungles, too, scientific racism sought to prove that they had emerged much earlier, and come much farther, than Black people.

In reality, the half of the nation that tried to hold the other half hostage was the Southern half, which had attempted to force the North, at the point of bayonet, to accept slavery in the South and its expansion across the West. The rapid political gains Black people in the Reconstruction South made, some rising quickly to high office, were resisted in the most brutal possible terms: more than one Black politician was murdered in broad daylight, while the Black population was stripped of newly gained property and voting rights. All this *Gone with the Wind* naturalizes, while insisting on the patriotic loyalty and principled stand of former enslavers, which underwrites the myth of white martyrdom that pervades the story.

The white South had self-governance restored with its ratification of the Fourteenth and Fifteenth Amendments, a supposed condition for readmission to the Union, and for the removal of Union forces after the war, although in the end neither condition could be fully enforced. After Union forces withdrew from the South, white dominance was sweepingly re-established below the Mason–Dixon line in local and state law – and in lawlessness.

Not until the civil rights movement led to the Voting Rights Act of 1965 did the United States attain anything close to universal adult suffrage, but in 2013, the Supreme Court gutted its key provisions in *Shelby County* v. *Holder*. The Voting Rights Act of 1965 had prevented regions with dubious voting-rights records, primarily the states of the former Confederacy, from unilaterally changing local electoral laws without approval from the US Department of Justice. But in 2013, Chief Justice John Roberts helpfully explained from the bench that racism in America was over, voting security had been permanently achieved, and therefore no further protections would be required: 'The conditions that originally justified these measures no longer characterize voting in the covered jurisdictions.' Time to move on.

Local Republican governments, including in Georgia, took their cue and moved on very quickly indeed from *Shelby* v. *Holder,* immediately enacting a raft of voter suppression measures targeted not only at African Americans, but also at Democrats – often conflated in the current political discourse, just as during Reconstruction Republicans and Black voters were held to be synonymous. The 2020 Georgia presidential primary reported widespread chaos in polling places in Black neighbourhoods, with long lines, late openings and early closings, insufficient machines, insufficient supplies, insufficient staff.[3]

As late as 1932, Southern Democrats in Florida, Tennessee, and Texas were introducing measures to 'exclude the negro'[4] as a class from voting in Democratic primaries, in direct contravention of the Constitution and four years before *Gone with the Wind* would celebrate the white South's pluckiness in excluding Black people from American democracy. It's a slippery slope, as defenders of 'extreme democracy' like to point out: without extreme democracy, before you know it, voting might be excluding you.

11

Cruel and Vicious Invaders

I t is a matter of pride for all the white men in the novel that they refuse to be reconciled with the Union after the war. Scarlett hears the same sentiment 'over and over until she could have screamed at the repetition: "I'd have taken their damned oath right after the surrender if they'd acted decent. I can be restored to the Union, but by God, I can't be reconstructed into it!"'

What to do with the unreconstructed South remained an unresolved question for Congressional leaders as Reconstruction • took hold. The radical wing of the Republican party favoured revolutionary policies that included permanent disfranchisement of former Confederates, confiscation and redistribution of Confederate property to landless people (Black or white), and universal suffrage, while the moderates argued for building pragmatic electoral coalitions that relied upon white Southerners.

Reconstruction governments sought to enforce civil rights with the Freedmen's Bureau, established by Congress at the end of the war as a relief effort for newly freed people, and to assist them in achieving full citizenship. Formally known as the Bureau of Refugees, Freedmen and Abandoned Lands, it provided Black Americans and impoverished whites with food, housing, medicine, education, and legal aid, as well as working to find dislocated people homes on abandoned or confiscated land.

And so, naturally, *Gone with the Wind* reviles it. Scarlett has 'a few unpleasant experiences with the Freedmen's Bureau' in the early months after the war, and soon loathes it for having 'told the negroes they were as good as the whites in every way and soon white and negro marriages would be permitted, soon the estates of their former owners would be divided and every negro would be given forty acres and a mule for his own. They kept the negroes stirred up with tales of cruelty perpetrated by the whites', so that in an area 'long famed for the affectionate relations between slaves and slave owners, hate and suspicion began to grow'. In reality those affectionate relations had numbered at least seventeen separate occasions of organized slave rebellions or resistance in Georgia before the war.

Dunning School history perpetuated the myth of the benevolent enslaver, maintaining that the planter class had the best interests of their former slaves at heart during Reconstruction. The Freedmen's Bureau was criticized for not trusting former enslavers to continue 'looking after' the people they had enslaved and blamed as manipulators who convinced gullible freed people that Southern whites were not their friends. 'The negroes must be turned against their former masters', Bowers wrote in *The Tragic Era,* as if slavery had been insufficient to the task. 'They should be taught to hate – and teachers of hate were plentiful', Bowers adds. 'Many of these were found among the agents of the Freedmen's Bureau… the simple-minded freedmen were easy victims of their guile.'

The premise of white paternalism and the perversity of Lost Cause history created a widespread assumption that the white people best entrusted with the care of childlike Black people were the ones who had gone to war to keep them enslaved. 'Left to themselves, the negroes would have turned for leadership to the native [Southern] whites, who understood them best', Bowers wrote. But 'their new friends from the North [had] been at pains to teach them these were the enemies', instead of 'hearken[ing] to the advice of their former masters and mistresses'.

Gone with the Wind, as ever, conforms closely to Bowers's unquestioning acceptance of inverted Lost Cause logic. Members of the Freedmen's Bureau were 'fixing the rules to suit themselves', Mitchell's narrator complains, as if the white South had not been founded and violently defended on precisely that standard. Scarlett thinks the Freedmen's Bureau was 'organized by the Federal Government to take care of the idle and excited ex-slaves', and 'fed them while they loafed and poisoned their minds against their former owners', an objection that implies Black people shouldn't eat unless they are working for white people, and blames the Yankees for freed Black people's hatred of their former enslavers, instead of admitting that maybe enslavement had something to do with it.

Although it is certainly true that enslavers accused freed people of parasitical idleness, this also conflates the Freedmen's Bureau with Roosevelt's New Deal, projecting 1930s debates about building a welfare state back onto Reconstruction. The New Deal created the nation's first sweeping federal support systems and was viewed by many prosperous white Americans as an incursion into their rights by an interventionist government. This meant the New Deal also got bound up in the idea that states' rights were a principle for which the South had fought the Civil War. Conservative Americans across America saw in the New Deal a pilot scheme for socialism and collectivizing the economy.

In the South, this perspective often confirmed a general belief that the federal government would continually seek to intervene in local affairs, an interpretation that retrospectively validated Lost Cause dogma of Confederate secession as valiant resistance to federal overreach. This allowed for accounts which, while supporting the New Deal policies that benefited white Southerners, also saw in it a worrying incursion against states' rights, while paternalistically encouraging laziness, discouraging competition, and disrupting meritocracy.

In real terms, historians have long argued, the New Deal was effectively positive discrimination for white Americans, carefully constructed to protect the structures of white dominance.[1] White Southern segregationists shaped its policies to benefit white and disadvantage Black Americans.[2] But white Americans did not always see it that way, just as they did not see that during Reconstruction the Freedmen's Bureau worked to extend civil rights across the South, including women's legal rights, and supported progressive economic reforms such as debt relief, while raising taxes on white property owners.[3]

Many of the despised carpetbaggers were in fact abolitionists who came South to help establish the rights of newly freed African Americans. Among them were educators working with the Freedmen's Bureau to expand the literacy of former slaves and open free schools for Black children. Black literacy was a clear threat to white dominance, both because knowledge of civil rights tends to lead to their assertion, and because it directly challenged the racist myth of biological inferiority that justified white governance. This is why the first Ku Klux Klan burned schools and attacked teachers.

But in *Gone with the Wind* the carpetbaggers and scalawags are equally contemptible, and interchangeable, a value system the film absorbs wholesale. Any doubts that Lost Cause history had been embraced by the entire nation are dispelled by the film, which reproduces the novel's vilification of the Northerners who cheerfully flocked to movie theaters to see themselves vilified. The film describes carpetbaggers in a notorious screen title as 'another invader... more cruel and vicious than any they had fought' in the war.

The carpetbaggers descend with their counterparts, the scalawags, whom Mitchell calls 'Southerners who had turned Republican very profitably': the possibility that any white Georgian might have voted for Lincoln to support the principle of racial equality, or to hold the United States together, is not even entertained by the story.

Corruption was indeed rife during the chaos of Reconstruction (including among Confederate Democrats), but many so-called scalawags were fighting for the Union cause and abolition, often at great personal risk. One of Georgia's most prominent scalawags, George Ashburn, who worked for the Freedmen's Bureau, lived among African Americans, and fought for their civil rights, became the first recorded victim of Klan violence in Georgia in 1868, when he was assassinated in full public view. Political corruption in Georgia was so rampant that year that eleven counties with Black majorities recorded not a single vote for a Republican candidate in the presidential election, although the Republican party, the party of Lincoln, was at that time the party of Black civil rights.

But even Mitchell acknowledges how many of the carpetbaggers were educators from the North. The Old Guard debates whom they hate more, 'the impractical Yankee schoolmarms or the Scallawags... The schoolmarms could be dismissed with, "Well, what can you expect of nxxxxr-loving Yankees? Of course they think the nxxxxr is just as good as they are!" But for those Georgians who had turned Republican for personal gain, there was no excuse.' In other words, one of the most popular stories of the twentieth century characterizes American schoolmistresses who taught Black children in public schools as vicious and cruel invaders who destroyed the gentle South.

*

The language of the Northern invader frames the Civil War as an act of aggression against the defenceless South, conquered by the alien rule of its own federal government. It was not, in fact, unreasonable to argue that people who had fought a treasonous war against a government they characterized as alien should be restricted from voting in that government's elections or holding office in it, but that is not the Lost Cause view.

It was no easy matter to agree what penalties, if any, should be imposed upon the millions of people who had engaged in an armed rebellion against the United States government, and now had to be re-established under it. The problem was so intractable that a reasonable argument could be made that it never was resolved, only endlessly deferred, as we just kept moving on, to avoid further divisiveness.

Most Southern states experienced temporary restrictions on white voting during the early years of Reconstruction, a circumstance upon which the men in Scarlett's circle are fixated, to her frequent exasperation. Mitchell's narration affirms that disfranchisement was motivated by Northern vindictiveness: 'The South must be kept down and disfranchisement of the whites was one way to keep the South down. Most of those who had fought for the Confederacy, held office under it or given aid and comfort to it were not allowed to vote, had no choice in the selection of their public officials and were wholly under the power of an alien rule.'

But alien rule is also a coded reference, what today we would call a dog whistle, a phrase that echoes 'negro rule' for a reason: this is the alien rule of what Scarlett's circle calls 'nxxxxr-loving Yankees'. African Americans had been described as an 'alien race' since the colonial era, and it was a phrase still commonly in use through the 1920s and 1930s. When a Black athlete was described as 'bearing the burden of his alien race' in 1927, for example, the New York Age sharply objected: 'The Negro is an American by birth and assimilation… the Negro is not an alien race, but has won his place in America, along with the other races of mankind.'[4] A decade later, the Southern press was decrying Europeans fascists' laws and propaganda against the 'alien race' of Jews without a hint of irony.[5]

The idea that Black people are an alien race, and not really American, aligns with the law of hypodescent, known more colloquially as the one-drop rule, which said that one drop of 'black blood' – that is, any known Black ancestor – made a person legally Black, and subject to enslavement or racial subjugation.[6] Its origins stretched back to the colonial era: in 1656, deciding that a 'mulatto [was] held to be a slave', a judge issued the first expression of American laws of hypodescent.[7] Within a few years, another more famous Virginia law established in 1662 that a mixed-race child 'shall be held bond or free only according to the condition of the mother', a ruling that underwrote chattel slavery and incentivized centuries of rape.

Comprehensively denying the citizenship rights of non-white Americans, these laws said that mixed-race people would be defined by the legally subordinate part of their heritage. By the same token, so-called white purity – being 100 per cent of 'white blood' – was necessary to make someone fully white, and thus a full citizen, with all the rights and privileges that whiteness bestowed.

Not until the 1920s and 1930s, however, were these laws and practices fully codified by the federal government: adopting the one-drop rule for the first time, the 1920 census defined 'white' as 'persons understood to be pure-blooded whites', whereas a 'Negro' was legally 'Negro regardless of the amount of white blood'.[8] In 1924, Virginia defined as white a person with 'no trace whatsoever of any blood other than Caucasian', and in 1930 a Black person as anyone 'in whom there is ascertainable any negro blood'.[9] The only thing pure about any of this was the double standard it created.

The nativist slogan '100% American', as popular in the 1920s as 'Make America Great Again' became in the 2020s (and as 'America First' was in both decades), was thus also racially encoded, a reverse claim to 100 per cent whiteness by asserting full citizenship, in a country where being 100 per cent American required being 100 per cent white. This same logic, reinforcing the idea that Black Americans are not fully American, drove the 'birther' conspiracy that Donald Trump rode to political power, claiming that Barack Obama, whose mother was a white

American and whose father was a Black Kenyan, was not 'really American' and therefore not legitimately president – because he was a member of an 'alien race'.

In addition to being alien savages, freed Black people in *Gone with the Wind* are uniformly depicted as the credulous dupes of one white master or another, dismissing out of hand any possibility that Black people might have exerted political self-determination. 'Formerly their white masters had given the orders. Now they had a new set of masters, the Bureau and the Carpetbaggers, and their orders were: "You're just as good as any white man, so act that way. Just as soon as you can vote the Republican ticket, you are going to have the white man's property. It's as good as yours now. Take it, if you can get it!"' This, too, was Dunning School dogma, that Black Americans were the pawns in struggles between white Americans, without the wit or agency to fight for their own emancipation or exercise their vote.[10]

Although Dunning School history taught white Americans like Margaret Mitchell that ignorant or deceitful Black voters were allowed to register multiple times (a Milledgeville, Georgia newspaper complained at the time that it was impossible to tell if African Americans had registered more than once because 'negroes look so much alike'[11]), more recent historiography repudiates that depiction. Up to 80 per cent of eligible Black voters in the former Confederacy enrolled in 1867, showing an eagerness to vote that surprised most white Americans, while the newly expanded franchise also helped poor white people exercise their right to vote.[12]

That year, local elections in Georgia were multiracial for the first time, with about 75 per cent of those registered Black male voters turning out at the polls to call for a postwar constitutional convention, electing a new General Assembly for 1868 that was mixed race, with thirty-seven Black delegates.[13] All of those Black members were expelled before the end of the year, and then reinstated by Congress, before the election of 1870 began restoring white governance. Within a few years the plantation class across the South had reclaimed power, often with extreme violence, and begun systematically stripping Black Americans of their newly acquired voting rights.

*

The slavocracy retaliated against the extension of the franchise to Black men with intimidation, threats (financial as well as physical), and race-based voter suppression laws. These 'black codes' – what James Baldwin called the 'slave codes' – included grandfather clauses (making the franchise conditional on having a lineal ancestor who had voted), poll taxes, whites-only primaries, felon voting restrictions, and literacy tests matched to inadequate educational provision, all of which effectively prevented Black people from voting in the South and laid the foundations for Jim Crow segregation.

At the same time a wave of mob violence swept the South, as lynching increased through the 1880s and peaked in the 1890s, when the Supreme Court legitimized Jim Crow segregation, thus imposing by law the racial subordination that vigilante violence sought to enact by force and terrorism. But although summary violence began to wane in frequency, its ferocity endured through the 1930s, as white mobs continued to use violence to maintain their status and power. Historians have also pointed out that lynching often enabled the seizure of Black land.[14] Certainly economic motives drove mob violence, as Black investigative journalism by writers including Ida B. Wells-Barnett established more than a century ago when they began campaigning against the 'unwritten law' of the land. 'Lynching is the aftermath of slavery,' Mary Church Terrell, a civil rights campaigner and co-founder of the NAACP, declared in 1904; it enforced 'the new slavery called "peonage".'[15]

In the early years of Reconstruction the South developed an entire ecosystem of vigilante groups designed to subjugate newly emancipated Black Americans, of which the Ku Klux Klan was only the most famous. There were also the Knights of the White Camellia, Pale Faces, Constitutional Union Guards, the Red Shirts, the White Brotherhood, and the White League, among many others. The Knights of the White Camellia began in New Orleans and spread through the Carolinas and west to Texas.[16] They were more elite, more secret and rumoured to be more effective than the Klan, while many of the group's members subsequently joined the White League.

The White League, also originating in New Orleans, helped overturn the 1872 gubernatorial election in Louisiana, as widespread electoral fraud led to ongoing violence and several attempts to oust the Republican governor by force. In 1873 at least 150 Black Americans were killed by a white paramilitary group in the Colfax Massacre, the bloodiest incident of racial violence in the Reconstruction South. Nearly half of the victims had already surrendered when they were slaughtered. Estimates of the death toll vary, but one Black observer at the time said the sun went down on Easter Sunday, 1873, 'on the corpses of two hundred and eighty negroes'.[17]

The unrest continued with the Battle of Liberty Place in 1874, when the White League, which avowed the violent restoration of white supremacy and plotted to assassinate Republican officials,[18] led an armed rebellion to unseat the state's Republican governor and install a Confederate Democrat, John McEnery. That effort failed, but the White League, like the Confederates, faced no repercussions for their attempted coup.

Amid the uproar that followed, Senator Oliver H. P. T. Morton, a staunch Republican and former ally of Lincoln's, warned against the consequences of allowing such a violent insurrection to occur without sanction. The state of Louisiana's seizure by the McEnery faction was effectively a coup, he said, adding that 'if McEnery had been placed in office it would have been by a fraud unequaled in extent and wickedness'.[19] It would also, he admonished, have given permission to further insurrections if it had been allowed to succeed.

Along the way Morton offered an account of the end of Reconstruction that would be vindicated by later historians, and stands in stark opposition to the version proffered by *Gone with the Wind* sixty years later:

> So far as reconstruction has failed, it has been by the conduct of its enemies, not because of the intrinsic defects of the system... [which] is based on the broadest principles of justice, equality and republicanism... The resistance to reconstruction grows out of the fierce opposition to the abolition of slavery and to the elevation of the negroes to civil and political rights. The proposition to establish a white man's government, excluding the negro from participation, is at war not only with the system of reconstruction but the Fourteenth and Fifteenth Amendments. The White Leagues are an armed organization, having but a single principle, which is that all political power, State and National, shall be vested only in white men, excluding negroes totally. They recognize no line of demarkation [sic] in politics except the color line; their weapons are murder and perjury, and they point to their own deeds of murder as evidence that the system of reconstruction is unsound and a failure.[20]

A Chicago editorial denounced one partisan account of the White League in Louisiana as a lie so outrageous that it was almost impressive, 'as strong a combination of falsehood and audacious impudence as ever came to our notice.'[21] The *St. Louis Times* had endorsed a conspiracy theory, informing its readers that the 'terrible scenes that have been forced upon the people of New Orleans were deliberately planned in Washington', a 'vile plot' to support the Republican party for the purpose of 'defeating the election in Louisiana.'[22]

Under the headline 'Unmitigated Falsification', the Chicago editorial observed of that conspiracy theory: 'There are lies so stupendous as to force a qualified respect, and there is a degree of impudence so overwhelming as to be almost sublime.'[23] It was a big lie recognized in terms that almost exactly anticipated Hitler's notorious formulation from *Mein Kampf*, that people are readier to 'fall victims to the big lie than the small lie', because the sheer scale of the audacity disarms suspicion. The bigger the lie, the more people fall for it.

The *Republic Magazine* placed blame where it belonged: former Confederate leadership's support for sectionalism had 'formed the Ku-Klux into horrible reality. It is their continued hatred of national ideas based upon the civic equality of all – that cardinal principle on which alone the Republic can stand – that has fomented the race issue and organized the iniquitous "White Leagues".'[24]

Reconstruction did not fail so much as it was overthrown. The *Republic* concluded that the problem was with a politics that had no strategy except to 'arouse race-hatred and fan into renewed flames the fires of sectional strife... It knows nothing but the dead past. It can only hinder, and then cry aloud in scorn at the troubles which itself has largely fomented. Its chief strategy is to raise false issues... "They raise the whirlwind" and reap, but cannot control, the storm.'[25]

America would continue to struggle between those who would raise the whirlwind and reap the storm of hatred. Some celebrate the coming of the storm, and put their faith in the leaders who promise to control it; others build shelters, instead.

*

When white governance was restored in Louisiana in 1876, it promptly made the White League its official state militia. Twenty years later the state erected a monument in New Orleans to commemorate the death of white supremacists during the Battle of Liberty Place, which was not removed until 2017. New Orleans also has a plaque memorializing the Colfax Massacre, describing it as 'the end of carpetbag misrule in the South', which remains in place.[26]

The great-grandson of John McEnery was interviewed by the *New York Times* after the removal of the Battle of Liberty Place monument in 2017, during which he declared that taking down an obelisk glorifying his ancestor's failed insurrection against the US government was morally equivalent to enslaving him:

> The name of that war, the most accurate name was the War of Northern Aggression, of the Northeastern establishment slave trader robber barons… My ancestors are being reviled as evil and bad people, and they are good people. We're condemned because we fought the federal government, right? What about the Native Americans? They waged war also and they also owned slaves. Are we going to tear down their monuments? This monument is a monument to greatness and nobility and the sublime purpose of the human race, and they vilified it through a massive lying campaign…

> Because I'm a student of history and I know how things work, I know that when you are going to conquer a people, subjugate a people, it's very important to remove their cultural foundations because their strength comes from that. The bad guys know that, which means they have to destroy our culture, our history. And when they do that, they destroy your identity, they destroy your soul. They come back and they replace it with the personality and the soul of a slave or a serf.[27]

This is where the lies of the Lost Cause have taken much of popular American memory a century and a half later: to an upended history that believes the Civil War was caused by the 'aggression' of 'Northeastern establishment slave trader robber barons', a claim that displaces even slavery itself onto Northerners in terms that would make Edward Pollard proud. McEnery defends the Confederacy's right to go to war against the nation's government and protests against their being 'condemned' for the trivial matter of having started a civil war, without mentioning that they were fighting in defence of the slavery he thinks is now destroying his dead white supremacist great-grandfather's soul.

In 1932, four years before *Gone with the Wind* appeared, a plaque was added to this monument to 'the sublime purpose of the human race' that declared: 'The national election in November, 1876 recognized white supremacy and gave us our state.'[28] A century after the Battle of Liberty Place, in 1974, the plaque affirming white supremacy was amended with an additional inscription: 'Although the "Battle of Liberty Place" and this monument are important parts of New Orleans history, the sentiments in favor of white supremacy expressed thereon are contrary to the philosophy and beliefs of present-day New Orleans.'[29]

History is endlessly revised, even when it's been chiselled in stone. Newly discovered facts can improve our understanding of the past, and sometimes people even ask new questions about the same old facts.

The plaque honouring the 'recognition' of white supremacy in Louisiana was removed before the monument to the Battle of Liberty Place was taken down in 2017, but the great student of history doesn't mention that fact, either.

12

The Deliverance of the State

When Scarlett returns to Atlanta in 1866, as Reconstruction takes hold, she views the city and thinks: 'They burned you, and they laid you flat. But they didn't lick you. They couldn't lick you. You'll grow back just as big and sassy as you used to be!' as she feels her 'blood sing' in response to 'the resurrecting town'. Atlanta's resurrection, rising from the ashes of Sherman's fires, mirrors Scarlett's own recovery: both survive but are hardened and degraded by the costs of that survival. After it finishes with the chaos of war (it's worth noting that Mitchell's military history is far more accurate than her political and racial history), *Gone with the Wind*'s focus shifts, along with that of its protagonists, to the single-minded restoration of white wealth and power.

Over the next seven years, Scarlett fights to reclaim her lost status and wealth, and although she is perfectly prepared to marry for money, Mitchell does force her heroine out into the marketplace, where Scarlett discovers she has a head for business. Rhett's financial prowess is part of his general masculine dominance: he masters money as well as he masters everything – apart from Scarlett, whom he never manages to control.

The novel ends in 1873, the year of the Colfax Massacre, which it never mentions (the only events outside Georgia recognized by *Gone with the Wind* are a handful of Civil War battles and Lincoln's assassination), but which marked the resumption of white control of Louisiana. The state of Georgia in fact ended Reconstruction a little earlier, by successfully ousting its own Republican government with less bloodshed than Louisiana, a history that *Gone with the Wind* incorporates into its plot. The only happy ending in *Gone with the Wind* belongs to white supremacism.

Rhett takes an active role in reclaiming white power from the biracial government in Georgia, as he predicts that people will 'remember for years' how he 'helped run the Republicans out of this state'. Scarlett doesn't believe the planter class will be able to regain power ('All they do is talk big and run around at night Ku Kluxing'), but Rhett knows Georgia's slavocracy better. 'If they've got to fight another war to get back, they'll fight another war. If they've got to buy black votes like the Yankees have done, then they will buy black votes. If they've got to vote ten thousand dead men like the Yankees did, every corpse in every cemetery in Georgia will be at the polls.'

When white Southerners reclaimed power after violently thwarting the efforts of Reconstruction, they called the period that followed Redemption, as white supremacists and plantation aristocrats redeemed the South from 'negro rule'. Redemption was counter-revolutionary, restoring what they saw as legitimate governance and ousting the radical forces of Republicanism; Du Bois called it a 'counter-revolution of property'.

After the Democrats reclaimed power in Georgia in the winter of 1871, Mitchell writes of white Georgia's 'deliverance' from misrule. They felt

> a deep-souled feeling of thanksgiving, and the churches were filled as ministers reverently thanked God for the deliverance of the state. There was pride too, mingled with the elation and joy, pride that Georgia was back in the hands of her own people

again, in spite of all the administration in Washington could do, in spite of the army, the Carpetbaggers, the Scallawags and the native Republicans... The negroes had frolicked through the legislature, grasping aliens had mismanaged the government, private individuals had enriched themselves from public funds. Georgia had been helpless, tormented, abused, hammered down. But now, in spite of them all, Georgia belonged to herself again and through the efforts of her own people.

Those people of Georgia's 'own' do not, of course, include the alien race of freed Black people.

Scarlett, who had pragmatically thrown in her lot with the Republicans despite her hatred of the Yankees, is disturbed by the outcome: Rhett, previously reviled for war profiteering, is now the most popular man in Atlanta, 'for he had humbly recanted his Republican heresies and given his time and money and labor and thought to helping Georgia fight her way back' – to white governance. Thus is Rhett personally redeemed, by helping Georgia's white leaders redeem white supremacism.

'Through poverty and oppression, we have gradually struggled upward from the ashes of defeat, throwing off bayonet rule, and redeeming our land from negro and carpetbag domination,' wrote the *Atlanta Constitution* twenty years later, as it warned at any cost against a return to Reconstruction, 'when white supremacy and white civilization and white home rule were menaced'.[1] They had brought about salvation, 'redeeming' the South from vindictiveness, corruption, and incompetence through the martyrdom of defeat.

*

The metaphor of redemption was pointed, as Mitchell's description of the prayers of thanksgiving for the state's deliverance and Rhett's atonement for past heresies underscores. The Christian overtones are clear: this was a judgement that meant their faith in white supremacy had been redeemed in the eyes of the Lord. This belief was consistent with a long tradition in American thought of seeing power as proof of God's grace, a crassly reductive version of the Calvinist idea of the Elect in which Americans have long traded, the childishly self-righteous view that if you are rich and powerful it's because God loves you more.

The idea of redemption runs throughout *Gone with the Wind* in both the economic and moral senses of the word, creating a moral economy. When Scarlett primly tells Rhett while he is blockade-running during the war that 'the only way to redeem yourself is to enlist', he responds: 'Suppose I don't want to redeem myself? Why should I fight to uphold the system that cast me out?' Scarlett doesn't know what he's talking about, saying she's never heard of any system, not recognizing the structures that underwrite her power.

The system that Rhett believes cast him out is currently engaged in enriching him, as he proceeds to explain to Scarlett. Just as the war started, he bought up thousands of cotton bales at pre-war prices and stored them in Liverpool to sell when England grew sufficiently desperate for raw material. 'I'm going to be a rich man when this war is over,' he ends, 'because I was farsighted – pardon me, mercenary. I told you once before that there were two times for making big money, one in the upbuilding of a country and the other in its destruction. Slow money on the upbuilding, fast money in the crack-up,' a fine explanation of the tenets of disaster capitalism.

The blockades Rhett is running are Union blockades of Southern ports, meant to stop the Confederates from trading the cotton produced by chattel slavery for international arms. By circumventing those, Rhett acquires the arms to defend slavery by selling the crops produced by slavery. But he also sails straight into New York harbour and does business with Northern firms ('sub rosa, of course'), and then down to the Bahamas where he buys the goods Northern merchants have sent for Southern blockade-runners to buy.

Blockade-running was rife during the war, with many Southern merchants pocketing the proceeds, including a small brokerage firm called Lehman & Brothers in Alabama that supplied the army with cotton and wool for uniforms – and were pardoned by President Johnson for doing so. That was a form of redemption, too. Redemption is tied up in the invisible economic system that people like Scarlett are rewarded for not recognizing, as in a debt that has been redeemed, a promissory note stamped 'paid' – in a structure that discourages its citizens from recognizing it as one. Lehman Brothers became one of the biggest banks on Wall Street, and eventually an object lesson in the failures of reckless capitalism.

First, however, they all benefited – as did the system that redeemed them. Scarlett's purpose is to redeem Tara, in the economic sense, from the risk of foreclosure, but the story works hard to redeem the system Scarlett represents. Scarlett's political obtuseness means that she doesn't understand the costs of her choices – but Rhett does, and soon enough is fighting for the system that he believes cast him out, and against Scarlett, because he knows the source of his power.

Many white Southerners felt they had paid their debts by losing the war they started. That is certainly Scarlett's view: 'The war was over, peace had been declared, but the Yankees could still rob her, they could still starve her, they could still drive her from her house.' This worldview admits no penalty for taking arms against the federal government, believing that wealth created through slavery should endure: 'I thought our troubles were all over when the war ended!' Scarlett cries. Having faced an invading army, the loss of family and friends, and the destruction of her home, Scarlett realizes her only fear is poverty – and so begin her mercenary adventures.

By contrast Black Americans are left arguing that they are the ones owed by a nation which has yet to redeem the promises it makes to them. That is the entire import of Dr King's 1963 'I Have a Dream' speech, a metaphor of redemption that he makes explicit, and explicitly economic: 'We've come to our nation's capital to cash a check', King said, on the 'promissory note' signed by the 'architects of our republic', a promise of 'unalienable rights' to 'life, liberty, and the pursuit of happiness'. But America has 'defaulted on this promissory note', King charged: 'America has given the Negro people a bad check, a check which has come back marked "insufficient funds".'

When King concluded his speech by listing the states in which he dreamed that the promise of racial equality might one day be redeemed, he began with Georgia ('I have a dream that one day on the red hills of Georgia the sons of former slaves and the sons of former slave owners will be able to sit together at the table of brotherhood') and returned to it near closing, after naming Mississippi, Alabama, and moving up to New York and Vermont and across to California. 'But not only there; let freedom ring from the Stone Mountain of Georgia!' – the place where the second Klan was born.

Redemption is central to America's value systems in a broader sense: it's how we keep redeeming our sense of innocence after all the unconscionable things we do. Redemption is the point of starting over, America's perpetual faith that it can reinvent itself. At some point in that process, identity becomes purely mythical, a concoction of stories and rhetoric.

A century after the Civil War ended, a truism had emerged: the North won the war, but the South won the peace.[2] Historians have often remarked that the American Civil War seems to provide an exception to the rule that victors write the history of wars. But perhaps that proposition is backwards: what if history is indeed always written by the victors, and therefore we should look to who wrote the histories if we want to know who really won a war?

For if the South won, the North didn't lose. The end of war did bring peace to white Americans – tenuous, bitter, ravaged, but peace. For Black Americans, though, it merely opened a new door in an old hell.

PART FOUR

A TRAGIC NECESSITY

13

Alleged Outrages

'They ride around at night dressed up like ghosts and call on Carpetbaggers who steal money and negroes who are uppity,' Aunt Pittypat tells Scarlett when she comes to Atlanta after the war in early 1866. 'Sometimes they just scare them and warn them to leave Atlanta, but when they don't behave they whip them and,' Pitty adds in a whisper, 'sometimes they kill them and leave them where they'll be easily found with the Ku Klux card on them.'

Taxes have been raised on the plantation class, sending Scarlett to Atlanta in search of enough money to avoid foreclosure on Tara. Recalling that Rhett amassed a fortune blockade-running and war profiteering, she decides to seduce him, marry him, or sell herself, as circumstances require. But when she arrives she learns from Miss Pittypat that Rhett has been imprisoned by the Yankees as an example, because they are 'upset' about the rise of the first Ku Klux Klan, who are undermining postwar military authority. Scarlett hasn't yet heard of the Klan when Aunt Pitty first mentions it, but Pitty is certain that Ashley must be a member: 'Ashley just doesn't tell you girls anything about it. Klansmen aren't supposed to tell.'

Rhett is not, in fact, a Klansman, but Pitty is correct in her surmise about Ashley, who as the novel's spokesman of the Old South must lead Atlanta's Klan, just as Melanie hosts the Confederate leaders. (Near story's end Mitchell disavows his membership, as Rhett belatedly reveals that 'Ashley never believed in the Klan because he's against violence of any sort,' a resistance Ashley heroically overcame for over a decade). Rhett has been mistaken for a Klansman because he murdered a Black man for being 'uppity' to a lady – the correct reaction, all in the Old Guard agree. The Yankees have imprisoned Rhett for what Scarlett's circle all treat as a minor infraction, but they are not alone in being unable to distinguish whether white supremacist violence marked a Southerner out as a Klansman or not.

Just as the gentlemen of the Old South would never abuse a slave and wished freed people well, so did Klansmen, Miss Pitty avers, merely dress up and 'call on' their targets – who were only white thieves and 'uppity negroes', and therefore deserved what they got. Only in a whispered, reluctant afterthought does Pitty admit that 'sometimes they kill them' – but even then the Klan leaves calling cards, because they are Southern gentlemen. Later admitting his guilt, Rhett reinforces the point that he was upholding racial and social hierarchies: 'I did kill the nxxxxr. He was uppity to a lady, and what else could a Southern gentleman do?' Rhett's irony does not make the statement any less chilling: white supremacist homicide was not a distinction of the Klan; it was required of every Southern gentlemen.

The first Ku Klux Klan, created at the end of 1865 in Pulaski, Tennessee, was wiped out thanks to aggressive intervention by the Grant administration by the early 1870s, after spreading across the South as disorganized bands of vigilantes who sometimes (but not always) disguised themselves with various grotesque costumes. Some wore elaborate masks, headpieces or helmets, occasionally embellished with antlers or horns, adapted from local minstrel and carnival traditions. They carried pistols and whips, and neither burned crosses to intimidate their victims, nor wore the later uniform of white robe and peaked hood. They might wear white, red, black or calico robes, various other disguises, or no disguise at all.[1]

The first Klan did not make its way to Georgia until around 1868; it was certainly not there in January 1866, when Mitchell has the Yankees imprison Rhett because of it. All the other men in Scarlett's circle are Klansmen, apart from Rhett. While perfectly happy to murder Black people, Rhett is too modern and too much of a renegade to join the Klan – but only because he thinks 'it's damned foolishness and not the way to get what we want'. Scarlett opposes the Klan on a similarly pragmatic basis; always impatient with questions of morality, she mostly worries about the harm to her fledgling business if the Yankees retaliate against the Klan. But when Rhett decides at the end of the story to win over the Old Guard, he remarks that 'he would even join their damned Klan to be respectable', because that, too, is just what a Southern gentleman does.

Although he does not claim to have saved a woman from rape per se, Rhett's act of vigilante violence reinforces the standard pretext for lynch culture, that it was created to safeguard white women from being 'outraged' by Black men, a nineteenth-century euphemism for rape. But as Rhett's example reveals, one of the (many) problems with this construction was that white women could be outraged by so much less.

The standard Lost Cause account held that the misrule of Reconstruction compelled the creation of the Klan, particularly through the need to protect the sexual purity of white women: 'It was the large number of outrages on women and the ever-present fear for the safety of their wives and daughters that drove Southern men to cold and trembling fury and caused the Ku Klux Klan to spring up overnight,' Mitchell declares. The historical reality, as ever in *Gone with the Wind*, was the precise opposite – it was the Klan who were committing outrages in the South, as Congress affirmed when they began investigating the 'alleged outrages' in the 'late insurrectionary states', a mandate later broadened to an investigation into the situation in the South at large.

Trying to avoid the obvious question – if white supremacism is so natural, why does it require so much violence to uphold? – white supremacists shifted the ground, claiming the violence was not about race, but about sex. The specific sex they cared about was interracial sex – and not because they cared about women's sexual safety. On the contrary. (It was, after all, an era when marital rape was not only legal, but frequently justified, by women as well as by men.) The purity they cared about was racial – the fears of racial 'pollution' that Robert E. Lee had warned about. The surest way of nullifying white supremacy is with racial mixing, because genetics don't respect human fantasies about race – or the vast economic structures teetering on those castles in the sand.

The Klan has had many iterations in American life since it emerged in 1866, and not one of them was ever motivated by the sanctity of womanhood. The Klan has always, quite obviously, been driven by the conspicuous racism its members exhibit. But women gave the Klan an alibi, enabling them to claim that white Southerners were reluctantly backed into vigilante violence, and that the Northern press was sensationally whipping up resentment against them. This is the version Mitchell endorses when Scarlett returns to Atlanta after the war:

> And it was against this nocturnal organization that the newspapers of the North cried out most loudly, never realizing the tragic necessity that brought it into being. The North wanted every member of the Ku Klux hunted down and hanged, because they had dared take the punishment of crime into their own hands at a time when the ordinary processes of law and order had been overthrown by the invaders.

White supremacist violence was a 'tragic necessity' forced upon unwilling white Southerners by Northern perfidy and Black violence – this, too, was an article of faith. It was also a barefaced lie, although one in which Margaret Mitchell certainly believed.

In her letters, Mitchell insisted that one of the Klan's 'earliest purposes' was 'to protect women and children. Later it was used to keep the Negroes from voting eight or ten times at every election. But it was used equally against the Carpetbaggers who had the same bad habit where voting was concerned.'[2] Her use of the passive voice turns the Klan into an impersonal weapon used by unknown agents for the good of society, rather than a very specific bunch of white people fixed on protecting their economic and political interests at any cost.

Miss Pitty similarly explains that the Yankees are prosecuting Rhett because 'so many uppity darkies have been killed recently' – a fine use of the exculpatory passive voice, to suggest that killing Black people just happens. That evasion has persisted into the twenty-first century, as police violence is routinely described as 'officer-involved shootings' in which 'a weapon was discharged' – by the officer, into a person who died, and was statistically likely to be Black.[3]

*

'The Yankees are very angry about it,' Miss Pitty tells Scarlett, in one of the novel's few accurate descriptions of the first Klan. One of the others is Rhett's assurance that the Klan was respectable: although popular memory would assume that the Klan was comprised of backwoods rustics and hoodlums, it was always led by former enslavers and supported plantation hierarchies, its membership including local officials and professionals such as doctors, ministers, and lawyers.

Northern Republicans were indeed angry about the first Klan, and for good reason. The Klan and their white supremacist allies in the South spread a reign of terror against Republican leaders, regardless of race. Republican legislators in Arkansas, South Carolina and Louisiana were assassinated, while white mobs roamed the streets in Southern cities, a paramilitary force intimidating Black citizens and enforcing the interests of the plantation class. Instead of rebuilding peace after the Civil War, white supremacists in the Reconstruction South sustained the conflict, fighting a proxy war through vigilante violence.

The Klan's purpose was not, as Mitchell believed, to keep Black people from voting multiple times in every election: it was to keep them from voting at all. One of the ways that white governance has historically maintained its grip on power is by circulating false claims of rampant multiple voting, while working furiously to suppress the legitimate vote. This is what white nationalists did during Reconstruction and Jim Crow, and it was what they did under Donald Trump, as they whipped up fears that the 2020 election had allowed unparalleled voter fraud among non-white voters (which is the only kind of fraud they recognize). According to a December 2020 survey, more than 75 per cent of Republican voters were convinced that voting machines in the 2020 election were rigged, and that millions of fraudulent ballots were cast, including thousands of votes in the names of dead people – much as Margaret Mitchell believed that the Klan had stopped Black people from voting multiple times at every election.[4] In reality, the only systematic fraud in the 2020 election was perpetrated by the Republicans.[5]

The first Klan made no secret of their motives, because their unquestioning white supremacism was its own justification: Black people did not deserve citizenship, and therefore the Klan would oppose it by whatever means necessary, from disfranchisement and stripping them of economic and property rights to intimidation, torture, and murder. Before the war, the economic value of enslaved people incentivized keeping them alive, creating financial, if not legal, inducements to keep from murdering them outright (although slave mortality obviously remained high). Once Black people were free to become an economic and political threat, white Southerners began eliminating them by any means available, while continuing to use spectacular violence as a deterrent.

At least three Republican candidates for the state legislature in South Carolina were assassinated in 1868, including Benjamin F. Randolph, one of the nation's first Black electors, who was gunned down by three white men on a crowded South Carolina train platform. Randolph's assailants were not pursued when they rode away, and despite the large number of witnesses, none of his killers was ever identified.

The Klan did not have a monopoly on white supremacist violence, as the example of Rhett Butler accurately suggests. But the Klan was its most vocal proponent and its most prominent face, rapidly becoming synonymous with it. As a Georgia man explained to Congress in 1871: 'These outrages now are spoken of commonly as Ku-Klux.' When asked for a 'definition of Ku-Klux', he responded: 'My understanding is that it is synonymous with lynch law.'[6]

The Klan soon became a byword for summary violence, joining another coinage adopted from a Spanish term for lynch mobs in the West, 'vigilantes', also sometimes rendered in English as 'vigilants'. As early as 1868 a Pennsylvania paper shared with its readers one of many 'dispatches from the South to the Northern press', which had announced: 'A party of vigilants took a stranger from a house in the edge of Gentry county, at daylight this morning, and it is supposed they have hung him. No particulars.' The paper offered a translation: 'For the enlightenment of our readers who don't know, we will tell them that word "vigilants" in this case means "Ku Klux"; the word "stranger", interpreted, is "Union man", and the word "supposed" means "known." Of course, in all such cases there are "no particulars".'[7]

The names given to people who perpetrated vigilante violence would change over the next 150 years; their victims mostly would not. Klan offshoots were called Conservative Clans, Constitutional Union Guard (or C.U.G.[8]), White Brotherhood, and Invisible

Empire. But regardless of the names they chose, what they stood for was clear. A South Carolina Republican paper wrote a scathing account of what 'Kuklux Law' meant in the summer of 1870, imagining a Klansman setting down his beliefs:

> The Constitution and Government of this State, formed under the reconstruction acts, must be overthrown by any means which are available... Having been unsuccessful in open rebellion by day, we are justified in resorting at midnight to masks, assassination and scourging; to perjury in the witness stand and jury box, and every species of outrage... As we have often been defeated at the free ballot, we have a right to use every species of intimidation to carry the election. The end justifies any means which we may see proper to adopt... So much of the law as protects us is the inalienable right of a freeman, but so much as interferes with our plans or punishes our acts is despotic, and ought to be disregarded. We are the virtuous, good and Christian men of the country and ought not to be governed by Republicans, and it is no great harm to kill and whip scallawags and nxxxxrs. (See constitution and by laws of Constitutional Union Guard, White Brotherhood and Invisible Empire.)[9]

This was very much the view of the American right after the 2020 election: they suborned and defended and excused perjury, claimed that voter suppression was necessary to keep them from being defeated at free and fair elections,[10] insisted that the end justifies the means, and claimed the law protects them but not their opponents.

*

Atrocities committed throughout the former Confederacy in the name of the Klan in the late 1860s and early 1870s prompted Congress to commission a report from its investigation into the disorder. Now known as the Klan Report, it ultimately ran to thirteen volumes and upwards of 10,000 pages, documenting firsthand testimony of white supremacist terror throughout six states in the postbellum South: North Carolina, South Carolina, Alabama, Mississippi, Florida, and Georgia. It is the most authoritative contemporary document about the first Klan, and it makes for harrowing reading.

The monstrous details of the testimony Congress heard in 1871 are not adequately rendered by words like 'lynching', 'torture', or even 'mutilation'. What became known in euphemistic terms as 'lynching' was by no means limited to hanging, although that certainly happened with dreadful frequency. But Black Americans in the postbellum South were routinely subjected to sadistic, unrestrained savagery, from whipping and beating to rape, castration, disembowelment, shooting, flaying, drowning, and burning, as well as myriad other acts of torture. The Freedmen's Bureau recorded a Mississippi case in which a Black man was 'murdered, beheaded, skinned, and his skin nailed to the barn'.[11] Klansmen openly displayed skulls and human limbs as trophies.

The first Klan didn't bother with elaborate rationales for their violence; they sought brutally and crudely to keep newly emancipated Black Americans in their (menial) place. 'People justify it upon the ground that it is necessary to keep the negroes in subjection,' a solicitor general in Georgia told the Joint Select Committee under oath in 1871. 'The idea of the liberation of the slaves, and the conferring upon them universal suffrage, is so obnoxious to the people of that country that I think that is the cause of the whole of it.' The Klan, he added, was 'intended to control the colored race', 'to keep the colored people down, to keep them in subordination'.[12]

The testimony corroborated the large number of white schoolteachers who were murdered in the company of Black people they were helping to educate. One former Klansman testified that the first Georgia Klan, headquartered in Atlanta, had between 10,000 and 12,000 members, and that 'the object of the organization was to control the negro vote and defeat the Republican party in obtaining offices'.[13] He had joined the Klan, he said, to help ensure the arrest of a white man who had raped his daughter, who was eleven or twelve; he left the Klan after the Klan had the rapist released because they owed him a favour.

So much for preserving the sanctity of white womanhood. Unsurprisingly, Klansmen were more likely to commit rape than to protect women from it. Another lawyer from Georgia stated that he knew of white women who had been 'very badly used in my immediate county'[14] by Klansmen, while the newspapers chronicled multiple charges that the Klan was raping both white and Black women, as well as the not infrequent 'mobbing of a white woman for living with a negro',[15] as it policed the biological boundaries between the races with sadistic brutality.

Lynching numbers are difficult to verify, less because it was secret, which it mostly wasn't, than because it was extralegal. But between 1877 and 1950, there were 4,084 documented instances of lynching across the United States, and there must have been many, many more that went unrecorded. The vast majority of cases were never prosecuted.

In nine counties of South Carolina, the 1871 report found that the Klan had 'lynched and murdered 35 men, whipped 262 men and women, otherwise outraged, shot, mutilated, burned out, etc., 101 persons'. One historian of racial violence in the Jim Crow South identified 460 victims of lynch mobs in the state of Georgia alone between 1880 and 1930, 441 of whom were Black.[16] No body count or statistical breakdown, as the historian Leon F. Litwack famously observed, could accurately capture the savagery and depravity of the assaults made on freed people in the name of restraining their savagery and depravity.[17]

Early in Reconstruction Scarlett hears of 'a negro who had boasted of rape' and was 'quietly hanged' by the Klan, as if it would be unseemly to lynch someone noisily. The qualification is revealing because, as Mitchell knew perfectly well, lynching was often very loud indeed. This was true both figuratively – the point of summary violence was to send a message – and literally, as roaring mobs bayed for blood. Insisting that it was quiet helped launder the Klan into a 'respectable' fraternal organization. For all their self-styling as the 'invisible empire', the Klan had no interest in invisibility. Their whole purpose was to intimidate and terrorize.

*

A few unspeakable examples from Georgia give an indication of the first Klan's barbarity. One man testified that he knew of an incident in which ten or eleven Black men were hauled out of their homes, one murdered outright, two whipped so severely that one later died, and another killed. Seven more had their ears cut off. He then told of a case in which a Black man and white woman were accused of cohabiting:

> He said that the colored man was taken out into the woods, a hole dug in the ground and a block buried in it, and his penis taken out, and a nail driven through it into the block; that a large butcher or cheese knife, as they call it, very sharp, was laid down by him, and lightwood piled around him and set on fire; the knife was put there so that he could cut if off and get away, or stay there and burn up. Doctor Swinney said that he cut it off and jumped out...

> After the colored man did this, they took the woman, laid her down on the ground, then cut a slit on each side of her orifice, put a large padlock in it, locked it up, and threw away the key, and then turned her loose. She went so for two or three days, and then sent for Doctor Swinney to cut it out.[18]

A Black man named Henry Lowther testified that he had been abducted by more than twenty Klansmen from a raid of 180 men, taken to a swamp, and given the choice 'to be altered or to be killed'. He chose castration and almost bled to death. 'Naked and bleeding very much', nearly frozen, Lowther walked over two miles to the house of the nearest doctor, who was not at home – because he was out on the raid.[19]

Lowther's crime was also having sex with a white woman, 'one of those low-down tramps who are scattered about the country', said another witness. Lowther had later said that she 'voluntarily followed him into the woods and... solicited him to have intercourse with her'. The chairman asked the witness, pertinently: 'Have you heard of any white man being castrated for visiting low-down characters?'[20] He had not.

Most of this testimony was actively suppressed by the white Southern press, who were themselves often Klansmen, and used their papers to excuse, justify, diminish, or flatly deny Klan sadism, further distorting the historical record. An Alabama editor, for example, responded to the Klan Report in early 1872 by calling it a malicious confection of Northern falsehoods – just as Edward Pollard had claimed of slavery itself. Republican leaders in the South and in Washington were conspiring, the editorial charged, 'to manufacture the pretext' for restoring 'the corrupt men' of Reconstruction governments: 'To this end, the flagrantly false and infernally malicious stories of ku klux outrages and "rebel" violence which in the fall and winter of 1870–71 filled northern republican newspapers and formed the staple of northern republican speeches, were invented, told, published, and retold and republished through the press.'[21]

Rhett says the same thing, when he tells Scarlett that the Republican governor during Reconstruction, Rufus Bullock, is so determined 'to keep in power [that] he's been desperately manufacturing Klan outrage stories where none exist, telling of loyal Republicans being hung up by the thumbs and honest darkies lynched for rape'. According to history as told by *Gone with the Wind*, the idea that 'honest darkies' were ever lynched is a fabrication, meaning that all lynching victims deserved their fates – everything else is an anti-Southern lie.

In short, they said, Klan violence was fake news, a conspiracy theory, as they worked to push white supremacist violence down an Orwellian memory hole, when the alteration of the public record succeeds in obliterating historical actuality.

This was so successful that in 1937, when the success of *Gone with the Wind* inspired the *Chicago Tribune* to run a serious feature on the history of the Klan, it told its readers that stories like *Gone with the Wind* and *The Birth of a Nation* gave 'a pretty good idea of the activities of the Ku Klux Klan', although both stories omitted 'the cruel and bad side of the situation'. That bad side of the Klan (implying there was a good side) included, according to the article, flogging, occasional whippings, some people put in 'coats of tar', and burned buildings, while 'here and there a murder was committed'.[22] But then 'organizing the Negroes for political purposes', the *Tribune* added, had 'naturally aroused the south to a white heat'. Thus is white supremacist rage normalized: such 'white heat' was only natural.

In truth, between 1865 and 1876, at least 2,000 Black freed people were murdered in the South, including thirty-four documented cases of mass lynchings; in all likelihood, there were hundreds or even thousands more undocumented victims. Many of these outbreaks of mass violence were around election days or when Black groups were marching or otherwise organizing to protect the franchise. This vicious reality was almost entirely obliterated from American historiography for the best part of the next century.[23]

*

The Congressional investigation into the first Klan gave the federal government power to act, and Grant's administration moved swiftly to crack down on the Klan across the South, arresting and jailing its leaders; within a year or so the first Klan was a spent force. But America has never been willing to do without the Klan for long. The first Klan lasted from 1866 to 1871; after what would prove its longest hiatus, it returned in 1915 for its second iteration, which peaked in the mid-1920s. Although the second Klan was in decline by the 1930s, it launched again after the Second World War, quickly reviving as a backlash against the civil rights movements of the 1950s, since when it has never disappeared. The Klan's membership is reportedly dwindling again in the twenty-first century, although white nationalism flourished under the Trump administration. Interest has shifted to newer far-right groups, including militias such as the Proud Boys, Three Percenters and Oath Keepers, who helped organize the Capitol siege.

But history has shown that it's a mistake to count the Klan out. In February 2019, the editor of a local Alabama newspaper declared: 'It is time for the Ku Klux Klan to night ride again,' because he wanted to lower his taxes. When asked about Klan violence, the editor shrugged. 'They didn't kill but a few people.'[24]

14

Dancing with Jim Crow

arly in the war, the recently widowed Scarlett attends a charity bazaar and scandalizes the Old Guard by dancing with Rhett Butler all night. The orchestra plays reels, waltzes, and polkas: Mitchell doesn't say whether they danced the Jim Crow Polka, but they could have. Named for the most famous minstrel act in America, it had been a popular dance since the 1840s. Minstrel shows were originally musical entertainments, sung by white performers in blackface, featuring songs with titles that say everything about the pleasure of minstrelsy for white people: 'Happy Are We Darkies', 'Oh! Mr. Coon', 'Darkies, Our Master's Gone to Town', 'My Pretty Yaller Gal', and the 'Jim Crow Polka' – the comic minstrel figure who would name the tragedy of racial segregation.[1]

The enormously popular blackface entertainments of nineteenth-century America appear only in passing in *Gone with the Wind*, when Melanie and Scarlett put out a fire at Tara set by Sherman's army on its march to the sea. As they survey each other's blackened faces, Scarlett tells Melanie, 'You look like a nxxxxr,' and Melanie responds, 'You look like the end man in a minstrel show.' Minstrelsy never explicitly returns, but its shadow hovers over the entire novel.

In October 1860, a few months before *Gone with the Wind*'s story begins, newspapers around the country reported the death of Thomas D. Rice, widely hailed as the 'author of "Jim Crow"' and 'father of Ethiopian minstrelsy',[2] a white performer said to have imitated a Black man in Pittsburgh who was known locally for singing and dancing a rhyme about the trickster figure Jim Crow. 'Before his time negro songs attracted but little attention,' an Ohio paper noted in reporting on Rice's funeral. 'He is certainly entitled to the distinction of being the founder of Burnt Corkdom.'[3]

Soon Jim Crow's legacy had extended far beyond burnt-cork blackface entertainments. As emancipation was replaced with segregation, the trickster figure of Jim Crow was increasingly invoked, as white Southern excoriations of 'accursed negro rule' were accompanied by cartoons of Jim Crow 'darkies'.[4] By 1891, the name had been applied to segregated trains, the so-called Jim Crow Car Laws, and within a few more years would name the whole system of racial segregation.

The word minstrelsy itself had travelled to blackface entertainments via the medieval romances of Sir Walter Scott, whose writings became a national mania in the nineteenth century. Towns across the United States changed their names to Ivanhoe and Waverley, while Scott's poem *The Lady of the Lake* gave America both its presidential anthem, 'Hail to the Chief', and the surname of its first great Black civil rights activist, Frederick Douglass, who renamed himself when he fled from slavery to freedom.

The medievalist revival was generally credited to Scott's *Ivanhoe*; there were other sources but their combined popularity left wandering troubadours roaming the American countryside as far north as Brooklyn's Prospect Park, which hosted a 'Grand Tournament' in 1870, where 'each knight, in costume' was to ride at the ring three times, while 'tilting' at each other.[5] (Sadly for Prospect Park locals, their champion, 'the Knight of New York city, S. Price Maury, was sick and refused to ride'.)[6]

But the fad for tournaments particularly captivated the Confederate South, where it lasted from the antebellum period until the 1880s. Plantation aristocrats mounted on armoured horses displayed their skills at tilting, jousting, and heraldry, competing for the privilege of crowning the 'Queen of Love and Beauty'. They paraded in velvet tunics with braided trim, ostrich feathers in their caps, talking of gentility and chivalry, and affected ersatz titles, such as the 'Knight of the Golden Lance' or the 'Knight of Kingstree'. At least some of these jousting knights in the postbellum South were known Klansmen.[7]

The popularity, thanks to Scott, of both knights and highlanders in the Old South is responsible for the peculiar farrago of cultural references eventually used by the Ku Klux Klan. While 'Ku Klux' likely derived from Kuklos, the Greek for circle, it was Scott's tales of the Highlands, glorifying many Southerners' Scottish–Irish ancestry, that helped inspire the idea of the 'clan'. But Scott's medieval legends left America's Klan incongruously peopled by knights and wizards, rather than chieftains or highlanders. And his sentimental medievalism meant the Klan felt entitled to declare itself 'an institution of chivalry', despite its penchant for homicide.

All this was more than playacting, or a forerunner of today's medieval re-enactment societies. These tropes actively helped the Confederate South define itself against the North and romanticize the inherent violence of its system into a chivalric code. The South's pastoral nostalgia was set in conscious opposition to the industrialized modernity of the North. Its aggressive feudalism recast Black slaves as loyal serfs, bound by devotion to the land and the family they served. An ascendant Southern nationalism absorbed this self-serving mythical genealogy, defending race-based slavery as a venerable feudal tradition, with the plantation merely its latest incarnation.[8]

At the same time, it reinforced the cult of Southern white womanhood, their chastity defended by gallant plantation aristocrats. The myth of hypersexual Black people underwrote this romance, in claiming that white purity must be defended from Black debauchery by any means necessary.

*

The folk roots of the eccentric branches of American culture are consistently more surprising than our histories allow: the unusual name for Jim Crow is one offshoot, the more unusually named Ku Klux Klan another. Both developed ostensibly comical names partly as misdirection, to camouflage their dark designs. Comedy began increasingly to offer plausible deniability.

After it was eradicated in the 1870s, references to the Klan appeared only occasionally in the local Southern press, for the most part to deny that it had anything to do with white supremacist violence. The Klan's outlandish name and violent behaviour had soon made it internationally notorious; in the 1880s and 1890s histories began to emerge chronicling 'that infamous society', in the words of London's *Pall Mall Gazette*.[9] An 1892 Sherlock Holmes story, 'The Five Orange Pips', featured the Klan; although Arthur Conan Doyle's focus was on its secrecy, not on its racial violence, the Klan was still Holmes's enemy, its 'infamy' definitional.

The recuperation and glorification of the Klan began with Thomas Nelson Page's popular novel *Red Rock*, published in 1898. Page, born in antebellum Virginia to an aristocratic slaveholding family, was a teenager when the Klan rode through the South, and idolized Robert E. Lee. Page's idealized tales of chivalric aristocratic gentlemen, genteel ladies, and faithful slaves – including the devoted Mammy and other comic minstrel figures – created the archetype of plantation fiction. A minstrel song, 'Carry Me Back to Ole Virginia', gave Page his title for *In Ole Virginia* (1887), the six tales of which comprise the classic example of the plantation school, exalting the disgraced South.

Plantation fiction, wildly popular across the country at the turn of the twentieth century, blended the pro-slavery plantation myth with Black minstrelsy. On the page, the minstrel tradition was defined for many white Americans at the turn of the century by the stories of Joel Chandler Harris. As a poor white youth in antebellum Georgia, Harris spent hours listening to the trickster stories of Brer Rabbit told by older slaves on a nearby plantation and later immortalized them as the tales of Uncle Remus. Such trickster tales, in which trapped figures outwit their captors and laugh all the way to freedom, were one of the oral traditions enslaved people adapted from traditional African cultures to share survival strategies, and which white people misread as simple entertainment. The Little Colonel novels of Annie Fellows Johnston, published from 1895 to 1912, were another phenomenon, ending in a 1935 film starring America's little darling, Shirley Temple, whose dance with Bill 'Bojangles' Robinson remains one of the last classic cinematic records of the minstrel tradition.

'Moonlight and Magnolias', recorded in 1935 by Al Jolson, a Jewish entertainer who made his reputation in blackface, helped popularize another name for plantation fiction, still one of the shorthands most commonly used to characterize *Gone with the Wind's* romance with the Old South. Its Black characters are purest minstrelsy, straight out of the plantation fiction Mitchell loved as a girl. Reinforcing white superiority with its stylized Black stereotypes, minstrelsy turns Black characters into puppets who exist to entertain white people and validate the status quo. Treating Blackness as comic relief, a respite from white suffering, is at the heart of minstrelsy.

Gone with the Wind is funnier throughout than its popular reputation suggests – in fact Mitchell's acerbic humour remains one of the novel's more enjoyable qualities – but for its first audiences, much of its comedy derived from minstrelsy. The film sharpened Mitchell's comedy, with Clark Gable offering a masterclass in the adroit delivery of sardonic one-liners and Hattie McDaniel's Mammy consistently undercutting Scarlett's pretensions and tantrums with mordant grumbling. The film's most famous comic performance, however, undoubtedly remains Butterfly McQueen's Prissy, the minstrel stereotype who trills and daydreams while Atlanta burns, promising Scarlett that she can deliver Melanie's baby, before confessing in a wild-eyed panic,

'Lordy, we've got to have a doctor. I don't know nothin' about birthin' babies!'

In the novel, Prissy's speech, like that of all the Black characters, is rendered in a dialect praised by many white reviewers at the time as 'superb',[10] 'Negro dialect set down 100 per cent accurately'.[11] Mitchell was gratified, replying that she 'sweat blood to keep it from being like Uncle Remus': 'I wanted it easily readable, accurate and phonetic. And I scoured the black country of this section routing out aged darkies who were born in slavery days' (a fine version of admitting they were enslaved).[12] The film's primary screenwriter, Sidney Howard, wrote to Mitchell complimenting her particularly on her Black characters: 'Those are the best written darkies, I do believe, in all literature. They are the only ones I have ever read which seem to come through uncolored by white patronising.'[13]

The preposterous idea that Prissy is 'uncolored by white patronizing' bespeaks the degree to which white America had normalized Black caricatures by the 1930s, for Prissy was quite obviously invented to be patronized: she exists only to highlight Scarlett's competence (as when 'the sight of Prissy's abject terror helped steady her').

Although in the novel the fight with Prissy over Melanie's labour is not particularly played for laughs, the spelling is: 'Fo' Gawd, Miss Scarlett! We's got ter have a doctah. Ah–Ah– Miss Scarlett, Ah doan know nuthin' 'bout bringin' babies. Maw wouldn' nebber lemme be 'round folkses whut wuz havin' dem.' There would presumably have been little appreciable difference between the way Prissy and Scarlett pronounced 'doctor', but only in Prissy's case is the word misspelled. There is similarly no need to spell 'what was' as 'whut wuz', apart from patronizing, and racializing, her – just as Uncle Peter's pronunciation of 'w'ite' is somehow mysteriously different from 'white'.

The use of 'comic', supposedly phonetic spelling of dialect is another form of minstrelsy – language performed in blackface. As Toni Morrison noted, phonetically spelled dialect renders

Black characters alien, and deliberately unintelligible.[14] It chokes off African American speech at its source, estranging its speakers from normative American language (and culture), and forestalling the possibility of communication between white and Black.

'I didn't like being a slave,' Butterfly McQueen later made clear, but she tried to cooperate, before setting firm limits. 'I did everything they asked me to,' she said, 'except I wouldn't let them slap me and I wouldn't eat the watermelon.'[15]

*

The minstrel figure, as later Black writers including Toni Morrison, Ralph Ellison, and James Baldwin kept trying to explain to white America, was a figment of white imagination, not Black. 'The country's image of the Negro,' Baldwin wrote in *Nobody Knows My Name*, 'which hasn't very much to do with the Negro, has never failed to reflect with a kind of frightening accuracy the state of mind of the country.'

Because America was a social drama with the fact of Black slavery at its moral heart, Ralph Ellison wrote in 1958, the figure of the minstrel evolved into national iconography. Ultimately the performer could be white or Black; their racial identity did not matter. What mattered was the mask of the minstrel, which worked to veil the humanity of Black Americans and reduce them to an empty symbol, 'to repress the white audience's awareness of its moral identification with its own acts'.[16]

That repression was so successful that in the early twenty-first century, white politicians kept being discovered in blackface at parties, because the comedy of racism had not yet worn thin. There were so many that CNN published a list of politicians 'who got in trouble over blackface' in 2019, including Canadian Prime Minister Justin Trudeau, the governor of Virginia, the attorney general of Virginia, half a dozen state legislators, and two policemen who had blacked up to go undercover in Louisiana.[17]

Mitchell's Black characters are all, without exception, dressed up in comedy racism to go to her fictional party. They are minstrel figures in precisely the way Ellison means, projections created to obscure the immorality of *Gone with the Wind*'s entire worldview from its audience.

The mask of the minstrel is another cover story, one of the many fantasies shielding white America from its own ugly truths, encouraging it to laugh at the tragedy it created. Newspapers often reported lynchings with humorous headlines, and not only in the South. 'NEGRO TREADS KENTUCKY AIR', quipped an Ohio paper in 1909, while one popular wisecrack was recycled for at least twenty years in headlines across the country: 'NEGRO MURDERER GIVEN SHORT SHRIFT', editors from Los Angeles to Boston joked.[18]

By the time Mitchell was writing *Gone with the Wind*, decades of such stories had helped desensitize the nation to its own brutality. 'It was the show of the countryside,' said a reporter of a 1930 lynching. 'Men joked loudly at the sight of the bleeding body, riddled with bullets. Girls giggled as flies fed on the blood.'[19]

15

Years of Terrorism

Like the rest of her circle, Scarlett is highly indignant at the Yankees for cracking down on the Klan, furious at the prospect of summary justice for members of an organization created to inflict summary justice. 'Suspected complicity in the Ku Klux Klan, or complaint by a negro that a white man had been uppity to him were enough to land a citizen in jail. Proof and evidence were not needed. The accusation was sufficient.' In reality this is the exact system that pertained first to the enslaved, and then to free Black people in the Jim Crow South.

This grievance appears within pages of Rhett Butler's admitting he murdered a Black man for being 'uppity', at which no one bats an eye. Scarlett's complaint is, in fact, one of the novel's many pure inversions of historical reality. Rhett's lynching a Black man for being 'uppity' is perfectly consistent with the historical record; the reasons given for lynching Black people in the Jim Crow South included 'insulting white woman', 'inflammatory language', 'writing insulting letter', 'bad reputation', 'unpopularity', 'giving evidence', 'refusing to give evidence', and many cases of 'unknown offense'.[1] These 'excuses for lynching' were publicized by the anti-lynching campaigner and journalist Ida B. Wells-Barnett as early as 1901.

There is not (*pace* Scarlett's indignation) a similar historical record documenting the lynching of white Americans for being uppity to Black. Instead, Scarlett believes that murdering Black men for being what white people consider uppity is generally the right thing to do: 'Even Rhett, conscienceless scamp that he was, had killed a negro for being "uppity to a lady".' Whatever defences of *Gone with the Wind* one may entertain, the fact is that it regards murdering a Black man as evidence of Rhett's residual morality. Rhett is redeemed by his willingness to act as judge, jury, and hangman, whereas the idea of anyone being imprisoned for lynching is an outrage to all the novel's protagonists.

This is why *Gone with the Wind* goes beyond fiction into propagandistic lies. 'The white people, unprotected by law, were terrorized,' Scarlett thinks more than once, when the Klan was created for the purpose of white terrorism, to debilitate or kill freed slaves and intimidate white Southerners who helped them. Even Southern newspapers admitted from the start that the first Klan worked 'with the expectation of making terrorism an auxiliary of social outlawry'.[2] By the 1920s the second Klan had named its officers 'Terrors', while references to 'Klan terrorism' had been commonplace since the 1860s,[3] and remained widespread through the 1920s and 1930s.[4] It was the obvious way to describe a paramilitary group that used violence and intimidation to maintain an entire class's control over the local population.

Throughout American cultural history white terrorism has been rewritten as self-defence, the summary executions of lynching as 'extralegal justice', the disfranchisement of Black people justified by their supposed corruption and incompetence, and all the structures of racial capitalism vindicated by this retrospective mythmaking. *Gone with the Wind* created 'a weapon of terror against black America', charged Earl Morris upon the film's release; it was a 'propaganda attack of the first magnitude against Negro America', offering a 'moral justification' of Jim Crow.[5] *Gone with the Wind* avoids acknowledging its own complicity with racial terrorism by projecting terrorism onto Black Americans. 'Three years of Reconstruction had passed and they had been three years of Terrorism,' Mitchell declares – the terrorism of 'negro rule' over white people.

Denial often entails simple and crude inversions of guilt, like a small child who hits a sibling and then claims to be the victim. At the collective level, blaming others for our own infractions becomes the politics of shifted blame. Racial scapegoating is not merely misplaced guilt – it is also displaced guilt, externalizing wrongdoing onto a different group to keep your own conscience clean and maintain your power, and moral high ground, over them. It creates a hall of mirrors: where white leaders demonstrably tampered with the polls, they accused Black voters of election fraud. Where they inflicted summary violence, they complained of it, their constant projection making every accusation a confession.

One of the key incidents in the novel, cut from the film, concerns the fate of Tony Fontaine after he lynches one of his freed slaves for frightening his sister, as he later explains:

> [The foreman] came to the kitchen door today while Sally was fixing dinner and – I don't know what he said to her. I guess I'll never know now. But he said something and I heard her scream and I ran into the kitchen and there he was, drunk as a fiddler's bitch… I shot him and when Mother ran in to take care of Sally, I got my horse and started to Jonesboro for Wilkerson. He was the one to blame. The damned black fool would never have thought of it but for him.

After murdering a Black man without even bothering to find out what he'd said, Tony decides he must also kill the 'white trash' scalawag Jonas Wilkerson, Tara's former overseer, for going 'too far with his nxxxxr-equality business', by saying 'nxxxxrs had a right to – to – white women'. (Anyone who supports Black equality is dismissed as 'trash' by the novel, whether the 'white trash' Wilkerson or the 'trashy free issue nxxxxxs' with whom he fraternizes at the Freedmen's Bureau.) When Scarlett protests, 'Oh, Tony, no!' at the very thought of interracial sex, Tony responds that he doesn't wonder she looks sick. The threat of miscegenation provokes Tony to further homicide – this time with the assistance of the honourable Ashley, who (despite deploring 'violence of any sort') argues with Tony for the privilege, but contents himself with holding back the onlookers as Tony stabs Wilkerson to death.

Scarlett and Frank Kennedy help Tony Fontaine flee to Texas after the murders, leaving Scarlett, in 'an agony of helpless fear', to wonder: 'What can we do with devils who'd hang a nice boy like Tony just for killing a drunken buck and a scoundrelly Scallawag to protect his women folks?' Punishing Tony's double homicide is an injustice, while the story literally demonizes as 'devils' those who institute laws against arbitrarily murdering a Black man for upsetting a white woman without even knowing what he'd said. It's pure projection: this is precisely what white Southerners were doing to Black from the 1860s to the 1930s – not the other way around.

A belief system that declares one group of people may commit summary violence at will, while another group of people cannot, by definition, be protected against it and have it called justice: this is what white supremacism looks like in action, a world of constant moral inversion – because the only justice the narrative recognizes is white dominance.

*

As part of its crackdown on the first Klan, Congress passed three Enforcement Acts between 1870 and 1871, empowering the president to defend with military force the citizenship rights conferred by the Reconstruction Amendments. The Enforcement Acts placed the administration of national elections under the supervision of Congress and authorized the government to supervise local polling places, expressly prohibiting interference with any citizen's right to vote, the bribery or intimidation of voters, or conspiracies to prevent citizens from enacting their constitutional rights. They also banned the use of terror or violent force to interfere with voting rights or with the ability of Congress to fulfill its constitutional duties.

The third Enforcement Act of 1871 was also called the Ku Klux Klan Act. It outlawed conspiracies and secret organizations, making it a federal crime to use 'force, intimidation, or threat' to interfere with people's civil rights. The president could use military force to prevent 'insurrection, domestic violence [i.e. terrorism], unlawful combinations, or conspiracies' if local governments did not.[6] Its passage was urged by President Ulysses S. Grant, who quickly used its powers to crush the first Klan.

The Klan Act thus enabled the federal prosecution of Klan leaders, some of whom were quickly imprisoned. Many more were given suspended or cursory sentences, even as Nathan Bedford Forrest, the first Klan's Grand Wizard and former Confederate general, repudiated the violence and issued orders that the organization should be disbanded. Historians dispute whether those orders were followed; most of the imprisoned leaders were released by 1875, and there is little evidence that the arrests changed anyone's minds. The first Klan did not last long, but its members' violent opposition to multiracial democracy endured, as did the legends it inspired.

When Donald Trump emerged as a presidential candidate in 2016, he was endorsed by the former leader of the Klan, David Duke, who announced he was 'overjoyed to see Donald Trump and most Americans embrace most of the issues that I've championed for years'. Challenged to disavow the support of America's most notorious Klansman, Trump prevaricated before claiming under pressure: 'I don't know anything about David Duke. OK? I don't know anything about what you're even talking about with white supremacy or white supremacists.'[7] Twenty years earlier, Trump had repudiated his affiliation with Pat Buchanan's Reform Party on the basis that 'the Reform Party now includes a Klansman, Mr.

Duke, a neo-Nazi, Mr. Buchanan, and a communist, Ms. [Lenora] Fulani. This is not company I wish to keep,' and then repeated the rejection a few days later: 'Well, you've got David Duke just joined – a bigot, a racist, a problem. I mean, this is not exactly the people you want in your party.'[8]

*

By 2021, it had become so axiomatic in the United States that terrorism was something Black or brown people did to white people, rather than the other way around, that one of the officers who testified before the Congress Select Committee about the 6 January insurrection said he 'came prepared' to defend his description of the Trump insurgents as terrorists. Officer Daniel Hodges, who himself was white and was injured that day, read from the US Statute Code that defines 'domestic terrorism' as 'activities that involve acts dangerous to human life', violate criminal law, and 'appear to be intended to intimidate or coerce a civilian population or to influence the policy of a government by intimidation or coercion'. Hodges added that he considered 6 January a 'white nationalist insurrection'.

At least some members of Congress agreed. Two Democrat Congressmen had immediately responded to the sacking of the Capitol by suing Donald Trump and some of his co-conspirators (his personal attorney, Rudolph Giuliani, as well as leaders of the Proud Boys and Oath Keepers) for violating the Klan Act of 1871 by conspiring to intimidate lawmakers and interfere with Congress's certification of the 2020 election.

Democrat Congressman Eric Swalwell brought a separate suit under the Klan Act against officials of the Trump administration, alleging violation of federal law by failing to prevent interference with citizens' voting rights. The Klan Act has a specific provision stipulating that 'it shall be lawful for the President and it shall be his duty' to protect those voting rights. And these are precisely the laws that Donald Trump broke in urging his followers to disrupt the certification of Joe Biden's electoral victory in the Capitol building on 6 January 2021 – the laws provoked by the explosion of white supremacist rage that was the first Ku Klux Klan, and that required him as president to stop 'insurrection, domestic violence, unlawful combinations, or conspiracies', rather than incite them.

16

A Giant Malicious Hand

'The South had been tilted as by a giant malicious hand' during Reconstruction, Scarlett thinks, 'and those who had once ruled were now more helpless than their former slaves had ever been', as Mitchell offers a perfect image of the malicious tilting of history, while denying the reality of whose hand did the tilting.

This statement is not only demonstrably false; it does some hard tilting of reality itself. The South wasn't passively 'tilted' by an invisible malicious hand: it actively seceded from the Union, precipitating the violence and chaos that followed. After the war the white South slammed its own giant malicious hand down on the scales once more, tilting power right back toward 'those who had once ruled'. As Ben Davis, Jr noted in his excoriating review of the film, *Gone with the Wind* also turned 'American history upside down'[1] – almost literally.

The characters in *Gone with the Wind* feel the same way, believing the natural order of things has been tilted topsy-turvy. Rhett says the postbellum South is now 'an upside-down world', while Scarlett sees inverted natural orders all around her. Glad that Atlanta is rebuilding, she reflects: 'The only trouble was that the soldiers crowding the streets wore the wrong kind of uniforms, the money was in the hands of the wrong people, and the negroes were living in leisure while their former masters struggled and starved.' Black people must work, white people must not.

Racial hierarchies have been overturned: 'The former slaves were now the lords of creation and, with the aid of the Yankees, the lowest and most ignorant ones were on top.' Mitchell strongly implies that it is this revulsion against the new order that sends Rhett at the end of the story in search of 'old towns and old countries where some of the old times must still linger'. He rejects Scarlett and the Atlanta she represents: 'Atlanta's too raw for me, too new.' Read this way, it is white supremacism that comes between Rhett and Scarlett – he can't live in a postbellum democracy, while she detests it no less, but compromises with it in search of power.

Railing against freed Black people, Scarlett thinks longingly of the old eugenicist, social Darwinist system, when plantation mistresses selected among their young Black slaves for 'the best of them', to be granted the easier and higher-status work in the house, while 'those consigned to the fields were the ones least willing or able to learn, the least energetic, the least honest and trustworthy, the most vicious and brutish'. Victim-blaming means that field hands deserved their fate, having been carefully rejected by wise and benevolent white mistresses. It is this class – 'the lowest in the black social order' – that Scarlett thinks Reconstruction put in charge.

The inverted guilt of the Reconstruction South shapes the entire psychology of *Gone with the Wind*, which endlessly transforms Black suffering into white martyrdom, Black wrongs into white justifications. As Scarlett begins to work after the war, taking over Frank's store and then buying a lumber yard, she thinks more than once that she is now worse off than the enslaved were:

Looking about her in that cold spring of 1866, Scarlett realized what was facing her and the whole South. She might plan and scheme, she might work harder than her slaves had ever worked, she might succeed in overcoming all of her hardships [only to have everything] snatched away from her at any minute. And should this happen, she had no legal rights, no legal redress, except... military courts with their arbitrary powers. Only the negroes had rights or redress these days. The Yankees had the South prostrate and they intended to keep it so.

This veers from absurd to appalling, starting with the fact that running a store for your own profit is not harder than being enslaved. Moreover, Scarlett's hardships, although real, were inflicted upon her by her own society's insistence on betting the farm on slavery, not by the Yankees; and the arbitrary powers of military courts were as nothing compared to the arbitrary powers of white Southerners. As false equivalence goes, this passage takes some beating.

But Mitchell keeps trying, as if to make it true through sheer force of will. Without a whiff of irony, Scarlett rages several times against being subject to arbitrary justice:

The commandants of the Yankee troops in the various cities had complete power, even the power of life and death, over the civilian population, and they used that power. They could and did imprison citizens for any cause, or no cause, seize their property, hang them... They regulated how, when and where they must dump their garbage and they decided what songs the daughters and wives of ex-Confederates could sing... They ruled that no one could get a letter out of the post office without taking the Iron Clad oath and, in some instances, they even prohibited the issuance of marriage licenses unless the couples had taken the hated oath.

Across the antebellum and postbellum South, white Southerners held power over life and death, controlling Black Americans' access to finances and property and language and history. They decided what enslaved people could sing, say, or read, and they outlawed marriage, while during Jim Crow, white people could and did imprison Black people for any cause, or no cause, seize their property, and they hanged them – or worse – with horrific and summary ease.

Asserting Scarlett's vulnerability, Mitchell ascribes to her precisely the experience of Black Americans in the Jim Crow South:

> She could be killed, she could be raped and, very probably, nothing would ever be done about it. And anyone who avenged her would be hanged by the Yankees, hanged without benefit of trial by judge and jury. Yankee officers who knew nothing of law and cared less for the circumstances of the crime could go through the motions of holding a trial and put a rope around a Southerner's neck.

The projection is so specific and spectacular that it is difficult to see it as unconscious, although its repetition also suggests the compulsive entrapment of an anxiety dream. Here are the seeds of white grievance, a nostalgic resentment that perceives only loss of individual power, refusing to consider the question of collective equality. Grievance is the politics of narcissism – the refusal to shift your ground, nursing your grudges, building spite into politics, while telling your enemies to move on in the interest of a unity in which you do not believe and for which you have no intention of compromising.

White Southerners did have some rights temporarily stripped from them in the immediate aftermath of the Civil War, although in point of historical fact many Black Republican leaders argued against punitive measures, both on democratic principle and because they feared precisely the white backlash that soon followed.[2] But the former Confederacy's opponents in the war that had just ended were not prepared to take their enemies' word that they had been reconciled to the nation they had fought so bitterly to leave.

The Fourteenth Amendment disqualifies from holding public office 'any individual who has taken an oath to uphold the US Constitution and then engages in an insurrection or rebellion against the United States, or gives aid or comfort to those who have', because Congress in 1868 did not think that public officials who had supported the insurrection against the United States government could necessarily be trusted to serve as its officers in future.

'The people of the North', an abolitionist Republican senator informed the Senate when they debated the Ironclad Oath, 'are not such fools as to fight through such a war as this… and then turn around and say to the traitors, "all you have to do is to come back into the councils of the nation and take an oath that henceforth you will be true to the Government."'[3]

That would be left to Democrats almost exactly 150 years later, who formed a government with the politicians who stoked the 2021 insurrection. As constitutional lawyers noted at the time, the language of the Fourteenth Amendment should bar Donald Trump from again holding public office, as well as members of the 'Sedition Caucus' who supported the insurrectionists, including Republican Senators Ted Cruz and Josh Hawley, and Republican House Leader Kevin McCarthy.

The two parties' representative relationship to civil rights has been turned as topsy-turvy as the depiction of slavery in *Gone with the Wind*. Over the course of the twentieth century, the Democrats increasingly became the party of civil rights, while the Republicans pursued the 'Southern Strategy' of exploiting white supremacism for electoral gain.[4] By 2021, the two parties' positions in respect of civil rights and multiracial democracy had flipped: the Republican party of Lincoln had become a party that defended insurrection, instead of fighting a war against it, while

Democrats welcomed back into Congress Republican leaders who had helped incite an insurgency.[5]

It was almost as if American politics had been tilted by a giant malicious hand – instead of turned upside down by the weight of its own historic lies.

17

A Nasty Place Like Shantytown

S carlett O'Hara has no morals to speak of, which is one of the things Rhett likes most about her. She worries about being caught and (having been raised Irish Catholic) fears the spectre of eternal damnation. But questions of right and wrong do not often trouble her, although she is surrounded by carnage, suffering, and the horrors of war. Survival and retaining Tara mean everything, at any cost.

When Gerald's valet, Pork, steals food for Tara during the war, he returns with minor gunshot wounds. 'The morals of the affair weighed lightly upon her,' the narrator comments. 'Instead of punishment or reproof, she only regretted he had been shot.' She feels the same way when she learns after the war that Big Sam has accidentally killed someone and must escape the Shantytown that has sprung up on the outskirts of Atlanta: 'She was not in the least alarmed or distressed that Sam had committed murder, but she was disappointed that she could not have him as a driver.'

Scarlett needs a driver because she has lost her backwoods white bodyguard, Archie, one of the characters the film eliminates. Archie is even more outspokenly racist than the other white characters, and Scarlett is shocked to learn that he was in Milledgeville Prison for forty years after killing his wife for adultery. 'A murderer!' Scarlett thinks, before the narrator characteristically blames the Yankees: 'They were responsible for a situation that forced a woman to keep a murderer at her side to protect her.'

It is one of the few times that Scarlett thinks in conventionally moral terms, and it's fairly unconvincing – for Scarlett appears to have forgotten that virtually all of her friends, lovers, and husbands are murderers, and so was her father, and so is she. 'Were there other ex-convicts at large, like Archie,' she wonders, 'murderers, desperadoes, thieves, pardoned for their crimes, in the name of the Confederacy? Why, any stranger on the street might be a murderer!' Well, quite – and all of the novel's heroes, from 'Little Alec' Stephens and John Brown Gordon to Rhett and Ashley, have been pardoned in the name of the Confederacy, too.

Rhett and Ashley both murder Black men in cold blood out of sheer white supremacism. So does Tony Fontaine. Gerald O'Hara is only sort of an exception, having killed an English absentee landlord's rent agent who is as negligible an entity in the novel's moral register as Black people ('a murder which was no murder to him or to his family'). Even weak Frank grows suddenly 'firm' and masculine when he declares that what matters most is 'scaring the darkies and teaching the Scallawags a lesson'.

Frank Kennedy's membership in the Klan and willingness to murder in defence of his wife is presented as his most redeeming quality, defining his masculinity, as India Wilkes explains to politically obtuse Scarlett: 'Of course, Mr. Kennedy is in the Klan and Ashley, too, and all the men we know... They are men, aren't they? And white men and Southerners. You should have been proud of him instead of making him sneak out as though it were something shameful.' Such robust defences of the Klan in the novel, a source of pride for Southern gentlemen, provoked Joel Augustus Rogers into angrily quoting the 1871 Klan Report to note that Mitchell was 'more Ku Klux' than the original Klan leaders who testified before Congress, producing a version of Klan history that was 'crassly prejudiced' in the Klan's favour. [1]

Ashley and Frank are both shot during the Klan raid; Frank is killed but Ashley is rescued by Rhett, who hastily concocts an alibi saying that all the men in the lynch mob were at Belle Watling's during the attack. Because all the Old Guard are members of the Klan, the news soon goes around Atlanta that all the respectable men in town were sneaking out to a brothel, much to the amusement of the Yankees. This is when the film euphemizes the Klan as a 'social club', a decision that has helped popular memory conveniently forget that the story's male protagonists are all Klansmen, except for Rhett, who nonetheless protects the Klan.[2]

Embarrassed by the scandal, the ladies of the Old Guard later object, believing 'if Rhett really had the good of the Klan at heart he would have managed the affair in a more seemly fashion'. And Scarlett agrees that the raid was admirably brave, if foolish, confessing to Rhett that the reason she didn't know Frank was in the Klan was that she 'never dreamed he had that much gumption'. Attributing gumption to the Klan associates lynching with resilience, as if they are morally equivalent. Gumption is what it takes to get by, whether that means digging for radishes or murdering your political opponents.

It is easy to miss a detail Mitchell adds in passing, as the Old Guard gathers, worried after Ashley's shooting that the Yankees won't accept Rhett's alibi, and they will all be caught: 'Not only those involved in the night's raid but every member of the Klan was ready for flight and in almost every stable along Peachtree Street, horses stood saddled in the darkness, pistols in holsters and food in saddlebags.' The local history she'd grown up absorbing taught Mitchell not only that the Klan was gallant, but that it had once occupied virtually every house on Atlanta's main street, and beyond. Some aspects of popular wisdom are probably more accurate than others.

Atlanta threw a parade in December 1939 to honour the film's premiere, after nearly a million Americans reportedly spilled into town in hopes of catching a glimpse of its stars. Opening day was declared a state holiday, while the city of Atlanta arranged several days of balls and luncheons, with locals encouraged to wear period costume, including Confederate uniforms and hoop dresses. The *Atlanta Constitution* reported that 300,000 people gathered to watch the white cast and crew parade triumphantly down Peachtree Street, while Atlantans in fancy dress pretended that the Civil War, and the slavery it defended, had never come to an end.

*

The scene of Scarlett's assault outside Shantytown has become notorious, not merely because it upholds the myth that lynching defended white women from sexual assault by Black men, but because of the extreme racism of Mitchell's depiction. Although both novel and film feature one white assailant and one Black, Mitchell's narration focuses on the horrors of the Black attacker.

'A big ragged white man and a squat black negro with shoulders and chest like a gorilla' come running after Scarlett. Smelling the Black man's 'rank odor' and seeing 'his black face twisted in a leering grin', Scarlett feels her dress ripped open. 'Then the black hand fumbled between her breasts, and terror and revulsion such as she had never known came over her.' She decides she would rather die than let 'that black ape' get his hands on her again, but Tara's foreman Big Sam is fortunately on hand to save Scarlett in the nick of time, concurring that the assailant was a 'black baboon'.

The filmmakers, made forcibly aware of how offensive Black Americans found this entire scene, reversed the emphasis, turning Scarlett's assailant into a white man with the Black man lurking sinisterly in the background. They also removed the worst of the language, but still depicted vigilante violence as a reasonable response from the film's white protagonists to this assault. This is why Ashley, Frank, Dr Meade and the other members of Atlanta's Old Guard form a lynch mob to kill both men and decide to 'wipe out that whole Shantytown settlement' while they're at it.

Mitchell stresses the perils of the shantytown, as well as white people's indignation at this 'dirty, sordid cluster of discarded army tents and slave cabins', where 'outcast negroes, black prostitutes and a scattering of poor whites of the lowest order' lived together 'in filth'. 'Even the Yankees admitted it was a plague spot,' she adds, while Scarlett particularly objects to the 'drunken negro slatterns' who sit along the road 'shouting coarse words' as she passes. As long as she has Archie to protect her, 'not even the most impudent negro woman dared laugh in her presence'. But Scarlett loses Archie to her determination to hire convicts for her lumber mills, and so must travel alone through this perilous spot, vulnerable to the terrible dangers of profanity and mockery, while 'averting her nose' and looking 'with distaste at the group of shacks squatting in the hollow'.

Mitchell carefully situates Shantytown on the road to Decatur, east of Atlanta, putting it in the vicinity of the Black neighbourhood she knew as 'Buttermilk Bottom' in the 1920s and 1930s, which had been called 'Butler Street Bottoms' before that.[3] Like many Black neighbourhoods in the Jim Crow South, it developed from the numerous transient Black settlements that arose around the periphery of cities like Atlanta after the Civil War. The shantytowns springing up all over the South were yet another symptom of a nation unprepared to fully integrate the 4 million people it had just emancipated into full citizenship.

An exodus of Black migrants abandoned Southern rural areas for urban centres during and after the war, seeking work and the safety provided by federal troops, as well as educational opportunities; between 1860 and 1870, Atlanta's population doubled, including its Black populace,[4] which had nearly trebled again by 1890.[5] These shantytowns, frequently known as 'Negro towns' or by the word Negro's more abusive derivative, were viewed by white city-dwellers exactly as Mitchell depicts them: colonies of 'squalid, starving, thieving blacks from the country, a large proportion of them living in unconceivable filth and destitution',[6] that had sprouted up illegitimately. 'Soon they were living like rats in ruined houses,' sniffed Claude Bowers in his 1929 *The Tragic Era*, 'in miserable shacks under bridges built with refuse lumber, in the shelter of ravines and in caves in the banks of rivers,' as if Black people preferred such surroundings.

These condemnations never mentioned that the properties in question were usually leased or sold to Black migrants by white landowners, who had hastily erected tumbledown dwellings on undesirable land, often in valleys and bottoms, while building their own homes and businesses on higher ground like Atlanta's prestigious Peachtree Street. Mitchell was perfectly able to see the offensiveness of such attitudes when she was on the receiving end of them, writing to a Southern friend that 'the Romans, after all, were politer than the Northern conquerors, for after they had sown Carthage with salt they never rode through it on railroad trains and made snooty remarks about the degeneracy of people who liked to live in such poor circumstances,' but this is precisely what she assumes about freed people.[7]

These Black neighbourhoods evolved into the tenements, segregated districts, and redlined residential areas that developed over the next century across the country, reflecting and reinforcing the social and economic distinctions between white and Black Americans, and impeding Black social mobility. By 1936, the shacks of 'Buttermilk Bottom' were being razed in the first of a series of 'low cost slum clearance[s]' for new urban developments; white flight to the suburbs would soon follow.[8]

In the 1940s an aspiring property developer in New York named Fred C. Trump took federal loans – which he was later hauled before Congress to admit he had wildly overstated, defrauding the taxpayer[9] – to build a property empire. His rental properties were so racially segregated that in 1973, when Fred Trump's son Donald took over running the business, they were both sued by Nixon's Department of Justice for racial discrimination.

(The Nixon administration was not distinguished by its eagerness to sue Americans for racial discrimination.)

A 2015 study ranked Atlanta as still the most racially segregated city in the South, and the second nationally.[10] It was published one month before Donald Trump announced his candidacy for president, telling Black Americans they had nothing to lose by voting for him.

PART FIVE

SOCIAL CLUBS

18

A Fetish Now

'Ahead of them was a tunnel of fire where buildings were blazing on either side of the short, narrow street that led down to the railroad tracks... A glare brighter than a dozen suns dazzled their eyes, scorching heat seared their skins and the roaring, cracking and crashing beat upon their ears in painful waves.'

The burning of Atlanta is the centrepiece of Selznick's *Gone with the Wind*, the red light of its flames still featured in marketing campaigns and on book covers, a cinematic extravaganza made possible by the torching of old movie sets on a Hollywood backlot in Culver City. Sherman's incineration of the city has become, along with the Battle of Gettysburg, one of the most culturally iconic episodes in the Civil War, carefully curated through popular memory.

Margaret Mitchell, born in 1900, grew up hearing stories of the burning of Atlanta, in a world steeped in nostalgia for the good old days of slavery. She spent her early years in the house of her grandmother, Annie Fitzgerald, who survived the city's destruction and showed young Margaret the path of the Confederates in 1864 as they retreated before Sherman's unrelenting march to the sea.

Mitchell later described listening as a child to her grandparents' stories of the war, including family visits from 'Little Alec'

Stephens, for whom Margaret's brother, Alexander Stephens Mitchell, was named. These events, Mitchell said, 'gradually became part of my life', which is another way of saying that she was raised by a family who had enslaved Black people and glamorized their support of the Confederacy with Lost Cause myths and legends. Even as a young woman, according to Mitchell's college roommate, she 'felt about Robert E. Lee pretty much as if he was the current film idol'.[1]

Margaret's great-grandfather, Philip Fitzgerald, was born in Ireland but his family fled after the rebellion of 1798; eventually he settled in Georgia. By 1854 he was a rich man, with a 3,000-acre plantation called Rural Home that held thirty-five enslaved people at a time when only a quarter of the white South owned slaves at all, and only about 10 per cent of enslavers owned more than twenty.

Philip Fitzgerald gave his basic outline to Gerald O'Hara, whose daughter Scarlett is loosely based on Annie Fitzgerald, inheriting her background, politics and rapacity, especially her lust for land. Annie Fitzgerald was born into the slavocracy in 1844, a year earlier than her fictional avatar Katie Scarlett O'Hara. Seventeen when the South went to war, Annie Fitzgerald married in the midst of it, and raised her family in Atlanta during Reconstruction. She regaled her granddaughter with tales of the plantation they'd lost, embittered accounts of Yankee treachery, vulgar carpetbaggers, and the corrupt incompetence of 'negro rule', all the while registering her obsessive determination to reclaim the family's lost wealth and status. By the time Margaret Mitchell was born, her family had re-established its affluence and respectability, but the resentment lingered – as did the determination of women like Mitchell's grandmother to pass on what they viewed as the hard-won lessons of survival.

Southern women of the planter class like Annie Fitzgerald could not join the first Klan, a deeply patriarchal organization, although they supported it in various ways, sewing costumes, spreading the word, offering alibis, and publicly advocating for lynching in the name of self-defence. But they also formed their own groups, the most influential of which was the United Daughters of the Confederacy (UDC), established in 1894, and by the 1920s had formed auxiliaries of the second Klan.

The UDC quickly became the dominant social club for Southern white women of the plantation class, with a membership of 100,000 by the early years of the twentieth century.[2] Where former Confederate leaders had shaped the political legacy of the Old South, the women of the UDC shaped its cultural legacy, glorifying it through educational and commemorative ventures that stamped the ennobled Lost Cause across the popular history and memory of the Confederacy, not only for the South, but for the nation at large.

As Mitchell was growing up groups like the UDC were fighting to keep schools free of any textbook that would teach that the South had fought to preserve slavery. They raised money to support pro-Confederacy history departments, insisting that the plantation legend be taught as fact, emphasizing the benevolence of slavocracy, the gallantry of white Southern men, the vulnerability of white Southern women, and the moral justice of white supremacy.

They also transformed the American landscape with monuments to the Confederate cause. The large-scale act of public commemoration that enshrined the Lost Cause embedded it in the United States physically as well as imaginatively: nearly 500 monuments to Confederate white supremacy were erected between 1885 and 1915, over half of which were built in just seven years, between 1905–1912, funded by these groups.[3]

Ultimately Georgia alone would dedicate around 175 public spaces to glorifying the Confederacy and intimidating Black citizens, who were constantly reminded of the power of white supremacy, their ancestors' enslavement, and their own vulnerability. At the same time, Atlanta's political leadership passed a law ensuring that no publicly owned military monuments could be removed, relocated, concealed, obscured or altered. That law was amended in 2004 to allow for alterations in the name of preservation, protection, or interpretation – but they still stand. In the early 2020s, the United States and Britain became engulfed in debates over the removal of statues as a way of 'rewriting' history, with scant attention paid to the ways that they had been erected, and protected, in order to do just that.

Through generations of careful curation, the Lost Cause gradually transformed into a secular religion, with its sacred objects (statues, shrines, swords, uniforms, relics, and, of course, the Confederate flag), its orthodoxies, its distinct morality, its heroes and its demons. Evangelists for the Old South, organizations like the UDC turned the story into a fetish, as Mitchell understood – the story demanded total devotion: 'The Lost Cause was stronger, dearer now in their hearts than it had ever been at the height of its glory. It was a fetish now. Everything about it was sacred, the graves of the men who had died for it, the battle fields, the torn flags, the crossed sabres in their halls, the fading letters from the front, the veterans'.

Admitting this is part of Mitchell's revisionist project. Melanie Wilkes, fiercely loyal to the Confederacy, is secretary for 'both the Association for the Beautification of the Graves of Our Glorious Dead and the Sewing Circle for the Widows and Orphans of the Confederacy'. But Scarlett impatiently rejects the nostalgic work of commemoration: 'Yes, the Cause was dead but war had always seemed foolish to her and peace was better.' She never shared 'the fanatic glow which made all these things endurable to others, if only the Cause prospered'.

Even during the war, Scarlett thinks heretically that the 'white heat of devotion to the Cause... just seemed silly!' and doesn't change her mind after the war. 'Why, they were fools!' she thinks on being shown expensive tombstones for the Tarleton twins, 'as indignant as if her own money had been squandered'. As ever

Scarlett points her face to the future, refusing to 'waste my money on tombstones or my time crying about the war'. She will keep every dime to buy back her power.

Mitchell never glorifies war, which is unsurprising given that she came of age with the First World War (and lost her fiancé, whom her brother called the love of her life, to it). *Gone with the Wind* repudiates the heroism of war and mocks the sacredness of the Lost Cause – but not its justice, never questioning the redemptive nature of white power.

*

In the wake of the insurrection in 2021 – after which Trump declared that his (non-existent) 'landslide victory' was 'sacred', and urged the insurrectionists to 'Remember this day forever!'[4] – Republicans began to increase their attacks on the teaching of history. These had been accelerating for some time: in 2015, for example, Republican school boards in Texas issued a textbook that called enslaved people 'workers' and 'immigrants'. They continue to insist on a curriculum that diminishes the role of slavery in causing the Civil War, while including sectionalism and states' rights as contributing factors to it, and conforming to Dunning School dogma that has been debunked for half a century.[5]

After the insurrection, the American right wing suddenly turned their attention to an academic subject called 'critical race theory', an interdisciplinary branch of legal theory taught in some specialized postgraduate courses, because a conservative activist had identified it as 'the perfect weapon' for inflaming culture wars.[6] Also known as CRT, it examines the ways in which legal systems not only upheld racist power structures, but have historically produced them. The law as an active agent that creates and sustains racism is, broadly, the concern of CRT courses, which examine that history with the purpose of undoing those systems. Local legislators and school boards responded by forbidding the teaching of what they referred to as CRT in schools.

By vaguely defining CRT as anything relating to the question of race in America, these laws could permit firing a teacher who told students that America had a history of racism, let alone a racist present, which is precisely what started happening. These laws were passed even as Congress turned Juneteenth, long an informal African American holiday celebrating the abolition of slavery, into a national holiday for the first time. The irony was not lost on observers, who pointed out that the United States now had a national holiday commemorating the end of a system that some schools would no longer be permitted to teach their students about.

One of the core tenets of critical race theory is that racist structures support the status quo – and one of the things *Gone with the Wind* reveals is how little that status quo has changed in certain key respects. Solutions like incrementalism are insufficient to alter those structures: legal and hard-won gains such as the Voting Rights Act of 1965 can be summarily reversed with the stroke of a conservative Supreme Court's verdict.

These tactics were buttressed by educational efforts at suppressing what they called CRT but defined far more expansively. Arkansas Senator Tom Cotton introduced a bill to withhold federal funding from any school district that teaches the *New York Times*'s controversial '1619 Project', which proposed reframing the history of the United States as founded upon the first violent importation of slaves in 1619, rather than upon the time-honoured, highly mythologized origin of the pilgrims landing in Massachusetts Bay in 1620.

In June 2021, Florida banned the teaching of both CRT and the 1619 Project. In signing the bill into law, Florida's governor, Ron DeSantis, denounced critical race theory as a system advocating racism, by teaching 'people to think of themselves more as a member of a particular race based on skin color, rather than based on the content of their character' – thereby appropriating the colour of Martin Luther King, Jr's famous rhetoric to argue against the content of his position.[7]

By the autumn of 2021, twenty-two states had introduced or passed legislation restricting the discussion of race in the classroom, saying teachers should not be forced to teach 'currently controversial issues' and that students should not be subjected to topics that might make them feel 'discomfort', 'guilt', or 'psychological distress' because of the social groups to which they belong.[8] Avoiding blame, guilt, or psychological distress is precisely what the Lost Cause enabled, prizing moral complacency above reality in a way that would make Scarlett O'Hara proud.

That summer, Republican state senators had also voted to remove Dr King's two most famous writings, 'Letter from a Birmingham Jail' and the 'I Have a Dream' speech, from Texas school curricula,[9] as school boards in Republican areas across the country decided that it is 'un-American' to teach the historical realities of racism in the United States – which in one sense, at least, is perfectly true.[10]

19

Georgia's Great Hero

One of the statues raised by the UDC in Georgia, unveiled in the spring of 1907 on the corner of the state's capitol grounds, was in honour of Confederate Major General John Brown Gordon. It was designed by Solon Borglum, whose brother, Gutzon Borglum (later the sculptor of Mount Rushmore), was soon commissioned by the UDC to create the largest Confederate memorial in the country on Stone Mountain, outside of Atlanta, carving white governance into granite in hopes it would last forever. The ceremony for Gordon's statue was walking distance from the Mitchell house; it's highly likely that six-year-old Margaret was taken to see the festivities.

Cast as 'Georgia's great hero' in *Gone with the Wind*, 'one of Georgia's best loved and most honored citizens', General Gordon is one of the Confederate leaders who gets a cameo at Melanie's political meetings, where Scarlett thinks they 'did little else except argue the merits of General John B. Gordon over every other general, except General Lee'. Gordon is a close enough friend of the Wilkes family to warn Ashley of his impending surprise birthday party in fraternal solidarity; the novel also mentions Gordon's 1868 defeat in a gubernatorial campaign against the despised Republican Rufus Bullock.

The novel does not, however, mention that John Brown Gordon was also the Grand Dragon of Georgia's first Klan, a man who adamantly defended slavery as 'morally, socially, and politically right' until he died in 1904.[1] A leading advocate of the Lost Cause and the New South, Gordon urged the South to build a new commercial marketplace in the ashes of the old. He also successfully campaigned for the US Senate in 1872, where he would help engineer the Compromise of 1877, which gave Republican Rutherford B. Hayes the presidency in exchange for removing federal forces from the South.

The 1907 ceremony consecrating Gordon's statue was reported nationally; it included a 'great military parade, in which national guardsmen, Confederate veterans, and other military and patriotic organizations' marched.[2] None of these reports appeared to notice the incongruity of describing Confederate veterans as a patriotic group, although many of them, like Scarlett's friends and family, had also violently refused to swear the Ironclad Oath of loyalty after the war. At the same time, and not incidentally, they were loudly complaining that they weren't paid federal pensions, resenting the nation's government all the more for its refusal to pay benefits to those who had taken up arms against it.

At the dedication ceremony, Gordon's Confederate comrade General Clement A. Evans spoke in memory of his lifelong friend, with whom he had served at Gettysburg. Instrumental in raising the money for Gordon's statue, Evans was another key architect in the creation of the Lost Cause and the promotion of the New South, publishing multi-volume Southern histories after the war. 'If we cannot justify the South in the act of Secession,' Evans wrote, 'we will go down to History solely as a brave, impulsive but rash people who attempted in an illegal manner to overthrow the Union of our Country.'[3] The motivation behind the Lost Cause was rarely put so explicitly: the need to justify their actions was acute.

There was no shortage of symptoms that the pressure was mounting. The project of commemoration was itself symptomatic, if only in its hysterical magnitude, as was the publication of Dunning's *Reconstruction, Political and Economic*, which legitimated Lost Cause justifications later that same year. They were responding in part to outbreaks of increasing racial violence, which gave the lie to these fables of peace and harmony, while spurring Lost Cause supporters into ever greater assertions of white supremacism.

One of the most consequential of these outbursts was the Atlanta race riot of 1906. Through the hot summer of 1906, a demagogic former newspaper editor – and close friend of the Mitchell family[4] – named Hoke Smith had been campaigning for governor by stoking racial tensions. Advocating 'the absolute disfranchisement of the negro',[5] Smith won Georgia's governorship, despite loud reminders from across the country that such campaign promises were flatly unconstitutional under the Fifteenth Amendment. Smith did his best to keep those promises, passing laws making literacy tests and property ownership a requirement for voting.

During the campaign, Atlanta's tabloid press whipped up racial hysteria by claiming the city was enduring not only a heat wave, but also a wave of sexual assault against white women by Black men, 'an epidemic of rape' that was part of the country's ongoing relentless, obsessive reiteration of the myth of the rampant Black rapist. On the night of 22 September 1906, thousands of white men and boys rampaged through the streets of the state capitol in a frenzy, destroying Black homes and businesses in Atlanta, which had one of the most prosperous Black communities in the country. Black Atlantans were beaten, stabbed, shot, hanged from lampposts, dragged from moving vehicles, assaulted in their homes and watched their businesses destroyed by white mobs; at least thirty people died in the violence, and hundreds of Black families fled the city soon after, migrating north toward what they hoped would be safety.

Mitchell, who was five during the Atlanta riots, remembered that 'they fought all day just a block behind our house'. She recalled rumours that 'negro mobs had been formed to burn the town', as white property owners warned each other to get their guns and stand guard , when in fact white mobs were rampaging.[6] She welcomed the coming of the militia, she said, and claimed to have recommended that her father use a neighbour's sword – presumably a Confederate relic – to protect the family.

Within a year, the South had erected thirty-three more monuments to white governance.

*

In the summer of 2021, President Biden commemorated the centenary of the terrible racial violence in Tulsa, Oklahoma, that had terrorized the Black community in 1921 only to be scrubbed from the historical record. Refusing to call it a race riot, as had been customary, Biden pointedly referred to it as the Tulsa Massacre, rejecting any implication that the violence was mutual, rather than a pogrom in which African Americans were slaughtered because a rumour started that a Black youth had raped a white girl. That was all it took to spark the murder of dozens, perhaps hundreds, of people, and the destruction of 8,000 homes and businesses.

Biden's speech was the latest in a long line of contests over how to remember racial violence in America. Four years earlier, the city of Charlottesville, Virginia had decided to remove a statue of Robert E. Lee in 2017, sparking a Unite the Right rally, at which right-wing groups including armed militias and Klansmen waved Confederate and Nazi flags while shouting, 'You will not replace us, Jews will not replace us.' People in 'Make America Great Again' hats chanted Nazi slogans of blood and soil.

During the violence, a peaceful white counter-protestor named Heather Heyer was murdered, and Donald Trump shocked the world by equivocating over the violence, insisting that there were 'very fine people on both sides' of the fight, although one side was entirely populated by white supremacists. The violence temporarily postponed the removal of Lee's statue, but soon precipitated the removal of other monuments to the Confederacy. Statues became the locus of public anger in both directions, but public memorials honouring the Confederacy go well beyond statues, including schools, universities, parks, forts, streets, prisons, and hospitals, scattering the names of insurrectionist leaders across the United States.

The demands to take down Lee's statue in Charlottesville had themselves accelerated in the wake of the 2015 shooting at a Black church in Charleston, South Carolina, when a white supremacist who posted photos of himself waving the Confederate flag went on a homicidal spree that left nine African Americans dead. A few years later, Nikki Haley, identified by many as a future Republican presidential hopeful, declared that until Dylann Roof 'hijacked' it for the Charleston shootings, the Confederate flag had symbolized 'service, and sacrifice, and heritage'.[7] It had also symbolized white supremacy, slavery, and secession, but all that was to be forgotten. America had moved on.

After the investigation into the church shooting revealed that Roof said he wanted to 'start a race war' to reclaim the United States from 'stupid and violent' African Americans, a Georgia state senator tried to pass a law that would remove official protection of Confederate symbols, including the statue of John Brown Gordon. Instead, in 2019, Georgia passed a law forbidding the removal of Confederate monuments.

A year later, Trump caused yet another outcry when he refused to allow US military forts that had been named for Confederate generals to be renamed in honour of less violently white supremacist Americans. One of those was Georgia's Fort Gordon, another monument honouring John Brown Gordon. Trump responded with fury that the forts were part of 'Great

American Heritage' and that 'Our history as the Greatest Nation in the World will not be tampered with. Respect our Military!'[8] That Trump was also demanding that the military respect seditionist traitors was observed at the time, some six months before he supported his own armed seditious movement against the US government.

*

Hunter Street, where General Gordon's statue was unveiled in 1907, was renamed Martin Luther King, Jr Drive in 1976, the year of the nation's bicentennial celebration – and the year the state of Kentucky finally ratified the Fourteenth and Fifteenth Amendments. The statue remains in the same place, meaning that a Confederate general who declared Black chattel slavery morally, socially, and politically right is venerated on the corner of a street named for the nation's greatest Black leader and civil rights activist.

Whether it truly honours King's memory, or his cause, to place a statue glorifying a white supremacist Klan leader on a street named for him is not a question white Americans like to ask, any more than we like to recall when we declare our reverence for Dr King that he was blasted in the throat with a high-velocity rifle because he spoke for racial justice in America.

20

A Better American

When Rhett and Ashley convince the rest of the 'hot heads' in Atlanta to retire the Klan, it's only indirectly because the Yankees will never otherwise leave them alone. This is when Rhett informs Scarlett that 'watching, waiting and working would get us further than nightshirts and fiery crosses', as Mitchell transfers the dubious honour of leading the first Georgia Klan from General Gordon to Ashley Wilkes.

The first Klan did not light fiery crosses. That was, instead, a hallmark of the second Klan, with whom Americans of Mitchell's generation were all too familiar by 1936, and who codified most of the group's now-famous features in the early 1920s, including its militant Christianity. The fiery cross itself did not come from the Bible, however, but was another importation from Sir Walter Scott. In Scott's *The Lady in the Lake*, the Chieftain Roderick Dhu lights a cross to signal an uprising against the English king, as Scott invokes an ancient Scottish custom for gathering the clans, known as the Crean Tarigh, or Fiery Cross. The burning cross thus associated the Klan with insurgency against the incursion of illegitimate rule, aggrandizing it as an extension of the revolutionary spirit that Jefferson Davis had claimed for the Confederacy.

Although much of the second Klan's gibberish ultimately derived from Scott, it arrived via the popular novels of Thomas

THE WRATH TO COME

Dixon, Jr, who endowed the Klan with an origin myth by literalizing its eccentric genealogy. In his Klan trilogy – *The Leopard's Spots: A Romance of the White Man's Burden, 1865–1900* (1902), *The Clansman: A Historical Romance of the Ku Klux Klan* (1905), and *The Traitor: A Story of the Fall of the Invisible Empire* (1907) – Dixon glamorized the Ku Klux Klan at the peak of the Lost Cause commemorative project, glorifying the restoration of Southern white governance after Reconstruction. *The Clansman* brought the cartoon of Reconstruction misrule to life, offering a lurid tale of lawlessness and corruption that forced persecuted white Southerners to retaliate with defensive terrorism, rescuing the South from 'African barbarism'. Its plot turns on – what else? – rescuing a white woman from the terrifying prospect of rape by a leering, savage Black man; she chooses death over the worse fate by jumping off a cliff.

The Klan's purpose, Dixon wrote in typical terms, 'was to bring order out of chaos, protect the weak and defenceless, the widows and orphans of brave men who had died for their country, to drive from power the thieves who were robbing the people, redeem the commonwealth from infamy, and reestablish civilization'. During a climactic moment in *The Clansman*, 'the old Scottish rite of the Fiery Cross' is re-enacted, to 'send a thrill of inspiration to every clansman in the hills'. The image of a clansman burning a cross as a call to arms would become all too real, as the old romantic idea of a local 'white knight' defending the Southern way of life, and especially Southern womanhood, took an even more a deeply vicious turn.

Not content with depicting white governance as the birthright of whiteness, Dixon went one better, celebrating Klansmen as the 'reincarnated souls of the Clansmen of Old Scotland', with the 'blood of Scottish kings' flowing through their veins. This may sound like a metaphor, but laws of hypodescent meant taking the relationship between blood and political entitlements all too literally – indeed, biologically. A radical white supremacist,

Dixon believed in total separation of the races, advocating for the compulsory return of Black Americans to Africa, as if what the United States had created by force it could expunge by equal and opposite coercion.

Dixon's Klan trilogy amounted to a folk saga in a Robin Hood vein, with mysterious, aristocratic 'night riders' saving the countryside from marauding bandits. The problem was that the bandits were writing the story and casting themselves as its heroes. *The Clansman* presented itself as 'the true story of the "Ku Klux Klan Conspiracy"', as Dixon assured the reader he had not taken 'a liberty with any essential historical fact' in describing his fearless freedom fighters who nobly saved the racial purity of the nation, offering 'one of the most dramatic chapters in the history of the Aryan race'.

Black leaders responded by calling Dixon 'the prophet of anarchy', warning that his stories would 'subvert the foundations of law and established order', leaving behind 'the greatest heritage of hate the world has ever known'.[1]

The Clansman was adapted into an equally popular play that toured across the nation in 1906, featuring as a dramatic centrepiece the lighting of the fiery cross while a white actor in minstrel blackface pretended to be lynched for the entertainment of a peanut-crunching crowd. Its plot hinged, of course, on saving an imperilled white woman from rape by a savage Black man foolishly liberated from his natural state of enslavement.

The play's popularity probably helped prime the white residents of Atlanta to go on a homicidal rampage in September 1906, in response to reports of Black men 'outraging' white women.[2] Within the next year, General Gordon's statue was erected, Dunning published *Reconstruction, Political and Economic,* and Dixon concluded the Klan trilogy with *The Traitor*, which treated the eradication of the Klan at the hands of perfidious federalists – otherwise known as the American government – as a tragedy for America.

It was in large part thanks to the popularity of Dixon's novels that the Klan re-emerged in 1915, having developed in and through fictions in almost every sense, providing a kind of pastiche of American history, a miscellany of cultural myths used to justify a white supremacist power grab. The cultural stories we tell do not merely reflect our world: they create it. Whatever mythical origins it liked to claim, the Klan burned real people at the stake.

*

But it was another adaptation of *The Clansman* that most radically affected American society, doing incalculable damage along the way. *The Birth of a Nation,* directed by D. W. Griffith and the first full-length cinematic narrative film in history, was released in early 1915. Although Dixon's novels were popular, Griffith's film was a cultural phenomenon. The most commercially successful silent film in history,[3] and very probably the most racist movie ever made, *The Birth of a Nation* thrillingly dramatized Dixon's genesis myth for the first Klan – because Griffith, himself the son of a Confederate colonel, had also grown up with the cult of the Lost Cause.

The Birth of a Nation makes its central claim in its title: that the real America emerged after the Civil War in the white supremacist violence of Reconstruction. As far as Griffith was concerned, the Ku Klux Klan hadn't just saved America, but created it. 'The birth of a nation began… with the Ku Klux Klans [*sic*],' Griffith declared. 'The Civil War was fought fifty years ago. But the real nation has only existed in the last fifteen or twenty years,' since Redemption transitioned into Jim Crow segregation. That 'real' nation was white Anglo-Saxon America, consolidating its power and insisting a new society could be born out of the ashes of defeat – that renewal and redemption would lead to the apotheosis of white sovereignty. This, after all, was the premise of the Lost Cause, that white dominance was not only natural, but glorious.

Black audiences boycotted the film, throwing rotten eggs and stink bombs at a Boston screening that ended in a riot, as white audiences emerged to clash with Black protestors outside the theatre.[4] Lynchings and racial violence spiked in counties across the nation after it was screened.[5] But white audiences flocked to Griffith's film. Advertisements quoted authorities like the reformer Dorothy Dix urging, 'See it because it WILL MAKE A BETTER AMERICAN OF YOU',[6] and a minister who maintained that 'only a bigoted prejudiced critic could accuse the producer or his picture of any ill-feeling towards or misrepresentation of the colored people',[7] although Griffith primarily used white actors in blackface, along with a handful of African American actors, to portray the evil, corrupt, drunken, incompetent and lascivious freed slaves who were destroying the vulnerable white South during Reconstruction.

Fifteen-year-old Margaret Mitchell, watching the film in Atlanta, immediately wrote her own theatrical adaptation of Dixon's *The Traitor*, making a Klan costume and casting herself as the lead. By then the Klan had been so thoroughly rehabilitated in popular memory that in its review of *The Birth of a Nation*, the *Atlanta Constitution* praised 'the welcome Ku Klux Klan call that fell so gratefully on the ear of southern whites, sorely oppressed by "the servants in the master's hall"',[8] an image of cultural hierarchies overturned.

Mitchell very likely read this review; the image recurs in *Gone with the Wind*. 'Servants in the master's hall' is exactly what Scarlett imagines as the worst possible outcome for Tara during Reconstruction. When Jonas Wilkerson and his 'white trash' wife Emmy Slattery try to purchase Tara, the very thought of 'these low common creatures living in this house, bragging to their low common friends how they had turned the proud O'Haras out' infuriates Scarlett – but the thought that they might 'even bring negroes here to dine and sleep' is worse than hiding from Sherman's army. The 'final insult to Tara' is the prospect that Black people might be welcomed to enjoy it.

*

Griffith drew the authority for his account of Reconstruction in *The Birth of a Nation* not from fiction, but from historiography. But the historian to whom he turned was not William A. Dunning or any of Dunning's acolytes – it was the president of the United States, Woodrow Wilson, who was also a segregationist and believer in the Lost Cause. Born in antebellum Virginia, Wilson was a historian (and president of Princeton University) before going into politics. His 1902 *History of the American People* validated the Lost Cause version of Reconstruction as a 'veritable overthrow of civilization in the South', one determined to 'put the white South under the heel of the black South' – and Griffith quoted from it liberally in the titles for *The Birth of a Nation*.

Griffith made clear that Wilson's authority had helped sway him: 'the Klansmen… according to no less than Woodrow Wilson, ran to the rescue of the downtrodden South after the Civil War. I could just see these Klansmen in a movie with their white robes flying.' But instead of saving a damsel in distress, this 'ride would be to save a nation', the Klan as the cavalry riding to the rescue of America.

In the same interview, Griffith claimed that 'a man we all revere, or ought to' had said at a screening that the film 'teaches history like lightning', a remark widely attributed to Wilson, and subsequently distorted into a misquotation that he'd described the film as 'like writing history with lightning'.[9] The difference is telling, for *The Birth of a Nation* did indeed 'teach' a version of history – an untrue one – and teaching the lessons of white supremacism was just what its creators intended. Dixon later said the film was conscious white supremacist propaganda, that it was designed to 'create a feeling of abhorrence in white people, especially white women, against colored men'.[10]

Most accounts of the role Woodrow Wilson played in the film's reception (including allowing it to be the first film ever screened at the White House) now also add Wilson's supposed conclusion

1. The Kekistan flag, paraded during the storming of the US Capitol on January 6, 2021. The flag of this imaginary nation has become a far-right symbol, its four Ks in the form of a square invoking both the Nazi swastika and the Ks of the Ku Klux Klan.

2. The US Capitol building, framed by a gallows erected by Trump supporters on the West Lawn as the insurrection gathered pace on January 6, 2021.

3. An insurrectionist strolls past the Senate Chamber parading the Confederate flag as the Capitol is being stormed. He was later arrested and faces grand jury indictments.

4. One of *Gone with the Wind*'s most iconic scenes: Scarlett O'Hara silhouetted against the flames of burning Atlanta in the distance, defiantly declaring: 'As God is my witness, I'll never be hungry again!'

5. A dust storm or 'black blizzard' approaches Stratford, Texas in 1935.

6. Vivien Leigh as Scarlett alone in a cotton field, evoking what had become familiar scenes of devastated farms during the Great Depression.

7. Registering Black voters in Macon, Georgia, September 1867.

8. 'One Vote Less', *Harper's Weekly*, 8 August 1868.

"ONE VOTE LESS."—*Richmond Whig.*

9. A plaque memorializing the Colfax massacre. At least 150 Black Americans were killed in Colfax, Louisiana on 13 April 1873, in what has been called the single bloodiest incident of racial violence in the Reconstruction South.

10. (below) Scarlett is accosted by a Yankee deserter intent on theft (with a threat of sexual assault): she shoots him and steals his money to protect herself and her family.

11. (above) Hattie McDaniel as Mammy looks over her shoulder in disapproval at Scarlett. McDaniel's performance, humanizing the novel's one-dimensional caricature of Mammy, made her the first African American to win an Academy Award.

12. Butterfly McQueen playing the enslaved Prissy with Vivien Leigh as Scarlett. McQueen resisted the minstrel 'comedy' she was asked to play and, along with co-star Hattie McDaniel, fought against the screenplay's inclusion of racist language.

TWO MEMBERS OF THE KU-KLUX KLAN IN THEIR DISGUISES.

13. 'Dress of the Original Klan', *Harper's Weekly*, 18 December 1868 and reprinted in 1936.

14. A scene from D. W. Griffith's *The Birth of a Nation*, 1915, in which a group of Klansmen prepare to lynch freedman Gus, played by white actor Walter Long in blackface.

15. The lynching of African American Charlie Hale on the courthouse square in Lawrenceville, Georgia on 7 April 1911. A sign hangs from his feet saying, 'Please do not wake him'.

16. Ida B. Wells-Barnett at the National American Woman Suffrage Association march in Washington DC, printed in the *Chicago Tribune*, 5 March 1913. Wells-Barnett stepped to the front of the Chicago delegation after African American women were told to march at the back of the parade.

17. Elizabeth Eckford, a member of the Little Rock Nine, ignores the hostile screams of fellow students and onlookers as she enters public school in Little Rock, Arkansas, on 6 September 1957.

18. 'Forty Acres and a Mule' was an iconic promise of land redistribution made by the US government to Black Americans during the Civil War. The slogan appears in *Gone with the Wind* behind a white carpetbagger as he dupes gullible Black people.

19. A chain gang in Atlanta, Georgia, 1895. These convicts and their guard pause in their work to have this photograph taken.

20. A German poster for *Gone with the Wind*. The novel and film were officially banned in Germany after 1941 but Hitler reportedly screened it at least three times, and it was as wildly popular in Nazi Germany just before the war as it was everywhere else in Europe during the war and beyond.

to the 'like writing history with lightning' remark: 'And my only regret is that it is all so terribly true.'

According to one film historian, however, this comment, now widely attributed to Wilson, was not appended to the story until 1937, twenty years later.[11] In 1936 Mitchell's novel breathed new life into *The Birth of a Nation*, prompting a spurt of profiles and a few revivals. It might be a coincidence, but given the renewed interest, it's likely that this desire to validate the supposedly tragic truth of its Lost Cause history was thanks to the influence of *Gone with the Wind*. The popularity of *Gone with the Wind* thus worked retrospectively to add a spurious authority – from a former president, no less – to the mythical account of Reconstruction told in *The Birth of a Nation* that *Gone with the Wind* recycled, creating a very efficient closed circle of mythmaking.

Two years later, Selznick's Technicolor extravaganza, with its good intentions of eliminating the 'blatantly objectionable', went even further toward normalizing this perspective in American popular culture. Selznick was determined to avoid the boycotts that had greeted *The Birth of a Nation* in trying to make *Gone with the Wind* palatable to Black audiences – while adamantly refusing to rethink its fundamental politics.

*

No scene in *The Birth of a Nation* would prove more consequential than Griffith's decision to retain from the stage adaptation of *The Clansman* the dramatic ceremony of a lynch mob gathering before a burning cross, as it prepares to execute a Black man for murder.

Six months after the film's release in 1915, while it was still making its way around the country, a group of men gathered on the summit of Stone Mountain outside Atlanta, lit an enormous fiery cross, and declared the Klan reborn. 'Weird Story That Ku Klux Klan is Come Back Again' read one headline, reporting that a 'mysterious yellow flame' had been seen burning brightly on the mountain, marking a 'revival of the mystic rites of the Ku Klux Klan'.[12]

On a stone altar the group 'erected the fiery cross' that had been popularized by Griffith's film a few months earlier and took an oath on bended knee 'to the service of country, homes and humanity'. Among those gathered were Georgia legislators and statesmen; at least two of the newly formed Klan were said to be surviving members of the original organization.[13] Burning crosses soon became the enduring symbol of the Klan, a sign of white supremacist terror. The state of Georgia, it was said at the time, 'was wisely and properly selected' as the right place to revive the Klan, for nowhere else 'could such a diabolical and lawless organization more securely carry on its wicked and proscriptive practices'.[14]

One member of the newly born second Klan had reportedly participated in the lynching of Leo Frank that August. Two years earlier Frank, a Jewish factory superintendent in Atlanta, had been found guilty of the rape and murder of a thirteen-year-old girl named Mary Phagan, and sentenced to death. A sensational, brutal story that quickly became a national *cause célèbre*, its details were sordid and murky, the case against Frank circumstantial.

After two years of controversy and inflamed tension, while audiences were becoming better Americans by watching *The Birth of a Nation*, Frank's death sentence was commuted to life imprisonment, sparking outrage across Georgia. Local officials calling themselves 'the Knights of Mary Phagan' dragged Leo Frank from his Atlanta jail and lynched him in Marietta, Phagan's hometown. After murdering him they debated whether to mutilate the corpse, afterwards congratulating themselves for the upright manner in which they resisted temptation and thus, they assured each other, had upheld law and order.

Although Frank's murder supposedly 'stirred the indignation of the country', within days three Black men accused of poisoning mules had been lynched in Alabama, followed shortly by two

Black men burned at the stake in Texas, provoking no similar outcry to the one that greeted Frank's execution.[15] That spring, in Waco, Texas, a Black man named Jesse Washington, accused of murdering his employer's wife, had been burned alive for two hours, raised and lowered over a bonfire, in front of a crowd of 10,000 spectators, including local officials and children on their school lunch break.

Even before the Klan officially reassembled on Stone Mountain in November 1915, Black Americans had recognized the Klan's 'bestial spirit' in Leo Frank's horrendous murder: 'The spirit and method of the Ku Klux Klan has once more triumphed in Georgia,' wrote the *New York Age*, 'celebrating the blood-lust of the Ku Klux Klan as a virtue.'[16]

Southern newspapers leapt to the defence of the Klan, insisting that although Frank's murder was an outrage (if not sufficiently outrageous to warrant prosecuting his killers, who had owned up to the murder), the first Klan was a noble organ of Southern chivalry. 'The original Ku Klux Klan was composed of the best blood of the South,' insisted the *Montgomery Advertiser* the day after Frank was murdered. 'No knightlier figure was known to the war period than Nathan Bedford Forrest, who was the highest officer in the original Ku Klux Klan.'[17]

It was pure cognitive dissonance: faced with a bestial murder, white Americans created another rationalization. Although the second Klan was 'unsavory,'[18] the first Klan consisted of honourable gentlemen in nightshirts 'calling on' disruptive local elements and protecting vulnerable white women from assault.

Scarlett does consistently detest the Klan, albeit usually for pragmatic, rather than moral, reasons. But there are a few moments of near-moral clarity, when Mitchell allows that Scarlett not only objects to the Klan's folly in antagonizing Yankees, but fears it – only for her position to collapse into hijacked victimhood: 'Let others go to jail for speaking their minds and get themselves hanged for being in the Ku Klux Klan. (Oh, what a dreaded

name that was, almost as terrifying to Scarlett as to the negroes.)'
Mitchell might have followed this intuition, allowing that white
women (much less Black people) could be legitimately terrified
by the Klan. Instead, Scarlett's fears are rebuked by the discovery
that the noble Ashley runs the Klan, India's public reprimand,
Rhett's quick-witted and daring rescue, and the whispered news
of 'the disaster to the Klan' caused by the botched raid.

The myth of the nobility of the first Klan, as distinct from the
second, was so widely believed that Selznick debated it during
production of *Gone with the Wind*, because the story's glorification
of the Klan was as problematic for the filmmakers as its use of
the racial slur. In regards to the second Klan the Jewish Selznick
was less forgiving, while being perfectly prepared to defend the
first. 'I personally feel quite strongly that we should cut out the
Klan entirely,' he told Sidney Howard, for 'it would be difficult,
if not impossible, to clarify for audiences the difference between
the old Klan and the Klan of our times.' This is presumably why
Selznick decided to euphemize the Klan as a 'social club' in the
film, because he believed in the nobility of the first Klansmen –
gentlemen who left a calling card, rather than thugs who tortured
and killed fellow citizens at will with impunity.

Selznick also removed explicit references to the Klan on the
basis that 'a group of men can go out to "get" the perpetrators of
an attempted rape without having long white sheets over them
and without having their membership in a society as a motive,'[19]
an argument suggesting that vigilante violence is fine as long as
it isn't perpetrated by Klansmen or by anyone wearing a sheet,
while the scare quotes around 'get' euphemize the ugly fact that
Selznick is talking about murder. It also assumes that women
were never involved in the Klan, although by the mid-1920s
white women were creating ladies' auxiliary groups such as the
'Klavanna', and marching in their own parades.

There were differences between the first and second Klans, but
relative nobility wasn't one of them. Through the 1920s, as the

second Klan gained in power and influence, its viciousness on full display, so did insistences that the first Klan was gallant and chivalrous, and that there was a categorical difference between the two groups – when in fact the two Klans even shared some of the same members, and the second Klan's founder, William Simmons, claimed that his father was a member of the first.[20] But by the late 1930s, the idea that the two Klans were distinct had become axiomatic. The logic of exception had come galloping, white robes flying, to save the nation once more.

21

Common Knowledge

'A s I had not written anything about the Klan which is not common knowledge to every Southerner, I had done no research upon it,' Mitchell told Stanley Horn, whose *Invisible Empire: The Story of the Ku Klux Klan, 1866–1871* was published in 1939 and validated Lost Cause dogma.[1] The author who boasted that she spent years establishing the accuracy of her research, and who claimed the novel's fact-checking identified 'exactly two minor errors, neither of which would ever have been found outside of Georgia', did not bother researching the Klan at all.[2] She was correct, however, in concluding that if she had, white historiography of the time would only have confirmed what she already believed.

A review by the progressive white historian Francis Simkins, for example, who broke from the Dunning School in the early 1930s, nonetheless described Horn's account of the first Klan as 'a moving narrative: the story of heroes who, bound together by a mystic symbolism, reestablished the southern standards of race relations'. also known as white supremacy.[3] That 'mystic symbolism' was so obviously bogus that in 1931 another historian had already dismissed the Klan's 'preposterous vocabulary' as simply 'a chance to dress up the village bigot and let him be a Knight of the Invisible Empire', but by 1939 supposedly serious accounts like Simkins's were still taking the Klan's puerile nonsense, used to veil their vicious savagery from themselves as well as others, at face value.[4]

The *New York Times* did not question Southern standards of race relations either, its review of Horn's history agreeing that the Klan's purpose was 'frightening obstreperous Negroes into good behavior, warning carpet-baggers out of the country, applying the lash when that seemed most effective, murdering if that remedy was demanded'. The Klan's activity, the *Times* added, often had 'abundant provocation'.[5] It's staggering to read: the American paper of record in 1939 calling the vigilante torture and murder of 'obstreperous' Black Americans a 'remedy' that was 'abundantly provoked'. Six months later, Selznick's version of *Gone with the Wind* premiered.

Apart from one year at Smith College, Margaret Mitchell lived her whole life in Atlanta. Mitchell's biographers stress that her family did not support the second Klan, distinguishing themselves from the rural Georgians of a 'crude agricultural background' who followed the new Imperial Wizard William J. Simmons. But Atlanta in the 1920s 'was a Confederate town', as her brother later said.[6]

Mitchell herself, according to one biographer, was 'considerably distressed by the racial situation' in Atlanta during the 1920s, when Black citizens, including Mitchell's domestic servants, were so terrorized by the Klan that they feared to leave the house.[7] But being distressed by the second Klan while writing a novel glorifying the first Klan was also consistent with the belief, by that point widespread, that the second Klan was an anomaly – an exception – instead of a deep and ugly abiding truth about white supremacy in America.

Atlanta was the national headquarters for the second Klan, an organization that swept the United States between 1921 and 1926, just as Mitchell was beginning to draft the novel. There were an estimated 5 to 6 million Klansmen in the United States by the middle of the decade, while Georgia's politics were dominated by them at the local, state, and congressional level. The state's governor addressed a 'Klonvocation' in full Klan regalia while in office, and promised to pardon any Klan member who was indicted.[8] The Chief Justice of the Georgia Supreme Court was also a Klansman. So was the mayor of Atlanta, which was not only Georgia's capital city, but also the Klan's Imperial City.

In the wake of the Red Scare, the second Klan maintained its white supremacism but expanded its list of enemies to include most foreigners, especially Catholics, Jews, Eastern and Southern Europeans, as well as communists, socialists and labour organizers, all of whom it generally equated. This broad-stroke nativism was strongly eugenicist, promising to protect the 'pure stock' of white American Protestantism from the racial 'pollution' of mixing with inferior breeds.

As the Klan's membership exploded across America in the early 1920s, its family resemblance to political movements across the Atlantic was all too clear to worried observers. The similarities between European fascism and the American Klan were remarked upon from the early 1920s, as Mussolini consolidated power in Italy and the reborn Klan spread across the United States. 'Has it occurred to you that our American Fascisti are the gentlemen of the Ku Klux Klan?' the *Washington Times* demanded of its readers at the end of 1922. It should have, as the comparison had been made all over the country for months, from Boston ('The Fascisti... are an Italian Ku Klux Klan, a Nationalistic, imperialistic, middle class, white collar, broadcloth mob, with plenty of money from the profiteers in their war chest')[9] to St Paul ('The signal success of the Fascisti or Italian Ku Klux Klan')[10] to Brooklyn ('The weapon of the radicals – terrorism – has been seized by the Fascisti... [who] are committing many excesses, just as the Ku Klux Klan committed many excesses')[11] to Tampa ('The klan... is the Fascisti of America').[12] The European press drew the same obvious conclusions: as early as 1923 German periodicals were referring to the 'Invisible Empire of the Ku Klux Klan' as an instance of 'Amerikanischer Faschismus'.[13]

The Klan was responding to an existential fear on the part of white Americans – by no means only Southerners – about losing their grip on power in the United States. This fear manifested itself in the restrictive anti-immigration laws of the 1920s, as the second Klan's support of 'America First' and '100% Americanism' helped it leverage widespread suspicion of foreigners. White Americans increasingly saw themselves as a victimized minority, a pure race under attack from foreign hordes, including the hordes they'd violently brought to America to work for them for free. They blinded themselves to their own dominance, insisting on their fragility and precarity.

Grand Wizard Simmons declared that 'the tremendous influx of foreign immigration, tutored in alien dogmas and alien creeds' was 'slowly pushing the native-born white American population into the center of the country, there to be ultimately overwhelmed and smothered', thereby 'threatening to crush and overwhelm Anglo-Saxon civilization'.[14] And so the Klan was forced, as always against its will, to fight back.

*

In September 1922, Margaret Mitchell married Berrien 'Red' Kinnard Upshaw, in limited respects probably a model for Rhett Butler. Their marriage was unhappy, violent, and brief. When it ended, Mitchell went to work for the *Atlanta Journal*, and began writing for the *Sunday Magazine* supplement, where she remained until 1926. After an ankle injury forced her to stay at home, she began composing what became *Gone with the Wind*. Two of the *Journal*'s founding partners were Hoke Smith, the race-baiting political boss, and Mitchell's great-uncle, Frank Rice.[15]

Red Upshaw was a cousin of Congressman William David Upshaw, who represented the state of Georgia from 1919–1927. 'Everyone knows', a Georgia reporter declared, 'that Rep.

Willie Upshaw is a Klansman.' 'This much certainly can be said of Upshaw,' added another: 'if he was never a Klansman in fact, he was always a Klansman in spirit.'[16] Upshaw provided Congressional testimony to the 'sterling character' of Imperial Wizard Simmons, saying he was 'incapable of an unworthy, unpatriotic motive, word or deed'.[17] Simmons always insisted that the Klan was not a group that supported 'race hatred', but rather one devoted to 'race pride' – another argument that has been taken up by white nationalists a century later, who insist that they are simply defending the white race.

The point is not that Mitchell was to blame for the racial politics of her ex-husband's cousin, or her family friends. It is, rather, to say that her own were less vicious than those of many people she knew: after she became wealthy, for example, Mitchell silently gave generous donations to Morehouse College, a historically Black university, to support scholarships. But her racial politics entailed constantly turning a blind eye to 'race hatred' even as she insisted that she supported Black people.

What Simmons liked to call 'racial pride in whiteness' led to some acts against Black people in the state of Georgia that are difficult to distinguish from race hatred, at a time when Mitchell was more than old enough to comprehend them. In May 1918, another national outcry was sparked when a heavily pregnant woman named Mary Turner was brutally murdered as part of a 'lynching orgy' in Georgia – five days of horrific violence that made national headlines around the country.[18] The rampage even made the *Atlanta Constitution*'s front page – but it downplayed the violence, informing its readers of only five victims, instead of the eleven identified in the national press (while historians later named at least thirteen). The *Constitution* reported that Mary Turner was hanged and her 'body riddled with bullets' after she made 'unwise remarks' following the lynching of her husband, Hayes Turner.[19]

Those 'unwise remarks' made by Mary Turner, who was eight months pregnant, were calls for her husband's murderers to face justice. In retaliation she was hanged 'head downward, doused with gasoline and set on fire. While she was still alive, one of the lynchers grabbed a knife and cut the unborn infant from her womb. Another man then crushed the baby's head with the heels of his boots. Finally the mob unloaded their guns into the dead woman's body,' according to the NAACP investigation.[20] No legal action was taken against the lynch mob, at least in part because the foreman of the local grand jury had been one of its leading members.[21] White Americans continue to make a point of protecting each other from being distressed by such details, which might challenge our collective complacency.

*

Although Southern newspapers could not always be trusted to report vigilante violence accurately after it happened, they were much more reliable sources of vigilante violence that was about to happen.

At the turn of the twentieth century lynchings were increasingly advertised ahead of time in the local press and on neighbourhood flyers, just as a fun fair or circus might have been. Headlines such as 'Will Burn the Negro at the Stake'[22] (1895), 'Texas Farmers Will Burn Negro Assailant at Stake'[23] (1901), 'Will Burn Negro: Officers Will Probably Not interfere in Texas'[24] (1905) blared premeditated homicide to readers – and law enforcement – around the country. An 1893 lynching in Louisville, Kentucky was carried out by a mob of thousands that had travelled from Missouri, Illinois, and Tennessee to join in the fun. For years they referred to these mobs as 'lynching bees',[25] likening homicidal mobs to the custom of gathering to help with a common task like sewing or quilting.[26] (By an even more obscene irony, the word 'bee' derives from the Old English for a prayer or favour.)

Minstrelsy and lynching were the comic and tragic masks of the American racial drama, both entertainments that unified white crowds over the degradation of Black people. Lynching provided a spectacular display of white power that terrorized the Black population and exhilarated white audiences with a sense of their own racial superiority. Whether through ostensibly comic mockery or overtly sadistic violence, both were performed for the pleasure of a crowd enjoying its political dominance by dehumanizing other people. As early as 1869, 'Klu-Klux [sic] Pantamorphs from the Wilds of Alabama' had been incorporated into circus entertainments to entertain locals in Maine.[27]

Such attractions were primarily capitalizing on the outlandish name, but the Klan always had a strong streak of theatricality, and before long it was clear that lynching had evolved into a barbaric form of mass entertainment. By 1917, the influential journalist H. L. Mencken was rightly observing that lynchings had become a local 'sport' that took 'the place of the merry-go-round, the theatre, the symphony orchestra, and other diversions' in larger communities. Street vendors sold popcorn and other snacks; postcards with grisly photos taken at the scenes of torture and murder circulated openly in the US mail; human remains were carried home as souvenirs. The Klan was also, by no coincidence, a money-making venture, a pyramid scheme populated by grifters and hucksters, literally setting up stalls at state fairs so that racial violence and economic resentment could make a buck.

Historians have traced the way lynching began to absorb aspects of modern showmanship in the early decades of the twentieth century. Just as the second Klan acquired its fiery cross from popular entertainments, so did public lynchings adopt some of the narrative forms of dime fiction, with exciting chase scenes, the satisfaction of capture and the supposed fulfilment of justice, and scenes of torture choreographed with gradually increasing care[28] – and they brought the frisson of fiction to exciting life. The carnivalesque aspects of Klan violence were vociferously denied even as they were on plain view in every local newspaper.

Defences that it never occurred to Margaret Mitchell and white Americans like her to think otherwise are not good enough. She claimed credibility as a revisionist truth-teller, while working extremely hard to avoid learning the truth about the Klan. If Mitchell wasn't actively 'endorsing' racial violence, as some have argued, this is a minimal defence: she was certainly apologizing for it.[29] Taken as a whole *Gone with the Wind* does endorse racial violence: every single white man in Scarlett's social circle voluntarily commits summary murder during Reconstruction to uphold racial hierarchies and is praised for so doing; their entitlement to murder is never questioned, even implicitly, by the highly opinionated narrator, and no one suggests for a moment that there might be anything objectionable in such behaviour.

Gone with the Wind actively helped white Americans pretend that the barbaric torture of spectacle lynching was exaggerated by Northern resentment, that white Southerners were forced into it against their better nature, that it was a quiet, occasional, regrettable, tragic necessity rather than a constant hysterical blood sport enjoyed by literally thousands upon thousands of white Americans less than a century ago.

Mitchell situates Tara and Twelve Oaks close to the real city of Jonesboro, Georgia, which today features the Road to Tara Museum. Jonesboro does not, evidently, commemorate the fact that in 1897 thousands of white people formed a lynch mob there to hunt down a 'Negro Ravisher' named Oscar Smith in order to burn him alive, an assemblage that made the 'peaceful community' look as 'warlike as at any time during the rebellion' of the Civil War.[30]

'Will Burn Him at the Stake', a Missouri newspaper told its readers, giving them plenty of time to get there to help.[31]

*

In 1931, one of America's most prominent Black journalists, George Schuyler, published *Black No More,* a scathing satire of racial capitalism and the violence that upholds it. The story centres on a scientific discovery that can turn Black people white:

its Black protagonist is the first in line for the process. Once he is sufficiently white, he ends up in Atlanta running a Klannish organization called the Knights of Nordics.

Schuyler dedicates the book witheringly 'to all Caucasians in the great republic who can trace their ancestry back ten generations and confidently assert that there are no Black leaves, twigs, limbs or branches on their family tree'.

By the end of the story, white supremacist politicians' efforts to racially discredit their opponents have backfired. Finding themselves in rural Mississippi, they black their faces to try to save their lives – as Schuyler satirically inverts blackface minstrelsy – but they are found out and brutally lynched by a furious mob: stripped naked, 'their ears and genitals cut off with jack knives amid the fiendish cries of men and women', their ears sewn onto their backs, and told to run. They are shot but not killed, and bound together to a stake, as the mob gathers kindling and kerosene and sets them afire. 'The odor of cooking meat permeated the clear, country air and many a nostril was guiltily distended', Schuyler adds, not pulling his punches.[32] This furiously graphic detail registers the ugly truth that by the 1930s lynchings remained all too horrifyingly common, their gruesome details shared in the pages of every newspaper.

According to one biography, it was probably in 1933 that Mitchell made the decision that Frank Kennedy would be 'dispatched' by way of the Klan raid – a year during which twenty-eight Americans were lynched. Earlier in 1933, a serious study called *Lynching and the Law* made the news when it revealed that only 'eight-tenths of one percent' of lynchings in the United States were followed by conviction, and that 99 per cent of lynchings were not met with any effort at prosecution at all. (Given that Mitchell did not feel it incumbent upon her to research the Klan, she probably didn't know this.)

Eight people were lynched in 1936, the year *Gone with the Wind* was published, including a forty-five-year-old Black farmer in Georgia who had been accused of sexual assault. He was seized by a mob of forty men with guns, his body found tied to a tree near where the alleged assault took place, 'pierced by shotgun, pistol, and rifle bullets'.[33] In April 1937 Robert McDaniels and Roosevelt Townes were tied to trees in Mississippi and tortured with blow torches, Townes burned alive. That autumn news began to spread that the Klan had revived in Florida and was growing.[34] Many Americans would have literally put aside *Gone with the Wind* and its paeans to the Klan only to open newspapers reporting the latest racist atrocity.

One of the most infamous of the last cases of American spectacle lynching occurred in 1935, as Mitchell was finishing *Gone with the Wind*. Rubin Stacy, a homeless former tenant farmer, was lynched after he knocked on a white woman's door in Fort Lauderdale to beg for food. She 'became frightened and screamed when she saw Stacy's face', and called the police, according to the NAACP report into his murder.[35] On his way to the jail Stacy was grabbed by a lynch mob and hanged outside the door where he'd had the temerity to frighten a white woman – just as Tony Fontaine kills a 'black buck' for frightening his sister in the novel. Rubin Stacy's murder was front-page news that summer across America, including in Florida, Alabama, Kentucky, and Louisiana. The *Atlanta Constitution*, by contrast, buried the story without a headline on page six, reporting under 'South-wide news' that two Black farmers were lynched in Mississippi, and that an unnamed man was lynched near Fort Lauderdale for having attacked a woman with a pen knife (a false report).[36]

Although Stacy's killers also photographed themselves in front of his corpse, the state of Florida did not prosecute them. One of the photographs shows Stacy's lynched body surrounded by five young white girls, one of whom is looking up at it with a smirk.[37] Anti-lynching activists once again mounted protests, trying to get a supine federal government to intervene. The *Pittsburgh Courier* reported that the photographs of Stacy's lynching had circulated in Nazi Germany in response to American protests against its persecution of Jews and other German citizens: 'Stop Lynching Negroes is Nazi Retort to American Critics', read the *Courier*'s furious headline.[38] It also reported that Mussolini had used lynching to deflect criticism from his invasion of Ethiopia: 'Negroes have enough concern with their brethren Christianly lynched daily in the United States without worrying about the blacks of Ethopia,' he wrote in a *Popolo d'Italia* editorial.[39]

But President Roosevelt, fearing the loss of Southern white votes in the 1936 election, refused to support the latest effort at passing a federal anti-lynching bill. Roosevelt rationalized his position by saying he could further advance the cause of Black people if he stayed in office. The New Deal had singularly failed to do that; in fact, it consistently sold out Black labourers to the white South (so that, for example, agricultural and domestic workers, a sizeable majority of whom at the time were Black, were specifically exempted from New Deal benefits).[40] Advancing the cause of civil rights would be left not to the New Yorker Roosevelt, but to his Southern successor, Harry Truman, whose support of civil rights broke up the 'Solid South' and incited the 1948 Dixiecrat rebellion that changed the political map of America for the next century.

'It doesn't seem to bother the Yankees whether folks are guilty or not, so long as they can hang somebody,' Aunt Pitty tells Scarlett, a jaw-dropping statement for a 1936 novel to put in the mouth of a white Southerner.

*

In January 2021, two weeks after the sacking of the Capitol, a Confederate monument was removed from its place in front of a courthouse in Lawrenceville, a suburb of Atlanta, one of the more than 150 Confederate memorials that were removed across the country in the year following the Black Lives Matter protests of 2020. The Lawrenceville statue, depicting a Confederate soldier and flag with the message 'Lest We Forget', made the news partly because it had been erected in front of the courthouse just thirty years earlier, in 1993. It would not seem that Atlanta was in much danger of forgetting the Confederacy, given that its suburbs were putting up monuments to it 130 years later.

Courthouses had become one of the South's favourite locations for Confederate statues, as opposed to the cemeteries that might seem more suitable places for commemoration, because in truth those statues symbolized not fallen soldiers, but white governance: they stood before courthouses and state government buildings for a reason.

The previous Gwinnett County Courthouse had been burned in 1871, the year that the first Klan was investigated by Congress. As part of its report about the new monument in 1993, the *Atlanta Journal-Constitution* offered a handy history of the courthouse, beginning in 1818, when 'the state of Georgia steals the necessary chunks of land' from the Creek and Cherokee tribes and a neighbouring county. It includes the burning of the courthouse, in 1871, 'purportedly' by a member of the Klan.

The history of Gwinnett Courthouse also mentioned the terrible lynching of Charlie Hale in 1911, immortalized, like so many lynchings in the early twentieth century, with horrifying photographs of self-righteous white men holding bloodhounds next to the person they've murdered. Hale's bare feet have a sign dangling from them: 'Please do not wake him.' His killers stare arrogantly into the camera, rightly confident that they decide the rule of law in Georgia.

A century after the lynching of Charlie Hale, a seventeen-year-old white man named Kyle Rittenhouse drove across state lines to join a self-styled militia patrolling a Black Lives Matter protest; he shot three (white) men he believed to be supporters of Black Lives Matter, two of whom died. Right-wing pundit Ann Coulter tweeted in response to Rittenhouse's mass shooting, 'I want him as my President', while Fox host Tucker Carlson professed to be 'shocked' that '17-year-olds with rifles decided they had to maintain order when no one else would.'[41]

This is precisely the alibi that was always offered for white supremacist violence, straight out of *Gone with the Wind* and the newspaper lynching reports that accompanied it. Scapegoating makes violence redemptive, as savagery is projected onto its victims, who deserve what they are getting. The Klan was a group shaped around projection and scapegoating, while apologists of white supremacists from Thomas Dixon and Margaret Mitchell to Tucker Carlson and Ann Coulter to the hyper-partisan mob that stormed the Capitol all insisted that they were defending 'extralegal justice', as if extralegal were not just another word for illegal.

In response to the failure of yet another attempt to pass a federal anti-lynching bill in 1938, the NAACP's Walter White gave a broadcast insisting that American democracy was under threat from 'mob rule'. It was misleading to claim that 'there were only eight lynchings in 1937', he argued, noting that hundreds of people had participated in those lynchings, meaning that hundreds of murderers were 'walking the streets of America, scot-free'. Ending lynching was not merely, White added, a struggle to save individuals from appalling violence and death: 'Fundamentally it is a struggle for the survival of law and order... It is just one step from unorganized mobs lynching helpless individuals to organized mobs lynching democracy itself' – for 'lynching is the open door to fascism'.

If the government didn't conquer the mob, White warned, the mob would destroy the government – 'that is the choice which America can no longer escape making', he concluded.[42]

But America would keep trying. In November 2021, Kyle Rittenhouse was acquitted of murder. A month later he headlined the conservative conference 'AmericaFest', where he was told, 'You're a hero to millions, it's an honor to be able to have you.' Rittenhouse walked onstage to his own theme song and a standing ovation, as the carnival continued.[43]

PART SIX

YOU, MISS, ARE NO LADY

22

What a Woman

'You, Miss, are no lady,' Rhett tells Scarlett, informing the audience in the story's opening scenes that its heroine is not a good Southern belle. Scarlett has just made an antebellum pass at Ashley by telling him that she loves him. When Ashley replies that he will honour his engagement to Melanie, despite having just told Scarlett that he 'cares', she denounces him as a cad and slaps his face. After he makes a dignified exit – in the novel, he kisses her hand, while in the film Leslie Howard turns an affronted cheek – she hurls a china bowl against the fireplace.

That is when Rhett Butler, highly amused, makes his presence known in the story. Scarlett tells him he is no gentleman for eavesdropping, and he responds that she is no lady, while making clear it's a compliment: 'Don't think I hold that against you. Ladies have never held any charm for me.'

Its sustained critique of nineteenth-century ideas of femininity remains by some way the most modern aspect of *Gone with the Wind*, its feminism frequently invoked in mitigation of its racism. This was no coincidence: Margaret Mitchell's mother, Maybelle, was one of Georgia's foremost campaigners for women's suffrage. She raised her daughter under the terms of a middle-class white feminism that consciously rejected Victorian separate spheres and the cult of ladyhood, fighting gender hierarchies and ignoring any others. A friend and colleague of Mitchell's from her time as a journalist considered her 'intensely feminist'.[1]

Scarlett O'Hara 'found the road to ladyhood hard', Mitchell tells us early on, making clear that one is not born but becomes a lady. For the first half of the story, Rhett tries to lure Scarlett off the road to ladyhood, until the war takes care of that for him. Scarlett is a modern woman confined in corsets and crinoline: she has a brain for business and resents being trapped by motherhood (in the novel she has three children, whom she spends most of her time ignoring; the film, likewise viewing them as encumbrances, dispensed with the first two). Scarlett seeks independence but lacks the financial autonomy that would let her determine her own fate.

She has been raised to be like her mother and Melanie, both of whom embody the gentle flower of Southern ladyhood: self-sacrificing, pious, politically submissive but morally indomitable, fiercely loyal and compassionate. Scarlett shares only their fierce loyalty, as Mitchell makes plain from the novel's opening words. The book begins (aptly) with a series of denials, telling us all the things Scarlett isn't. She is not beautiful, she is not modest, she is not demure, she is not quiet, she is not decorous: 'For all the modesty of her spreading skirts, the demureness of hair netted smoothly into a chignon and the quietness of small white hands folded in her lap, her true self was poorly concealed.'

In other words, Scarlett is not a conventional heroine of an antebellum romance. 'The green eyes in the carefully sweet face were turbulent, willful, lusty with life, distinctly at variance with her decorous demeanor.' These denials repudiate the tropes of plantation fiction, implying that the story will strip away illusions to show the reality beneath: 'Thanks to Mammy and Ellen, she looked sweet, charming and giddy, but she was, in reality, self-willed, vain and obstinate.'

Mitchell says explicitly that conventional femininity was a masquerade women were forced into playing: 'There was no one to tell Scarlett that her own personality, frighteningly vital though it was, was more attractive than any masquerade,' her narrator breaks in to explain. 'At no time, before or since, had so low a premium been placed on feminine naturalness.'

Gone with the Wind asks some good questions about the costs of white ladyhood. The problem is with the answers it offers; read one way, it is a thousand-page manifesto for selfishness. The story teaches that being a lady is a lesson to be learned, the end of a long road of study and training, an unnatural performance of submissiveness. A 'happy feminine conspiracy' made life easier for women, who

> knew that a land where men were contented, uncontradicted and safe in possession of unpunctured vanity was likely to be a very pleasant place for women to live. So, from the cradle to the grave, women strove to make men pleased with themselves, and the satisfied men repaid lavishly with gallantry and adoration...

Scarlett employs exactly these tactics, 'but with a studied artistry and consummate skill', never performing submission 'except to further her own aims'. Mitchell understood in so many words that women played up to and subverted the docility their society demanded – without ever questioning whether Black people might have been doing precisely the same thing, protecting themselves, making life easier, and trying to further their own aims. In *Gone with the Wind* being a lady is unnatural for white women, but being enslaved comes naturally to Black people.

Scarlett is so modern that she packs a pistol, which Vivien Leigh pats with satisfaction in the film (earning the ultimate 1930s accolade from Clark Gable: 'What a woman!'), able to broadly hold her own in a man's world. But the story's racial politics require fragile white ladies for its moral economy, to rationalize its outrage at Black people acquiring power. (If Black men aren't attacking white women, why else resist their equality so viciously?) And so even as Mitchell deplores the cult of femininity on one page for impeding Scarlett, she eulogizes it on the next in the character of Melanie, who embodies it. Melanie is to ladyhood what the novel's Black characters are to minstrelsy: they uphold the plantation hierarchies that provide the story's scaffolding.

This is why arguments that *Gone with the Wind* is redeemed by its feminism don't go very far – because neither does its feminism. In fact, Scarlett O'Hara's feminism is measured primarily by the tenacity of her quest for individual power, which she construes as purchasing power. *Gone with the Wind* has little interest in confronting complex realities and must disavow Scarlett's power as often as it avows it. In spotlighting the fall and rise of a white woman whose economic agency is purchased at the cost of Black people, *Gone with the Wind* replicates the historical reality of American power structures in more ways than one.

*

What it meant to be a lady, especially in the South, changed dramatically over the course of Margaret Mitchell's life. Raised in the Edwardian era by her suffragist mother, Mitchell grew up listening to debates over women's rights. She later said one of her earliest memories was of being taken by her mother to a rally led by a famous suffragist, who might have been Susan B. Anthony. As her mother spoke, the six-year-old sat on a platform wearing a 'Votes for Women' sash and, she said, blowing kisses at the men in the audience.

Georgia had taken a prominent place in national women's suffrage when Atlanta hosted the National Woman Suffrage Association convention in 1895 – its first meeting beyond the nation's capital – to counter the widespread view that white Southern women did not support suffrage. The Old Guard of the Georgia suffragist movement was outspokenly white supremacist; racism was central to the support they gained from rural populists, to whose bigotries they played. The struggle for women's suffrage in the South emerged as a battle between the political power of white women and Black men; Black women, as so often in American political discourse, were treated as an afterthought, despite driving much of the change.

Excluded from the 1895 Atlanta convention, Black women responded with the first annual convention of the National Federation of Afro-American Women in 1896, where together with the National League of Colored Women they formed the National Association of Colored Women, whose motto was 'lifting as we climb'. Several leading national Black suffragists were from Georgia, including Janie Porter Barrett, Adella Hunt Logan, and Mary A. McCurdy. In 1913, on the eve of Woodrow Wilson's inauguration, the National American Woman Suffrage Association organized a major march in Washington, DC, with thousands of delegates from all over the country. African American women were told to march at the back of the parade.

The journalist Ida B. Wells-Barnett intended to join the Chicago delegation but was informed that her presence in the front of the parade would alienate white Southern women. Wells-Barnett refused to be relegated to the back: she waited just until the Chicago delegation passed and then stepped into the front, where the *Chicago Tribune* featured her two days later.

For the best part of a century, popular history of women's suffrage in America similarly told a story that put white women at the front, marginalizing African American women historically just as they had once been physically sidelined.

The shortest constitutional amendment, just twenty-eight words ('The right of citizens of the United States to vote shall not be denied or abridged by the United States or by any state on account of sex'), the Nineteenth Amendment passed Congress in June 1919, six months after Margaret Mitchell's mother died from the influenza pandemic. Mitchell had been attending Smith

College in Massachusetts, but after her mother's death decided not to return.

There was much Mitchell disliked about Smith, including, apparently, its policy of admitting one or two African American woman each year.[2] Her roommate at Smith later recalled that when Mitchell entered a history classroom at the start of term to find a Black student there, she flew into a rage and demanded to be switched into another class, where she was safe from having to consider either the historical, or actual, existence of Black people.

In later years, Mitchell embellished and justified the tale, claiming that the white teacher had a grudge against Southerners, and that she had accused the teacher of hypocrisy at the time, demanding to know if she 'had ever undressed and nursed a Negro woman or sat on a drunk Negro man's head to keep him from being shot by the police'.[3] This is the same paternalistic defence Scarlett offers when the Yankee women insult Uncle Peter, and it was a standard one: that however objectionable Southerners' systemic racism might appear, in reality they were kinder and closer to Black Americans than Northern whites.

It is possible that African Americans considered such distinctions moot, or even that they might have disputed whether having a white girl sit on their head was an effective remedy for racist violence. But it also shows that by the time Mitchell told this story, racism was already mutating to conceal its structural roots in individual attitudes. It was shifting from the overt to the covert, enabling plausible deniability, so that a woman who had literally refused to sit in a room on equal terms with a Black person could still convince herself she was not personally racist.

The biographer who reported the story about the classmate, Darden Asbury Pyron, added in his 1991 account that there were 'one or two' Black women in Mitchell's class at Smith, "'quiet, fine girls", one alumna boasted'.[4] Given that he interpreted Black women's silence as something for white people to boast about, it is perhaps unsurprising that Pyron looked no further into the identities of these quiet, fine girls. But it is equally unsurprising that the handful of Black women who attended Smith and other elite colleges during the Jim Crow era were outstandingly talented – they had to be – and went on to lead distinguished and influential lives.

The four Black women attending Smith along with Mitchell were Catherine V. Grigsby, who matriculated with Mitchell in the class of 1922; she joined her older sister Pearl A. Grigsby, as well as Miriam L. Courtney and Eunice R. Hunton. The introduction to English history in which Mitchell had enrolled was a required class for students with her entrance qualifications and could be taken in either the freshman or sophomore year, which means that the woman whose existence provoked Mitchell's racist outburst in the autumn of 1918 was either Catherine Grigsby or Eunice Hunton.[5]

Catherine Grigsby Mayo became a French teacher and then an active local organizer of African American women in New Jersey, working to preserve Black history.[6] Eunice Hunton Carter had in fact been born in Atlanta a year before Margaret Mitchell, but her family was one of the many who moved north after the Atlanta race riot of 1906. Carter was the first Black woman to receive a law degree from Fordham University, and then one of the first Black women lawyers in New York in 1933.

Two years later, Carter became the first Black woman assistant district attorney in New York. She helped lead the team whose successful prosecution of the gangster Charles 'Lucky' Luciano for organized prostitution and racketeering made headlines across the country less than two weeks before the publication of *Gone with the Wind*. Margaret Mitchell does not appear to have noticed.

Carter later said she chanced to overhear a remark in court suggesting that nearly all cases against prostitutes were dismissed before being prosecuted, in a suspiciously systematic way. She spent months establishing that prostitution was an organized racket, but her boss, the district attorney Thomas E. Dewey, thought prostitution insignificant; it took protracted arguments and overwhelming evidence for Carter to finally convince him. She helped organize the sting operation that led to Luciano's arrest and eventual conviction in June 1936 on sixty-two racketeering charges of compulsory prostitution, the first ever such conviction on prostitution charges.[7]

While white men were dismissing prostitution, a Black woman recognized its significance. It's an utterly obvious point, and one we constantly forget: people with different perspectives do not share our blind spots.

23

Not a Very Nice Person

In the early days of the novel's success Mitchell claimed that Melanie was 'really my heroine, not "Scarlett"', whom the narrator frequently regards with exasperation. While knowing perfectly well that, as she put it, '"Scarlett" was not a very nice person',[1] Mitchell also defended her 'good traits' in another letter: 'Surely courage is commendable, and she had it. The sense of responsibility for the weak and helpless is a rare trait, and she had this, for she took care of her own even at great cost to herself. She was able to appreciate what was beautiful in her mother, even if she could not emulate her… She had perseverance in the face of defeat.'[2] The phrase 'her own' is doing a lot of work in this statement, for the weak and helpless to whom Scarlett might be said to owe an obligation very much include the humans her family has enslaved, and to whose labour she continues to feel entitled.

The first representative woman in American popular culture, Scarlett was a character with whom audiences around the world identified from the start, in her resilience and obstinate drive toward her own goals. Japanese audiences reportedly identified with her efforts to rebuild after losing a catastrophic war, as well as her familial loyalty, her strength, and the mannered conventions of her culture.[3] Vietnamese readers found in her 'what a woman had to be: selfish, ruthless, unkind, but practical, vigorous, and able to overcome difficulties through sheer force of will'.[4] Scarlett is, as Mitchell argued, admirable in many ways: she shoulders responsibilities with real fortitude when everyone around her fails, singlehandedly providing not only for her (large) immediate family, but for a huge extended family as well, including relatives in other cities and Ashley Wilkes's family, too. She certainly sees the people her family has enslaved as 'her own' – her responsibility, as well as her property.

While busily cutting her heroine down to a modern and realistic size, Mitchell does allow other characters to recognize her good qualities, which the narrator, with the scepticism she ascribes to Mammy, rarely shares. As Scarlett convinces the family to help make her green velvet dress from Ellen's curtains so that she can wheedle tax money out of Rhett, Mitchell abruptly (and uncharacteristically) shifts to Ashley's point of view, as he is 'wrenched with admiration' for Scarlett's courage:

> He knew she had no such word in her vocabulary as gallantry, knew she would have stared blankly if he had told her she was the most gallant soul he had ever known. He knew she would not understand how many truly fine things he ascribed to her when he thought of her as gallant. He knew that she took life as it came, opposed her tough-fibered mind to whatever obstacles there might be, fought on with a determination that would not recognize defeat, and kept on fighting even when she saw defeat was inevitable... he had never known such gallantry as the gallantry of Scarlett O'Hara going forth to conquer the world in her mother's velvet curtains and the tail feathers of a rooster.

It is easy to sympathize with Scarlett in such passages, and with Mitchell's human comedy here. Scarlett's indomitable strength of will is often moving, as she becomes 'a woman to whom nothing was left from the wreckage except the indestructible red earth upon which she stood'. Her identification with Tara's red earth, so complete that even her name invokes it, makes Scarlett as indestructible as the land she loves.

But Scarlett's obliviousness to the immensity of the history happening around her also makes her wildly self-centred. Scarlett resents the war not because of its horrors, but because it disrupts her pleasures: 'The war didn't seem to be a holy affair, but a nuisance that killed men senselessly and cost money and made luxuries hard to get.' The narration is critical of Scarlett in such passages, but because it never turns its own attention to those horrors or moves beyond Scarlett's solipsistic perspective, its criticism gains little purchase.

The film strikes a better balance between its heroine and history, making her resistance seem more humane, even conscientious, as Vivien Leigh portrays distress and revulsion at the vicious conflict rather than a solipsistic disregard of others' suffering. The power of Leigh's performance goes a long way to redeeming Scarlett in popular memory. Whereas Mitchell emphasizes Scarlett's insensitivity, obtuseness, and calculating nature, Vivien Leigh's tremendous charm elevates the character. Leigh delivered a performance that the film's first director, George Cukor, who cast her, said was 'charged with electricity' and 'possessed of the devil'.[5] The filmmakers retained some of Scarlett's sharpest lines, while never undermining her intelligence the way Mitchell does. The result is a character who is wilful, manipulative, and self-deceiving, but a shrewd observer of her society and someone who fights for herself and those she loves.

The assertive, scene-stealing performance of Hattie McDaniel as Mammy goes even further in some ways, because Leigh had so much more scope in the source material. Selznick responded to African American objections to the novel in part by expanding Mammy's role, giving her more time on screen than she gets on the page, and letting her dominate the scenes she was given, but it was McDaniel's performance that subverted the stereotype even while playing it.

McDaniel triumphantly transforms Mitchell's vaudeville cartoon into a forceful, sympathetic woman who is just as strong as Leigh's Scarlett, a woman who gives no more of a damn than Rhett Butler about what anyone else thinks. Mammy becomes the moral heart of the film (an opportunity the novel does not afford her), offering common sense and tough love where Scarlett struggles against her own constant misunderstandings and misreadings.

The substance of McDaniel's performance shifts the balance of sympathies in the film, working to overcome the novel's shrieking gaps in moral wisdom, while the comedic splendour of Butterfly McQueen's Prissy ensured that together the story's two Black women steal all their scenes. They transcend the minstrel stereotypes they were handed, while the Black male characters recede into the background. Mammy and Prissy were not granted interiority on Mitchell's page, but McDaniel and McQueen together claimed it on screen. While expanding the story's depiction of Black women, the film sacrifices almost all the novel's large, variegated cast of secondary white women, each of whom is sharply delineated.

Taken together, the two versions of *Gone with the Wind* offer one of the richer portraits of American womanhood to be found in its popular culture, an aspect of it that has been, by no coincidence, almost entirely overlooked.

*

Scarlett's mother, who symbolizes the virtues of the benevolent (and imaginary) plantation mistress, dies during the war – like Melanie, she will vanish with the passing of the world she embodies. A 'thrifty and kind mistress, a good mother and a devoted wife', Ellen brings 'order, dignity and grace into Gerald's household'. Mitchell allows that power-driven Scarlett can never achieve the 'selflessness' of her mother and the other women of the Old Guard, without acknowledging that such selflessness is itself a fiction, designed to erase the obtrusive selves of real women.

Although the novel only idealizes Ellen O'Hara and Melanie Wilkes, presenting its other female characters as decidedly imperfect, it does idealize (and universalize) all its white women in their treatment of the enslaved. None of these women, however flawed, the story insists, would dream of 'mistreating' a slave.

But the novel keeps slipping up. While maintaining that none of the Old Guard would even consider hurting a Black person, that the very idea is a vicious Yankee slur, Scarlett keeps longing to flagellate Black people. She threatens to whip Prissy at Tara after the burning of Atlanta and complains about the 'trashy' 'free issue darkies': 'If you so much as swear at them, much less hit them a few licks for the good of their souls, the Freedmen's Bureau is down on you.' To disown what Scarlett has just admitted, Mitchell has Frank Kennedy recoil in response at the very thought of violence against a Black worker, telling her he bets her father 'never hit a darky a lick in his life'.

Scarlett almost agrees ('well, only one') but maintains that 'it was different then. Free issue nxxxxrs are something else, and a good whipping would do some of them a lot of good.' Freed Black people are indeed 'something else', something other than enslaved Black people, and it is that difference – namely, their liberation and equality – to which Scarlett so vehemently objects. Exception turns difference into a justification: 'well, only one', 'it was different then', this is 'something else', that only applies to 'some of them'. The enslavers must constantly insist that slavery was different, because it was always the ultimate American exception – the country's 'peculiar institution'.

Sentimental maternalism was central to pro-slavery mythologies, corresponding to the paternalistic arguments that enslavement benefited (subhuman) Black people. Part of Mitchell's rejection of plantation fiction is letting Scarlett dislike motherhood – but then she surrounds Scarlett with idealized mother figures: not only Ellen O'Hara and Mammy, but also the maternal Melanie, and Dilcey, who nurses Melanie's baby and helps care for Scarlett. All these sentimental mothers are another way in which the mythological version of chattel slavery not only falsifies, but specifically reverses its cruel realities.

Gerald purchases Dilcey with her daughter Prissy at the start of the novel, to bring the family of his valet, Pork, to Tara. This generosity was quite atypical of antebellum slavery, which was far more likely to divide slave families than to reunite them. Indeed, Gerald has spent so lavishly to keep Pork's family together that Scarlett objects to his extravagant generosity: 'In the name of Heaven, Pa, three thousand! And you didn't need to buy Prissy!' Gerald responds by asking: 'Was there any use buying Dilcey if she was going to mope about the child? Well, never again will I let a darky on this place marry off it. It's too expensive.'[6] This passage is pure negation: enslaved families were constantly sold off for enslavers' profit, not kept together at enslavers' expense.

Chattel slavery often did not even admit the concept of slave families, because families belong to each other, according to standard rules of kinship, rather than to other humans who've purchased them against their will. Marriage was one of many civil rights sweepingly denied to enslaved people: not recognized as citizens under the law, they could not voluntarily enter into contracts on their own behalf. Many of the enslaved did choose to enter into conjugal unions, of course, but enslavers were under no obligation to recognize these, and mostly didn't. They sold their human property at will, without reference to familial bonds of any kind. The fundamental condition of chattel slavery was its systematic destruction of the bodily autonomy, sexual identities, and kinship relations of the enslaved: that was how it turned humans into property.

Chattel slavery thus also gave licence to every imaginable form of sexual violence. As Thomas Jefferson helpfully explained in 1820, 'a woman who brings a child every two years [is] more profitable than the best man of the farm. What she produces is an addition to the capital, while his labors disappear in mere consumption.'[7] The increase of what she 'produced' could be effected by enslavers like Jefferson very simply: women were raped by enslavers irrespective of their own marital status, or age, or relationship with their rapist (incest was not only common but incentivized). Enslaved women would also sometimes accept or seek out sexual relationships with enslavers in hopes of preferential treatment, or even of being freed, a promise that was frequently made to lure enslaved women into bed and infrequently kept.[8]

This reality does make it, glancingly, into the novel, when Scarlett objects to the Yankee women's 'very nasty and ill-bred interest in slave concubinage', a formulation that not only euphemizes rape and displaces any prurience about it onto the Yankees, but also shows how codes of Southern gentility enabled systemic sexual violence, not least by creating a lexicon designed to buffer those who used it from having to think about what they were talking about. Determinedly denying there was anything abusive in slavery, the story keeps slipping up and admitting such abuse into the tale – because the violence of chattel slavery was so endemic it could not, in fact, be kept entirely at bay.

Enslaved men were also raped, a fact that does not make its way into *Gone with the Wind*. In her classic narrative *Incidents in the Life of a Slave Girl* (1861), Harriet Jacobs describes the plight of her fellow slave Luke, chained to the bed of his 'cruel and disgusting' white master, a 'degraded wreck of manhood', who subjected Luke to 'the strangest freaks of despotism... of a nature too filthy to be repeated', in coded language that echoed the terms of contemporary anti-sodomy discourse.[9] And enslaved men were forced to rape enslaved women, to increase the unpaid labour force.[10]

Sexualized violence also included various forms of genital mutilation. Castration was not a new vengeance inflicted upon freed men after emancipation. During the antebellum period – and not only in the South – castration was not only wielded against the enslaved. It was all too common a punishment for any number of crimes, real or imagined, including sodomy, bestiality, and incest.[11] But castration was heavily racialized. For example, when one young white woman (allegedly) ran off with a Black slave in 1855, it afforded Huntsville, Missouri with 'the most extraordinary and revolting instance of female depravity', so 'utterly unfit for publication' that the local paper would only gasp out that she 'left her father's residence in company with one of his negroes'. Given 'the pernicious example this would be to other slaves if suffered to go unpunished', the town agreed 'he ought to be castrated – which conclusion was acted upon the same evening'.[12]

Sexual mutilation was explicitly used as a deterrent: the crime would not be spelled out, but the punishment was. Black men were also castrated for (alleged) sexual assault ('an outrageous rape and murder committed by a negro... the black wretch was first castrated', then hanged until 'nearly dead', then shot until completely dead), or (alleged) attempted sexual assault (after 'a fiendish outrage was attempted by two negroes', 'the free boy was castrated... Pity they were not hanged'), or the (alleged) 'gross and unmentionable proposals' that led to the castration of two Black men in Ohio in 1839.[13]

The symbolic implications of castration are obvious, as an assertion of total dominance, as well as the conspicuous demasculinizing and dehumanizing of its victims. But it also expresses the ways in which chattel slavery was deeply, and necessarily, implicated in human sexuality. Castration was a violent embodiment of the absolute control over Black sexuality that chattel slavery required. Enslaved men were castrated for perceived sexual rivalry, or for challenging white masters' sexual assaults upon enslaved women.[14] Not even always directly punitive, castration could also be used to ensure that the enslaved had no family ties other than the fondly imagined, but savagely imposed, devotion to the enslaving family. In Willa Cather's 1940 novel *Sapphira and the Slave Girl,* based on her memories of Reconstruction-era Virginia, the enslaved Till is forced into marriage with a castrated man – a 'capon man' – because the enslaver Sapphira doesn't want Till 'to be havin' chillun all over de place, – always a-carryin' or a-nussin' em', instead of attending to her own demands.

The Mammy stereotype works the same way, stripping the character of her own kinship bonds or desires to ensure that her only care is for the white child of her enslaver. Scarlett's Mammy, as has often been noted, has no life beyond the O'Hara clan, and is a strikingly desexualized figure (the mixed-race Dilcey, with the 'innate dignity' of her native heritage, is considerably more sexualized than Mammy). Enslaved women like Scarlett's Mammy were forced not only into becoming surrogate mothers, but into leaving their own children to be raised by surrogates, as chattel slavery created a chain of displacement across kinship bonds.[15] The endless insistence upon the devotion, loyalty, fidelity, love, and care of the Mammy figure is at once compulsive and reactive, part of American culture's endless attempt to naturalize a brutal racial hierarchy into the sentimental, oxymoronic myth of the 'willing slave'. The minstrel figure of 'Mammy' is there to hide these truths behind a substitute mother grinning and promising that slavery was all one big happy family.

*

The Mammy figure's 'devotion' to her enslavers is twinned, in the mythology, with the idealized plantation mistress's devotion to her slaves. Although histories of American institutional slavery have long disproved this image, thoroughly demonstrating that women were often just as sadistic in their treatment of slaves as masters and overseers, many factual accounts still assume that white women's power over slaves was only indirect. They construe institutional slavery primarily in terms of the master's power, admitting white women's deep investment in plantation slavery and capacity for cruelty within it, but depicting women's social and economic benefits from the slave system as mediated through patriarchy, so that white women were almost as thoroughly 'owned' by white men as were Black slaves.[16]

But more recent histories, including several by women of colour, have challenged this received wisdom, showing that enslaved people were one of the few forms of property that women in the South could hold in their own right, meaning that white women enslavers exercised more control over human property than any other form.[17] White women could buy and sell slaves, inherit and bequeath them, profit from their hire, determine the limits of their freedom and the brutality of their punishments, exercising direct control over their value, bodies, and lives. Female enslavers could also demand sex from enslaved men, a form of sexual assault that would not have been conceived as rape until very recently. Slavocracy offered white women forms of power they could not otherwise obtain in nineteenth-century America, deepening their investment (in every sense) in slavery's institutions.[18]

For white plantation mistresses, emancipation was thus no indirect grievance at the loss of social status and the financial security provided by patriarchy: it was direct and concrete – the loss of their only source of economic independence.[19] The women of the former Confederacy resented their loss of political and economic agency no less personally, and perhaps even more bitterly, than the men, as they had no other means of reclaiming it.

Chattel slavery let white women in the South build an identity around the idea that they were an exception to the general rule of Victorian coverture, under which women could not own property but were 'covered' by the legal and political rights of men in their families. Race-based slavery created an exemption for white women, a sense of personal exceptionalism that extends straight to the white women of the 2020s who argued that white patriarchy would protect their rights, even as it energetically worked to strip them away.

Gone with the Wind, like all Lost Cause fictions, works to veil this reality. That is its essence and origin: white women providing the cover story for the erasure of Black people that white sovereignty demands.

24

What Did Votes Matter?

Although the men of the plantation class all bitterly denounce the United States government for (temporarily) removing their franchise, for Scarlett the vote is a theoretical abstraction. 'Voting? What did votes matter?' she thinks, with her eyes fixed firmly on the concrete power of money. She is so apolitical and uninformed that she can't recall the word 'ratification' during these debates ('Why couldn't they have rati– radi– whatever they were supposed to do to it and smoothed the Yankees down instead of stirring them up again?') and never considers the possibility of women getting the vote.

In reality, American women of Scarlett's generation were, of course, fighting for the vote, and the complex trade-offs between abolitionists and suffragists over the moral fight against slavery, and for equal rights, were central to the way voting rights developed in the United States.[1] As ever, the negations in *Gone with the Wind* unwittingly reveal gaps in the politics of American memory, as Scarlett mentions the franchise only to dismiss it. But the question of women's suffrage plays a crucial role in the history that *Gone with the Wind* disavows. Although the Nineteenth Amendment was ratified in 1920, giving all American women the vote in theory, in practice it denied full suffrage to African American, Asian American, Hispanic American, and Native American women.

As pressure to pass the Nineteenth Amendment mounted, so did outbreaks of racial violence. Some of the most violent race riots in American history occurred just as women were securing the vote, including the terrible Chicago race riots of 1919, and the 1921 Tulsa Massacre, which left somewhere between 300 and 500 Black Americans dead in a twenty-four-hour period, a bloodbath that white leaders proceeded to scrub from the American record, deleting documents and newspaper accounts, denying that it occurred, and keeping it out of history books.[2]

A few weeks before the 1920 election, headlines in Orlando, Florida, about ten miles from a town called Ocoee, warned: 'TEN NEGRO WOMEN REGISTER HERE TO EVERY WHITE WOMAN'.[3] It was a call to arms, and it worked: the first election in which women voted has been called the 'bloody election of 1920', because of a massacre of African Americans in Ocoee on election day.[4] The fight over Black male suffrage had been successfully deferred in the South for fifty years, only to break out again in a proxy war over the rights of women.

Limiting the power of Black voters was crucial to sustaining white governance. Even as Black men were being systematically denied the vote in practice that they had been given in law in 1870, for the next fifty years white and Black women continued to fight for the franchise as well, meaning that debates over women's suffrage in the South were always entangled, explicitly, with debates over Black suffrage.

As women across the country were voting for the first time in the bloody election of 1920, women in the state of Georgia were barred from the ballot thanks to a rule requiring that voters register six months before an election. Most other states, including many in the Deep South, waived this rule so that women could vote, but not Georgia.

A century later, just before what became the bloody election of 2020, the American Civil Liberties Union found that the state of Georgia had 'incorrectly' purged 200,000 citizens from its voter rolls in 2019. As the delayed results of the 2020 election were finally decided in Georgia, where the organization of Black women activists like Stacey Abrams were widely acknowledged as having turned out the Black vote and pushed the Democrats over the line, Georgia's lawmakers responded with a raft of controversial voter suppression bills in the first months of 2021, including the prohibition of giving water to a voter standing in line.

Since gaining the vote in 1920, white American women have broadly supported socially conservative parties, a choice generally attributed to their traditional role as the moral guardian of the family. The single biggest voting group in the United States, at around 40 per cent, white women are perceived as swing voters, because their social and economic interests should align with progressive politics, yet American white women have voted reliably with social conservatives since 1952. As Republicanism increasingly consolidated around 'traditional family values', including normative patriarchal gender roles and religious beliefs, white women increasingly voted with them.

*

The movement for women's rights was always deeply entwined with abolition, as well as the temperance movement, all of them inspired by the great cultural wellspring that was the Second Great Awakening, the Protestant revival that swept the nation in the first half of the nineteenth century and generated many of the evangelical groups and ideas dominating American life to this day. Because of the political, economic, and moral urgency of slavery, abolition arrived sixty years ahead of its sibling reforms, legalized and realized by the Thirteenth, Fourteenth, and Fifteenth Amendments. The other two reforms, women's suffrage and Prohibition, having taken much longer, came into law in near lockstep, just six months apart in 1920, as the Eighteenth and Nineteenth Amendments.

Partly motivated by a sincere desire to lead a more Christian life, these movements were also inspired by less spiritual reasons. Prohibition derived from a complex mix of social motives: partly a women's rights movement, focused on the causal links between alcoholism, domestic violence, and poverty, it was also nativist, a way to criminalize the behaviours of immigrant communities, and thus had economic aims as well.

There was a similar complex of reasons driving the enfranchisement of women. An economic argument for women as wage earners and property owners was based on America's foundational promise to give representation where there was taxation (and the Sixteenth Amendment had recently legalized federal income tax, strengthening this argument). But the associations between abolition and women's suffrage also shaped the campaign for women's rights, especially in the South.

Women's suffrage constituted a direct threat not only to patriarchal but also to racial hierarchies, to the entire social order that was mystified and justified by Lost Cause fictions. White women were some of the fiercest advocates of maintaining the carefully constructed house of cards that upheld their own social and racial prerogatives. They feared that granting women direct political power might prove the pulled thread that unravelled the whole fabric of their social order – and they were right.

As early as 1867, one of the founders of the American Woman Suffrage Association, Henry Blackwell, told white Southerners explicitly that they should give women the vote to safeguard white supremacy. He said women's votes would effectively nullify the Fifteenth Amendment, helping to reunite the country by providing 'the only ground of settlement between North and South'. Because the North was as adamantly determined to create 'negro suffrage' as the South was to oppose it, Blackwell proposed a simple transaction: 'Your 4,000,000 of Southern white women will counterbalance your 4,000,000 of negro men and women, and thus the political supremacy of your white race will remain unchanged.'[5]

Fifty years later, the question was how to stop the extension of suffrage to women from retroactively undoing the denial of the franchise to Black men. In July 1919, the *Atlanta Constitution* boasted that Georgia was the 'First State Against Suffrage', warning: 'If you pass this nineteenth amendment you ratify the fifteenth, and any southerner, knowing what that means, is a traitor.'[6] The language of treachery, invoking the cult of the Lost Cause, was widespread in the debates over women's suffrage as a slippery slope to Black suffrage. A Georgia congressman agreed that any Southerner supporting the Nineteenth Amendment was 'a traitor to his section': 'If you pass this Nineteenth Amendment, you ratify the Fifteenth.'[7] A South Carolina senator concurred, saying that passing the Nineteenth Amendment would ratify the Fifteenth, 'a crime against civilization' that would enable 'an alien and ignorant race to be turned loose on us'.[8]

Women's suffrage, they argued, would undermine the patriarchal order of plantation politics, plunging the South back into racial chaos. The *Atlanta Constitution* denounced women's suffrage as a socialist platform that would spell 'the final ratification of the fifteenth amendment', of which 'Frederick Douglass was the father and Susan B. Anthony, who received the negro in her home, the mother', an image summoning the triple threat of abolition, feminism, and miscegenation.[9] Prophecies of a return to Reconstruction misrule routinely mixed sexual with racial freedom, as they continued to fight the spectre of racial 'pollution' that would bring down white supremacy.

Simple math meant Black enfranchisement would end the white Southern Democrat stranglehold on power: in 1920, there were over 200 counties in Southern states where the Black population outnumbered the white. A Florida senator helpfully spelled out the logic of voter suppression: 'In our state at present our elections are participated in almost exclusively by our white men and the Negro is not a factor in the election of our public officials. I am opposed to any proposition which would possibly invite greater and more extensive participation in our elections on the part of the Negro population.'[10] Some Southern politicians offered a compromise, promising to grant white women suffrage at the state level (which could be legislated locally without opening the door to federal enforcement) if white women would stop fighting for a constitutional amendment.

*

White women in the South divided over suffrage across the issue of race – but only over whether enfranchising women would help or hinder the white supremacist cause. Opponents of women's suffrage argued that their interests, including white supremacy, were better served under the protection of white patriarchs. Supporters of women's suffrage promised that white women would add their votes to the patriarchs' in upholding white supremacism. Either way, most of them were determined to maintain white supremacism. In Georgia, the white women on both sides of the debates were all leading members of the United Daughters of the Confederacy, meaning that although they differed over women's rights, they shared an allegiance to the old planter class and were united in supporting the cult of the Lost Cause.

Opponents of suffrage called it a Yankee import, associating it with carpetbaggers, invoking cultural motifs about white womanhood, benign patriarchal white governance, and states' rights, while accusing suffragists of betraying the cause: 'Woman's suffrage comes from the north and west and from women who do not believe in state rights and who wish to see negro women using the ballot. I do not believe that the State of Georgia has sunk so low that her good men cannot legislate for women,'[11] declared Mildred Rutherford, a prominent opponent of suffrage. She warned against 'Negro domination of the South', informing a legislative committee that the basis of Southern 'civilization' was 'the right to control our elective franchise', a statement that doesn't even pretend to be democratic.[12] Another anti-suffragist from Georgia, Dolly Lamar (who attended Wellesley College in Massachusetts only after being personally guaranteed there would be no Black women among her classmates), warned in 1914 that suffrage would mean 'the negroes put into office over our heads', invoking the same caricature of 'negro rule' that D. W. Griffith was busily validating as he began filming *The Birth of a Nation* that summer.[13]

But Southern white suffragists responded in the same terms, arguing that white women should get the vote so they could uphold white governance. Insisting that the disbarment of Black men from voting would easily extend to Black women, they played directly to the bigotries of rural populists. Where Rutherford spoke of the threat of 'negro domination of the South', Sallie Fannie Gleaton scoffed at the 'negro woman hoodoo',[14] promising that Black women's political power would remain limited. Another prominent suffrage campaigner, Georgia attorney James L. Anderson, published a pamphlet entitled 'Votes for Women as Bearing upon Negro Supremacy in the South', in which he made the same case as Henry Blackwell in 1867: white women outnumbered Black people, and so could successfully obliterate Black women's political agency.[15] 'Everyone knows that the enfranchisement of the women of the south will enormously increase white supremacy', another Georgia white suffragist campaigner maintained.[16]

*

One of the foremost figures in the Georgia fight for women's suffrage, Mrs Rebecca Latimer Felton, described by historians as having one of the best political minds of the nineteenth century, was also one of the nation's most famous advocates for lynching.[17] Felton would become the first female senator in the United States when the race-baiting demagogue Tom Watson (who also often urged oxymoronic 'lynch law', including for Leo Frank) died in 1922, and she was appointed to his seat. Felton was also the last person on the floor of the Senate to have personally enslaved people.

She was the subject of a 1923 *Atlanta Journal* profile by a young journalist named Margaret Mitchell, who praised the first woman in America to join the Senate as an exponent of 'the tradition of Georgia's noble womanhood', sharing their 'capacity for assuming difficult responsibilities when the need arose'. 'There has been no more interesting figure in Georgia for thirty years than she,' the young Mitchell wrote, praising Felton's 'indefatigable' letter campaigns and her defence against 'vitriolic newspaper attacks'.[18]

Many of the letters that the indefatigable Felton wrote were vitriolic newspaper attacks against Black people. She declared that 'the future of the South depends upon putting down the bestial blacks', on making 'a choice between the safety of the wives and daughters of white men, or coddling subserviency to the northern fanatics who have money to pay those who would thus betray their own race and color'.[19]

Felton was notorious for having urged the lynching of Sam Hose, a young Georgia farm worker burned at the stake in 1899 after being accused of bashing in the head of his employer and then raping his employer's wife. In fact, investigators found that an altercation between Hose and his employer over time off for Hose to visit his sick mother had led to violence: the employer pulled a gun, and Hose threw an axe, killing him.

Rumours that the employer's wife had been raped instantly erupted, and Rebecca Felton, already campaigning for women's suffrage, threw her energy into inciting a lynch mob to murder Hose. She publicly demanded that white women be protected from such 'negro fiends': 'If it needs lynching to protect woman's dearest possession from a raving human beast, then I say lynch a thousand times a week if necessary.'[20] Whether woman's dearest possession was her purity or her power, Felton didn't say.

A few days later, as Hose was running for his life, Felton reiterated her demand. 'I said, "Lynch 1,000 a week or stop the outrage,"' she wrote to the *Atlanta Constitution,* 'and I again repeat it,' adding:

> Sam Holt [*sic*] needs and deserves no trial. When such a fiend abandons humanity to become a brute, then he shall be dispatched with no more cavil than would prevail with a mad dog's fate, after he had bitten your child... In one case there is hellish intent, in the other a hapless disease. The dog is more worthy of sympathy.

Hose, she ended, was 'beyond the pale of human mercy'.[21] This justification for murder is precisely the one that *Gone with the Wind* offers in its defence of the Klan as a 'tragic necessity' provoked by the 'large number of outrages on women', and why it expects its audience to sympathize with Ashley and Frank as they race off to murder Scarlett's assailants.

Sam Hose was eventually caught by the lynch mob near Newnan, about thirty miles from where Mitchell locates Tara. A special train was commissioned so that 2,000 people could travel from Atlanta in 1899 and watch a twenty-four-year-old man be burned alive.

'The Black Beast Burned at the Stake',[22] read the Macon *Telegraph* front-page headline, reporting the atrocity with local pride. The *Telegraph*'s description of Hose's murder begins with the 'nearly two thousand people, who sent aloft yells of defiance and shouts of joy', as 'Sam Hose, a negro who committed two of the basest acts known to crime, was burned at the stake in a public road one and one-half miles from here this afternoon.' That yell of defiance is the same Lost Cause defiance that Mitchell praises in Scarlett, and ties to the 'spirit of her people, who would not know defeat'.

The next paragraph of the front-page account is almost impossible to read:

Before the torch was applied to the pyre the negro was deprived of his ears, fingers, and other portions of his anatomy. The negro pleaded pitifully for his life while the mutilation was going on, but stood the ordeal of fire with surprising fortitude. Before the body was cool it was cut to pieces, the bones were crushed into small bits, and even the tree upon which the wretch met his fate was torn up and disposed of as souvenirs. The negro's heart was cut in several pieces, as was also his liver. Those unable to obtain these ghastly relics direct paid their more fortunate possessors extravagant sums for them. Small pieces of bone went for 25 cents and a bit of the liver crisply cooked sold for 10 cents. One of the men who lifted the can of kerosene to the negro's head is said to be a native of the commonwealth of Pennsylvania...

Women and children joined in the cry of 'Lynch him,' 'Burn him.' [23]

White women posed for souvenir photos at the scene, just as men did. They scavenged for Hose's crushed bones; they ate his liver for a dime. They may not have poured the gasoline that killed Sam Hose and thousands like him, but the gentle flower of white womanhood lit the match.

25

All Alone, Little Lady?

'All alone, little lady?' the Yankee deserter asks, as he barges into Tara, intent on thievery. Scarlett, alone with the babies and Melanie, who is still recovering from childbirth, must defend the household by herself. So she pulls out a gun and shoots the Yankee in his 'startled, bearded face'.

It's one of Mitchell's funnier turns of phrase, part of the vengeful comedy of the scene, as Scarlett turns the tables on her assailant in a moment that plays as feminist amid the indiscriminate violence of war. Scarlett and Melanie bury the body, and steal his money – which, as Rhett later rudely points out, gives Scarlett her start in business. At first she is shocked by her own violence, but then she feels 'vitally alive again, vitally glad with a cool tigerish joy. She could have ground her heel into the gaping wound which had been his nose and taken sweet pleasure in the feel of his warm blood on her bare feet. She had struck a blow of revenge for Tara – and for Ellen.' It's neither the first nor the last time that Scarlett will feel joy in violence or justify it as defence of her home.

The Yankees make several depredations into Tara and the surrounding region, as Mitchell accurately depicts the foraging, pillaging, and pre-emptive elimination of enemy provisions that Union soldiers employed as they descended south into the Confederacy. Scarlett and her planter neighbours are outraged at what seems to them the wanton destruction of their homes, but as historians have shown, soldiers in Sherman's army targeted larger slaveholding plantations more often than small yeoman farms as it drove southward. This was a strategic decision, but it was also a moral one. Union soldiers were 'not averse to destruction', but wanted to visit it upon 'those who deserved it, and usually only in rough proportion to the extent of their sins'.[1] That rough sense of moral justice 'did not prevent destruction on a scale that desolated much of the South, but it channeled it in some directions and away from others', including toward the slavocracy.

The only rough justice that *Gone with the Wind* acknowledges is on the Southern side. The Yankee soldier conveniently turns out to have been a thief, assuaging their guilt, while the film goes further, with an extreme close-up as the soldier leers telegraphing that he intends sexual assault, making Scarlett's violence personal self-defence. But in the story she just shoots him rather than let him enter Tara.

Gone with the Wind frequently puts Scarlett in dangerous situations, but it's modern enough to let her defend herself, except for the climactic scene of Rhett helping her escape the burning of Atlanta, which he frames in ironically romantic terms ('And perhaps, I'm staying here to rescue you when the siege does come. I've never rescued a maiden in distress'). One might have predicted that the most popular romantic epic of the twentieth century would feature more brave men rescuing imperilled damsels, but *Gone with the Wind* is fundamentally a drama of vengeance, not of love.

Although Scarlett believes that her vindictiveness is solely targeted at the Yankees, her moment of greatest degradation – and source of bitterest resentment – does not arrive courtesy of Yankees, or at least not directly. When Scarlett returns home as Atlanta burns, she discovers everyone on the plantations around Tara destitute. The night she arrives, starving, she scrabbles for a radish in the dirt, retches on it, and vows never to be hungry again. In the film, all this takes place at Tara; in the distant background, at the very start of the scene, a slave cabin is visible, hinting at the depths to which Scarlett has fallen.

The novel, by contrast, equates her ignominy with blackness. Scarlett makes her famous vow not at Tara but at the aristocratic Twelve Oaks, the Wilkes family plantation, which has been burned to the ground. There is no food left in the vegetable gardens by the manor, where she belongs, but she finds some behind the slave quarters, where, Mitchell adds, 'the faint nxxxxry smell which crept from the cabin increased her nausea'. The racial slur measures the extent of Scarlett's debasement – but it also mitigates against it, by reinforcing the inherent difference between her and her surroundings. Scarlett shouldn't be retching and starving by a slave cabin, because she is white and deserves better. Only the Black people who created the nauseating smell belong in such an environment. Although poverty and Blackness are equated metonymically, it specifically isn't the smell of poverty that makes Scarlett retch, it's the smell of blackness.

It's an association Mitchell keeps making. Scarlett dresses up in her mother's green velvet curtains to visit Rhett in jail not because she is vain (she is, but that isn't why). It's because she is trying to raise her value, and that depends on deceiving Rhett into believing she has not been farming the land – 'working like a nxxxxr', as he tells her contemptuously when he sees the revealing calluses on her hand.

Once again the racist slur is not casual, but definitional; it marks the point where Scarlett's value to Rhett is explicitly defined in racial terms. Having removed the racial slur from its language, the film has Clark Gable angrily tell Vivien Leigh her hands 'don't belong to a lady. You've worked with them like a field hand', making the question merely of social status, and not also of racial purity. But in the novel, Scarlett's white ladyhood, which she offers to Rhett in exchange for money, is an identity that depends upon Black labourers to uphold its value.

Scarlett fixates on this recognition that her valuc has been depreciated because she has been working like a Black slave. Later that night, attending a party, she suddenly realizes what it will take for her to feel like a lady again:

> She knew that she would never again feel like a lady until her table was weighted with silver and crystal and smoking with rich food, until her own horses carriages stood in her stables, until black hands and not white took the cotton from Tara... 'Ah!' she thought angrily... 'That's the difference.'

Wealth and luxury alone will not suffice to make her a lady again: this is no mere demand to be restored to the leisure class. The necessary extra ingredient is explicitly racial: dark hands must work, and white hands must not. Racial power is purely zero-sum: the image of Black hands picking cotton renders an entire political economy that demands white dominance be underwritten by Black labour, because without slaves, no one is a master.

The next moment Scarlett forgets her own epiphany, dismissing the women of the Old Guard as fools who don't understand that 'you can't be a lady without money!' But as Scarlett just registered, the difference is not money alone. The difference is the exclusionary whiteness of money, the racialized economics that American society continues to disavow. The point is important enough that Mitchell reiterates it several times: Scarlett was 'ashamed that she was poor and reduced to galling shifts and penury and work that negroes should do'.

When Black Americans unambiguously rejected this idea during the civil rights movement, as James Baldwin observed, it left white people 'mystified', 'betrayed', 'baffled and demoralized'. Without the image of Black subservience 'the whites were abruptly and totally lost. The very foundations of their private and public worlds were being destroyed'.[2] If some whites responded to resistance merely with hurt bafflement, many lashed out with violence. Rhett is, after all, in jail for having lynched an 'uppity' Black man when he tells Scarlett what her hands resemble. Scarlett's fantasies of whipping and enforced labour are not categorically different from Rhett's casual murder: both violently enforce plantation hierarchies. Scarlett is infuriated by freed people's refusal to acknowledge her superiority by right: 'She hated the impudent free negroes as much as anyone and her flesh crawled with fury every time she heard their insulting remarks and high-pitched laughter as she went by.'

The very word 'uppity' emerged in the United States, by no coincidence, during Redemption. There is little trace of the word in antebellum culture because submissiveness was an obvious survival tactic for the enslaved. Like miscegenation, the word uppity was conjured to ward off the spectre of equal standing, trying to put people back in their places; it makes hierarchies literal. Words like 'insolence' were used when the enslaved were deemed disrespectful, but as white governance returned after Reconstruction 'uppity' exploded into the culture, from the Uncle Remus stories of Joel Chandler Harris, to Southern editorials arguing against 'uppity negroes' being permitted into white train carriages even as servants for white people.[3] (It is once again no coincidence – remember that there are no coincidences in this story – that *Plessy* v. *Ferguson*, the notorious Supreme Court decision that legalized Jim Crow segregation in 1896 by declaring that separate could be equal, was fought over the right of a man who was seven-eighths white but legally 'Black' to ride in a white train carriage.)

Just as Black Americans don't become 'uppity' in the public record until after emancipation, so women didn't start being called 'uppity' until the 1920s and 1930s, when they began exercising political and economic freedoms. When Rhett calls Scarlett 'uppity' in the late 1860s, as he does a few times, it is anachronistic – 1930s attitudes placed in the mouths of planter aristocrats.

When she leaves the jail, having told Rhett she hopes he hangs, the episode comes full circle as Scarlett herself is subjected to the 'insolence' of 'black apes' on the street, prompting more racist slurs and vengeful, violent fantasies:

> The negroes she passed turned insolent grins at her and laughed among themselves as she hurried by, slipping and sliding in the mud… How dared they laugh, the black apes! How dared they grin at her, Scarlett O'Hara of Tara! She'd like to have them all whipped until the blood ran down their backs. What devils the Yankees were to set them free, free to jeer at white people!

For someone raised on a plantation where violence against Black people was unheard of, Scarlett imagines it vividly: she would never dream of whipping a Black person, apart from all the times she dreams of whipping a Black person. The hot drama of racial vengeance inspires far greater emotion from Scarlett than either her supposed love for Ashley, or eventually for Rhett – because her deepest romance is with her own power.

*

After Scarlett is assaulted on the road to Decatur by a Black assailant whose race highlights her own vulnerability, she abruptly repudiates her proud individualism, realizing that she is part of a system – of white victimhood. Having hitherto found white ladyhood vexing, she suddenly decides that white women are helpless after all, as the novel swings into a ringing endorsement of 'gallant' racist paternalism:

> Scarlett O'Hara, frightened and helpless, was not all that mattered. There were thousands of women like her, all over the South, who were frightened and helpless. And thousands of men… stood ready to risk their necks on a minute's notice

to protect those women… She remembered the old story how her father had left Ireland, left hastily and by night, after a murder which was no murder to him or to his family. Gerald's blood was in her, violent blood. She remembered her hot joy in shooting the marauding Yankee. Violent blood was in them all, perilously close to the surface, lurking just beneath the kindly courteous exteriors. All of them, all the men she knew, even the drowsy-eyed Ashley and fidgety old Frank, were like that underneath – murderous, violent if the need arose.

This is about the only moment in the entire twelve years of her story that Scarlett concludes she is not the only one who matters: when she realizes that what unites her and the people she loves is a mutual propensity for homicidal violence. Presumably most people can be 'violent if the need arose' – the problem is how little is required for these particular people to decide violence is needed.

This, finally, is the story's value system: not merely justifying, but naturalizing, the brutality that lurks just beneath the supposed gentility. If violence is only natural, then of course white people slaughter Black people. (That they do so in the name of protecting gentle white civilization from 'black savages' is what we might want to call irony, or we might want to call it something worse.) Everyone Scarlett knows nurses homicidal rage, and it makes her proud. Vengeful violence is a 'hot joy' in Scarlett's blood, as it is, we are told, in the blood of all white Southern men – not only romanticizing violence, but eroticizing it. Their most bitter regret is for the loss of glamour that veiled the savagery of the ruling class from itself, but the violence remains jubilant.

The immorality of this shouldn't need saying, but it does. It is not merely the value system of the Lost Cause, but of the country that normalized it, and the millions of white readers around the world who saw nothing objectionable in it, or at least nothing that stopped *Gone with the Wind* from being one of the bestselling novels and the highest-grossing film in the world for a century.

During Reconstruction, Melanie tells Scarlett that she intends to cultivate her hatred of the American government. 'The same people who have set the darkies up to lord it over us, who are robbing us and keeping our men from voting! I can't forget. I won't forget. I won't let my Beau forget and I'll teach my grandchildren to hate these people – and my grandchildren's grandchildren if God lets me live that long!' Scarlett is startled to hear 'the quivering note of violence' in Melanie's voice. That violent hatred was indeed kept alive through generations, just as women like Melanie intended – 'those whose motto was "No surrender"'.

When Rhett admits to lynching the Black man, he adds that he also killed a Yankee in a barroom. Mitchell pays brief lip service to 'moral indignation', before Scarlett remembers that she killed her own Yankee. 'He had not been on her conscience any more than a roach upon which she might have stepped. She could not sit in judgment on Rhett when she was as guilty as he.'

This is an evasion of historical responsibility dressed up as moral relativism: if everyone murders Yankees, is murdering Yankees wrong? Well, yes. In fact, what Scarlett's false equivalence shows is not that no one was guilty, but that the guilty were everywhere, loudly protesting their innocence.

Guilt is the great leveller in American life – violence justified by dint of its sheer ordinariness. If everyone is guilty, then guilt ceases to matter; it shifts the burden of guilt onto the victim, or disperses it into the social ether, where it can euthanize the nation's conscience.

26

The Packed, Hysterical Mob

'She pushed her way swiftly through the crowds, past the packed, hysterical mob surging in the open space... As she rounded the corner of the Atlanta Hotel and came in full view of the depot and the tracks, she halted appalled. Lying in the pitiless sun, shoulder to shoulder, head to feet, were hundreds of wounded men, lining the tracks, the sidewalks, stretched out in endless rows under the car shed...'

As Sherman's army marches upon Atlanta, Scarlett races to the Atlanta depot in search of a doctor to help with Melanie's labour, only to be confronted with hundreds of wounded soldiers. Dr Meade is exasperated by her request that he leave dying men to help deliver 'a damn baby', and tells her to find a woman to help.

A striking scene of tension and the horror of war in the novel, it becomes in the film an unforgettable panorama of human suffering, perhaps this iconic movie's most visually iconic tableau: thousands upon thousands of wounded and dying soldiers spread across the ground as far as the eye can see. (Selznick enlisted so many extras – a few of whom can be seen lounging on a bored elbow behind Vivien Leigh in some of the stills – that a Paramount executive from the South told the producer he'd overdone it. 'If we'd had anywhere near that many men in our army we'd have whipped all the damn Yankees,' he remarked at the 1940 Oscars ceremony.[1])

Scarlett's expression of horror at the carnage of war is the focus of the scene – until the camera gradually pulls back to reduce her to an anonymous participant in a panorama of suffering. It perfectly encapsulates the story's worldview, for only white people are suffering; there are no Black people discernible in the frame at all.

The novel, meanwhile, never offers such a panoramic view, although it does report that Scarlett is appalled at the sight of hundreds of wounded and dying men in the pitiless Georgia sun. The realism of the scene was surprising enough in an epic romance for critics at the time to remark it: Mitchell includes the stink of soldiers' sweat and excrement, the flies swarming in their faces, the bloody, filthy bandages, admitting the suffering of white soldiers briefly into her tale.

But within two sentences even the description of dying white soldiers has returned to Scarlett's nausea at the stench, thereby discounting the perspectives of everyone else in the world. Other people's suffering is kept resolutely in the margins. It is not just denied, it is inverted, turned into Scarlett's suffering, her victimhood. This is the politics of narcissism, a little lady who is always alone, despite being surrounded by a sea of suffering people.

Her plight as a woman on her own is contrasted on either end of the scene with the spectre of the mobs she encounters as she runs back and forth to the depot: first the hysterical mob that impedes her progress to Dr Meade, and then another mob on her way home:

> There were women in the mob near Decatur Street, garishly dressed women whose bright finery and painted faces gave a discordant note of holiday. Most of them were drunk and the soldiers on whose arms they hung were drunker. She caught a fleeting glimpse of a head of red curls and saw that creature, Belle Watling, heard her shrill drunken laughter as she clung for support to a one-armed soldier who reeled and staggered.

When she had shoved and pushed her way through the mob for a block beyond Five Points the crowd thinned a little and, gathering up her skirts, she began to run again... If there were only someone in this mad place to whom she could turn.

Why, she had never had to do a thing for herself in all her life... There had always been friends, neighbors, the competent hands of willing slaves. And now in this hour of greatest need, there was no one. It was incredible that she could be so completely alone, and frightened, and far from home.

In the midst of war, Scarlett does not see herself as part of a collective. The drunken mob highlights Scarlett's frail but heroic individualism, just as prostitute Belle Watling's implicitly sordid dependence upon drunken men accentuates Scarlett's American self-reliance. But that self-reliance is itself a myth, as the story soon confesses: it has always been propped up by other white people, and by the oxymoronic 'willing slaves' who eagerly endorse her entitlements.

Mitchell remarks upon the presence of white women in the mob, whose appearance on the streets bespeaks their fallen status. Scarlett is implicitly surprised to see them there, because national myths held that mobs were made up of men, while women waited sweetly at home. The fact that women have consistently taken part in American mobs continues to surprise American culture.[2] Throughout Reconstruction and Jim Crow, headlines were regularly remarking on the fact that women were inciting mobs, a fact to which they never seemed to accustom themselves.

'Women Join the Mob', a Kansas paper ensured its readers knew in 1899, as it recounted in detail 'the terrible fate of a negro ravisher in Kentucky' called Richard Coleman.[3] Accused of raping and murdering his employer's wife, Coleman was taken to a deep pit, tied securely to a tree and brush piled about him, saturated with coal oil and set on fire. Cayenne pepper was thrown in the eyes of the negro, vitriol was poured over his face and head, his skull was crushed and the body horribly mutilated. His death was slow and his agony terrible, yet while he writhed and screamed and pleaded for mercy the crowd hooted, cheered and danced, taunting the unfortunate. Many women were in the mob and cheered the men on to their work of cruelty.

Lest anyone get the wrong idea about this Kentucky lynch mob, however, the article hastened to reassure: 'The mob, outside of its treatment of Coleman, was orderly, being composed of the best people of Mason County.' Sometimes American history is little more than a sick joke.

Lynch mobs were always composed of the best people, as civil rights campaigner Mary Church Terrell observed in 1904: 'According to the reports of lynchings sent out by the Southern press itself, mobs are generally composed of the "best citizens" of a place, who quietly disperse to their homes as soon as they are certain that the negro is good and dead.'[4] Scarlett and Rhett and Ashley and Melanie are the best people, too.

The *New York Age* sounded mostly weary when it reported yet another lynching in 1926: 'As usual there were a number of white women in the mob.'[5]

*

A century later, when Trump supporters sacked the American Capitol, observers were surprised all over again to discover white women in the centre of the rage. Even the Anti-Defamation League, which studies hate crimes, was startled, declaring that 'the one female white supremacist who has been charged for her actions at the Capitol is certainly an outlier; white supremacists are profoundly sexist.'[6] That white supremacists are generally sexist is perfectly true – and yet female white supremacists are not outliers, and never have been. An MSNBC journalist claimed that 'women among the Jan. 6 attackers are the new normal of right-wing extremism', a perspective on right-wing extremism that is historically truncated, to say the least.[7]

From the United Daughters of the Confederacy to the Klavannas, from the Mothers' Movement of 1939, an ultra-conservative isolationist group launched by Elizabeth Dilling within months of *Gone with the Wind*'s film premiere, to Phyllis Schlafly fighting the Equal Rights Amendment in the 1970s, to Moms for America in 2020, to whom Congresswoman Mary Miller declared that Hitler was correct about the importance of mobilizing the nation's youth, white women in America have consistently thrown their power behind nativist, white supremacist movements.

After Trump's election in 2016, American media went into hysterical overdrive, producing stories about white male grievance and demands for sympathy with their loss of power. Meanwhile a majority of white women – 53 per cent – voted against Hillary Clinton, the first female candidate to win a major party nomination. Many said that Hillary Clinton's decision not to speak out against her own husband's history of sexual abuses motivated them, while voting for a male candidate with a history of personal sexual abuse and harassment. These included many credible accusations of rape and assault, as well as a recorded confession in which he bragged that he liked to grab women 'by the pussy', and that 'when you're a star, they let you do it. You can do anything,' released only days before the 2016 election.

The right-wing assault upon Hillary Clinton, vastly amplified by the national media, was virulently misogynist, overtly anti-feminist, and often graphically violent, speaking a patriarchal language of white male entitlement that became viciously maddened when questioned. It sounded much like white governance unleashing the full force of its rage against Black people when they most clearly breached its prerogatives.

In the 2020 election two white women who rapidly became notorious were voted into office; they supported the Capitol insurrection while endorsing right-wing disinformation, anti-Semitic and anti-liberal conspiracy theories, and the politics of white martyrdom and white nationalism. Both Marjorie Taylor Greene and Lauren Boebert frequently appeared in public with avowed white supremacists. Greene represents the 14th District in Georgia, 85 per cent of which is white – and where she moved in order to run against a Democratic platform she characterized as socialist. Greene grew up in Milledgeville, mentioned several times in *Gone with the Wind* as the location of the state prison, and the source of the convicts that Scarlett leases for her lumber yards.

In launching her political career, Greene advocated for the execution of Democrat leaders, including the lynching of Barack Obama and Hillary Clinton, and agreed with a recommendation that Nancy Pelosi should get 'a bullet to the head'. She said Black Americans should be 'proud' of Confederate monuments (and in her spare time endorsed claims that California wildfires are caused by Jewish-financed space lasers). Boebert tweeted her support for 'Real Americans' during the Black Lives Matter protests of 2020 and compared the 6 January insurrection to the American Revolution in 1776. Greene and Boebert also brought the QAnon conspiracy with them to Congress.

For a while, the white woman at the Capitol insurrection who received the most attention was the one who did not survive the attempt. In the immediate aftermath of the insurrection, the right-wing media sphere had made very little noise about the death of Ashli Babbitt. But gradually they realized that she could be turned into a martyr for their big lie, a decision they made consciously and discussed openly with journalists. Her killing was compared to that of George Floyd, who was murdered by a police officer after a store clerk suspected that Floyd had used a counterfeit twenty-dollar bill; Floyd did not resist and was choked to death on camera for nine long minutes. Babbitt, by stark contrast, was shot by Capitol police as she burst through a smashed window as part of a violent mob that was attempting to storm the chamber with military-grade weaponry and had already beaten some officers bloody.

Her death inspired vigils and slogans ('Justice for Ashli', 'Ashli Babbitt, American Patriot'). One right-wing organizer told reporters that invoking Babbitt had made it easier to stoke outrage over the prosecution of the insurrectionists. 'It made others feel emboldened, which helps me,' said another organizer, who had told a large rally that the word 'insurrectionist is no longer going to come up' when Ashli Babbitt's name was mentioned in five years. 'They will not rewrite history,' he shouted, busily rewriting history. 'She's a martyr, okay?'[8]

Using Ashli Babbitt's name worked because protecting white women is the foundational script of American white supremacy, and the martyrdom that sanctifies it.

*

Gone with the Wind is a story about white female grievance. It demands identification with Scarlett's sense of injury at her own loss of status and her willingness to blame everyone but herself. Scarlett's panicky belief that Black people have been liberated to assault and rape her is also narcissistic: paranoia always is, because it means believing you're important enough for the world to target you.

White supremacism is a politics of collective narcissism, justified by racism, enabling its adherents to believe they are the moral police while engaging in the most brutally selfish acts. For many years the story's defenders argued that 'race, and politics too, are essentially negligible' in *Gone with the Wind*, providing only a 'backdrop' for Scarlett O'Hara's struggle 'against the confines of Southern womanhood'.[9] The enslaved, as Pyron puts it in his biography, serve as 'chiefly social decorations for upwardly mobile white farmers'.[10] But that's not a defence – it's the indictment.

'Slavery as a social or economic system hardly exists in the novel,' Pyron adds, which is neither quite true given how much time Mitchell spends defending its benevolence, nor defensible in a novel about the Civil War and the plantation class.[11] How can you tell a story about enslavers and not talk about slavery?

The story only cares about the discomfort of Scarlett and her friends – Mitchell criticizes Scarlett's individual narcissism, while constantly replicating the narcissism of her worldview. The film renders a fuller world, with the strength of the Black women in particular working to resist Scarlett's self-centredness, while Rhett's famous final line is a flat rejection of Scarlett's self-absorbed response to his ending their marriage: 'If you go, where shall I go, what shall I do?' No wonder he tells her he doesn't give a damn.

Our society likes to claim that fiction teaches empathy, but what *Gone with the Wind* reveals is that fiction may only show us the bars of our cage. When Scarlett O'Hara sees herself as the victim of Black equality, when she bitterly resents having inflicted upon her all the things she feels entitled to inflict upon Black people, it does not teach her empathy. She does not begin identifying with Black people, or suddenly register their suffering. It simply provides more evidence of what she already believes, confirming all of her deep and blinding biases.

The solipsism of the novel grows suffocating, as it demands we identify with a woman surrounded by devastation who only thinks of how it impacts her. *Gone with the Wind* urges moral complacency through self-justification, and distorts reality to do so. It turns a vast tragedy into the petty struggles of one individual who never understands that tragedy gains its meaning from our moral interconnectedness. Great writers have tried to teach us this, from John Donne's belief that no man is an island but part of the continent of mankind, so that every death diminishes us, to Ralph Ellison's Invisible Man telling his reader, 'Who knows but that on some frequency I speak for you.' *Gone with the Wind* believes that meaning is radically individual, which taken to absolutes becomes moral idiocy – because there can be no morality where other people don't matter.

White women actively benefited from race-based slavery and actively supported the structures that upheld and succeeded it. White women owned and profited from enslaved Black people. They incited lynch mobs. They enforced the teaching of eugenicist biological racism, created boycotts of 'un-American' businesses run by Jews or Catholics or Black people, tried to get Catholic teachers fired, campaigned for racist politicians, and baked goods for state fairs where the Klan recruited new members. Fiercely opposing the integration of public schools – as did Margaret Mitchell herself – they were the screaming faces behind frightened, determined Black girls asserting their rights at Little Rock in 1957.

On 6 January 2021, as darkness fell on the US Capitol, the police were pushing back the rioters in earnest, with tear gas and truncheons. As clashes escalated, a reporter on the scene wrote the next day, 'it became a mob set against itself'. Watching the rioters begin to fall back against police resistance, he spotted a white woman on the edge of the mob. Weeping hysterically, she cried out in disbelief: 'This is not America! They're shooting at us. They're supposed to shoot BLM!'

She had accidentally blurted out the truth: the police were only supposed to shoot Black people, or white people who defended Black people. Another rioter became notorious when she tweeted after the attacks: 'Sorry I have blonde hair white skin a great job a great future and I'm not going to jail.'[12] She was wrong – a judge sentenced her to sixty days – but not by much.

The rioter who thought the police would only shoot Black protestors and their supporters also believed that her whiteness secured her political virtue. 'They're shooting the patriots,' she added, as she stood in the middle of a seditious insurrection she had joined, convinced of her own patriotism even as she tried to overthrow democracy at the command of a con artist. Another man told her not to worry: 'We showed them today. We showed them what we're all about.'[13]

This is what Baldwin called the wrath to come – the moral derangement spinning the nation off its axis. Beyond the bars of our foolish little cages, a reckoning looms, at a scale we can't assimilate.

PART SEVEN

HOME TO TARA

27

The Indestructible Land

In the end, Scarlett goes home to Tara. Because her deepest romance is with power, neither Ashley nor Rhett can ultimately supply it. Power comes from Tara, the plantation she is always fighting to save, the supposed survival of which justifies everything she does. But survival is just a euphemism for ownership. The land will survive: Scarlett is fighting to keep it. That is the novel's happy ending: men come and go, but retaining land is what matters. And so she returns to it, and the loving embrace of wish fulfilment in the form of 'willing slaves' who have been freed but choose to stay.

What rouses the story most is not war, which happens off the page. It is the arrival of entrepreneurial capitalism, as agrarian idylls yield to urban opportunity. Scarlett's saving grace, according to the story, is her affinity for hard work, an aspirationalism rooted in her immigrant heritage, which easily triumphs over her half-hearted performance of Southern belle. Scarlett not only isn't afraid of hard work, she thrives on it, becoming a hustling opportunist who exploits any situation she can.

Gone with the Wind is playing recognizable chords of the American Dream, but in a different arrangement. Scarlett is in flight from desperation and in pursuit of happiness. She has no idea where to find it, although everyone keeps telling her. From her father explaining in the film's opening scene that one day she will realize her love of the land ('Land is the only thing in the world worth working for. Worth fighting for, worth dying for. Because it's the only thing that lasts') to Ashley telling her she loves Tara 'even better than you love me', to Rhett declaring, 'It's this from which you get your strength – the red earth of Tara', the men who love her all repeat the lesson.

The film ends as Scarlett hears a montage of voices eulogizing Tara, urging her home. The screenplay's stage directions dictate not only Scarlett's interior thoughts and emotions, but also the audience's:

> A beautiful smile of hope crosses Scarlett's face as the realization comes to her that she still has Tara… She lifts her chin higher. We see the stuff of which Scarlett O'Hara is made, and we thrill with the knowledge that she won't be defeated for long… As the speech progresses we see and hear her strength return – her voice accelerates in power and volume and we must believe completely that what Scarlett O'Hara wants to do, she can do.

There's little doubt the filmmakers achieved their intentions. For almost a century audiences have reported that they do indeed thrill to the certainty that defeat is temporary, that strength returns, that what we want to do, we can do. That is the message that universalizes this character's resilient response to adversity, while insisting upon the importance of home as a source of renewal. From the sanctuary of home Scarlett can rebuild once more. 'I'll think of it all tomorrow, at Tara,' she tells herself as the novel ends. 'I can stand it then. Tomorrow, I'll think of some way to get him back. After all, tomorrow is another day.' Home is not retreat, but hope: it's where the future is recovered.

When audiences at the end of 1939 watched for the first time as Vivien Leigh lifts shining eyes beneath her tears and declares,

'Home! I'll go home. And I'll think of some way to get him back. After all, tomorrow is another day!' it was less than four months after moviegoers had first heard Judy Garland affirm at the end of *The Wizard of Oz* that there's no place like home. Although Scarlett's home is not Dorothy's sepia-tinted Kansas farm, or the archetypal little white house with a picket fence, but a Technicolor plantation estate, the association of home and happiness is the same. Both endings sent an identical message: women might have their adventures, but home was where they belonged.

But the return to domesticity is subtext: what drives the story is its affair with real estate. As *Gone with the Wind* was published, the country was just beginning to link the idea of 'the American Dream', a phrase only recently popularized, with homeownership. In 1937 President Roosevelt urged Congress 'to save the American dream' – the only time he used the phrase in a public speech – a dream he framed in Jeffersonian terms as a yeoman farm, 'the American dream of the family-size farm'.[1] The association is inscribed in the Declaration of Independence when Thomas Jefferson converted John Locke's promise of 'life, liberty, and the pursuit of property' into 'life, liberty, and the pursuit of happiness'. The ghost of that erasure lingered in the country's popular memory, associating liberty and happiness with property.

The story's devotion to property rights spoke to readers facing widespread homelessness during the Great Depression, when white people reduced to living in the shantytowns known as Hoovervilles had become emblematic of the nation's economic struggles in a way that poor Black people never have. The 1930s were marked not only by brothers asking each other for a dime, but also by the promise that prosperity was just around the corner – the promise that drives Scarlett's story. Scarlett's overwhelming need for money is destroying her reputation and her relationships, but material security still supplies the story's happy ending. Mitchell forces her heroine through the familiar stages of the immigrant American Dream: she must lose everything, start all over again, and achieve prosperity. It's a Horatio Alger success story without the moral improvement: in nineteenth-century popular American culture, wealth was the reward for virtuous behaviour. Mitchell is honest enough to admit that Scarlett gets rich because she's unvirtuous, not in spite of it. Indeed, *Gone with the Wind* was a milestone on American culture's journey toward transforming money from a useful convenience into a virtue – from one kind of fetish into another.

Scarlett's determination to acquire money by any means possible to protect her home is perhaps where the story is most ambivalently American. The rewards of upward social mobility prove more important to Scarlett than their high cost. Her devotion to the 'red earth of Tara' means that everyone thinks Scarlett loves property more than anything else – and they're right.

28

Swelling Acres

Scarlett's struggle to pay the unfair taxes on Tara drives much of the story's plot – property taxes lead directly to Scarlett's decision to marry Frank Kennedy, and indirectly to her marrying Rhett and to the death of Gerald. Taxes, as much as Yankees and free Black people, become Scarlett's antagonist after the war, not a civic obligation but a petty and arbitrary punishment of the hard-working. During Reconstruction, when she learns that 'the Yankees could evict her from Tara', Scarlett declares: 'I'm going to have money enough so the Yankees can never take Tara away from me.'

Its enduring hostility to taxation is part of *Gone with the Wind*'s argument with the New Deal – it is, in one sense, a treatise against New Deal economics of wealth redistribution. Scarlett is not only fiercely individualist, as well as pathologically self-centred – she is also archetypally libertarian. Mitchell herself, whose politics her brother described as 'extremely reactionary', railed against Roosevelt and the New Deal,[1] and eventually supported Herman Talmadge, an avowedly racist opponent of desegregation and civil rights, who would later boycott the Democratic National Convention in response to Lyndon B. Johnson's support of the Civil Rights Act of 1964. Mitchell maintained a 'Red' file on Southerners she suspected of communist sympathizing – before

McCarthyism had flowered – including Lillian Smith, and toyed with the idea of writing a major essay on 'why the communists attack the South and attempt to inflame the Negro press and public against the South'.[2]

Gone with the Wind often criticizes Scarlett's selfishness, but not in the case of taxes. It agrees they are unfairly levied on the white propertied class who had fought a war to protect their property, lost the war, and still had all their property, apart from the humans they had turned into property, restored. Pyron remarks in passing that the Mitchell family, like 'most of Atlanta's old families[,] had made their money in real estate',[3] a history he never extends beyond noting that Annie Fitzgerald's obsession with buying land stemmed from the loss of her father's plantation, as if it were merely an individual psychodrama, instead of a story about collective power. Real estate was inextricable from plantation economics.

Real estate was also entangled with women's rights, as women gradually owned property and paid taxes, but still could not vote. Maybelle Mitchell argued for women's suffrage in these very terms: white women, she noted, paid property taxes in Atlanta but were not allowed to vote, while 'drunken bums… on the sidewalk', 'because they were men, though they haven't paid a dime', were 'entitled to vote and we are not. Is that fair?'[4] It was not – but Rebecca Felton had earlier asked an identical question in explicitly racist terms: 'I do not want to see a negro man walk to the polls and vote on who shall handle my tax money while I myself cannot vote at all. Is this fair?'[5] As Du Bois wrote in *Black Reconstruction*, 'No matter how degraded the factory hand, he is not real estate', whereas under chattel slavery the enslaved person was 'purely and absolutely property'. The same applies to white women: their rights were sharply curtailed, their bodily autonomy violently interfered with, but they were not purely and absolutely property.

Gone with the Wind exalts the rise (and moral justification) of unscrupulous capitalism, celebrating Scarlett's shrewdness in leveraging land ownership into wealth and power, and applauding the survival of the oligarch class. Mitchell took great pains to differentiate the yeoman O'Haras from the planter aristocrats typified by the Wilkes family. Twelve Oaks is the patrician manor in the neighbourhood, whereas Tara is a working farm, sprawling, irregular, ugly and crude, a far more accurate depiction of antebellum plantations in blackbelt Georgia than popular ideas, stoked by Selznick's film over Mitchell's objections, of porticoed mansions.

Trying to convince the producers to depict the film's plantations with a modicum of historical accuracy, Mitchell took them to a house in Milledgeville called Stately Oaks. Now a heritage museum filled with *Gone with the Wind* memorabilia, Stately Oaks is an 1830s timber farmhouse fronted by a veranda with square wood pillars, not imposing columns. 'I grieve to hear that Tara has columns,' Mitchell wrote during filming; in another letter she said she feared Selznick's Twelve Oaks would resemble 'Grand Central Station', and that when she learned it would have two staircases, she couldn't help 'yelping with laughter'.[6]

Mitchell may have hooted at exaggerated ideas of plantation aristocrats, but her story shows Scarlett's transformation, through real estate and her lumber business (also part of the postbellum property boom), from one of the enslaving minority (roughly 30 per cent of Southern whites held enslaved people, according to the 1860 census)[7] to the oligarchy of 8,000 white elites who emerged after the Civil War in political and economic control of the New South.

*

In the United States white wealth was built upon a series of land grabs as well as upon slavery. This included not only the many seizures of land from indigenous tribes across the nation's history of settler colonialism and westward expansion, but also the betrayal of the promise to give land to freed people after the

Civil War so they could be economically self-sufficient as well as politically emancipated.

One of the most significant omissions in *Gone with the Wind*'s mythmaking is the genocide of indigenous peoples, which took place in Georgia at the same time that Gerald O'Hara was acquiring the land for Tara. The death marches known as the Trail of Tears began in 1831 with the forcible displacement west of five tribes, the Choctaw, Cherokee, Seminole, Muskogee, and Chickasaw, and continued for almost twenty years. *Gone with the Wind* ends in 1873; a year later gold was discovered in the hills of South Dakota, leading to the immediate repudiation of treaties with native peoples. The infamous Battle of Little Bighorn, once known as 'Custer's Last Stand', in which General Custer and his troops were defeated and killed in battle by Chief Crazy Horse, Sitting Bull and the Lakota Sioux and Cheyenne warriors they led, took place in 1876, three years after the action of *Gone with the Wind* finishes. General Custer, like so many American military men who led the incursions against native peoples, was a Civil War veteran, who took part in the Battle of Gettysburg. His first major incursion against the Cheyenne people took place in 1868, the year that Rhett and Scarlett marry, while Scarlett's beloved Tara is built upon land that was stolen from indigenous Americans a mere decade before her birth. In fact, much of the land in the Deep South to which the planter class so fiercely clung had only been in white hands for a few decades when the Civil War began.

Gone with the Wind never questions Scarlett's moral entitlement to ownership of Tara: it is her heritable, natural right. Having returned home at war's end, Scarlett reflects that 'when she looked at Tara she could understand, in part, why wars were fought'. Recalling the half-truth Rhett once told her, that 'all wars are in reality money squabbles', and that slavery and states' rights were both mere pretexts for fighting the Civil War (as if slavery were distinct from money), Scarlett decides Rhett was wrong.

Not because she suddenly understands that slavery was indeed the cause of the war, but because wars were fought over land, not money:

> Rhett was wrong when he said men fought wars for money. No, they fought for swelling acres, softly furrowed by the plow, for pastures green with stubby cropped grass, for lazy yellow rivers and white houses that were cool amid magnolias. These were the only things worth fighting for, the red earth which was theirs and would be their sons', the red earth which would bear cotton for their sons and their sons' sons.

Just as Rhett's argument sets up a false distinction between money and slavery, so this makes a false distinction between money and land. The swelling acres and pastures green mystify the land's true value as property Scarlett can bequeath to little white patriarchs for generations to come. This is why she will fight so hard to keep Tara – because unjust agents are trying to wrest it from her rightful, permanent ownership. Scarlett's clinging on to the plantation is presented as a triumph of individual will over a corrupt and illegitimate occupying force that is spitefully raising her taxes – namely, the American government.

Property taxes were raised on white Southerners after the war partly to fund social programmes, including free education, but also as a means of weakening the white hold on the land and furthering Black ownership. Poorer citizens, white and Black, hoped that taxation would force white property onto the market and enable redistribution of real estate.[8] Many Republicans supported outright confiscation of Confederate landowners' property, following promises during the war to give freed Black slaves land to work – the fabled 'forty acres and a mule'.

This famous guarantee features in the film as a sign behind a glib white carpetbagger rooking a group of gullible Black people (one of whom, accoutred with the corncob pipe that marks an

American yokel, even utters in incredulous delight, 'A *mule?* Gee!') into voting Republican, 'because we're your friends', while Mammy passes by with a look of disgust. The entire scene invokes the imagery of the grifter and the mark – the carpetbagger as confidence man, implicitly contrasted against the honourable white Southerners who generously enslaved Black people for their own good.

The promise of forty acres and a mule had been made first by General Sherman, as he marched across Georgia to the sea, followed by the Freedman's Bureau Act of 1865 and the postwar Southern Homestead Act of 1866, which said that confiscated Southern land would be offered for lease to freed male citizens for three years, after which it could be purchased by the occupant. Fiercely opposing measures that might lead to Black self-determination, President Johnson undermined the promises and restored property to white Southerners.

The nation's failure to enable the economic self-sufficiency of some 4 million newly freed Americans who were emerging from generations of unpaid labour condemned the vast majority of them to the system of sharecropping that had been established by the early 1870s. Freed people were forced back into farming the land they had once worked in bondage, renting small plots ('shares') from the same masters and delivering a portion of the crop each year to the landowner. Barely adequate for survival, sharecropping never afforded Black Southerners economic independence.

Whether it constituted a swindle to promise economic redistribution to emancipated slaves is a question *Gone with the Wind* never addresses, but that is what the slogan of forty acres and a mule meant in real terms. The novel acknowledges the truth, albeit backhandedly, when it condemns the Freedmen's Bureau for giving Black people ideas above their station in promising that 'soon the estates of their former owners would be divided and every negro would be given forty acres and a mule for his own'. More recent historians have suggested that the real swindle was perpetrated by the US government, which never fully adopted a programme of land redistribution.[9]

It's not really 'the Yankees' to whom Scarlett doesn't want to give up the land and house she inherited, in other words – it's Black people.

29

The Land Lottery

I f *Gone with the Wind* is a story of the American Dream reclaimed, it is worth noticing that the O'Hara family does not acquire Tara by any of the customary methods: Gerald does not inherit the plantation, marry into a family that owns it, or purchase it through hard work. Merit never comes into the story, in one of Mitchell's more historically accurate touches. Gerald O'Hara wins Tara in a poker match around 1833, when Georgia's final land lottery took place. The land lotteries distributed the land seized from indigenous peoples to any white male citizen who put his name into the draw.

Gerald wins Tara from a man who 'had been one of the winners in the land lottery conducted by the State to divide up the vast area in middle Georgia, ceded by the Indians the year before Gerald came to America'. (Native Americans 'ceded' land in the sense that 60,000 people were forcibly displaced by systematic ethnic cleansing – another fine use of the exculpatory passive voice.) Gerald thus acquires in a game of chance a piece of land first obtained in an earlier game of chance after being confiscated from the people who lived on it first. Mitchell's rewriting of the land lottery as a poker game obscures the degree to which it was a rigged game that only white men could play: Gerald O'Hara should have won Tara in a fixed match against a Native American and a Black man, with women looking on, unable to play. Not incidentally, Gerald also wins his first enslaved person in another poker match: 'the first step upward toward his heart's desire. Gerald wanted to be a slave owner and a landed gentleman,' just as his daughter would one day realize that she depended upon enslaved Black people to maintain the status of Southern lady.

The rigged logic of the land lottery was further expanded by the subsequent Homestead Act of 1862, passed in the middle of the Civil War to encourage white settlement westward into seized native territories. The Civil War battle that was most decisively won was for the free labour policies championed by the Republicans, who successfully framed the West as the land of American freedom, and helped strengthen national assocations between political and economic self-determination. The two Homestead Acts meant in theory that any citizen who had not borne arms against the United States could escape the consequences of war and claim western land after several years of 'improving' it. In practice it was overwhelmingly white people who claimed and kept land in western territories, plenty of whom had borne arms against the United States.

Meanwhile, white landowners in the South were also given political inducements: not only did they get to keep their land, but they were offered reparations for the damage their war had done to their property if they signed the Ironclad Oath. In the novel Scarlett's sister Suellen gets Gerald drunk to trick him into signing it; although Scarlett loathes Suellen almost as much as the Yankees, when she learns the offer is for $150,000, she agrees that lying would be worth it. But Gerald discovers Suellen's deception, charges off on his horse in outrage, and breaks his neck.

The filmmakers, evidently questioning the commercial viability with American audiences of a scene in which the heroine's father dies rather than swear an oath of loyalty to America, at a time when most schoolchildren recited the pledge of allegiance every morning, instead made the 'white trash' carpetbagger Wilkerson the source of Gerald's fatal rage, as ever concluding (correctly) that where racial or sectional politics were problematic, basic snobbery would serve.

*

White wealth through property ownership is what *Gone with the Wind* wants to exalt – while trying, less than successfully, to ignore the role of slavery and its aftermath in the creation of that wealth. Rhett insists that half his postwar fortune was 'honestly' acquired, while the other half he took in good faith from the Confederacy to sell for supplies and kept when the Confederacy collapsed. 'There is no Confederacy now,' he observes. 'Whom shall I give the money to? The Yankee government?' a suggestion of voluntary taxation so risible that Scarlett doesn't bother responding to it.

Rhett also enumerates how he acquired the money that is 'honestly mine' – from various investments in slave cotton that he sold across the blockade and banked in Liverpool as part of the triangle trade. Rhett's war profiteering and capital from cotton create the vast wealth that lets him buy up much of Atlanta after the war and help restore white governance at story's end. The evolution of Rhett's financial power, as he leaves slavery behind but not its profits, is the true story of modern American capitalism.

In similar terms, by going into the lumber business, Scarlett finds in her hands the material conditions of reconstruction, and thus helps Atlanta boom again, even as Mitchell partially recognizes the unscrupulous nature of the bargains she strikes. Scarlett's drive for wealth at any cost is justified over and over, as she decides during Reconstruction that 'money was the only protection against fresh calamities'. She frankly admits to Rhett that she no longer thinks about anything but money, and adds that if he'd been through her experiences, he wouldn't either. 'Money is the most important thing in the world. I've found out that and, as God is my witness, I don't ever intend to be without it again.' She uses money she stole from the Yankee she killed to help keep Tara afloat, so that this property won in a lottery is retained through murder and theft – and all of this exalted as resilience.

As Scarlett says it, she recalls the moment of her greatest deprivation, and Mitchell returns to the earlier racial slur to remind the reader of the depths of her abasement: 'She remembered the hot sun, the soft red earth under her sick head, the nxxxxry smell of the cabin behind the ruins of Twelve Oaks, remembered the refrain her heart had beaten: "I'll never be hungry again. I'll never be hungry again."'

The retention of Tara justifies Scarlett's unrelenting pursuit of property rights, itself depicted as success at all costs. Acquisitiveness is rationalized by the devastation suffered by the South, while the realities of depressions and wars continued to ensure audiences around the world identified with her determination to cling on to her home.

Less sympathetically, Scarlett's pursuit of lost wealth could be described as a grim resolve to evade the devastating consequences of the war her society started for reasons everyone around her continues to defend. A battle over exclusionary white power was the whole point of the Civil War that the white South lost, while the whole point of *Gone with the Wind* is to justify the white South's violent reclamation of that power, thus turning defeat into victory not only rhetorically, but also economically and politically. That is what Redemption meant in real terms.

The problem is not that Scarlett won't accept defeat – as the screenwriters understood, that is what makes her story universal, her character so appealing despite her flaws. The problem is that Scarlett represents a worldview that should have admitted defeat, that cannot be redeemed. In a historical context, rather than an individual one, admiring *Gone with the Wind* for Scarlett's determination is precisely equivalent to praising a story about an unrepentant Nazi who never admitted defeat because we so admire his spirit, while ignoring the question of whether he ever repudiated fascism. It means accepting the equivalent of Holocaust denial, agreeing that Jews weren't persecuted, much less slaughtered, and that Germany did indeed go to war for *Lebensraum*. Tara thus symbolizes far more than a sentimental attachment to home, or even to the soil that is in Scarlett's blood – although the story of *Gone with the Wind* will indeed take us to 'blood and soil', and soon.

Gone with the Wind shows how the mythology of American success stories, including those of immigrants, were also inculpated in the bloody history of institutionalized slavery. The triumphalism of the immigrant success story has worked to obscure the question of complicity: the supposed underdog in this tale making good does so at the expense, in more senses than one, of an entire other, racially marked, underclass. Tara denotes property ownership in a story that is entirely about who is entitled to own what property – and what kind of property.

In fact, immigration is the only context in which the word 'America' appears across the half a million words of *Gone with the Wind*, where it is never used to describe a national identity, but only nativist hierarchies, identifying when various families in the story 'came to America', to measure how American they were. One of the most popular stories in American history thus mythologizes white people's ownership of the land, offering a history of survival through racial capitalism and inherited property, while disavowing the central role slavery and a hatred of the United States as a political entity played in that history.

In the process it becomes a kind of parable of American popular memory, which has done exactly the same thing.

30

Survival of the Fittest

After Scarlett confesses to Rhett that she no longer cares about anything except money and asks him for a loan to help buy her mills, she fantasizes about what being rich again will mean: 'When she was rich, she wouldn't stand anything she didn't like, do without anything she desired or even be polite to people unless they pleased her.' In Scarlett's mind, wealth simply enables selfishness, but Mitchell's narrator and Rhett both see her somewhat differently.

'I have a deep and impersonal admiration for your endurance, Scarlett,' Rhett announces, as he agrees to give her the loan. *Gone with the Wind* continually asks if the cost of survival is worth the price to Scarlett's character. Gradually all her superficial refinements are stripped away, revealing only the obdurate will beneath. Mitchell gave interviews when the book was published making the 'central theme' of her book explicit: 'The theme is survival of the fittest,' she said. Although Mitchell had not consciously elaborated the motif at first, by the time she finished the novel it was central and deliberate. 'What makes some people able to come through catastrophes and others, apparently just as strong, able and brave, go under?' It was a question, she added, prompted by 'conditions in the present depression. They happen in every panic, every war, every revolution… I wrote about the people who had courage – "gumption" – and those who didn't.'[1]

The theme of endurance was certainly on everyone's mind during the Great Depression, as Mitchell remarked, although not everyone subscribed to her characters' social Darwinism. Bitter endurance is the lesson in survivalism that Grandma Fontaine teaches Scarlett when Gerald dies, that the white South will bide its time: 'We've survived a passel of things that way, smiling and biding our time, and we've gotten to be experts at surviving.' It is so important to the ethos of the novel that Mitchell has Grandma Fontaine repeat the phrase three times in the same scene, ending: 'We work and we smile and we bide our time. And we play along with lesser folks and we take what we can from them. And when we're strong enough, we kick the folks whose necks we've climbed over. That, my child, is the secret of the survival.'

Playing along with lesser folks, taking from them what you can, and then kicking them to the kerb is also the secret of social Darwinism, which is inextricable from the novel's racism. Both preach survival of the fittest, defining fitness through biological determinism, as heritable traits that mean survivalism is a question of innate character, rather than environmental good fortune. These ideas are fundamentally eugenicist, claiming not only that some human 'stock' is biologically superior to others, but that such groups come racially and ethnically pre-sorted. Presumptions of lesser and greater beings, the right of merit to rule, was at the heart of the argument: an aristocratic entitlement that claimed privilege was founded on inherited superiority, rather than on brute force or the dumb luck of circumstance.

The enslaving women who are the O'Haras' neighbours serve primarily as exponents of eugenicist ideas of tribalism – the notion of 'good stock' and 'breeding' that underpinned scientific racism. Neighbouring Mrs Tarleton compares people to racehorses, delivering a broadside against the inbred degeneracy of the Wilkes family's aristocratic 'stock', making clear that they are not fit enough to survive the crisis to come: 'They are overbred and inbred too... I believe the stamina has been bred out of them, and when the emergency arises I don't believe they can run against odds.'

Rhett, the story's most brutal realist, also tries to teach the 'natural law' of opportunism to Scarlett in eugenicist terms of 'breeds' like the Wilkes family: 'His breed is of no use or value in an upside-down world like ours,' Rhett declares:

> They don't deserve to survive because they won't fight – don't know how to fight... They should go under. It's a natural law and the world is better off without them. But there are always a hardy few who come through and given time, they are right back where they were before the world turned over... We saw opportunity in the ruin of a civilization and we made the most of our opportunity, some honestly, some shadily, and we are still making the most of it.

Making opportunism a 'natural law', one as supposedly funda-mental as survival of the fittest, is another way the story naturalizes its value system, insisting that its power structures are only natural. *Gone with the Wind* pays lip service to the nobility and honour of Melanie and Ashley Wilkes – but ultimately seems as unconvinced as Scarlett herself, not least because the story kills the Wilkeses off, literally and figuratively. Rhett, always proved right in his reading of the novel's world, is a white supremacist social Darwinist who uses eugenicist thinking to justify his self-enrichment. Melanie dies and Ashley fades away, as the story ends on Scarlett's dogged endurance.

But endurance was also strongly racialized as the conventional trope for Black suffering in America. Six weeks before the publication of *Gone with the Wind*, the first film version of the Broadway musical sensation *Show Boat* was released, a story about racism and opportunism in the antebellum South based on Edna Ferber's bestselling 1926 novel (to which *Gone with the*

Wind owes several generally unacknowledged debts). The film's show-stopping centrepiece features the great civil rights activist Paul Robeson singing 'Ol' Man River', a song in which Black people endure suffering, endure oppression, and, like the river that might offer freedom, just keep enduring:

> You and me, we sweat and strain,
> Body all achin' and racked with pain,
> Tote that barge! Lift that bale!
> You gets a little drunk
> And you lands in jail
> I gets weary
> And sick of tryin'
> I'm tired of livin'
> And scared of dyin'
> But ol' man river,
> He just keeps rollin' along.

As the *Chicago Defender* rightly noted of *Gone with the Wind* in 1937, 'Negroes in the book sing "Go Down Moses" but the author seems not to understand what they mean.'[2] They were absolutely right, for that spiritual – as Mitchell certainly knew – describes the enslaved Israelites in Egypt, 'oppressed so hard they could not stand', while every other line repeats the refrain: 'let my people go'. How can anyone hear enslaved people compare themselves to the enslaved Israelites while singing 'let my people go' and conclude they're willing? And yet Mitchell's internalization of white victimhood was so absolute she thought the oppressed people who needed liberation were not the Black enslaved, but the white Southerners 'toiling' under the Northern yoke of the American government that forced racial equality upon them against their will. Mitchell originally intended to call *Gone with the Wind* 'Tote the Weary Load', another slave spiritual, again transforming Black suffering into white martyrdom: the people toting weary loads in her novel are always the white plantation class, never the Black enslaved.

The guarantee of African American stoic endurance was more projection, part of how white America gave itself permission for its own structures and attitudes. It meant that William Faulkner could declare in *The Sound and the Fury*: 'They were black: – They endured.' It is why Frederick Douglass noted: 'The limits of tyrants are prescribed by the endurance of those whom they oppress.' Endurance may be necessary, but eventually it is taken as licence. If Black people are better at endurance, it follows that they are less sensitive to oppression, just as brute animal strength and childlike simplicity were likewise imputed to Black people to rationalize chattel slavery and Jim Crow.

When the Yankee women insult Uncle Peter, Scarlett is indignant, partly because of the childlike 'tenderness' of Black people ('negroes had to be handled gently, as though they were children, directed, praised, petted, scolded'), but also because of their 'qualities of loyalty and tirelessness and love in them that no strain could break'. Tirelessness is certainly a quality to be valued in an enslaved labourer – one that white America constantly attributed to Black Americans to justify their exploitation.

The romanticization of survival is morally vacuous – survival is not an ethic. But pretending that endurance is meritocratic allowed America to reclaim its innocence and continue to deny the suffering it veils with lies. It claims honesty while being self-deceiving, just as Mitchell declares in the same sentence that Scarlett has a 'hard self-honesty' and also that she continually worked at 'trying to justify herself to herself – a task which she seldom found difficult'. Neither has America.

Rhett tells Scarlett after the war that the Old Guard 'just aren't smart, Scarlett, and only the smart deserve to survive'. Well-educated Ashley reinforces the lesson, while understanding that it means his own demise, as he tells Scarlett that 'the people who have brains and courage come through and the ones who haven't are winnowed out', as they endure the *Götterdämmerung*, the twilight of the gods. Scarlett repeats it uncomprehendingly ('something about the strong coming through and the weak being winnowed out') just as she can't recall Rhett's exact phrase: 'something he calls the survival of the fitting'.

Mitchell's use of these phrases registered as an anachronism to reviewers in 1936 – '"*Götterdämmerung*", and "survival of the fittest" sound very strange upon the tongues of Civil War Southerners,' the *New York Times* observed that summer, alluding to the fact that Wagner's opera *Götterdämmerung* was not performed until 1876. Mitchell defended her use of *Götterdämmerung* in her letters, insisting she'd spent three weeks establishing its plausibility for Southerners who'd done the Grand Tour in the 1850s and that the phrase 'dusk of the Gods' was ancient.[3]

Regardless of whether her slavocrats would have used these phrases in the 1860s and 1870s, however, they were certainly current in the mid-1930s, not only in the United States, but also in Europe. 'The survival of the fittest' was invoked in debates about the rise of fascist nationalism, while Hitler's fondness for Wagner was widely reported in the American press, including rumours that he would marry Winifred Wagner, Richard Wagner's English-born daughter-in-law.[4] The collapse of the Nazi regime would ultimately be accompanied by a Wagnerian soundtrack, as the 'twilight of the gods' finale from the *Götterdämmerung* was played during the final performance of the Berlin Philharmonic on 12 April 1945, amid reports that audience members were offered cyanide capsules on their way home.

'At least, it has been interesting, if not comfortable, to witness a Götterdämmerung,' Ashley tells Scarlett. When she asks what the word means, he translates: 'A dusk of the gods. Unfortunately, we Southerners did think we were gods.' The phrase is probably more familiar now than the bloody revenge drama that precedes it in Wagner's opera, the story of how a lesser race proves the downfall of the gods. The inspiration behind the Ring Cycle was an Old Norse epic about a heroic, barbaric, mystic world, ruled by fear and greed, destroyed by treachery, dissolving in violence, that ends in blood and fire as Valhalla burns. The twilight of the gods is no gentle decrescendo, but a violent self-annihilation, a mythic vision of historic fatality.

It's an 'interesting, if not comfortable' comparison for Ashley to make, as he implies that the South may, in fact, be fated to die. There are few such moments in the story – and the implication that the South's political system was barbaric, self-destructive, and treacherous remains submerged at best, cloaked in myth and allusion. Less mystically, we might observe that neither the word democracy nor the word republic occurs in the most famous novel about the American Civil War, while the word equality only appears once, to assert that 'this nxxxxr-equality business' had gone too far – far enough for those who thought they were gods to discover the power of the lesser races.

The screenplay of Gone with the Wind stripped out the reference to the Götterdämmerung, having Ashley only rhetorically ask an abridged social Darwinist question: 'What becomes of people when their civilization breaks up? Those who have brains and courage come through all right. Those that haven't are winnowed out.'

The Jewish actor who played Ashley Wilkes, born Leslie Howard Steiner in Upper Norwood, London, categorically refused to read Gone with the Wind, and so would not have known that he had been spared the indignity of singing Hitler's tune four years before he would be killed in the RAF, fighting to stop the Nazis.

31

Buying Men Like Mules

'It looks like folks have gone crazy about rebuilding,' Frank tells Scarlett soon after she arrives in Atlanta, explaining that 'anyone who owns a sawmill owns a gold mine, for nowadays you can ask your own price for lumber'.

The period of 'Reconstruction' acquired its name from the political efforts of the country to rebuild its constitutional democracy into a nation that would embrace rights and freedoms for all its citizens, rather than just for the few. But it also suggests the more literal work of rebuilding the South after the devastation of war. The idea of rebuilding was central to how the nation reconciled itself, turning toward the bustle of commerce.

Reconstruction is also the form that Scarlett's commerce takes: she buys a lumber yard as soon as the war ends and reclaims her affluence thanks to the building boom. Making Scarlett's business 'reconstruction' is perhaps Mitchell's most aesthetically satisfying choice, reconnecting her to the nation's mercantile roots, while also fusing her story with rags-to-riches themes of hardworking immigrants thriving in a land of opportunity.

Scarlett succeeds amid the hustle and bustle of modern economic competition thanks to her amoral embrace of radical free market capitalism. She understands the world in typically transactional terms, thinking constantly of the 'bargains' she makes, from her understanding of Catholicism ('Religion had always been a bargaining process with Scarlett'), through her marriage with Frank Kennedy, a 'bargain' she intends to keep, to her marriage with Rhett ('They had made a bargain and she was quite pleased with her side of the bargain. She hoped he was equally pleased but she did not care very much whether he was or not').

Scarlett's mercenary drive makes most of her society un-comfortable and embarrasses Frank, but she sees it as a matter of economic necessity, repeatedly insisting that she will give up business once she ensures her family's security. That was another bargain, one women increasingly made during the Great Depression as they became household wage earners. With 'the usual masculine disillusionment in discovering that a woman has a brain', Frank dislikes that Scarlett is good with numbers and is embarrassed by her doing math in public. Worst of all, her mill is making money: 'No man could feel right about a wife who succeeded in so unwomanly an activity.'

Mitchell's satirical feminism mocks Frank's backwardness to highlight Rhett's heroic modernity: he is proud of Scarlett's business sense. Scarlett's sudden 'revolutionary thought' that she is better at business than Frank arrives with 'a violent longing' 'to make money for herself as men made money', to buy her security and independence. Rhett will fulfill that violent longing, too (he would fulfill all her violent longings, if only she knew): 'I'm ill bred enough to be proud of having a smart wife,' he says when he tells her to keep running the businesses with his blessing. That sense of equality defines their meeting of minds and their battle of the sexes: they are matched in a fight that in one sense Scarlett wins, as Rhett surrenders and walks away, leaving her the field of a pyrrhic victory.

*

Scarlett's struggle to make money from the lumber mill drives most of the second half of the novel. She tries briefly to hire freed Black labourers, before deciding they aren't worth it: 'How could anyone get any work done with free nxxxxrs quitting all the time?' That's one of the more conspicuous benefits of chattel slavery – your labourers can't quit if you treat them badly.

This question is another evasion, however. Scarlett isn't struggling to get work done, she's annoyed that she's not making money more easily. 'Free darkies are certainly worthless,' she declares, complaining that she 'just can't depend on the darkies any more. They work a day or two and then lay off till they've spent their wages… Thousands of them aren't working at all and the ones we can get to work at the mill are so lazy and shiftless they aren't worth having.' The problem with 'free darkies', in other words, is that they are not free enough – their political freedom has removed Scarlett's power to claim their labour for free. Slavery was so much cheaper.

Emancipation doesn't enter Scarlett's calculations – free here means only free of charge, not the political or moral freedom of enslaved people. This was a dynamic Du Bois had remarked on a year earlier in *Black Reconstruction*: the white South still instinctively thought of the Black American as property, revealing 'an ingrained feeling that the blacks at large belong to the whites at large', because 'whites esteem the blacks their property by natural right'. During the war, Scarlett tells Rhett that it would have been better for everyone if the North had just paid the South for their slaves, or even for the South 'to give them the darkies free of charge', and thus prevented the war. In 1936 the white Southern mindset Mitchell typified still thought in terms of the economic value of Black people to the extent of describing abolition as a question of 'giving' Black people to the North.

Scarlett finds a solution to the problem of paying freed people, and not being able to beat them when she wishes, by leasing convicts instead. When Scarlett tells Ashley in the film that she's going to have money enough so the Yankees can never take Tara away from her (as ever using Tara to rationalize her avarice), she adds: 'And I'm going to make it the only way I know how!' – by recreating slavery as nearly as she can.

Everyone in Atlanta's Old Guard is horrified at convict-leasing. Frank considers it immoral, 'a traffic in human bodies on par with prostitution', a system 'far worse than slavery had ever been'. While he and his friends 'realized the necessity of the system, they deplored it just the same': convict-leasing is just another tragic necessity, like the Klan. Moreover, 'Many of them had not even believed in slavery.' To imply in 1936 with a straight face that it's a mark of personal character to not 'even' believe in slavery is not just moral relativism, it is a moral vacuum. But although the enslavers intone that 'it was wrong to take advantage of the miseries and misfortunes of others', Mitchell is at least honest enough to allow Scarlett the obvious rebuttal that they 'didn't have any objections to working slaves!'

To which the Old Guard responds that slavery was 'different', because 'slaves were neither miserable nor unfortunate. The negroes were far better off under slavery than they were now under freedom.' Scarlett has no rejoinder to this, as exceptionalism comes racing once more to the rescue, insisting that slavery is defensible because it was 'different'.

Evidently unpersuaded by her own preposterous argument, Mitchell repeats it nearly verbatim almost 200 pages later, when Scarlett sells the mills to Ashley. He duly, and piously, announces that he will return the convicts, like so many unwanted goods, because he refuses to 'make money from the enforced labor and misery of others'. Scarlett once more points out the obvious. 'But you owned slaves!' To which Ashley can only trot out the same insistence: 'They weren't miserable… This is different.' Mitchell has him add another lame excuse for good measure: 'And besides, I'd have freed them all when Father died if the war hadn't already freed them… I do not believe that happiness can come from money made from the sufferings of others.'

Mitchell seems driven to repeat this argument because the contradictions are clearly about to overwhelm the mythmaking. Stuck in a totally illogical corner, she substitutes repetition for persuasion. Denying that there was anything abusive in the slave system is another categorical false distinction that upholds the fraudulent social order the story depicts. For a former enslaver to say he can't make money from 'enforced labor' is beyond hypocritical – it is the pathological denialism at the heart of the fable of virtuous, meritocratic, bootstrapped white wealth that *Gone with the Wind* is peddling, the deadening flat lie.

To get herself out of the corner she backed the story into, Mitchell has Rhett suddenly remind everyone that money isn't everything. As Scarlett tries to defend her choices, enumerating her businesses, Rhett turns on her: 'Don't forget murdering that Yankee,' he adds. 'He really gave you your start... And the money has made you very, very happy, hasn't it, darling?' And that is what finally leaves Scarlett speechless, the only way Mitchell can find out of her dead-end argument that slavery was better than convict-leasing. Money doesn't buy happiness, everyone's a criminal anyway, and therefore we can leave the moral debate about slavery behind.

The narrator takes the opportunity to offer another erroneous history lesson, displacing guilt about slavery onto convict-leasing, so that it can be blamed on the Yankees: 'This new system of leasing convicts had come into being because of the poverty of the state after the war. Unable to support the convicts, the State was hiring them out to those needing large labor crews in the building of railroads, in turpentine forests and lumber camps'.

In reality, the state of Georgia during Reconstruction was not 'unable to support' its prisoners – but it found that by leasing them out for hire it could make vast profits (nearly 375 per cent of penal expenses),[1] while also enriching the white owners of private industry. They were able to reclaim cheap labour and undercut the wages and rights of freed Black people, making convict-leasing one of the greatest generators of personal wealth for many white Southerners after the war.

Mitchell never identifies the race of Scarlett's convicts but strongly implies they are white, calling them 'men' rather than any of the racial labels by which she uniformly denotes Black people. When Scarlett visits the convicts she's leased and finds them being mistreated by her foreman, Mitchell mentions the 'mulatto' serving them, also referring to her as the 'negro woman', while the convicts have no racial markers in a world of presumptive whiteness. The film makes this impression explicit, casting all white actors as convicts in Scarlett's gang.

This casting choice makes the moral economy much clearer: everyone in the Old Guard responds to convict-leasing with horror because it means treating white people like Black people. Scarlett's poor white bodyguard, Archie, himself a former convict, quits working for her in outrage:

> I knows about convict leasin'. I calls it convict murderin'. Buyin' men like they was mules. Treatin' them worse than mules ever was treated. Beatin' them, starvin' them, killin' them. And who cares? The State don't care. It's got the lease money. The folks that gits the convicts, they don't care. All they want is to feed them cheap and git all the work they can out of them.

Buying men like mules, feeding them cheap, and getting all the work possible out of them becomes immoral only when the men being treated like mules are white.

The imagery of slavery cannot be escaped; endlessly repressed, it endlessly returns. (White people in *Gone with the Wind* don't know what they're dreaming about, but it definitely isn't slavery.) It shapes all the novel's thoughts, but unless it is denied, the iniquity of slavery must also be admitted – and consequential moral and economic debts along with it. This is the 'difference' they keep invoking but won't name. When Scarlett thinks 'that's the difference', as she realizes she needs Black slaves to make her a lady again, when Frank and Ashley insist that slavery was 'different' from convict-leasing: the difference is racial. It's the difference that must be asserted but not named, because it underwrites their power. It's the difference that lets Scarlett O'Hara rebuild her fortune on the foundations of the American carceral state.

32

Criminal Emancipation

Freedom 'has just ruined the darkies', Scarlett complains, without a trace of irony. According to *Gone with the Wind*, freedom must be protected at all costs for white people – whereas Black people must be protected from it. 'The more I see of emancipation the more criminal I think it is,' Scarlett adds, in another symptomatic phrase – for emancipation led directly to the criminalization of the Black population.

If Scarlett had leased convicts in Reconstruction Georgia in reality, she'd have received not white convicts, but Black. After abolishing slavery in 1865, the United States put African Americans back in chains by putting them in chain gangs. Slavery mutated not only into Jim Crow, but into the mass incarceration that led, eventually, to the perpetual imprisonment of a huge majority of America's Black male population.

Georgia passed its first postbellum felon disfranchisement laws in 1868, the year it ratified the Fourteenth Amendment, and then proceeded to invent reasons for charging Black men with felonious crimes. Prisons were built upon the literal ground of former plantations, including in Mississippi, Florida, and Louisiana, where state penitentiaries are still known colloquially by the names of the old plantation owners: Mississippi State Penitentiary is referred to locally as Parchman, while Louisiana

State Penitentiary is more familiarly called Angola, the Angola Plantation, or just The Farm. Many prisons in the Deep South still have Black inmates picking crops. There is a kind of malicious ingenuity to it that becomes staggering in its historical scope: white Americans keep finding ways to keep Black Americans in shackles and irons, working the land for free. And they are motivated to believe that this is a justice system, so that they don't have to question a system that benefits them.

Convict-leasing, like the Klan, comes to Scarlett's Georgia a little early. She leases convicts from the Milledgeville state penitentiary at the end of 1866, although Georgia did not award its first convict lease until 1868, when the Georgia railroad system received 150 African American convicts for one year, during which time sixteen prisoners died.[1] State leaders were informed that prisoners were being cruelly abused, whipped, starved, overworked, and casually murdered, but profits outweighed all other considerations.

Cheap penal labour thus built a new system of racial capitalism on the economic and physical foundations of plantation slavery. White private industry could abuse Black prisoners at will without risking their human capital – meaning that chattel slavery created more protections for its Black labourers than Jim Crow convict-leasing. (In one of the novel's typical half-truths, Big Sam tells Scarlett that he was never beaten, because Gerald would not let anyone beat a slave as expensive as him.)[2] Felon disfranchisement laws helped close a vicious circle that contained multiple incentives for the incarceration of Black Americans, creating economic and political gain for white people every time they found an excuse to lock up a Black person.

By 1880, out of 1,200 prisoners in the state of Georgia, almost 1,100 were Black.[3] And from the start they were given longer sentences than white convicts: an 1882 investigation into the Georgia penal system found that Black people were serving twice as long for burglary and five times longer than white people for larceny, the two most frequently charged crimes. Over the next thirty years, the convict population in Georgia soared, as did the proportion of Black people among them.[4] Between 1908 and 1936, four white women were sentenced to chain gangs in Georgia – along with nearly 2,000 Black women.[5] Sexual assault was commonplace and, to all intents and purposes, authorized.[6]

Convict-leasing upheld plantation politics while extending their reach and embedding them ever more deeply into the South's social, juridical, and economic systems. White capitalists, including railroad owners and lumber merchants, whose ranks Scarlett O'Hara soon joins, built enormous personal wealth for political and business leaders during Redemption, in response to popular demands for financial 'retrenchment'[7] after the impoverishment of Reconstruction.

When Rhett finally, near story's end, provokes Scarlett into selling her lumber mills to Ashley, she immediately regrets it, feeling bereft, 'as though she had sold one of her children', in one of the most extraordinary of all the novel's slips of the tongue, an involuntary recollection that enslavers routinely sold off their own enslaved children for profit.

Mitchell even extends the metaphor: 'The mills had been her darlings, her pride, the fruit of her small grasping hands', which Scarlett 'nursed' through the dark times of early Reconstruction. It is the only time in the entire novel that Mitchell describes forward-looking Scarlett as 'nostalgic': not for the days before the war, nor for her lost family, friends, or childhood – but for the 'bitter, harsh' period in her life during which she had built her lumber business, 'one which she recalled with nostalgic satisfaction'. Scarlett does love property as much as (if not more than) she loves humans, and finds it increasingly difficult to differentiate the two.

*

Public indignation at the inhumanity of the convict-leasing system grew during the early decades of the twentieth century, spurred on by investigative journalism and cinematic exposés. Georgia outlawed convict-leasing in 1908, but not chain gangs, which continued to provide forced labour for public works, especially road projects. It also mutated into a system of debt peonage, whereby white property owners could pay a convicted criminal's fine and then claim that person's labour to pay off the debt. Landowners were known to trawl courthouses to 'buy up' the labour of petty criminals who couldn't afford their fines, forcing them into indentured servitude to work off the payment.

It was a dispute between one such indentured worker, Sidney Johnson, and his white employer after a particularly brutal beating, that led to the Georgia 'lynching orgy' of 1918 and the murder of pregnant Mary Turner. Having been jailed when he couldn't pay a $30 fine for playing dice, Johnson was indentured to a man named Hampton Smith, who routinely abused his workers, including Mary Turner and her husband Hayes. After Mary was beaten with especial severity, Hayes Turner threatened Smith and was sentenced to a brief term on a chain gang. Upon release, he was returned to Smith's employ, where the abuse continued. Smith's Black workers eventually plotted his murder, and the ensuing violence culminated in the thirteen lynchings that included the slaughter of Mary and her unborn child.[8]

In 1932, the film I Am a Fugitive from a Chain Gang (based on a book called I Am a Fugitive from a Georgia Chain Gang), a nonfiction account of a white man who was wrongfully convicted and escaped, only to be captured and reincarcerated, brought nationwide attention to the inhumane conditions of convict labourers in Georgia. By 1937, Georgia's chain gang system had become the subject of widespread national criticism, as the state promised reforms to eliminate convict labour.[9]

By the time Gone with the Wind appeared, American culture had long absorbed tropes of the fugitive fleeing from gangs of men with guns and hounds, hiding in swamps and in trees – first as slaves running from patrollers, then as criminals running from lynch mobs, and then as convicts escaping from prisons and chain gangs. Mitchell uses the image of the hunted man running from hounds like a frightened animal to describe Scarlett's fear of poverty, which makes her feel 'as hunted as a fox, running with a bursting heart, trying to reach a burrow before the hounds caught up'. Scarlett the slaveholder and convict-leaser becomes the hunted slave and convict, another image of white victimhood that compulsively reverses historical reality.

Within forty years, Nixon had declared a 'war on drugs' that his advisors later admitted was racially motivated; a decade after that the Reagan administration began locking up young Black men in unprecedented and staggering numbers, making of American society a fairly efficient factory geared to creating Black prisoners, with the highest incarceration rates in the world. Mass imprisonment of the American Black male population has exploded by 500 per cent since 1975, representing yet another retrenchment of white power against the gains of the civil rights movements in the 1960s. As of 2019, Black Americans were still being imprisoned at five times the rate of white Americans: one in every fifty Black American men is incarcerated, and Black men between the ages of twenty-five and forty-four are imprisoned at a current rate of one in every twenty-five.[10]

The prison system became increasingly profitable for the state, while in the 1980s the modern private prison industry emerged; as of 2019, 116,000 state and federal prisoners were held in privatized prisons.[11] America's carceral systems continue to ensure the profitable imprisonment of the country's Black population, while relieving the nation, with dreamlike efficiency, of its guilt for the profit motive.[12]

33

Hot Joy

During the war Rhett tells Scarlett, 'There's just as much money to be made in the wreck of a civilization as in the upbuilding of one,' and when she comes to Atlanta during Reconstruction she understands. 'This is the wreck he foresaw,' she thinks, 'and he was right. There's still plenty of money to be made by anyone who isn't afraid to work – or to grab.' Scarlett grabs.

Scarlett's evolution from agrarian wealth to commercial mercantilism mirrors the Old South's transformation into the New South. But although Scarlett is apolitical (mostly because she is amoral), her mercenary ambitions are not. Debates in *Gone with the Wind* about political freedom under the Yankees have a way of turning into twentieth-century arguments for free market capitalism. In the 1930s this was becoming known as libertarianism,[1] the most fundamental rejection of federalism (and a way of aggrandizing what Toni Morrison called the parasitical nature of white freedom).[2] The calculating cynicism of the story turns it into a romance with brute force, as the confected plantation myths drop away and reveal what lurks behind: the desire to grab.

Scarlett's acquisitiveness is part of what the narrator bluntly calls her 'predatory nature' at the start, her rejection of everything except material luxury, with no spiritual understanding or higher ideals. Materialism provides Scarlett's greatest erotic frisson – her love for Ashley is profoundly sexless, and she feels more lust for revenge than for any man. There is plenty of lust on display for the piratical, swaggering Rhett, but it's mostly expressed by the narrator: Scarlett responds physically to him without understanding her own reactions. There is only one sex scene in America's most famous romance novel; if the story concerns, as Lillian Smith said in 1936, Scarlett's 'amorous and monetary adventures', the amorous takes a decided backseat to the monetary.[3]

Scarlett's and Rhett's carnal desires are triangulated over the accumulation of wealth, as they embrace laissez-faire capitalism instead of each other. His cynical justifications for gambling, her obsession with money, the mutual erotic appeal of taking what you want, lead ultimately to the story's insistence that the ones who are taken either deserve it or like it. This dictum applies equally to the fools and weaklings who deserve to be exploited by unscrupulous business practices, as to Scarlett's own pleasure at being 'taken' by Rhett in *Gone with the Wind*'s sex scene – one now commonly described as marital rape, primarily because of how it is depicted in the film.

After being humiliated by Scarlett's (friendly) embrace with Ashley, Rhett gets drunk and carries her up the stairs, informing her: 'We are both scoundrels, Scarlett, and nothing is beyond us when we want something.' Just as he taught her to grab money from the wreckage, so Rhett now gets to grab Scarlett – literally, as he 'swung her off her feet into his arms and started up the stairs'.

This avowal of winner takes all leads the novel to their one night of implied mutual passion. Although Scarlett is briefly 'wild with fear', thinking he 'was a mad stranger and this was a black darkness she did not know, darker than death', in an instant the 'savagery' of his kisses 'wiped out everything from her mind but the dark into which she was sinking and the lips on hers', 'evoking feelings never felt before':

> She was darkness and he was darkness and there had never been anything before this time, only darkness and his lips upon her. She tried to speak and his mouth was over hers again. Suddenly she had a wild thrill such as she had never known; joy, fear, madness, excitement, surrender to arms that were too strong, lips too bruising, fate that moved too fast. For the first time in her life she had met someone, something stronger than she, someone she could neither bully nor break, someone who was bullying and breaking her. Somehow, her arms were around his neck and her lips trembling beneath his and they were going up, up into the darkness again, a darkness that was soft and swirling and all enveloping.

Waking up with 'the memory of rapture, of the ecstasy of surrender', she thinks: 'He had humbled her, hurt her, used her brutally through a wild mad night and she had gloried in it.' A night of wild thrills that include joy, excitement, rapture, and ecstasy in which a woman gloried may be many things, but rape is not a very good word for them. Before he carries her up the stairs, Rhett 'released her abruptly', after telling her that he loves her and that her delusional idea that she loves Ashley is just a child crying for the moon. That is what makes Scarlett run away – she is running from the truth, not from fear of Rhett. When he swoops her up, the novel's language quickly becomes orgasmic – up, up into the darkness that was swirling and all-enveloping, ending in a memory of rapture and ecstasy – and typical of the way women's sexual pleasure was encoded in popular romance fiction before the sexual revolution helped liberate fictional language as well as nonfictional women.

The film's depiction in 1939 is more ambiguous: Rhett simply carries Scarlett as she fights him, and perhaps by implication her own desires, upwards into the darkness of the Hays Code. But when Scarlett awakes next morning, she is smiling and singing a happy tune, implying the same reciprocal pleasure as in Mitchell's scene, again in terms that audiences at the time were accustomed to decoding. After shutting the bedroom door, Hollywood routinely opened it to post-coital signals, whether cigarettes, coy smiles, or cooing babies, none of which indicated sexual violence.

If we restrict 'rape' to denoting a non-consensual, non-reciprocal act of sexual violence which the victim finds traumatic and not pleasurable, then neither version of the scene is coded as rape, but rather as (vaguely) rough sex that Scarlett enjoyed, a pleasure that neither she in 1871 nor her story in the 1930s was able to openly admit. The point is that it's a code.

Mitchell is not afraid to name rape in other scenes, and has Rhett teach Scarlett to 'be frank' and speak plainly about it. When she hints at what she thinks the Yankees would do to her, Rhett cuts her off, calling a spade a spade: 'Rape you? I think not. Though, of course, they'd want to.' When Scarlett objects to his language, he tells her: 'Be frank. Wasn't that what you were thinking? … No use getting mad at me for reading your thoughts. That's what all our delicately nurtured and pure-minded Southern ladies think. They have it on their minds constantly. I'll wager even dowagers like Mrs. Merriwether...'

> Scarlett gulped in silence, remembering that wherever two or more matrons were gathered together, in these trying days, they whispered of such happenings, always in Virginia or Tennessee or Louisiana, never close to home. The Yankees raped women and ran bayonets through children's stomachs and burned houses over the heads of old people. Everyone knew these things were true even if they didn't shout them on the street corners. And if Rhett had any decency he would realize they were true. And not talk about them.

When it happens to white women, it's a rape that the women compulsively discuss; when it happens to Black women, it's a nasty and ill-bred interest in 'concubinage'. Rhett's role as buccaneering seducer is partly to liberate Scarlett from the traps of priggish conventionality, to get her to admit that women talk and think about sex, too. This exchange does not insinuate that Scarlett would enjoy being raped – but it does allow that talking or thinking about sexual violence might have been titillating, particularly in an era of sexual repression. And it makes clear that the story is not afraid to name rape, or to consider illicit forms of desire.

The other code in Rhett and Scarlett's sex scene, by contrast, is considerably more problematic than the implication that Scarlett may like rough sex without knowing it. Its endless repetitions of 'darkness' are far more hysterical than the sex, as if all the novel's denials and displacements of its own anxieties about race, having been pushed out of their proper places in the story, swirled madly around its pages until they accumulated and settled, like a black blizzard, on this one climactic scene.

All that 'hot joy' at the thought of murdering the Yankee, all Scarlett's violent longing for money, her fantasies of whipping Black people, here get tangled up in the savage embrace of the swarthy man who embodies a compelling darkness that cannot be resisted. And that is one of the many reasons why there is so much 'darkness' here, because power and mastery in Jim Crow America were inescapably entangled with race, whether as money, or sex, or slavery, or the erotics of wealth. Darkness, with all its racial connotations, is where moral, social, and erotic disorder collide: the terror and thrill of raw power unleashed.

Its extravagant assertions that Scarlett enjoyed being bullied and broken are very much on a spectrum with the story's insistence that the enslaved are equally enraptured by their own enslavement. Such submissive masochism does glorify violence, by eroticizing sadistic domination. And it offers another kind of redemption, as submission to violence relieves the guilt of the oppressor with a dreamlike ease that Scarlett's erotic joy vindicates. Scarlett's violent longings are finally fulfilled: for money, for revenge, for power, or perhaps just for violence itself.

The subject of the dream, as Toni Morrison said, is always the dreamer: that's what projection means. Once again it is the great Black writers who help explain what is happening, with their profound understanding of the collective white imagination – as Black Americans keep saying, they are forced to understand white America if they want to survive it. Motives of race, status, economics, and guilt are always clustered, Ralph Ellison observed, pointing to moments when American writers cannot see beyond the moral tangle symbolized by race in their society but remain profoundly disturbed by it. Instead of disentangling the symbolism, he explained, some writers instead leap right into it, yelling out their most terrifying name for chaos, which in America is blackness.

That is surely what Mitchell is doing here with all this darkness – yelling out of the racial nightmare her most terrifying name for chaos, while admitting the erotic frisson of power grappling with power. Darkness is where power in America is exercised, as it soars upwards and becomes ecstatic.

34

The Confidence Man

'What a gambler you are, Scarlett,' Rhett tells her when her ruse at the jail fails to deceive him into handing her the tax money for Tara. Rhett is a gambler, too – a professional gambler, one of the reasons he begins the story an outcast from polite society. Even as *Gone with the Wind* insists that the fittest survive, it also constantly depicts Rhett and Scarlett as risk-takers, wavering between determinism and contingency in its life philosophies.

Rhett starts out as a professional river-boat gambler, before turning blockade-runner, war profiteer, and food speculator. His betting on starvation is just a more sophisticated version of Scarlett's crude price-gouging: they're both enriching themselves in a disaster economy. Atlanta's Old Guard continues to hate Rhett after the war because of his food speculation ('making money out of our hunger', as Mrs Merriweather tells Scarlett) and Rhett freely admits he is a speculator more than once.

Scarlett, always less than self-aware, is also a speculator without realizing it. As she consorts with Republicans and scalawags during Reconstruction, putting her beyond the pale of Atlanta society, her new power goes to her head. 'To her had come that pleasant intoxication peculiar to those whose lives are a deliberate slap in the face of organized society,' Mitchell breaks in to explain: 'the gambler, the confidence man, the polite adventuress, all those who succeed by their wits. She said and did exactly what she pleased and, in practically no time, her insolence knew no bounds.'

When Scarlett discovers that 'you can't be a lady without money', she decides to embrace her heritage as a gambler, setting her sights on rebuilding her fortunes, just as her father had done: 'She wasn't going to be poor all her life. She wasn't going to sit down and patiently wait for a miracle to help her. She was going to rush into life and wrest from it what she could. Her father had started as a poor immigrant boy and had won the broad acres of Tara. What he had done, his daughter could do'.

The immigrant American Dream here is rewritten not as hard work, but as winner-take-all. Scarlett will not farm her way to success. She will gamble, and she will win – everything except the love and esteem she seeks.

Her immigrant Irishness also romanticizes Scarlett's grim determination to hang on to her land. The first scene of the film ends with Gerald informing Scarlett that 'land is the only thing in the world worth working for, worth fighting for, worth dying for, because it's the only thing that lasts', before adding: 'To anyone with a drop of Irish blood in them, why the land they live on is like their mother... It will come to you, this love of the land. There's no getting away from it if you're Irish.' The final frame of the film shows her standing once more in silhouette against the land, with Tara in the background, sentimentalizing the plantation aristocrat's ownership of the big house.

In between, her vows against hunger and poverty reflect not only the immigrant experience generally, but Irish immigrants fleeing famine specifically – and in Gerald's case, murder. In America he marries Ellen Robillard, a Southern aristocrat from Savannah, but Mitchell emphasizes on the first page that Scarlett inherited her father's volatile passions as well as his unscrupulous determination, and that it sits uneasily beneath the thin veneer of ladyhood bestowed upon her by Ellen.

Gerald's Irishness also works to distance the novel's image of the South from the guilt of slavery. In cultural stereotypes, the Irish symbolize not the colonial oppressor, but the oppressed – first by the English and then as immigrants in the United States. The Irish are not feudal aristocrats but small tenant-farmers, meaning that Tara has not been granted to an effete English grandee – it has been carved out of nothing. Boasting that Tara was 'built by slave-labor', Mitchell also declares that 'Tara's bloom was not the work of a planter aristocrat, but of the plodding tireless "small farmer" who loved his land', neglecting to mention that the 'small farmer' in question may have loved his land, but also had a hundred slaves who worked it for him.

The classic American immigrant success story of hard work rewarded by prosperity is superimposed over the labour of slaves, whose subjugation enabled Irish immigrants like the O'Haras to enjoy the prosperity that the enslaved were so absolutely denied. The stark racial hierarchy of the South, divided into its ruthless binary of black and white, made it easier for Irish immigrants like Margaret Mitchell's great-grandfather Philip Fitzgerald to assimilate – owning Black slaves could help the so-called 'black Irish' ensure that they counted in American society as white.

Rhett later underscores the point, saying he is returning to the Old Guard so their daughter Bonnie isn't left consorting with Scarlett's new friends: 'Irishmen on the make, Yankees, white trash, Carpetbag parvenus – my Bonnie with her Butler blood and her Robillard strain… The O'Haras might have been kings of Ireland once but your father was nothing but a smart Mick on the make. And you are no better.' But Scarlett is also no worse: being on the make was by no means unacceptable to American audiences in the 1930s.

This means deciding that morality is a luxury she can't afford, as Scarlett becomes the most exploitative of capitalists. She turns a blind eye to her manager's abuse of the convicts they lease, and price gouges. She undersells her competitors and deliberately traffics in shoddy goods. She becomes a swindler and neither Mitchell nor Rhett can decide how much they should object. Rhett loves Scarlett's renegade spirit, although he deplores her lack of awareness and recognizes what it will cost her.

Scarlett's thinking is always on the shortest terms available. She insists that once she is rich, she will behave better, while suppressing memories of her mother, a figure for Scarlett's (dead) conscience:

> Momentarily, Scarlett cringed as she pictured the look on her mother's face. And then the picture faded, blotted out by an impulse, hard, unscrupulous and greedy, which had been born in the lean days at Tara and was now strengthened by the present uncertainty of life. So she passed this milestone as she had passed others before it—with a sigh that she was not as Ellen would like her to be, a shrug and the repetition of her unfailing charm: 'I'll think of all this later.'

Shrugging off morality as an inconvenience, she adheres to capitalism's justifications of its own amoral practices, offering a plausible rationale for venality and promises of a liberal reform that never comes. The kind of rapacious capitalist Scarlett typifies will always think about the costs of their greed later. That, too, is representative of her society.

Warning her that morality, once lost, is hard to reclaim, Rhett demands: 'If you must steal, Scarlett, why not steal from the rich and strong instead of the poor and weak? From Robin Hood on down to now, that's been considered highly moral.' It's another evasion, enabling Mitchell to imply that Rhett's cynicism masks a kind heart while deflecting attention from the fact that the ultimate predation on the poor and weak was chattel slavery. Goaded, Scarlett answers with motivated reasoning: 'I know I'm not as - scrupulous as I should be these days. Not as kind and as pleasant as I was brought up to be… What else could I have done? What would have happened to me, to Wade, to Tara and all of us if I'd… been – kind and scrupulous? Where would we all be now?'

Gone with the Wind ends in 1873, the year of one of the greatest financial panics of the nineteenth century, inaugurating what was known as the Great Depression until the 1930s.[1] Although Mitchell never mentions it, she was certainly aware of the context. Rhett keeps telling Scarlett she should be ashamed of being manipulative and exploitative, while being entirely ruthless about his own wealth. This ambivalence reflects the moral relativism of the society being depicted: in a culture in which everyone is exploited, criminality comes to seem both universal and tolerable. Just as everyone murders Yankees, so is every American a profiteer.

In Walt Whitman's 1871 *Democratic Vistas* – published as Scarlett and Rhett are buying up Atlanta and Scarlett is building the vulgar mansion that Rhett tells her is 'just the kind of house a profiteer would build' – Whitman warned that America needed to 'look our times and lands searchingly in the face, like a physician diagnosing some deep disease. Never was there, perhaps, more hollowness at heart than at present, and here in the United States.' The 'hectic' activity could not dispel the 'atmosphere of hypocrisy': 'money-making' had overtaken the nation, filling it with 'a mob of fashionably dress'd speculators and vulgarians', creating a 'colossal' empire 'with little or no soul'.

It sounds strikingly like Mitchell's description of Scarlett's mercenary narcissism: 'It was an era that suited her, crude, garish, showy, full of over-dressed women, over-furnished houses, too many jewels, too many horses, too much food, too much whisky.'

America's commercial depravity, Whitman concluded, was not less than people imagined, but infinitely greater.

*

Whitman's description of American commercial depravity also sounds strikingly like the man who would become president in 2016, who liked to photograph himself surrounded by gold, trying to convince the world, and himself, that he had the Midas touch.

In early 2017, soon after Donald Trump's inauguration, Philip Roth was asked by the *New Yorker* if his 2004 novel *The Plot Against America* had predicted Trump's presidency. Roth replied that the novel best able to capture the character of Trump was not his own, but Herman Melville's *The Confidence-Man*, 'the darkly pessimistic, daringly inventive novel – Melville's last – that could just as well have been called "The Art of the Scam"'.

A story that was published, as per Melville's request, on April Fool's Day in 1857, four years before *Gone with the Wind* begins, *The Confidence-Man* can be read as a satirical allegory of the American Dream, in which the Confidence Man dupes all the passengers on a steamboat, exposing American society as a ship of fools, a carnival of hucksters and hypocrites, speculators and counterfeits, dupes and imposters, all in thrall to market forces and profiteering. *The Confidence-Man* depicts a society characterized by misplaced trust and pervasive suspicion, a self-seeking and self-interested collective, always on the brink of disintegration.

Trump, Roth explained, was perfectly familiar to American history 'as a character, a human type – the real-estate type, the callow and callous killer capitalist'. The problem comes when a society admires a confidence trickster so much they make him president.

When Trump announced his presidential campaign in June 2015, he declared that the American Dream was dead, but that he would bring it back from the losers, because he was a winner. Casting himself as the classic exemplar of the American Dream, who had bootstrapped his way to success, he announced: 'I've done an amazing job... I started off in a small office with my father in Brooklyn and Queens… I'm really proud of my success… I made it the old-fashioned way. It's real estate. You know, it's real estate.'

After (untruthfully) declaring that he was worth $9 billion, give or take, Trump added:

> I'm not doing that to brag, because you know what? I don't have to brag. I don't have to, believe it or not. I'm doing that to say that that's the kind of thinking our country needs. We need that thinking. We have the opposite thinking. We have losers. We have losers. We have people that don't have it. We have people that are morally corrupt. We have people that are selling this country down the drain.

Credibly accused of serious financial crimes, and of stripping the country down and selling it for parts, Trump is projecting in this speech to a degree that would make Scarlett O'Hara blush, but she would recognize his compulsive need to see himself as a winner – and his instinct that winners must conjure the spectre of losers to imagine themselves into existence.

Throughout his campaign and presidency, Trump continually espoused his eugenicist faith in what he called the 'racehorse theory', which explained (he said) his genetic superiority over lesser people, the same theory of 'good stock' and 'breeding' that is advocated by Grandma Fontaine and Mrs Tarleton in so many words, and was devised to justify winners taking everything from losers.[2]

Confidence tricks exploit the good faith of the victim – the whole point is to make the dupe believe in the trick (that's where the confidence comes in). Fiction is another kind of confidence trick, in which the audience willingly participates. Politics are even more of a confidence trick; so is the reality television that made Trump a star and taught him how to deceive audiences on a mass scale.

He already knew how to deceive himself. In truth, Trump had not started out small; he inherited millions from his father's real estate empire, which Fred Trump had acquired thanks to loans paid for by the high taxes levied primarily from the white propertied classes under the New Deal, the taxes against which Americans like Mitchell so violently railed, and from which they so often profited. When Black Americans left rural farms in the South, trying to escape the cycle of debt peonage that was sharecropping, they migrated to cities where they were exploited by predatory landlords like Fred Trump, who bequeathed his wealth to his sons, and his sons' sons.

That Donald Trump was a charlatan had become clear to all but his most devoted followers by the end of his presidency, but along the way he had passed himself off as a tycoon and a showman, a reality television star, a saviour. He even managed to persuade the faithful that he was a conservative (he was nothing of the kind, he just didn't like paying taxes), and then a devout Christian, before convincing millions he was the Second Coming – all the while playing along with lesser humans, taking from them what he could, and then kicking them to the kerb.

This version of the American Dream is the ultimate confidence trick, a collective hoax promising that everyone can be rich, when really you have to make it the old-fashioned way – with real estate you inherit from your father, after he won it from the government in a fixed game.

PART EIGHT

DEEP INTO THE
BLOOD-COLORED SOIL

35

The Blood-colored Soil

'War, war, war; this war talk's spoiling all the fun at every party this spring. I get so bored I could scream. Besides… there isn't going to be any war.' After more than two years of preparation, and seven months of filming, *Gone with the Wind* ended production with retakes in late August, 1939.[1] Selznick had decided to reshoot the very first scene, as Scarlett sits on the veranda of Tara, complaining at talk of war. Days after they finished filming, the Second World War had begun.

Gone with the Wind's portrait of the Civil War had suggested the conflict brewing in Europe to audiences from the start, the story's anti-war sentiment matching the mood of a broadly isolationist America in the 1930s. Watching 'practically the entire world feverishly, insanely, preparing for war', a 1936 Oregon editorial hoped the novel's popularity might strengthen Americans' determination to avoid another world war at all costs. If not, it warned, 'gone with the wind' might be as perfect an epitaph for modern civilization as it was for the Old South.[2]

Scarlett's primary response to the war is impatience with its posturing heroics and rage at the lives it destroyed. Although there is certainly solipsism in the story's refusal to look beyond Scarlett's perspective to the carnage of battle, that refusal is also resistant, part of what defined it at the time as a woman's novel focused on the domestic and civilian costs of war. Inasmuch as the story reviles war, its sympathies are humane. The problem is that *Gone with the Wind*'s politics put it clearly on the wrong side of the war to come – and the wrong side of history.

*

At the end of her arduous, life-changing journey back to Tara as Atlanta burns, Scarlett has an epiphany, realizing for the first time the truth of what her father repeatedly told her, that 'her roots went deep into the blood-colored soil' of the plantation. This is a literal description of Georgia's deep red clay, coloured by iron oxides, although Mitchell may have also intended a metaphorical allusion to the Confederate dead ('Their blood poured down all in vain for us / Red, rich, and pure, like a rain for us,' as Father Ryan, the poet-priest of the Confederacy, put it). Mitchell almost certainly did not intend a figurative reference to the blood of the enslaved soaking the soil, but it applies nonetheless.

Scarlett dedicates herself from that point forward to Tara's salvation – because a mystical bond connects her to the land, linking blood and soil. Mythmaking is caught in the act here (red-handed, as it were), for Scarlett's roots do not, after all, go especially deep into a farm her father won in a poker game thirty years earlier. Having previously stressed the plantation's decidedly unheroic origins, here Mitchell decides that Scarlett's lineage, her blood and breed, tells otherwise, mixing the soil of Tara with the ancestral blood that 'flowed in Scarlett's veins'.[3]

By 1936 Americans were familiar with Nazi Germany's 'tenets of race, blood, and soil',[4] its fervent belief in a nativist 'aristocracy of blood and soil'[5] – and *Gone with the Wind* certainly believes in its own aristocracy of race, blood, and soil. Scarlett's blood-and-soil connection to the land designates both her power and her race purity: it turns white farmers into the lifeblood of the nation, not just socio-economically, but spiritually and culturally, and views all other groups as a threat to that cultural and political purity.

This was not something its first readers overlooked. 'The Fascist implications of "Gone with the Wind" and its nostalgia for the old, old South are fairly palpable,' declared the celebrated columnist Heywood Broun in the spring of 1939, six weeks into Selznick's production, and six months before war was declared in Europe.[6] The story's fascist overtones were equally palpable to the Jewish Selznick, son of immigrants from what is now Lithuania, who had no difficulty seeing the resemblance between fascism and the second Klan. He urged Sidney Howard to exclude the Klan from the screenplay from the start; as he believed in the categorical difference between the two Klans, he feared that aggrandizing the second Klan might serve as 'an unintentional advertisement for intolerant societies in these fascist-ridden times'.[7]

The affinities between the second Klan and European fascism had only grown clearer since their simultaneous start in the early 1920s, with their shared cults of paramilitary violence, legal apartheids, eugenicist ideologies, and paranoid cultures. Mussolini called it fascism's 'common denominator'[8]: a master narrative about the sacredness of the cause, the purity of the nation, and the exaltation of violence to defend against the enemy within. Only 'the historic destiny of the group' matters to fascists, as historians have explained: 'their only moral yardstick is the prowess of the race, of the nation, of the community. They claim legitimacy by no universal standard except a Darwinian triumph of the strongest community,' the survival of the eugenicist fittest.[9]

A few months after Selznick privately told Howard he worried that Gone with the Wind's sympathetic depiction of the Klan might advertise for fascism, the Chicago Defender said reading the novel would make 'many minds more friendly' to fascism.[10] A Jewish actor wrote to Selznick when his production was announced to protest that the story would inevitably create a 'Negro baiting film' that would only embolden groups like the Klan to 'continue their terrorism'. It was, he added, sure to 'be welcomed by the Fascists

... of this country'.[11] As publicity for the film intensified, Black readers became more concerned at the likely effects of a major Hollywood movie validating the dangerous stereotypes that justified the violence of Jim Crow America. Protests continued during filming with a stream of letters denouncing the story as 'un-American, anti-Semitic, anti-Negro, Reactionary, Pro-Ku Klux Klan, pro-Nazi and Fascist'.[12]

Selznick acknowledged the issue more than once, saying, 'I feel so keenly about what is happening to the Jews of the world that I cannot help but sympathize with the Negroes in their fears about material which they regard as insulting and damaging.'[13] Making clear that he had 'no desire to produce any anti-Negro film', Selznick added, 'I think we have to be awfully careful that the Negroes come out decidedly on the right side of the ledger.' But as Selznick also insisted upon being scrupulously faithful to the novel, rebalancing the ledger of its skewed racial politics was impossible.

Selznick had told his screenwriters that his 'ideal script' would be 'one hundred percent Margaret Mitchell', just rearranged, without a word of original dialogue added. (Scott Fitzgerald, for one, found this absurd, telling his editor: 'I was absolutely forbidden to use any words except those of Margaret Mitchell; that is, when new phrases had to be invented one had to thumb through as if it were Scripture and check out phrases of hers which would cover the situation!'[14]) This extreme fidelity made it possible to omit problematic details such as racist language and characterizations, but impossible to remedy the story's entire value system.

It may seem unsurprising that Black audiences recognized broad similarities between the bigotry in Mitchell's novel and bigotries abroad, or even as if they were comparing *Gone with the Wind* to European fascism for polemical reasons. That was certainly Mitchell's view (after all, she said Black critics of her story were 'Professional Negroes' stirring up trouble) but it was not only Black critics, and the arguments went beyond general comparisons. Mitchell equally scoffed at criticism from whites, declaring herself thrilled at the white liberals who also condemned the story, saying she would have been appalled if they liked it, and privately mocking those who objected to its depiction of slavery and Black people.[15]

Heywood Broun's remark about the story's fascism was in response to the publication of a play by Clare Boothe the previous year, a hit comedy that parodied Selznick's search for Scarlett, as a producer seeks an actress to play Velvet O'Toole in his adaptation of a bestselling novel about the Old South. When Boothe published the text of *Kiss the Boys Goodbye* in early 1939, she added an introduction explaining that she had intended more than a satire of Hollywood, and that the play was 'meant to be a political allegory about Fascism in America'. Upon learning this, Mitchell 'whooped with laughter'.[16]

But Boothe was getting at the essential fascism of glorifying the Old South, rather than at *Gone with the Wind*. 'We are warned,' she observed in her introduction, '(though not loudly, not often enough) when – or if – Fascism comes to all America she will come so prettily costumed in red, white and blue' as to be mistaken for a 'Fourth of July performance'. Reflecting on American fascism, Boothe said she directed her attention not to 'dangerously alien' aspects of American life, but to those 'which we most eagerly gloss with the sentimentality of the familiar'. This had become a familiar warning: because all fascism is homegrown, Americans were explaining that an American fascism would be all-American, arriving wrapped in a flag and waving a Hearst newspaper.[17] 'Fascism cannot be imported,' warned one lecturer in 1937, repeating the lesson Mussolini had taught: fascism must, by definition, be 'particularly suited' to a given 'national life'. Logically, 'the anti-Negro program' would provide a 'rallying cry for American fascists', just as anti-Semitism had for Germans. A century later, Americans revived some of these quotations, applying them to Donald Trump's administration in the summer of 2020, as he staged a photo opportunity in front of a church, while ordering federal troops to attack protestors.[18]

What she called 'Southernism' was, Boothe said, 'a particular and *highly matured* form of Fascism with which America has lived more or less peacefully for seventy-five years. Indeed "Southernism" may possibly have been the inspiration or forerunner of Fascism.'[19] This fact, she added, was one of which Americans were 'not, perhaps, sufficiently aware'. In the aftermath of slavery, 'the Southerner has evolved a benevolent Fascism, which is to say a *relatively* tolerable, politically pragmatic form. His Jim Crow laws and his Jim Crow spirit have, on the whole, been accepted as the moral and political norm even at last by the North.'[20]

Mitchell was not the only one who ridiculed this idea. Boothe's introduction was met with widespread derision, several critics asking outright if they were meant to take it seriously, but she had a point, and others, including Heywood Broun, agreed. 'The word "Fascism" is new,' he said. 'The political philosophy is not. There have been scores of potential Fascists in the political and economic life of America ever since the beginning of the republic. And so, instead of looking under the bed for the foreign invader, it might be a good idea for every American to look into hearts nearer home… who protest too often that they alone are patriots.'[21]

Steeped in Lost Cause history, glorifying the first Klan, blind to her depictions of slavery and race, Mitchell could only have seen this perspective as absurd, but that doesn't make it wrong. Fascism rationalizes the local politics of hate, seeking the eradication of entire scapegoated groups in the name of cultural purity and in the interests of consolidated ethno-nationalist power. Any society in which violence has become idiomatic will not find fascistic politics alien, whatever name they give it.

*

Historians continue to debate to what extent the first Klan can, or should, be regarded as the world's original fascist movement, in part because there is no clear consensual definition of fascism. As all fascisms are native, they must take locally specific forms: none of the interwar fascisms in Italy, Germany, Spain, France, Britain, Ireland, Brazil, or the United States (among other places) were identical in ideology or practice. But there is a strong case for the fascism of the Klan, with its paramilitary violence, its extralegal assertions of power, its uniforms and rituals, its love of esoterica, its nostalgic racial fantasies, its conspiracy theories, and its existential rejection of the legitimacy of any government that opposes it, as historians of fascism have pointed out.[22]

The assumption that American nativist, xenophobic, white supremacist, conspiratorially anti-Semitic and anti-communist paramilitary groups were categorically different from their European counterparts was less likely to be made during the interwar years – not least because it was clear how they were all leveraging existing bigotries on behalf of state violence, consolidating power for one small group while dehumanizing, persecuting, and annihilating others.

Fascism and the Klan shared more than eugenicist exaltation of certain 'bloodlines' over others, white grievance displaced onto racialized enemies within. The Klan was also a self-appointed militant force that declared itself the arm of the *herrenvolk* (literally, 'master race') and a parallel moral authority. It terrorized through mass gatherings, stoked nativist invocations of the people's bond with the land, and created systems that delegitimized, incarcerated, and murdered those it deemed inferior.

The Klan saw itself as counter-revolutionary, not merely reactionary, supporting a cause so ultra-nationalist it had formed its own nation within a nation, and then was glorified as having regenerated the country. It was ennobled by myths of national purity, performed by masculinist cults of the leader, and sold as the will of the people.

The phrase the 'master race', made notorious by Hitler, was in fact popularized by an American eugenicist he much admired. In his immensely popular 1916 *The Passing of the Great Race*, subtitled *The Racial Bias of European History*, Madison Grant announced that Black people were 'willing followers who ask only to obey and to further the wishes and the ideals of the master race', the 'Nordics', or people of Northern European descent. The Civil War, Grant wrote, had 'shattered the prestige of the white race, and it will take generations and perhaps wars to recover its former control'.[23] The sinister offhandedness is chilling – if war is required, so be it – and what makes its message fundamentally fascistic: the call to violence to protect racial prerogatives.

The wealthy Grant was also a founder, and funder, of the American eugenicist movement, and a leading proponent of the immigration restriction laws that led to the imposition of nativist quotas in the early 1920s, all to protect the 'superiority' of white American racial 'stock'.[24] In 1921, he took a leading role in the Second International Eugenics Congress, inviting his friend, the French eugenicist G. Vacher de Lapouge, who told the assembled audience of leading citizens that the United States needed to safeguard the master race: 'America, I solemnly declare that it depends on you to save civilization and to produce a race of demigods', he declared, to protect 'the whites, the wealthy, and the intellectually superior elements' from the 'barbarism' of savage races.[25]

The Passing of the Great Race, implying a twilight of the gods in its title, influenced a generation of Americans and more. It was soon joined by Henry Ford's circulation of *The International Jew* in his *Dearborn Independent* throughout the United States in the early 1920s, disseminating the notorious anti-Semitic forgery *The Protocols of the Elders of Zion* and its lurid details of a global cabal of vampiric Jewish leaders drinking the blood of Christian children, while controlling the world's economy, governments, and media. Hitler and Goebbels later built their propaganda machine using not only the *Protocols,* but also German translations of *The International Jew.* Hitler called Ford his 'inspiration' and hung a portrait of the industrialist over his desk, while Ford reportedly distributed swastika pins at the *Dearborn Independent* in the early 1920s, and forced Jewish employees to wear them.[26]

The mutual influence of the racial theories of American white nationalism and its European counterparts during the interwar period is historically well established, including Hitler's explicit use of American race laws as a precedent for the Nuremberg laws.[27] As historians have shown, Hitler praised US racial policies in various writings, including its racial segregation, immigration quotas, and eugenicist policies.[28]

Some historians of fascism argue that it is not properly understood as an ideology, but better viewed 'as a type of politics – the coercively nationalist recourse to political violence and exclusionary authoritarianism under worsening pressures of governing paralysis and democratic impasse',[29] a description that equally applies to the Reconstruction South as to interwar Europe. W. E. B. Du Bois, also watching the first wave of European fascism, agreed: twice in *Black Reconstruction* he calls the socio-economics of white governance during Reconstruction, in which 'the few control the many', 'fascist'.

What has become a standard description of fascism was offered by historian Robert O. Paxton, who characterized it as a politics

> marked by obsessive preoccupation with community decline, humiliation, or victimhood and by compensatory cults of unity, energy, and purity, in which a mass-based party of committed nationalist militants, working in uneasy but effective collaboration with traditional elites, abandons democratic liberties and pursues with redemptive violence and without ethical or legal restraints goals of internal cleansing and external expansion.[30]

Fascism depends on political fantasies, replacing the historical past with a mythical past, actively destroying the difference between the two.[31] Reclaiming the mythical past justifies violence in making the myth come true in the present, imposing its ideology on reality. Mythical histories lay the groundwork for fascist politics.

Black Americans saw more than affinities between Nazi Germany and Jim Crow America: they saw causal connections. 'Hitler Learns from America', the *Pittsburgh Courier* declared in 1933, reporting that German universities under the Third Reich were explaining that 'racial insanities' in America provided Nazi Germany with 'a model for oppressing and persecuting its own minorities'.[32] The *New York Age* wondered the same summer if Hitler had studied 'under the tutelage' of Klan leaders, perhaps as 'a subordinate Kleagle or something of the sort'.[33] In a follow-up, headlined 'Hitlerism and Kukluxism', the *Age* reported that the 'striking resemblance' between Hitler's policies and 'the propaganda used by the Ku Klux Klan' had also been 'noted by Americans abroad in their discussions of Hitlerism': 'the racial dogmas of Chancellor Hitler were found to smack strongly of American origin, but in his practical application of them he was pronounced but a poor imitator of Southern methods'.[34]

But American popular memory would erase these discomfiting observations, too. By the time the Second World War was over, the country had convinced itself that fascism was a uniquely European pathology, an alien disease against which American democracy was inoculated.

36

Roots That Go Deep

When Rhett leaves Scarlett at story's end, he says he's had enough of Reconstruction Atlanta and wants to return to his roots. Unlike Scarlett, with her immigrant Irish blood, Rhett comes from the aristocratic Old South of Charleston, and although he is his family's black sheep, he never questions the superiority of his heritage. He will return to one old world or another, 'perhaps to England – or to Paris. Perhaps to Charleston to try to make peace with my people,' as he's reached an age to value 'the clannishness of families, honor and security, roots that go deep'.

If Rhett did leave Scarlett for Europe, he would not have been the only Southerner after the Civil War to do so hoping to live a more clannish, or Klannish, life. Many Confederates who couldn't accept living in a multiracial society chose to sever their deep roots with their country instead, and went into exile in Europe and South America.

The Confederacy had established diplomatic connections across Latin America in its search for international alliances, while various European monarchies had exploited the conflict by trying to install puppet regimes across the western hemisphere. The most notable of these was Napoleon III's effort to take the Hapsburg empire to Mexico in the early 1860s, in part at least to capitalize on the political chaos of the United States. These plans, which included a Franco-Confederate alliance, collapsed after the Union, which had continued to recognize the government of Benito Juarez, won the war in 1865. The Confederacy had also explored its own imperialist ambitions south of the border.[1]

After the war, there were reports that unreconstructed Confederates had been given land by Emperor Maximilian to establish a colony in Mexico called 'New Virginia', into which they were importing munitions and smuggling slaves, although slavery was banned under Mexican law. These efforts were abandoned after Napoleon III withdrew his troops in 1866, and Maximilian was killed by firing squad at Querétaro in 1867.[2] Confederates also tried to continue plantation slavery in South American countries including Brazil, where they established colonies such as Americana.

Among the estimated 20,000 Confederates who chose exile over concession was Commodore Thomas Jefferson Page, who served in the Confederate Navy, refused to swear the oath of allegiance, and moved his family first to Argentina and then to Rome after the war. His younger cousin was the novelist Thomas Nelson Page, the progenitor of plantation fiction, who later served as Woodrow Wilson's ambassador to Italy from 1913–19, where his cousins were already living. Thomas Jefferson Page's grandson, George Nelson Page, who grew up in a Roman palazzo decorated with Confederate flags and his grandfather's Lost Cause relics, caused a minor scandal in America in 1933 when he renounced his US citizenship in support of Mussolini's fascism. Page would go on to become the head of Mussolini's propaganda bureau, helping to produce Ezra Pound's pro-fascist broadcasts. He was 'the most fascist of fascists', according to an American reporter in Rome at the time.[3]

The American press, accustomed to Italians seeking American citizenship and not the other way around, launched a fusillade against George Nelson Page.[4] The *Richmond Times-Dispatch*, for one, found it incongruous that 'from the library lined in flags and marked with the crossed swords of Confederate heroes', Page had 'marched one day to Mussolini. His attempt to be an American had failed,' it concluded.[5]

The reabsorption of the Confederacy into the United States was sufficient for 'crossed swords of Confederate heroes' to have been read as signs of Page's Americanism, instead of as diehard hostility to Americanism. The *Richmond Times-Dispatch* couldn't see any difference, any more than the woman sobbing at the Capitol insurrection almost a century later could understand why the police were firing at her, given that she was a patriot who was merely storming government buildings to overturn a democratic result she didn't like.

We might conclude instead that George Nelson Page's attempt to be an American hadn't failed so much as his attempt to be a Confederate had succeeded: whether America absorbed the Confederacy or in important respects the Confederacy absorbed America remains a question worth asking. Most Americans, then as now, did not want to see how few steps it took to get from Confederate swords to the broadcasting offices of Italian fascism.

The point is not to overlook the obvious differences between the Confederacy and interwar fascism – it is, rather, to acknowledge how resolutely, and for how long, we've been disregarding the similarities.

*

If George Nelson Page had spent more time in the United States, he might have realized that there was plenty of homegrown American fascism for him to support without renouncing his citizenship. By 1933 a proliferating host of extremist right-wing groups were blending Christian nationalism, anti-communism, conspiratorial anti-Semitism, paramilitary organization, and patriotic symbolism while advocating violent ethno-nationalism. Soon there were enough hybrid groups in the United States combining 'European [fascist] movements and the old Ku Klux

Klan' for worried observers, including the ACLU, to try to measure them.[6] In a series of 1933 articles for the *New Republic*, Harold Loeb and Selden Rodman identified 103 separate groups they considered fascist, which seemed to be waiting for the fabled 'man on horseback' to unite them under dictatorial rule, a charismatic modern Caesar capable of assuming the mythical character required for heroes of fascist narratives.[7]

The black and brown shirts of European fascism were met by America's own 'clothes line politics',[8] all declaring sympathy with European fascism and espousing the rights of the white Christian American *herrenvolk* to dominate their nation, too. The American right-wing 'haberdashery brigade' included William Dudley Pelley's Silver Shirts, George Christians' White Shirts, the Khaki Shirts, the Dress Shirts, and the Gray Shirts. They were joined by the Black Legion, the Order of '76, as well as Christo-fascist groups including Gerald Winrod's Defenders of the Christian Faith, and soon by Father Coughlin's Christian Front, whose members called themselves Brown Shirts. The Friends of the Hitler Movement, the official Nazi association in America, was established in 1933, eventually becoming the German-American Bund.

The American Fascisti Association and Order of Blackshirts, also often called just the Atlanta Black Shirts, was established in Atlanta in 1930 by a former Klan candidate for state governor. Although, like all American fascist organizations, the Atlanta Fascisti claimed to be anti-communist, in practice their purpose was to intimidate white employers out of hiring Black workers, and to replace them with white workers. The association claimed its purposes were 'white supremacy', 'charity', 'patriotism', and job assistance, *Time* magazine reported under the headline 'Blackshirts v. Blackmen',[9] but in fact it was 'simply and solely an "anti-negro" organization', with the stated purpose of 'putting negroes out of all jobs, and putting white men in them'.[10] In a month it claimed to have acquired over 21,000 members, although subsequent reports revealed these numbers were inflated. After it was hit with a grand jury investigation for breaking employment laws, the Atlanta Fascisti Association and Order of Blackshirts were enjoined from operating under that name, so they said they would rename themselves the Order of Patriots.[11]

The Atlanta Black Shirts did not last long, and most of the paranoid right-wing anti-Semitic groups that bloomed in America during the 1930s remained on the fringe. But Father Coughlin's virulently anti-Semitic radio broadcasts reached 22 per cent of the American public, making his audience the largest in the world at the time. Coughlin's Catholicism antagonized some stalwarts of the 'Old Christian Right', the protestant evangelicals like Gerald Winrod's Defenders of the Christian Faith and William Pelley's Silver Shirts, partly because of their anti-Catholicism. Sadly for their efforts at organizing, their conflicting hatreds kept neutralizing each other; but they all saw in Roosevelt's New Deal a 'Jewish–Communist plot' and 'the Hidden Hand of Zion'. Calling him 'Rosenfeld', in service to a cabal of 'international bankers' led by the Rothschilds, they said Roosevelt was leading America into the 'Jew Deal'. (A 'Jewish–Communist plot' was also accused of organizing the kidnapping and murder of the Lindbergh baby, and was, of course, also Hitler's pretext.) Within a decade of Ford's *International Jew* series, conspiratorial anti-Semitism had become commonplace in American elite right-wing circles.

The nation's most prominent Black critics and writers, including Du Bois, Langston Hughes, Joel Augustus Rogers, George S. Schuyler, and Kelly Miller publicly enumerated, in Miller's words, the 'striking analogy between the legal manifestations of race prejudice against the Negro in America and the Jew in Germany'.[12] These included not only racially motivated violence, but also denial of citizenship rights, residential and educational segregation, laws prohibiting intermarriage and free travel, and racially determined mass incarceration. In 1933 George Schuyler bluntly called the Nazis 'the German Ku Klux Klan'.[13]

By 1936, Joel Augustus Rogers was declaring: 'American

Fascism Already Has Negroes in Grip.' 'Not only is there Fascism in America now but Mussolini and Hitler copied it from us,' Rogers insisted. 'What else are Jim Crow laws but Fascist laws? Indeed Hitler's laws against the Jews are so much like American Jim Crow laws that it is difficult to believe that Hitler to save time did not copy them directly from the Southern statutes and from the unwritten laws of America against the Negroes.'[14] As historians would later show, that is precisely what Hitler did, although he did it in the interests of legitimacy, not expediency.

Langston Hughes agreed: 'America has its own brand of fascism,' he told audiences.[15] Fifteen million Black Americans, said Hughes, knew 'in actual practice the meaning of the word fascism... In America Negroes do not have to be told what fascism is in action. We know. Its theories of Nordic supremacy and economic suppression have long been realities to us. And now we view Fascism on a world scale,' including 'Hitler in Germany... with his tyranny over the Jews, and the sterilization of the Negro children in Cologne,' and 'Mussolini in Italy, with his banning of Negroes on the theatrical stages, and his expeditions of slaughter in Ethiopia'. At the same time Germans were offering advice on racial purification to the United States: one Nazi scholar suggested America solve its racial problems by abolishing racial equality, repealing the Fourteenth and Fifteenth Amendments, and expelling Black people from the nation.[16]

*

Gone with the Wind thus emerged into a debate about American fascism that had been building for fifteen years, and by 1936 was active and urgent. In 1935, Sinclair Lewis had published *It Can't Happen Here,* a satirical vision of an American fascism, 'of the profits, for the profits, by the profits', that took over the US government. His fictional dictator was widely assumed to have been based on Huey Long, the recently assassinated Louisiana governor whose strong-arm methods and corrupt consolidation of power led him frequently to be described as an American fascist, although his political platform also included the redistribution of wealth. But the name of Lewis's all-American dictator, Buzz Windrip, strongly suggests Gerald Winrod, whose anti-Semitism and fascistic views earned him the nickname the Jayhawk Nazi, and who ran for the Republican nomination in 1938. (Winrod's son, also Gerald, was arrested in 2001 for kidnapping his grandchildren with the express intention of indoctrinating them in his anti-Semitic evangelical faith; he refused to speak to the media after his arrest, saying it was controlled by the Jews.[17])

It Can't Happen Here was one of the most popular books of 1936, sharing the bestseller lists with *Gone with the Wind*. It was the same year the Black Legion, a paramilitary white supremacist group, made headlines after it was accused of murdering as many as fifty people, most of them African American; its resemblance to European fascism was widely remarked. Their leader vowed to seize Washington, DC in a coup he likened to the Russian Revolution, and espoused the extermination of American Jews by means of poison gas dispensers in synagogues on Yom Kippur. 'If Americans would like to know what fascism would be like in this country,' said a widely syndicated editorial just weeks before *Gone with the Wind* appeared, they need only look at the Black Legion, with its 'odor of Hitlerism', its 'anti-Catholic, anti-Jewish, anti-Negro, anti-labor platform, its whips, clubs and guns, its brazen defiance of law and order and the due processes of democracy... These are the attitudes and equipment of fascism.'[18]

There was similar widespread concern that the newly formed Liberty League was proto-fascist, preparing to join 'the brief and unlovely history of fascism' as 'the deus ex machina of the American fascism when and if it comes. Once it finds its man on a horse, its Hitler or Mussolini, it will change its name, merge with his colored shirts, or dissolve into an invisible regency.'[19] Within a few months, Langston Hughes was declaring: 'Fascism is what the Ku Klux Klan will be when it combines with the Liberty

League and starts using machine guns and airplanes instead of a few yards of rope.'[20]

The most famous fascist in America, Lawrence Dennis, published a much-discussed book called *The Coming American Fascism* in 1936, which was reviewed next to bestseller lists touting the success of *Gone with the Wind*.[21] 'America's number one fascist intellectual' in 1940 according to *Life* magazine, Dennis defined fascism as a 'revolutionary formula for the frustrated elite' that would catalyze the embittered desperation of the middle class during a period of capitalist crisis into a reactionary movement. 'An arrow-collar Mussolini' who 'believes that it can and should happen here',[22] Dennis met both Hitler and Mussolini, attended Nuremberg rallies, admired Hitler's qualities as a leader, and rejected the possibility of an international consensus defending bankrupt liberalism. Believing 'the Ku Klux Klan showed the possibilities' for fascists in America, Dennis identified Huey Long as 'the best example of our nearest approach to a national fascist leader' because he understood that 'in this country, the full force of powerful regional and sectional feelings can be exploited in the struggle for power'. America was ripe for fascism, Dennis argued, because 'no country boasts more militarized organizations'. A century later, that ripening continues to bear fruit.

There were rumours, as Walter Winchell reported at the time, 'that the author of Lindbergh's talks is Lawrence Dennis, who denies he is part Creole'.[23] That surprising final negation is crucial: Dennis, it turns out, was an African American passing as white, and many suspected it. In 1940, *Time* magazine described Dennis as the 'wooly-haired, swarthy' 'dabbler in "native fascist" politics'.[24] Even the Lindberghs, neither of whom can be called astute, noticed his 'bronzed' skin and wondered if his 'ancestors came from the Near East'.[25]

Dennis's fascism was clearly a defensive reaction against Jim Crow America; he often warned that America's racist structures were destroying liberal democracy from within. The apparently astonishing fact of America's foremost interwar fascist being an African American passing as white is, in the end, perfectly symptomatic of America's wilful denials of the realities of its racism. Being Black meant that Dennis frequently pointed out, as his biographer put it, that 'what was called democracy in the United States was a quite limited *herrenvolk* democracy'.[26] Fascism seemed inevitable to Dennis because he knew just how powerful white supremacist ethno-nationalism was, and how insubstantial the promise of American democracy was proving. He decided to ride what he called the 'wave of the future', seeing fascism as America's unfinished business.

But although worrying signs of an incipient American fascist movement abounded, many insisted on a categorical difference between innocent American prejudice and the more sinister European kind. In the summer of 1936, a *New York Times* editorial responded to criticism of American racial politics from the Berlin Olympics: 'In that city they have a cheerful habit, whenever American citizens criticize the peculiarities of Nazi race philosophy, of turning around asking how about the way Negroes are treated in the United States. The answer is simple,' it responded. Although Black Americans were the victims of discrimination and 'in not too many cases, let us hope, injustice and cruelties', few 'decent' Americans were 'proud about it'. Given that three years later the same paper would agree in its review of Stanley Horn's Klan history that Black Americans offered 'abundant provocation' for the 'remedy' of murder, its hope that Black people were the victims of cruelty 'in not too many cases' would seem misplaced.

Racial bigotry in America, the *Times* insisted, was just unthinking, in 'the good, old, thick-headed, prejudiced, irrational human fashion'.[27] Whether unthinking racism is preferable to thinking racism is probably immaterial to its victims, as if lynching would be less objectionable if it weren't defended on the grounds of rationality.

In any case that's precisely what the history of scientific racism in the United States did, espousing what George Schuyler called 'the biological superstitions' shared by the United States and Nazi Germany.[28] As far as the *New York Times* was concerned, racial injustice in America was an exception, the nation's innocence so unquestionable that even American racism was by definition morally superior to foreign racism. 'We do not reach into the laws of science and history and yank out an alibi for our hates and election requirements,' the *Times* insisted, adding that few 'literate Americans have made a philosophy of the thing'.[29]

The page before this editorial featured a large advertisement for *Gone with the Wind,* a thousand-page alibi for America's hates and election requirements, claiming that racial equality was against the laws of science and history and making a philosophy of the thing.

*

The shared logic of the 'master race' was even less clear to defensive Southerners, who rejected comparisons between American white supremacism and European fascism even more vehemently. Although many, including the Nazis, expected Southern political leaders to embrace fascism as a philosophy, few did, not least because it would have invalidated the myth of white benevolence and Black contentment. The Southern press consistently denounced Nazi racism as incompatible with American values.[30] They condemned Nazi racism – the *Atlanta Constitution* supported an American boycott of the 1936 Berlin Olympics, for example – while flatly denying the legitimacy of any comparison. A Nazi consul general in California tried to purchase the Klan, with the idea of plotting an American putsch. His price was too low – the Klan was nothing if not mercenary – but, as journalists remarked after the story came to light in 1939, the Klan could not afford to seem foreign; 'to be effective', its nativist agenda had to be pursued 'in the name of 100 Percent Americanism'.[31]

The white South's total control of their *herrenvolk* democracy meant they could deplore European fascism as a foreign dictatorship, while never being forced to question whether they would continue to support democratic processes if such processes overthrew their own power. Instead, they denounced Nazism as a self-evidently bigoted system that bore no resemblance to the cordial arrangement enjoyed by Black and white in the Jim Crow South.

The Klan, to be sure, bore an unfortunate resemblance to fascism, they acknowledged – but it was a regrettable exception to an otherwise peaceful coexistence. Fascism, they insisted, was a system as alien to the South as to the rest of America. An Alabama paper admitted that although the Klan had never gone as far as Nazism, 'its general outlook was quite similar to the one represented by Adolf Hitler', and suggested that Germany under the Nazis resembled 'what might have happened in the United States if the Ku Klux Klan, after increasing considerably in ferocity and irresponsibility, had actually gained control of the United States government', without admitting how many local and state governments the Klan had controlled until very recently, and not only in the Deep South.[32]

They made a similar distinction between the Nazi regime's persecution of Jews, which German law mandated, and the extra-legal practice of American lynching, protesting that it, like the Klan, was an exception. 'Decent white men in the South no more approve these lynchings than they do the official persecution of Jews in Germany,' declared a North Carolina editorial. However, 'in Germany the hoodlum attacks are incited by the State. In the South lynching is a crime against the State,' a shameless denial of the fact that such crimes were rarely charged, less often prosecuted, and regularly took place in front of courthouses and jails, with public officials often eager onlookers or participants. The editorial ended by insisting that German propaganda 'exaggerate[s] lynching here'.[33]

Just 'because we are unwilling for the negro masses to vote and have a part in governing us', a South Carolina paper argued, did not mean that white Southerners were 'as hostile to democracy as Hitler',[34] although it's not clear what the limits of their hostility to democracy were. Certainly this assertion belies Southern arguments that only Nazi Germany created legal systems that persecuted racial minorities. A Tennessee newspaper went further, insisting the racial politics of the South were meliorist and exemplary: 'Leaders of Negro thought in America realize that in the South an experiment in gradual solution of racial problems is being made on a scale which might well be a model for the World. There are hot-heads and bigots and lynchers, of course, but the progress of the Negro up from slavery is being solved, while in Germany, an alien race is being sold into a new slavery.'[35] Exceptionalism continued to work its magical thinking, to suggest that the 'hot-heads and bigots and lynchers' were the exception, not the rule, and that incrementalism was effectively solving America's racial crisis.

It was obvious that lynching gave the Nazis a devastating rebuttal against American criticism, one that the Germans did not hesitate to use, as we saw in the case of Rubin Stacy. By 1938, the Nazi journal *Völkischer Beobachter* was deflecting criticism of the murder of hundreds of Jews during Kristallnacht by pointing at the Jim Crow South, where Black Americans were 'free game'.[36] Meanwhile Father Coughlin was validating the Nazi pretext for Kristallnacht to his audience of tens of millions of Americans.

Within a few months America's most popular magazine, the *Saturday Evening Post*, published a cover story called 'Star-Spangled Fascists', noting that 'Nazi family features are too plain to be missed' in American fascist groups. They represented a 'revival of the Ku Klux Klan', with many leaders who were 'products of the Klan and readily admit their debt to it', including the man who had resurrected the Reconstruction-era Knights of the White Camellia by 1934. Insisting that the Klan deserved credit as the world's first fascist group, George Deatherage declared: 'Fascism is America's only solution.'

'Thanks to the Klan,' Deatherage added, 'America started toward Fascism long before Germany.' He also saw the affinity between Nuremberg race laws and American white supremacists: 'Nazi policy toward the Jews,' Deatherage maintained, 'is only a copy of the Klan's program for the Negroes,' while 'even the Nazi salute is a straight steal from the Klan'.[37]

His critics agreed: 'One gets the same flavor of skunk in the revelations about the Knights of the White Camellia and other American fascist organizations… The general pattern is that of slick schemers on the make, feathering their own nests by taking advantage of the credulity and prejudices of the angry and the ignorant – just the old Ku Klux racket over again, with various colored shirts instead of a bed-sheet.'[38]

*

It was impossible to miss the similarities between the two systems; far easier to shift the blame. 'Like the Nazis who have been so eager to disprove charges of war guilt, the articulate South has been engaged for a century in a long, shrill and persistent campaign to prove that the slavocracy bordered on Utopia,' wrote George Schuyler in a 1939 review of a new Dunning School history. Trying to prove 'that maintaining white supremacy is justified' was 'the burden of almost every tome written by a Southern white writer, whether it be "The Tragic Era" or "Gone with the Wind"'.[39] Defences of the Lost Cause, he added, perpetuated 'super-Goebbels propaganda', declaring 'the blame is on the North for whatever happened during the Civil War and afterward'.

The comparisons began to seem inevitable, as fascism irresistibly reminded Americans of the Civil War, and vice versa. When Roosevelt gave a speech in Georgia endorsing a liberal Democrat senator rather than the conservative incumbent, he sparked local outrage for interfering in local politics, leading to furious charges that he was behaving like Hitler (by endorsing a candidate they didn't like).[40] Supporters of the conservative senator filled the airwaves, Margaret Mitchell wrote to a friend, with 'so many yells of "state rights" and "Northern oppression"' that she 'wondered whether this was 1938 or 1861. I feel that if I look out the window I will see the Confederate troops, headed by General John B. Gordon, marching towards Washington.' But when she read the responses of 'Northern commentators of pinkish tinge', she found it astonishing that anyone could think

> that Appomattox settled beautifully and peacefully and justly all the problems, economic and social, for which the South was fighting. Their idea seems to be that might made right in 1865. Common sense should show that many of the problems that sent us to war have never been settled, and the same injustices persist – tariff, freight rates, et cetera. As far as I can see Appomattox didn't settle anything. We just got licked.[41]

The same injustices did persist, including the problem for which the South had in truth fought the war – the screaming injustice that Mitchell and her friends were so determinedly disregarding, while seeing themselves as its victims. Appomattox settled something – the question of slavery, which she persisted in viewing as a distraction from the central matter of white Southern entitlements.

In the summer of 1937, as the Nazis were opening Buchenwald and mounting their 'The Eternal Jew' propaganda exhibition, Margaret Mitchell was still vindicating the Reconstruction Klan in letters to her readers, never questioning its political justice. She assured a reader in Minnesota that the first Klan formed 'to protect women and children', and to stop Black people from committing voter fraud. 'But it was used to equally against the Carpetbaggers who had the same bad habit where voting was concerned,' she added. 'Members of the Klan knew that if unscrupulous or ignorant people were permitted to hold office in the South the lives and property of Southerners would not be safe.'[42] In other words, by claiming voter fraud, the Klan was justified in ignoring the democratic and legal process and the votes of Northerners (carpetbaggers) with whom it disagreed, and installing its own politicians to protect the property interests of white Southerners.

The Klan had Mitchell's permission to overturn the outcome of an election, and to use violence to impose its will. Arguing that the material interests of the *herrenvolk* override any pretext at democratic process, and that they are entitled to install their own leaders by fiat and force when they choose, is a straightforwardly fascist argument – and it is precisely the argument that was made by the insurrectionists and self-styled 'patriots' who stormed the US Capitol on 6 January 2021 expecting only Black people to be shot.

*

Gone with the Wind defends counter-revolution on behalf of a *herrenvolk*; its entire ethos endorses a eugenicist version of survival of the fittest, and all of its protagonists believe that granting power to the racial underclass creates a *Götterdämmerung* for the master race.

Margaret Mitchell did not sympathize with European fascism, but that isn't the point. She sympathized with the structures that upheld American fascist systems while denying their similarities to European fascism, comfortably inhabiting a double standard. Mitchell supported American politicians like Herman Talmadge, who publicly sympathized with Hitler (the summer that *Gone with the Wind* came out the *Atlanta Constitution* reported that Talmadge said he'd read *Mein Kampf* seven times[43]).

Talmadge's race-baiting was extreme, as he urged Georgia's white voters 'to restore the white primary' and exclude Black voters in 1946, or 'you will see Negro mayors, Negro school superintendents, Negro congressmen, Negro judges, and Negro sheriffs… Negro solicitors will try white people before Negro judges and white men and white women prisoners will be subject to the orders of Negro sheriffs and their Negro jailers.' Calling this a 'grave situation' and 'not a pretty picture', Talmadge warned: 'Our forefathers faced this same grave situation here in Georgia following the War Between the States… But our forefathers did not take it lying down!' This was an open call to lynching in 1946, urging white Georgians to revive the widespread racial violence of the Reconstruction South. The *Atlanta Journal* reported that Talmadge had received the support of the Klan, which had revived once again on Stone Mountain in 1946 – and Mitchell, who supposedly did not support the Klan, was supporting Talmadge.[44]

There are two important ways in which *Gone with the Wind* does resist fascism: its rejection of the sacredness of the cause, and its clear anti-war politics, whereas interwar fascism exalted violence as sanctifying the cause. *Gone with the Wind* doesn't glorify military violence in fascistic terms, but it both normalizes and justifies the violence of slavery and its aftermath. The denial of chattel slavery's violence is a predicate for claiming a legitimate role for it in government, which then de facto supports its intrinsic violence at every turn. That is a fascistic logic, as is the eternal fantasy that racist violence was nationally redemptive. The story rejects organized warfare, while still believing in the redemptive possibilities of violence. It embraces state-sponsored vindictiveness and scapegoating, and endorses power for the master race at whatever cost.

If *Gone with the Wind* is broadly fascistic in its outlook, the Lost Cause is even more so, in its glorification of the Confederate casus belli, its cults of its leaders and of its dead, its propaganda, its wars for territorial expansion and its insistence on the sacred rebirth of the nation in the ashes of Reconstruction, the new order founded on the ongoing defiance of the federalist government of the United States and a fundamental rejection of pluralist democracy.

American fascism was never exorcised, but merely obscured beneath romantic mythmaking that displaced a reckoning with vicious aspects of the nation's past. To conclude that American interwar fascist groups were always on the 'lunatic fringe', and could never have consolidated power, is to decide that what did not happen could not happen, replacing the contingency of history with the certainty of retrospection. It is to deny the possibility that they were just biding their time.

Insisting that European fascism was categorically distinct from American white supremacism turned American racism into another exception that has exempted America from the same historical reckonings as other countries and helped white supremacism flourish even as fascism was discredited domestically after the war: because American white supremacism was just good old-fashioned thick-headed American prejudice.

Gradually Americans became blinded by their faith in an achieved democracy to the realities of their own white supremacist structures and the persistence of their nation's fascist factions. *Gone with the Wind,* with its Depression-era themes but historical setting, offered white Americans sweeping disavowals, pretending that all this was in the past – that white supremacism, too, was gone with the wind, instead of going deep into the blood-covered soil of the nation.

37

A Fatal Parallel

'At the throat of black America, "Gone with the Wind" is poised like a dagger. And men in the highest places of the government are strangely silent. Is this to be the course of our boasted civilization in the years immediately ahead? This is Fascism.'[1] So wrote the *Chicago Defender* in its review of Selznick's film in January 1940, two months after 600 masked men in Klan regalia marched on the offices of the *Atlanta Constitution*, bearing signs that announced: 'The Klan is riding again.'[2]

Gone with the Wind premiered two weeks later at Loew's Grand Theatre, half a mile away. Even as the film was released, Black writers angrily observed, the Klan was coming back out of hiding. As 8,000 Klansmen gathered in Atlanta, the journalist Earl Morris warned, 'undoubtedly they have called for "Gone with the Wind".'[3] The film vindicated homegrown American fascism, the *New York Age* declared: 'The picture openly refers to the Negroes as "simple-minded darkies", resurrecting all the racial inferiority theories which science has discarded, and which Hitler and his fellow imperialistic have picked up against Jews and other minorities.'[4] 'Hollywood Goes Hitler One Better',[5] agreed the African American *Los Angeles Sentinel*. The film preached 'racial inferiority', while legitimizing 'Ku Klux Klan slanders against Negroes'.

African Americans widely protested against the film upon its release, as picketers marched with signs reading 'Gone with the Wind Incites Race Riots' and '"Gone with the Wind" slanders the poor whites of the south'.[6] In Illinois they distributed pamphlets saying the state of Lincoln 'should not be disgraced by having this apology for slavery shown anywhere within its borders'.[7] 'You'd be sweet too under a whip!' read another sign.[8]

The *Chicago Defender* lambasted the film as 'the voice of the lyncher coming from the screen',[9] the 'lies and slanders of the landlord slave owning, lynch inciting South are being sold on a country-wide scale'. It was 'pure propaganda, crude propaganda'. It 'glorified slavery' and 'martyred the southern plantation owner',[10] and was liable to 'create a mad lust for a lynch holiday'.

By the autumn of 1940 even Southern newspapers were acknowledging that 'the Klan itself represents native Fascism, complete with storm troopers, irresponsible vigilantism, racial and religious intolerance, xenophobia, and spurious patriotism', as it reported Klan meetings with the German-American Bund, the American interwar Nazi movement.[11]

*

As fears that the United States would be drawn into the war in Europe mounted, the film connected with American audiences torn, like Scarlett and Rhett, between the self-protection of isolationism and the heroism of joining a conflict to fight for one's values. The novel was sweeping the world in translation at the same time as the film: in France *Autant en emporte le vent* was 'on everyone's lap in 1939',[12] Norwegians had bought almost 50,000 copies by the same year,[13] and *A hverfanda hveli* was reportedly a bestseller in Reykjavik by 1941.[14]

It was equally popular as *Vom Winde verweht* in Nazi Germany, where some critics praised its depiction of 'patriarchal, well-defined relations between black and white' in the Old South.[15] They approved its characters' nativist desire 'to become a Volk', noting that 'a new spirit rejecting foreign immigration was leading the United States from mixed races to a national community (*Gemeinschaft*) – a biological entity worthy of approval by National Socialist Germany'.[16] Its Nazi detractors deplored the German public's enthusiastic embrace of decadent American *kitsch*, unworthy of a master race who should have been reading exalted German masterpieces, but agreed that its portrayal of slavery as a benign institution offered a 'useful corrective' for readers whose only knowledge of chattel slavery came from *Uncle Tom's Cabin*.[17] One aspiring German translator informed Margaret Mitchell that her novel did 'not contain any ideas which could displease the Hitler government'.[18]

In 1941, the book's publisher was reported to have said that 'when Hitler entered Paris he insisted upon seeing this film of "Gone with the Wind"', adding that the book had been a bestseller in Nazi Germany for five years, along with everywhere else in the world.[19] Although both novel and film were officially banned in Germany after 1941 for the story's endorsement of resistance in the 'occupied' South during Reconstruction, the Nazi elite continued to hold private showings, angering Goebbels, who felt it engendered sympathy with the enemy.[20]

Hitler reportedly screened it at least three times, telling Goebbels after watching it, 'Now that, that is something our own people should also be able to do,'[21] while several of his aides mentioned his enjoyment of the film. One source claimed that Hitler had said as he took power in 1933 that 'it was not the Southern States, but the American people themselves who were conquered' by the Civil War: 'The beginnings of a great new social order based on the principle of slavery and inequality were destroyed by that war, and with them the embryo of a future truly great America that would not have been ruled by a corrupt class of tradesmen, but by a real Herren-class [master class] that would have swept away all the falsities of liberty and equality.'[22]

The novel remained popular in occupied France, circulating underground after it was banned in 1940, as a tale of defiant resistance against a conquering force. Mitchell reported that she was also told it was popular in occupied Poland, where 'they used *Gone with the Wind* for "morale-building purposes".[23] In 1944, the American press reported that *Gone with the Wind* had become the most popular black-market book in occupied France: 'Passed from hand to hand until the covers were torn and the pages dogeared, sold "under the counter" for three and four times its original price, an American romantic novel of the Civil War was the most sought after book during the German occupation of France.' The book had become 'a symbol of freedom', the article added, without managing to remember that its story literally justified slavery.[24]

The film played uninterruptedly in Leicester Square for four years, 'Blitz or no blitz',[25] with audiences reportedly queuing seven days a week from the early hours of the morning while fires still burned from the bombs that fell the night before.[26] The novel made it to Franco's Spain after being published in Latin America, and the film was shown in Europe to exultant crowds after liberation, who found in it a parable for survival and endurance, but also for the persistence of a value system after a civilization was threatened. Mitchell noted in 1949, just before her death, that it had become even more popular after the war, because every country in Europe had experienced what it meant to be 'occupied by an enemy or besieged by an enemy'.[27]

At the end of 1944, she told a correspondent, with some pride, that *Gone with the Wind* had been banned in Germany and occupied countries, but that the Nazis had acquired a print of the film, 'where it had a private showing before a group of five – Hitler and his four closest boy friends. I've wondered since what they thought of it. They did not think a story or a movie which had to do with a conquered people who became free again would be a good thing to show in Germany or occupied countries.'[28]

Mitchell did not, presumably, learn how much they enjoyed the politics of her story.

No one seems to have noticed during the noise and chaos of war that *Gone with the Wind* is on the side of the fascists. In early 1941, before the United States joined the war, the film critic for the *New York Times*, Bosley Crowther, published a reassessment of *Gone with the Wind*. Extolling the film as a 'glowing and pertinent', 'tortured and realistic account', Crowther could clearly see in its story a 'fatal parallel' with war-ravaged Europe: 'Today we are grimly aware of the horrible realities of destruction... The Civil War was an "inevitable conflict", just as the present war between the democracies and the Fascists was also inevitable. The consequences of the latter may some day prove as shattering.' Watching 'the tragic collapse of a civilization in "Gone with the Wind"', he added, left him reflecting 'ruefully upon the monstrous waste and degradation of warfare'.[29]

If the inevitable conflict between North and South over slavery mirrored the inevitable conflict between democracy and fascism, then the South was against democracy, unless the *New York Times* in 1941 was putting Lincoln on the side of fascism. *Gone with the Wind* casts the white South as the oppressed, when they were just oppressors enraged at their loss of total power. But white Americans, whether from the North or South, simply couldn't let themselves draw this obvious conclusion. Crowther had to ignore the implications of his own analogy or be left admitting that *Gone with the Wind* is, by his own logic, comparable to a story that glorifies the 'tragic collapse of a civilization' fanatically devoted to Nazism.

The *Richmond Times-Dispatch* said the same thing a few months later. In reporting that *Gone with the Wind* had broken all box office records, it praised the film for 'a definite relation between historical fact and presentation', before commenting: 'England today fights the same fight but, God willing, there will be no "Lost Cause" there. It is small wonder the South remembers. To an England weary and war-ridden there must be much in *Gone with the Wind* that is heartening.'[30] In fighting off Nazi Germany, England did not fight the same fight as the Southerners in *Gone with the Wind* – but a moral equivalency between anti-fascism and pro-fascism is the endgame of Lost Cause mythmaking.

It's a consummate moment in the wilful blindness of American popular memory, as the national press looks straight at the moral inversion of its myth of white victimhood, and still refuses to see it. *Gone with the Wind* had turned the nation's political values as topsy-turvy as its history.

38

Thought Experiments

I n the summer of 1934, a widely syndicated feature explained to Americans how Nazism had taken power in Germany by means of an analogy to the Klan. Headlined 'Had Ku Klux Klan Won Rule of Country, It Might Have Been "American Nazism"',[1] the thought experiment asked readers to imagine that the Klan had not collapsed into financial and sexual scandals in the late 1920s, and that the United States had confronted the same postwar crises as Germany: a crashing economy and prolonged depression, with an embittered, unemployed populace who had more than a decade to search for a scapegoat. The Klan would gain popularity as it expressed more of the electorate's rage, and before long could abandon its secrecy to become a political party, electing representatives 'on its platform of "America for the Americans; down with the Jews and Catholics"', and advocating 'Buy American.'[2]

As Klan rallies become larger and more vociferous, the police begin to defer out of fear, or join its forces, cooperating with their marches by shutting down public opposition. Money starts to flow in from members, media owners, and wealthy far-right sympathizers. Street fights with the left regularly break out, keeping Klan members energized and making them feel heroically militant. The Klan's demagogic leader, supported by this 'private army', begins pressuring the president. The Klan gains a political majority in Congress, and faces only a formless coalition of its opponents, who are constantly deadlocked from internal conflicting agendas. These deadlocks make Congress dysfunctional, unable to legislate for an increasingly tense and impatient country. The president puts Klan leaders in the Cabinet as a concession, and fears calling out the regular army against armed Klansmen roaming the streets at will. With the president and Congress paralyzed, the Klan leader shifts his private army into regular troops on the government payroll. The forces of conservatism, 'while not wholly approving, was close enough in sympathy to agree to co-operate rather than fight'. That was how Nazism took over Germany, the article concluded, and it is how American fascism, if circumstances had been slightly altered in the 1930s, could have taken over the US government.

Or it might be how an American president attempted to consolidate his power almost a century later.

*

Here's another thought experiment. Imagine a *Gone with the Wind* in which Scarlett's journey was not toward restoring white oligarchy, in which the object of her quest was not learning which patriarchal slavocrat she should desire. Imagine a *Gone with the Wind* that began with a slaveholding white woman, followed her shattering passage through Civil War and Reconstruction, and ended with her coming to apprehend the injustice of slavery. Imagine a Scarlett O'Hara who went on a moral journey like Huck Finn's.

There were white women who went on that journey, or similar ones. The screaming white girl in the photo of Little Rock in 1957 was named Hazel Bryan, and she grew up to be deeply ashamed of her behaviour that day. Having become a symbol of bigotry who shouted 'go back to Africa' at a Black girl, Bryan tried to redeem herself. She later apologized to Elizabeth Eckford and educated herself about civil rights. Many years later, the photographer who had taken the now-iconic image effected a reunion, and Bryan and Eckford reportedly struck up a friendship for a while, although it was, unsurprisingly, a conflicted one, and didn't last.[3]

Margaret Mitchell was honest enough to recognize that no truly happy endings were possible in the American romance. But she didn't begin to understand why.

*

In the summer of 2021, a right-wing think tank published a podcast in which influential conservatives put forward their own thought experiment, arguing for the necessity of an 'American Caesar' to seize power, a hypothetical figure to whom they soon gave the less than hypothetical name Trump. They discussed strategies such as declaring a national emergency in the inaugural address, communicating directly with supporters using a 'Trump app', and encouraging them to mobilize once more at the nation's Capitol – this time, using social media to communicate directly with all 75 million Trump voters, and not just with the thousands who appeared at the 'Stop the Steal' rally on 6 January. They would create a paramilitary force enabling the Caesar-Trump to establish a dictatorship.

This is precisely what the White League attempted in the Battle of Liberty Place. And it is what Mitchell herself rationalized in her discussion of the first Klan, when she declared that they had the right to control politics because 'if unscrupulous or ignorant people were permitted to hold office in the South the lives and property of Southerners would not be safe.'[4] The Proud Boys and Oath Keepers who led the 2021 insurrection made exactly the same argument and offered exactly the same defence. They were the inheritors of Pelley's Silver Shirts and Father Coughlin's Brown Shirts, of the Khaki Shirts who recruited Mussolini supporters, while their wealthy funders were not far different from J. P. Morgan, Jr, who secured a loan of $100 million to the Mussolini government.

A retired Marine Corps major general named Smedley Darlington Butler testified before Congress that he had been approached in 1933 by a group of the nation's plutocrats and financiers to lead a coup against Franklin Roosevelt, a plan backed by the American Liberty League. Butler said that he was asked to mobilize an army of disgruntled veterans to march on Washington and install a military fascist dictatorship, and reported the 'Wall Street Putsch' to J. Edgar Hoover.

When the story came out in 1934, Butler was widely accused of being a fantasist and conspiracist, and historians later followed suit in suggesting that the 'Business Plot', as it was also called, was mere bloviating, empty threats that were foolish to take seriously.[5] They said the same thing about all the other fascist groups, which never gained electoral legitimacy but were prosecuted by the Roosevelt administration for sedition, a decision historians long dismissed as a hysterical 'Brown Scare'. Many said the same thing about Trump, too – until the events of 6 January 2021. Historian Robert O. Paxton, for example, America's pre-eminent expert on fascism, had long resisted calling Trump a fascist, but wrote in the wake of the insurrection that he had changed his mind.[6] Members of the Trump administration agreed: 'Senior Trump Official: We Were Wrong, He's a "Fascist"', as a *New York Magazine* headline succinctly put it.[7]

After Trump left office (with great unwillingness, by force of law) in January 2021, members of his former administration began speaking publicly about things he had said that troubled them at the time. John Kelly, Trump's former White House chief of staff, was reported by several journalists to have said that Trump told him Hitler 'did a lot of good things'. Trump denied it; Kelly did not. During the Black Lives Matter protests in the summer of 2020, Trump reportedly told his generals to 'beat the fuck' out of protestors, to 'crack their skulls', and to declare that whoever revealed that he had hidden in a bunker during part of the protests should be 'charged with treason' and 'executed'.

When Trump hatched a plot with his final chief of staff, Mark Meadows, to fire the acting attorney general in order to overturn the election results, he further stoked concerns that he was willing to stage a coup. Mark Milley, one of Trump's former joint chiefs of staff, was quoted as saying the military would not support him in a coup attempt – a statement never before required in over two centuries of the peaceful transfer of US power – and that he feared the insurrection on 6 January 2021 would be Trump's Reichstag moment. As the congressional investigation into the insurrection revealed, Trump spoke to many people about overturning the election. His lawyers had drawn up a plan for a coup. Senator Mo Brooks of Alabama issued a statement in the spring of 2022 declaring: 'President Trump asked me to rescind the 2020 elections, immediately remove Joe Biden from the White House, immediately put President Trump back in the White House, and hold a new special election for the presidency.'[8] Trump had done everything he could think of to seize the laurel crown and declare himself an American Caesar.

As one commentator writing about the Trump-Caesar thought experiment noted, it indicated that in conservative circles the Overton window determining the acceptable sphere of public discourse had 'shifted far beyond the boundaries of democratic self-government to a place broadly coterminous with fascism'.[9]

American history has many instances of movements that were broadly coterminous with fascism in just this way. By insisting they were not really fascist but merely bore something of a resemblance in a more American way to something that might elsewhere or at another time be called fascism, American culture allowed them to spread from local government to federal, to be absorbed into official state militias, police, and the National Guard, to shape the media culture, electorate, and national leaders.

American fascism has always been broadly coterminous with fascism, but American exceptionalism continues to keep us from seeing it.

*

A final thought experiment. If civil war comes again to the United States, if it hasn't already, it will not mean mustered armies squaring off against each other in the blood-soaked fields of the republic, any more than it will mean cavalry charges or cannonades. That's not how wars are fought in the twenty-first century.

It will be another information war, with street skirmishes between armed militias, outbreaks of vigilante violence, and spontaneous mob violence. We know this because we are already seeing it. The Capitol was literally stormed by people enraged at losing an election, but after 160 years of denialism, pretending that wasn't the beginning – or continuation – of a Civil War was easy. The mythmaking had already done the work, and a majority of Americans were ready to believe it.

If violence breaks out around the elections of 2022 and 2024, as seems all too likely, it will look like the conflicts around the elections of 1872 and 1876, with local outbreaks of mob violence using the weapons that are available. In the nineteenth century, that meant muskets and swords retrieved from the battlefields. Today, thanks to half a century of corrupt lobbying by the NRA, military-grade automatic weapons across the country are easier to buy than some cold medicines, and much of America's population is armed to the hilt.

The battles will look different, but the conflict will be the same: those fighting to keep power limited to people like them, and those fighting to share power across a plural democracy. The politics of racial terror will continue to shape the fight.

The process was outlined in the 1934 thought experiment about American Nazism. The armed militias, the political pressure, the economic power, the complacency, the appeasement: all of this was predicted a century ago. But we disregarded it and read historical mythology that flattered us – because disregarding it was the point. An achieved American democracy comes to seem mere wishful thinking, tilting the poignancy of democratic faith toward pathos: a *Götterdämmerung* for the American demigods.

39

A Growing Wrath

E ight months before the film of *Gone with the Wind* premiered in Atlanta, John Steinbeck published *The Grapes of Wrath,* which would become the most popular novel of 1939. Widely hailed as a testament to human endurance, the novel took its title from 'The Battle Hymn of the Republic', Julia Ward Howe's mighty 1862 Civil War anthem.

> Mine eyes have seen the glory of the coming of the Lord:
> He is trampling out the vintage where the grapes of wrath
>   are stored;
> He hath loosed the fateful lightning of his terrible swift
>   sword:
> His truth is marching on.

The song was an abolitionist call to arms, urging its listeners: 'let us die to make men free'. Howe's Bible-steeped language comes from the Book of Revelation, invoking divine justice, when God's truth will force the wine of freedom from the grapes of wrath. It is an image of anger accumulated, even cultivated, over the long march of time.

The Grapes of Wrath appeared the same year as Selznick's film and serves as a kind of rebuke to *Gone with the Wind,* denouncing exploitative capitalism and sympathizing with its (actual) victims. Ironically, however, American audiences distilled exactly the same message from both stories. Although Steinbeck's novel is profoundly critical of American capitalism, it was transformed by popular memory into an inspiring chapter in our national mythology, 'an iconic tale of "noble" individuals who face poverty in the American way with hard work and determination'.[1]

Rushing to capitalize on the novel's success, Hollywood released a film version of *The Grapes of Wrath* in March 1940, while Selznick's *Gone with the Wind* was still triumphantly sweeping across America. The studio's advertising campaign sold it as a story about a woman holding her family together in the face of adversity. Whittaker Chambers praised the film version for removing 'the novel's phony conclusions' about greedy capitalism, turning it into a 'saga of an authentic U.S. farming family who lose their land. They wander, they suffer, but they endure. They are never quite defeated, and their survival is itself a triumph.'[2] *Gone with the Wind* drew much phonier conclusions about farming families who lose their land, wander, suffer, and endure – but almost all of them were overlooked.

In his novel, Steinbeck reworked Howe's famous image of the growing rage of judgement to describe the poor farmers betrayed by big business and corporate agriculture, left to choke in the Dust Bowl. Precarious lives collapsed into poverty, their farms foreclosed and the nation's promises forsaken: 'In the eyes of the people there is a failure; and in the eyes of the hungry there is a growing wrath. In the souls of the people the grapes of wrath are filling and growing heavy, growing heavy for the vintage.' The grievances caused by inequality and injustice were mounting, stoking a 'hopeless anger [that] began to smolder' and would, Steinbeck predicted, burst forth into violence, even revolution – a wrath to come.

A month after *The Grapes of Wrath* appeared, Nathanael West, who had already seen that violence in America was idiomatic, published *The Day of the Locust*. It made a similar prediction in telling a story of dispossessed characters orbiting around Hollywood while fantasizing about violence and fame and power. A Hollywood set designer who aspires to be a great artist toils away at a painting he calls *The Burning of Los Angeles,* a modern-day bonfire of the vanities, in which 'the people who come to California to die', lured by false promises and real delusions, turn into a 'crusading mob', carrying baseball bats and torches. Hollywood is filled with 'savage and bitter' people who

> realize they've been tricked and burn with resentment. Every day of their lives they read the newspapers and went to the movies. Both fed them on lynchings, murder, sex crimes, explosions, wrecks, love nests, fires, miracles, revolutions, war ... Nothing can ever be violent enough to make taut their slack minds and bodies. They have been cheated and betrayed. They have slaved and saved for nothing.[3]

And so they await the spectacular violence that will vindicate their grievances with a drama of vengeance. West's original title for his novel was *The Cheated*, a brief, terrible story of Americans whose resentment at broken promises burns as brightly as the torches they are lighting.

'All those poor devils who can only be stirred by the promise of miracles and then only to violence' came together, 'marching behind [a] banner in the great unified front', an assemblage of crackpots and cranks determined 'to purify the land. No longer bored, they sang and danced joyously in the red light of the flames.' Only one conclusion to the story of modern America was possible: 'There would be civil war.'

*

In the months after the insurrection, American cultural discourse consolidated around Trump's big lie about the election, linking his propaganda efforts to Hitler and Goebbels's famous 'big lie' that Germany had been betrayed by an internal enemy, the Jews. During the opening of the investigation into the insurrection, which began in late July 2021, there was a clear effort to implicate Trump's project in fascism, a term that (Jewish) Congressman Jamie Raskin put into the record twice in his statements on the first day. 'Those who attacked you and beat you are fascist traitors to our country,' he told Capitol Officer Hodges, 'and will be remembered forever as fascist traitors.'[4] Asked by another Democrat member of Congress what he was fighting for that day, Officer Hodges responded: 'Democracy.'

At the same time Trump's disinformation campaign was likened to the Lost Cause by some of America's most eminent historians of the Civil War and Reconstruction, including Eric Foner, David Blight, and Karen L. Cox, who wrote within days of the insurrection making the comparison. By the summer of 2021, most major American outlets had run a piece on Trump and the Lost Cause: the *New York Times, Washington Post, The Atlantic, Rolling Stone, Slate, Salon, Politico,* and on and on.

The media oscillated between making fascist and Lost Cause analogies because neither seemed quite sufficient on its own to describe Trump's aggressive lies and disinformation – and because they are far more similar than we have been accustomed to think.

Just before the insurrection, Tucker Carlson warned Fox News viewers that Democrats were trying to foist a 'new version of Reconstruction' onto Americans, resurrecting the myth of carpetbag misrule.[5] Within weeks right-wing apologist Dinesh D'Souza was calling the Capitol sacking itself 'a big lie', denying that 'there were these seditious Trump supporters trying to overthrow the constitution mounting an al-Qaeda-style attack'.

These inversions continue to flip the script, insisting that the truth is the 'big lie', and that reality can be whatever they want it to be. The insurrection, they now say, was defending 'election integrity' and the 'purity of the ballot box'. But in the same way

Gone with the Wind's notions of justice are simply incompatible with Black governance, so does Trumpism maintain that election integrity can only elect Trump, because there is no other legitimate outcome. Hence the ultimate projection, 'Stop the Steal', as the name given to the violent effort to steal the election from Biden. 'We were just there to overthrow the government,'[6] as the Trump insurrectionist said in her own defence.

On 2 March 2022, Oath Keeper Joshua James pleaded guilty to seditious conspiracy, admitting that he and his fellow militia members stormed the Capitol with the express purpose of overturning the 2020 election results. Charged with intending 'to oppose by force the lawful transfer of presidential power', James agreed in court that he was 'trying to influence the conduct of the United States government or retaliate against the United States government'.

After the insurrection, in discussing whether to take further action, James had told another Oath Keeper: 'If nothing happens... its war... Civil War 2.0.'[7]

*

What defined fascist propaganda was never its lies, wrote Hannah Arendt in 1945, for all propaganda is based on lies. What distinguishes fascist lies is that they are intended to negate reality, making 'that "true" which until then could only be stated as a lie'. Fascists don't lie to deceive; they lie to change reality.

The lies about the Lost Cause did just that, using fiction to displace a reality until the fiction had become a reality. Soon that fiction spread beyond the cult of true believers, normalizing itself in the body politic for the best part of a century, a cancer legitimating unreason that metastasized long ago. Mythology replaced history as the arbiter of American truth.

The lie is not only the Hitlerian big lie of propaganda, but a culture of pervasive lying, what Arendt called 'lying as a way of life' and 'lying on principle'. It is a systematic dishonesty that destroys the collective space of historical-factual reality. That dishonesty was necessary to enable the country to pretend to be a liberal democracy while systematically disfranchising large swathes of its population. Wishful thinking replaced political thought, as lying became so normalized that even people who wanted to know the truth were hard-pressed to discover it.

In his first inaugural address in 1861, a month before America plunged into war, Lincoln explained the problem of minority rule: 'A majority held in restraint by constitutional checks and limitations, and always changing easily with deliberate changes of popular opinions and sentiments, is the only true sovereign of a free people. Whoever rejects it does of necessity fly to anarchy or to despotism. Unanimity is impossible. The rule of a minority, as a permanent arrangement, is wholly inadmissible; so that, rejecting the majority principle, anarchy or despotism in some form is all that is left.'

The minority then was the slaveholding Confederate states, trying to impose their viewpoint on the American majority who opposed the spread of slavery. Now much of white governance across the country is equally prepared to entrench itself as minority rule. Republicans no longer oppose Democrats politically: they are opposing them existentially, as an enemy within. This, too, is part of the Lost Cause, the absolute rejection of the opposing viewpoint, and it is consistent with fascism.

It has often been said that America had to imagine itself into existence; less often remarked is the corollary, that America is, in a very real sense, merely a story the nation tells itself. That makes the US singularly subject to the meanings of stories and myths – all nations tell stories about themselves, but America has little to hold it together beyond those stories (which is one of the reasons it fetishizes its founding documents). If *Gone with the Wind* is one of the most popular stories America has ever told about itself, then it matters that it is profoundly antidemocratic, and a moral horror-show.

Gone with the Wind ends on resistance and delusion, not reunion and forgiveness. Scarlett thinks she can reshape reality, until reality in the shape of a weary, angry Rhett Butler walks away. Those who think that the wrath is coming believe reality will win the war against fantasy in the end. But like all delayed reckonings, the cost will mount.

In the Bible, the wrath to come is specifically what Jesus saves us from – the hellfire of judgement. When Baldwin warned that he could see the shape of the wrath to come spinning above the thoughtless American head, he did not mention it might end in redemption, presumably for a reason. Judgement has been markedly absent from the stories we tell about ourselves.

The truth is marching on, I learned to sing as a child. Judgement may bring damnation or salvation – but it requires revelation, that we see the truths from which we have been blinded too long. If not, our defeat will stop being but apparent, and we won't be able to disregard it.

Until then, it appears we will keep moving on. Just move on: the American creed. Light out for the territory, head for the frontier, sail after the white whale, reach for the green light, escape your past, hit the road, Jack, don't think about it now, think about it tomorrow. Forget slavery, forget injustice, keep chasing the American Dream. Just move on, keep on movin' on, and maybe you can outrun the wrath to come.

London, 2022

Acknowledgements

This is not the book I thought I was going to write when I began thinking about it in 2018. I had just finished a book about the history of the expressions 'America First' and 'the American Dream', drawing on my work as a cultural historian of the 1920s and 1930s, which included coming to grips with the histories of American conservatism, nativism, and fascism that threaded through the period. As I finished *Behold, America* I envisioned a short book that used *Gone with the Wind* to explain the controversies around the Confederate statues that were coming down across America (and their counterparts in many other postcolonial societies). But it was not, in the end, possible to write a short book about what *Gone with the Wind* has to teach us about the American political situation today, not least because that situation – for all its fluidity – continues to cleave ever closer to *Gone with the Wind* as it unfolds. And so my short book grew into what is now my longest.

I incurred a great many debts during that expansion, which happened primarily during the two years of global pandemic and lockdown. For discussions, both formal and informal, debates, conferences, symposia, and shared readings that deepened my thinking around this topic I would like to thank (in alphabetical order) Sanders Isaac Bernstein, Kristin L. Canfield, Quassim

Cassam, Philip Davies, Federico Finchelstein, Bradley Hart, Rafael Hernandez, Chet Lisiecki, Volker Langbehn, Michael Lynch, Amanda Minervini, Peter Pomerantsev, Marc Redfield, David Runciman, Barry Smith, Jason Stanley, Richard Steigmann-Gall, Matthew Stratton, Helen Thompson, Lynne Tirrell, Kay Wells, Asa Wikforss.

I am fortunate to be upheld by a circle of exceptional women writers and thinkers; for their moral, professional and intellectual support, especially during the dark days of lockdown, my thanks to Helen Carr, Hannah Dawson, Lindsey Fitzharris, Kate Kirkpatrick, Suzannah Lipscomb, Joanne Paul, Hallie Rubenhold, Naomi Steinberg, Alex von Tunzelmann and Kate Williams.

In 2019 and 2020, I published a series of essays that began shaping this research and thinking in the *New York Review of Books*, the *New Statesman*, *Prospect*, the *Guardian*, and the *Times Literary Supplement*, portions of which are reprinted here. My thanks to the editors, including Tom Clark, Prudence Crowther, Tom Gatti, and Matt Seaton for their assistance, and thanks to Matt for his work on one essay in particular that sharpened not only my writing but also my thinking around the topic.

The Eccles Centre for American Studies at the British Library has been supporting my published and unpublished work since 2015, for which I am extremely grateful, especially to Catherine Eccles for her generous adaptability and faith in the creative process. Thanks to my agent, Zoe Waldie, for her help navigating the unusual voyage this project has taken, and to the team at Head of Zeus for their flexibility and support throughout its evolution, especially to Georgina Blackwell, who has been steadying, encouraging, and frankly tolerant, in addition to her editorial skills, and to the design team for a cover we all think is exceptional.

Thanks to Sadaf Betts, Tim Galsworthy, and Nick Greenwood for research assistance and help with fact-checking and citations, and to Nanci Young, archivist at Smith College, for research assistance. I owe debts of gratitude to Helen Brocklebank, Michell Chresfield, Mike Churchwell, Erin Glade, Bonnie Greer, Rachael Kerr, and Keri Leigh Merritt for reading drafts and for greatly improving them along the way. Heartfelt thanks to Lindsey Fitzharris and Suzannah Lipscomb not only for reading drafts but for stepping into various breaches, for incisive editorial and intellectual advice, and for their friendship.

I embarked on writing this book at the same time my friend Lyndsey Stonebridge began writing a (superb) book about Hannah Arendt, and we ended up on an extraordinary creative and intellectual journey together. It is not hyperbole to say I don't think I could have done this without her friendship, and I certainly wouldn't have wanted to try.

But most of all thanks to Wyndham, who makes everything better.

Bibliography

'Best-Sellers: "Gone with the Wind" Passes Million Mark in Six Months', *Literary Digest* 122 (26 Dec 1936).

'Blackshirts v. Blackmen', *Time* (8 September 1930).

'Blizzard of Black Sweeps Over Kansas', *Charleston Daily Mail*, WV, 17 April 1936.

'Condition of Affairs in the Southern States', Reports of Committees: 30th Congress, first Session; 48th Congress, second Session, Klan Report, Georgia, vol. 1 (1871).

'Confederate States of America: Georgia Secession', Lilian Goldman Law Library, Yale Law School (29 January 1861).

'Florida Board of Education Passes Rule Banning Critical Race Theory in Classrooms', NBC News (10 June 2021).

Letter from Thomas Jefferson to John Wayles Eppes, 30 June 1820.

'Miss Mitchell, 49, Dead of Injuries', *New York Times* (17 August 1949).

'Mutilation is Laid to Klansmen: Five Suspects in Cargell Case After Year's Investigation of Florida Terrorism', *Hartford Courant* (Hartford, CT) (10 April 1936).

'Scarlett O'Hara, So Help Us, Will be Named This Week', *Pittsburgh Post-Gazette* (10 January 1939).

'State of the Union Interview with Presidential Candidate Donald Trump', CNN (28 February 2016).

'Stepping Inside the Fox Hole: The Media Echo-Chamber of Fox News', Navigator Research (21 March 2019).

'Texan Republican Cancel Culture Targets the Teachings of the Rev. Martin Luther King Jr.', *The Nation* (21 July 2021).

'The Women Facing Charges for January 6, 2021', Anti-Defamation League (6 April 2021).

'Trump Calls Critical Race Theory "un-American". Let's Review', *Washington Post* (2 October 2020).

'Trump Downplays Insurrection but Tells Supporters to "Go Home"', NPR (6 January 2021).

'Whose Heritage? Public Symbols of the Confederacy', Southern Poverty Law Center (1 February 2019).

Adams, Amanda. 'Painfully Southern: *Gone with the Wind*, the Agrarians, and the Battle for the New South', *Southern Literary Journal*, vol. 40, no. 1 (2007), pp. 58–75.

Adkins, Katherine Christina. 'Slavery and the Civil War in Cultural

Memory,' Harvard University PhD Dissertation (2014).

Allen, Frederick Lewis. *Only Yesterday: An Informal History of the 1920s*, classics edition (New York: Open Media Publishing, 2011).

Allen, Patrick (ed.), *Margaret Mitchell, Reporter: Journalism by the Author of Gone with the Wind* (Charleston: University of South Carolina Press, 2000).

Allerfeldt, Kristofer. 'The KKK is in Rapid Decline – But Its Symbols Remain Worryingly Potent', *The Conversation* (1 March 2019).

Ang, Desmond. 'The Birth of a Nation: Media and Racial Hate', *American Economic Review*, working paper under revision.

Antolini, Katherine Lane. 'Scarlett O'Hara as Confederate Woman', *West Virginia University Philological Papers*, vol. 51 (2004), pp. 23–35.

Apel, Dora. *Imagery of Lynching: Black Men, White Women, and the Mob* (New Brunswick: Rutgers University Press, 2004).

Aptheker, Herbert. 'American Negro Slave Revolts', *Science and Society*, vol. 1, no. 4 (1937), pp. 512–538.

Aptheker, Herbert. *American Negro Slave Revolts* (New York: Columbia University Press, 1943).

Arendt, Hannah. 'Thinking and Moral Considerations: A Lecture', *Social Research*, vol. 38, no. 3 (1971), pp. 417–446.

Atchison, R. Jarrod. *A War of Words: The Rhetorical Leadership of Jefferson Davis* (Tuscaloosa, AL: University of Alabama Press, 2017).

Baldwin, James. 'The Dangerous Road Before Martin Luther King', *Harper's Magazine* (February 1961).

Baldwin, James. *No Name in the Street* (London: Michael Joseph, 1972).

Baldwin, James. *Notes of a Native Son*, second edition (Boston: Beacon Press, 1984).

Baldwin, James. 'Notes for a Hypothetical Novel' in James Baldwin (ed.), *The Price of the Ticket: Collected Nonfiction, 1948–1985* (London: Michael Joseph, 1985).

Baldwin, James. 'The White Man's Guilt' in Toni Morrison (ed.), *James Baldwin: Collected Essays* (New York: Literary Classics of the United States Inc., 1998), pp. 722–727.

Barker, Deborah E. and Kathryn McKee (eds). *American Cinema and the Southern Imaginary* (Athens: University of Georgia Press, 2011).

Barnes, Rhae Lynn. 'Yes, Politicians Wore Blackface. It Used to be All-American "Fun": Minstrel Shows Were Once So Mainstream That Even Presidents Watched Them', *Washington Post* (8 February 2019).

Barnett, Ida B. Wells. 'Lynching and the Excuse for It', *The Independent*, vol. 53 (1901), pp. 1133–1136.

Bean, Annamarie, James V. Hatch, and Brooks McNamara. *Inside the Minstrel Mask: Readings in Nineteenth-Century Blackface Minstrelsy* (Middletown: Wesleyan University Press, 1996).

Beck, Earl R. 'German Views of Negro Life in the United States, 1919–1933', *The Journal of Negro History*, vol. 48, no. 1 (January 1963), pp. 22–32.

Beckert, Sven. *Empire of Cotton: A Global History*. (New York: Knopf, 2014).

Beckert, Sven and Seth Rockman, (eds). *Slavery's Capitalism: A New History of American Economic Development*. (Philadelphia: University of Pennsylvania Press, 2016).

Beckett, Lois and Vivian Ho. '"She Was Deep into It": Ashli Babbitt,

Killed in Capitol Riot, Was Devoted Conspiracy Theorist', *Guardian* (9 January 2021).

Behlmer, Rudy (ed.). *Memo From David O. Selznick: The Creation of Gone with the Wind and Other Motion Picture Classics, As Revealed in the Producer's Private Letters, Telegrams, Memorandums, and Autobiographical Remarks* (New York: Viking, 1972).

Benbow, Mark E. 'Birth of a Quotation: Woodrow Wilson and "Like Writing History with Lightning"', *The Journal of the Gilded Age and Progressive Era*, vol. 9, no. 4 (October 2010), pp. 509–533.

Berg, Manfred. *Popular Justice: A History of Lynching in America* (Lanham: Rowman and Littlefield Publishers, 2015).

Bethea, Charles. 'Georgia Betrays Its Voters Again', *The New Yorker* (9 June 2020).

Bevilacqua, Kathryne. 'History Lessons from *Gone with the Wind*', *The Mississippi Quarterly*, vol. 67, no. 1 (2014), pp. 99–126.

Blackmon, Douglas A. *Slavery by Another Name: The Re-enslavement of Black People in America from the Civil War to World War II* (New York: Doubleday, 2008).

Blackwell, Henry B. 'What the South Can Do: How the Southern States Can Make Themselves Masters of the Situation', in Elizabeth Cady Stanton, *et al.* (eds), *History of Woman Suffrage*, vol. 2 (Rochester: Charles Mann, 1887), pp. 929–930.

Blakemore, Erin. 'The Story Behind the Famous Little Rock Nine "Scream Image"', History.com (1 September 2017).

Blight, David W. *Race and Reunion: The Civil War in American Memory* (Cambridge: Harvard University Press, 2001).

Bonekemper, Edward H., III. *The Myth of the Lost Cause: Why the South Fought the Civil War* (Washington, DC: Regnery History, 2015).

Boothe, Clare. 'Introduction to *Kiss the Boys Good-bye*' in Richard Harwell (ed.) *Gone with the Wind as Book and Film* (Columbia: University of South Carolina Press, 1983), pp. 90–7.

Brennan Center for Justice, 'The Myth of Voter Fraud' (2020).

Brockell, Gillian. 'A Republic If You Can Keep It', *Washington Post*, (18 December 2019).

Brown, Ellen F. and John Wiley, Jr. *Margaret Mitchell's Gone with the Wind: A Bestseller's Odyssey from Atlanta to Hollywood* (Lanham: Taylor Trade Publishing, 2011).

Brundage, W. Fitzhugh. *Lynchings in the New South: Georgia and Virginia, 1880–1930* (Urbana: University of Illinois Press, 1993).

Budiansky, Stephen. *The Bloody Shirt: Terror after Appomattox* (New York: Viking Press, 2008).

Bullock, Charles, Scott Buchanan, and Ronald Keith Gaddie. *The Three Governors Controversy: Skullduggery, Machinations, and the Decline of Georgia's Progressive Politics* (Athens: University of Georgia Press, 2015).

Burgett, Bruce. *Sentimental Bodies: Sex, Gender, and Citizenship in the Early Republic* (Princeton: Princeton University Press, 1998).

Burns, Robert E. *I Am a Fugitive from a Georgia Chain Gang!*, reprint edition (Athens: University of Georgia Press, 1997).

Burt, John. *Lincoln's Tragic Pragmatism: Lincoln, Douglas, and Moral Conflict* (Cambridge: Cambridge University Press, 2008).

Campbell, Edward. '*Gone with the Wind*: Film as Myth and Message' in Walter J. Fraser and Winfred B. Moore (eds), *From the Old South to the New: Essays on the Transitional South* (Westport: Greenwood, 1981), pp. 143–151.

Cardon, Lauren S. '"Good Breeding": Margaret Mitchell's Multi-Ethnic South', *Southern Quarterly*, vol. 44, no. 4 (2007), pp. 61–82.

Cardyn, Lisa. 'Sexual Terror in the Reconstruction South' in Catherine Clinton and Nina Silber (eds), *Battle Scars: Gender and Sexuality in the American Civil War* (New York: Oxford University Press, 2006), pp. 140–167.

Carlson, Tucker. 'Democrats Pushing Unity Through Domination of Their Opponents', *Fox News* (15 January 2021).

Carson, E. Anne. 'Prisoners in 2019', *Bureau of Justice Statistics*, US Department of Justice (October 2020).

Chalmers, David. *Hooded Americanism: The History of the Ku Klux Klan*, third edition (Durham: Duke University Press Books, 1987).

Chalmers, David. *Notes on Writing the History of the Ku Klux Klan* (Cambridge: Orange Grove Books, 2013).

Churchwell, Sarah. *Behold, America: The History of America First and the American Dream* (London: Bloomsbury Publishing, 2018).

Churchwell, Sarah. 'American Fascism: It Has Happened Here', *New York Review of Books* (22 June 2020).

Churchwell, Sarah. 'White Lies Matter', *Prospect* (10 July 2020).

Clayton, Bruce. 'Dixie's Daughter: Margaret Mitchell Reconsidered', *Georgia Historical Quarterly*, vol. 76, no. 2 (1992), pp. 393–409.

Coates, Ta-Nehisi. 'The Great Schism', *The Atlantic* (18 October 2011).

Cockrell, Dale. *Demons of Disorder: Early Blackface Minstrels and Their World* (Cambridge: Cambridge University Press, 1997).

Coleman, Nancy. 'Why We're Capitalizing Black', *New York Times* (5 July 2020).

Collins, Kristin A. 'Illegitimate Borders: Jus Sanguinis, Citizenship, and the Legal Reconstruction of Race and Nation', *Yale Law Journal*, vol. 123, no. 7 (2014), pp. 2134–2235.

Coski, John. *The Confederate Battle Flag: America's Most Embattled Emblem* (Cambridge: Harvard University Press, 2005).

Cowley, Malcolm. 'Going with the Wind', *The New Republic* (16 September 1936).

Cox, John and LaWanda Cox. 'General O. O. Howard and the "Misrepresented Bureau"', *Journal of Southern History*, vol. 19, no. 4 (1953), pp. 427–456.

Cox, Karen L. *Dixie's Daughters: The United Daughters of the Confederacy and the Preservation of Confederate Culture* (Gainesville: University Press of Florida, 2003).

Cox, Karen L. *Dreaming of Dixie: How the South was Created in American Popular Culture* (Chapel Hill: University of North Carolina Press, 2013).

Crank, James A. *New Approaches to Gone with the Wind* (Baton Rouge: Louisiana State University Press, 2015).

Cripps, Thomas. *Making Movies Black: The Hollywood Message Movie from World War II to the Civil Rights Era* (New York: Oxford University Press, 1993).

Dauphine, James G. 'The Knights of the White Camelia and the Election of 1868: Louisiana's White Terrorists; A Benighting Legacy', *Louisiana History: The Journal of the Louisiana Historical Association,* vol. 30, no. 2 (1989), pp. 173–190.

Dawsey, Josh and Paul Schwartzman. 'How Ashli Babbitt went from Capitol Rioter to Trump-embraced "Martyr"', *Washington Post* (30 July 2021).

Deyle, Steven. 'An "Abominable" New Trade: The Closing of the African Slave Trade and the Changing Patterns of U.S. Political Power, 1808-60'. *William and Mary Quarterly,* vol. 66, no. 4 (2009), pp. 833–50.

Diggins, John P. 'Flirtation with Fascism: American Pragmatic Liberals and Mussolini's Italy', *American Historical Review,* vol. 71, no. 2 (January 1966), pp. 487–506.

Dinnerstein, Leonard. *The Leo Frank Case,* second edition (Athens: University of Georgia Press, 2008).

Doherty, Thomas. *Hollywood and Hitler, 1933–1939,* reprint edition (New York: Columbia University Press, 2015).

Dornan, Inge. 'To "make a good Mistress to my servants": Unmasking the Meaning of Maternalism in Colonial South Carolina' in Lawrence Aje and Catherine Armstrong (eds), *The Many Faces of Slavery: New Perspectives on Slave Ownership and Experiences in the Americas* (London: Bloomsbury Publishing, 2019), pp. 88–110.

Dowd Hall, Jacquelyn. 'The Long Civil Rights Movement and the Political Uses of the Past', *Journal of American History,* vol. 91, no. 4 (March 2005).

Doyle, Don H. *The Cause of All Nations: An International History of the American Civil War* (New York: Basic Books 2014).

Drago, Edmund L. 'Georgia's First Black Voter Registrars during Reconstruction', *The Georgia Historical Quarterly,* vol. 78, no. 4 (Winter 1994), pp. 760793.

Du Bois, W. E. B. *Black Reconstruction in America: An Essay Toward a History of the Part Which Black Folk Played in the Attempt to Reconstruct Democracy in America, 1860–1880,* reprint edition (New York: Athenaeum, 1975).

Du Bois, 'The Souls of White Folk', in *Darkwater: Voices from Within the Veil* (Oxford: Oxford University Press [1920] 2007).

Eckert, Ralph Lowell. *John Brown Gordon: Soldier, Southerner, American* (Baton Rouge: Louisiana State University Press, 1993).

Edelman, Adam and Garrett Haake. 'Republican Loyal to Trump Claims Capitol Riot Looked More Like "Normal Tourist Visit"', NBC News (12 May 2021).

Edmondson, Taulby H. 'How the Wind Goes On: *Gone with the Wind* and the Imagined Geographies of the American South', Virginia Polytechnic Institute and State University PhD Dissertation (2018).

Edwards, Ann. *Road to Tara: The Life of Margaret Mitchell,* commemorative edition (Lanham: Taylor Trade Publishing, 2014).

Edwards, Laura F. *Scarlett Doesn't Live Here Anymore: Southern Women in the Civil War Era* (Champaign: University of Illinois Press, 2004).

Eggers, Andrew C., Haritz Garro, and Justin Grimmer. 'No Evidence for Systematic Voter Fraud: A guide to statistical claims about the 2020 election', *Proceedings of the National Academy of Sciences,* vol. 118, no. 45 (2021).

Eley, Geoff. 'What is Fascism and Where does it Come From?', *History Workshop Journal*, vol. 91, no. 1 (Spring 2021), pp. 29–50.

Eliot, Thomas. 'Review of *The Coming American Fascism* by Lawrence Dennis', *Social Forces*, vol. 16, no. 2 (December 1937), pp. 299–301.

Ellison, Ralph. 'Change the Joke and Slip the Yoke' in Ralph Ellison (ed.), *Shadow and Act*, reprint edition (London: Secker and Warburg, 1967), pp. 45–59.

Entzminger, Betina. *The Belle Gone Bad: White Southern Women Writers and the Dark Seductress* (Baton Rouge: Louisiana State University Press, 2002).

Equal Justice Initiative Report, 'Reconstruction in America: Racial Violence after the Civil War, 1865–1876.'

Farca, Paula Anca. 'And You, Miss, Are No Lady: Feminist and Postfeminist Scarlett O'Hara Rethinks the Southern Lady', *Southern Studies*, vol. 14, no. 1 (2007), pp. 73–90.

Farrow, Ronan. 'A Pennsylvania Mother's Path to Insurrection', *The New Yorker* (1 February 2021).

Faulkner, William. 'An Introduction to *The Sound and the Fury*', *Mississippi Quarterly*, vol. 26 (Summer 1973), pp. 410–415.

Faust, Drew Gilpin. *Mothers of Invention: Women of the Slaveholding South in the American Civil War* (Chapel Hill: University of North Carolina Press, 2004).

Fede, Andrew T. *Homicide Justified: The Legality of Killing Slaves in the United States and the Atlantic World* (Athens: University of Georgia Press, 2017).

Fierce, Milfred C. *Slavery Revisited: Blacks and the Southern Convict Lease System, 1865–1933* (New York: Africana Studies Research Centre, Brooklyn College, City University of New York, 1994).

Finchelstein, Federico. *A Brief History of Fascist Lies* (Berkeley: California University Press, 2020).

Fichelstein, Federico. *From Fascism to Populism in History* (Berkeley: University of California Press, 2017).

Finchelstein, Federico. *Fascist Mythologies: The History and Politics of Unreason in Borges, Freud, and Schmitt* (New York: Columbia University Press, 2022).

Fischer, Klaus P. *Hitler and America* (Philadelphia: University of Pennsylvania Press, 2011).

Fitzgerald, F. Scott. *A Life in Letters*, (eds) Matthew J. Bruccoli and Judith Baughman (New York: Charles Scribner's Sons, 1994).

Fleming, Walter J., John C. Lester, and Daniel Love Wilson. *Ku Klux Klan: Its Origin, Growth, and Disbandment* (New York: Neale Publishing, 1905).

Floyd, Josephine Bone. 'Rebecca Latimer Felton, Champion of Women's Rights', *Georgia Historical Quarterly*, vol. 30, no. 2 (1946), pp. 81–104.

Foner, Eric. *Reconstruction: America's Unfinished Revolution, 1863–1877*, updated edition (New York: Harper Trade, 2015).

Foner, Eric. *Gateway to Freedom: The Hidden History of America's Fugitive Slaves* (Oxford: Oxford University Press, 2015).

Foner, Eric. *A Short History of Reconstruction, 1863–1877*, revised edition (New York: Harper Trade, 2015).

Foner, Eric. *The Second Founding: How the Civil War and Reconstruction Remade the Constitution* (New York: W. W. Norton and Company, 2019).

Foster, Gaines M. *Ghosts of the Confederacy: Defeat, the Lost Cause, and the Emergence of the New South, 1865–1913* (New York: Oxford University Press, 1987).

Foster, Gaines M. 'A Respect for Confederate History' in Larry M. Logue and Michael Barton (eds), *The Civil War Veteran: A Historical Reader* (New York: New York University Press, 2007), pp. 376–396.

Foster, W. H. 'Women Slave Owners Face Their Historians: Versions of Maternalism in Atlantic World Slavery', *Patterns of Prejudice*, vol. 41, no. 3 & 4 (2007), pp. 303–320.

Franklin, John Hope. '"Birth of a Nation": Propaganda as History', *The Massachusetts Review*, vol. 20, no. 3 (1979), pp. 417–434.

Fraser, Mya. 'Stop Using "Officer-Involved Shooting"', *Columbia Journalism Review* (7 August 2020).

Fritzsche, Peter A. *An Iron Wind: Europe Under Hitler* (New York: Basic Books, 2016).

Gallagher, Gary W. *Lee and His Army in Confederate History* (Chapel Hill: University of North Carolina Press, 2001).

Gallagher, Gary W. and Alan T. Nolan, 'Introduction' in Gary W. Gallagher and Alan T. Nolan (eds), *The Myth of the Lost Cause and Civil War History*, reprint edition (Bloomington: Indiana University Press, 2010), pp. 1–10.

Gallagher, Gary W. and Alan T. Nolan (eds), *The Myth of the Lost Cause and Civil War History*, reprint edition (Bloomington: Indiana University Press, 2010).

Galsworthy, Timothy. 'Carpetbaggers, Confederates, and Richard Nixon: The 1960 Presidential Election, Historical Memory, and the Republican Southern Strategy', *Presidential Studies Quarterly* (2021), pp. 1–30.

Gates, Henry Louis, Jr. *Stony the Road: Reconstruction, White Supremacy, and the Rise of Jim Crow* (New York: Penguin Books, 2019).

Genovese, Eugene. *Roll, Jordan, Roll: The World the Slaves Made* (New York: Pantheon, 1974).

Gilmore, Glenda E. 'Gender and Origins of the New South', *Journal of Southern History*, vol. 67, no. 4 (2001), pp. 769–788.

Glancy, Mark. 'Going to the Pictures: British Cinema and the Second World War', *Past and Future: The Magazine of the Institute of Historical Research*, Issue 8 (October 2010), pp. 7–9.

Gleason, Glenda. *Defying Dixie: The Radical Roots of Civil Rights, 1919–1950* (New York: W. W. Norton and Company, 2008).

Glymph, Thavolia. *Out of the House of Bondage: The Transformation of the Plantation Household* (Cambridge: Cambridge University Press, 2008).

Godfrey, Elaine. 'It Was Supposed to Be So Much Worse', *The Atlantic* (9 January 2021).

Godfrey, Mollie. '"They Ain't Human": John Steinbeck, Proletarian Fiction, and the Racial Politics of "The People"', *Modern Fiction Studies*, vol. 59, no. 1 (2013), pp. 107–134.

Goings, Kenneth W. *Mammy and Uncle Mose: Black Collectibles and American Stereotyping* (Bloomington: Indiana University Press, 1994).

Graham, Chris. 'Facing Legacies: A Photo from Inside the US Capitol', The American Civil War Museum (7 January 2021).

Gramlich, John. 'Black Imprisonment Rate in the US', Pew Research (6 May 2020).

Greenwald, Marilyn S. and Yun
  Li. *Eunice Hunton Carter: A Lifelong
  Fight for Social Justice* (New York:
  Fordham University Press, 2021).
Greve, Joan E. 'Trump Would "Not
  Even Consider" Renaming Bases
  with Confederate Links', *Guardian*,
  10 June 2020.
Grimsley, Mark. *The Hard Hand of
  War: Union Military Policy Toward
  Southern Civilians, 1861–1865*
  (Cambridge: Cambridge University
  Press, 1995).
Haag, John. '*Gone with the Wind* in
  Nazi Germany', *Georgia Historical
  Quarterly*, vol. 73, no. 2 (1989),
  pp. 278–304.
Hale, Grace Elizabeth. *Making
  Whiteness: The Culture of Segregation
  in the South, 1890–1940* (New York:
  Vintage Books, 1999).
Haley, Sarah. *No Mercy Here: Gender,
  Punishment, and the Making of
  Jim Crow Modernity* (Chapel Hill:
  University of North Carolina Press,
  2016).
Hanson, Elizabeth I. *Margaret Mitchell*
  (Boston: Twayne, 1990).
Harcourt, Felix. *Ku Klux Kulture:
  America and the Klan in the 1920s*
  (Chicago: University of Chicago
  Press, 2017).
Hardwick, Kevin R. '"Your Old Father
  Abe Lincoln is Dead and Damned":
  Black Soldiers and the Memphis
  Race Riot of 1866', *Journal of
  Social History*, vol. 27, no. 1 (1993),
  pp. 109–128.
Hart, Bradley W. *Hitler's American
  Friends: The Third Reich's Supporters
  in the United States* (New York: St.
  Martin's Press, 2018).
Harwell, Richard (ed.), *Margaret
  Mitchell's Gone with the Wind Letters,
  1936–1949* (New York: Macmillan,
  1976).

Harwell, Richard (ed.) *Gone with the
  Wind as Book and Film* (Columbia:
  University of South Carolina Press,
  1983).
Haskell, Molly. *Frankly My Dear: Gone
  with the Wind Revisited* (New Haven:
  Yale University Press, 2010).
Haver, Ronald. *David O. Selznick's Gone
  with the Wind* (Liverpool: Outlet,
  1986).
Hickman, Christine B. 'The Devil
  and the One Drop Rule: Racial
  Categories, African Americans,
  and the U.S. Census', *Michigan
  Law Review*, vol. 95, no. 5 (1997),
  pp. 1163–1265.
Hoffmann, Carlee and Claire Strom.
  'A Perfect Storm: The Ocoee Riot of
  1920', *Florida Historical Quarterly*,
  vol. 93, no. 1 (2014), pp. 25–43.
Höhn, Maria. '"We Will Never Go Back
  to the Old Way Again": Germany
  in the African-American Debate
  on Civil Rights', *Central European
  History*, vol. 41, no. 4 (2008),
  pp. 605–637.
Horn, Stanley F. *Invisible Empire: The
  Story of the Ku Klux Klan, 1866–1871*
  (Montclair: Patterson Smith
  Publishing, 1939).
Horne, Gerald. *The Color of Fascism:
  Lawrence Dennis, Racial Passing, and
  the Rise of Right-Wing Extremism in
  the United States* (New York: New
  York University Press, 2009).
Hors Grill, Johnpeter and Robert
  L. Jenkins. 'The Nazis and the
  American South in the 1930s: A
  Mirror Image?', *Journal of Southern
  History*, vol. 58, no. 4 (1992),
  pp. 667–694.
Horwitz, Tony. *Confederates in the
  Attic: Dispatches from the Unfinished
  American Civil War* (New York:
  Pantheon, 1998).
Hsu, Spencer S., Tom Jackman, and
  Devlin Barrett. 'Self-styled militia

members planned on storming the U.S. Capitol days in advance of Jan. 6 attack, court documents say', *Washington Post* (19 January 2021).

Hsu, Tiffany. 'Tracking Viral Misinformation', *New York Times* (24 February 2022).

Hughes, Langston. 'Soldiers from Many Lands United in Spanish Fight' in Christopher C. De Santis (ed.), *The Collected Works of Langston Hughes, Vol. 9: Essays on Art, Race, Politics, and World Affairs* (Columbia: University of Missouri Press, 2002), pp. 181–7.

Hunter, Tera W. *Bound in Wedlock: Slave and Free Black Marriage in the Nineteenth Century* (Cambridge: Harvard University Press, 2019).

Janney, Caroline E. *Remembering the Civil War: Reunion and the Limits of Reconciliation* (Chapel Hill: University of North Carolina Press, 2013).

Jeansonne, Glen. *Women of the Far Right: The Mother's Movement and World War II* (Chicago: University of Chicago Press, 1996).

Johnson, Kenneth R. 'White Racial Attitudes as a Factor in the Arguments against the Nineteenth Amendment', *Phylon*, vol. 31, no. 1 (1970), pp. 31–37.

Jones-Rogers, Stephanie. *They Were Her Property: White Women as Slave Owners in the American South* (New Haven: Yale University Press, 2019).

Jones, Anne Goodwyn. *Tomorrow Is Another Day: The Woman Writer in the South, 1859–1936* (Baton Rouge: Louisiana State University Press, 1981).

Jordan, Winthrop D. *White Over Black: American Attitudes toward the Negro, 1550–1812* (Chapel Hill: University of North Carolina Press, 1968).

Karimi, Frank, and Doug Criss. 'Justin Trudeau Isn't the Only One. Here's a List of Politicians Who Got in Trouble Over Blackface', CNN.com (20 September 2019).

Katznelson, Ira. *Fear Itself: The New Deal and the Origins of Our Time* (New York: W. W. Norton and Company, 2013).

Kellogg, John. 'Negro Urban Clusters in the Postbellum South', *Geographical Review*, vol. 67, no. 3 (1977), pp. 310–321.

Kennedy, David M. *Freedom from Fear: The American People in Depression and War, 1929–1945* (Oxford: Oxford University Press, 1999).

Kennedy, Randall L. '"Who Can Say 'Nxxxxr?'" And Other Considerations', *Journal of Blacks in Higher Education*, no. 26 (1999), pp. 86–96.

Kennedy, Stetson. *Southern Exposure*, modern edition (Tuscaloosa: University of Alabama Press, [1946] 2011).

Klein, Charlotte. 'Tucker Carlson Defends Kenosha Shooter for Just Trying To "Maintain Order"', *Vanity Fair* (27 August 2020).

Krehbiel, Randy. *Tulsa, 1921: Reporting a Massacre* (Norman: University of Oklahoma Press, 2019).

Kühl, Stefan. *The Nazi Connection: Eugenics, American Racism, and German National Socialism* (Oxford: Oxford University Press, 1994).

Lambert, Gavin. 'The Making of *Gone with the Wind*', *Atlantic Monthly* (February 1973).

Lambert, Gavin. 'Studies in Scarlett' in Richard Harwell (ed.) *Gone with the Wind as Book and Film* (Columbia: University of South Carolina Press, 1983), pp. 132–37.

Lindbergh, Charles A. 'Aviation, Geography, and Race', *Readers' Digest*, vol. 35 (November 1939).

Linker, Damon. 'The Intellectual Right Contemplates an "American Caesar"', *The Week* (28 July 2021).

Lebsock, Suzanne. 'Women Suffrage and White Supremacy: A Virginia Case Study' in Susanne Lebsock and Nancy A. Hewitt (eds), *Visible Women: New Essays on American Activism* (Champaign: University of Illinois Press, 1993), pp. 62–100.

Leff, Leonard J. 'David Selznick's *Gone with the Wind*: "The Negro Problem"', *Georgia Review*, vol. 38, no. 1 (1984), pp. 146–164.

Leff, Leonard J. '*Gone with the Wind* and Hollywood's Racial Politics', *Atlantic Monthly* (1 December 1999).

LeFlouria, Talitha. *Chained in Silence: Black Women and Convict Labor in the New South* (Chapel Hill: University of North Carolina Press, 2016).

Leiter, Andrew. 'Thomas Dixon, Jr.: Conflicts in History and Literature', *Documenting the American South* (2004).

Levinson, Sanford. 'They Whisper: Reflections on Flags, Monuments, and State Holidays, and the Construction of Social Meaning in a Multicultural Society', *Chicago-Kent Law Review*, vol. 70, no. 3 (1995), p. 1079–1119.

Lichtenstein, Alex. *Twice the Work of Free Labor: The Political Economy of Convict Labor in the New South* (London: Verso, 1996).

Lincoln, Abraham. 'Second Inaugural Address' (4 March 1865).

Link, William A. *Atlanta, Cradle of the New South: Race and Remembering in the Civil War's Aftermath*, new edition (Chapel Hill: University of North Carolina Press, 2013).

Litwack, Leon F. *Been in the Storm So Long: The Aftermath of Slavery* (New York: Vintage, 1980).

Lybrand, Holmes, Katelyn Polantz, and Hannah Rabinowitz. 'Oath Keeper Pleads Guilty to Seditious Conspiracy and Will Cooperate With Justice Department', CNN.com (3 March 2022).

Mackey, Al. 'The Extent of Slave Ownership in the United States in 1860', Student of the American Civil War (18 April 2017).

MacLean, Nancy. *Behind the Mask of Chivalry: The Making of the Second Ku Klux Klan* (Oxford: Oxford University Press, 1994).

Mahar, William J. *Behind the Burnt Cork Mask: Early Blackface Minstrelsy and Antebellum American Popular Culture* (Champaign: University of Illinois Press, 1999).

Mancini, Matthew J. 'Race, Economics, and the Abandonment of Convict Leasing', *Journal of Negro History*, vol. 63, no. 4 (October 1978), pp. 339–352.

Mancini, Matthew J. *One Dies, Get Another: Convict Leasing in the American South, 1866–1928* (Columbia: University of South Carolina Press, 1996).

Mathews, James W. 'The Civil War of 1936: *Gone with the Wind* and *Absalom, Absalom!*', *Georgia Review*, vol. 21, no. 4 (1967), pp. 462–469.

McCormick, Andrew. 'Madness on Capitol Hill', *The Nation* (7 January 2021).

McGill, Ralph. 'Little Woman, Big Book: The Mysterious Margaret Mitchell' in Richard Harwell (ed.) *Gone with the Wind as Book and Film* (Columbia: University of South Carolina Press, 1983), pp. 66–76.

McPherson, James M. *Battle Cry of Freedom: The Civil War Era* (Oxford: Oxford University Press, 1988).

McPherson, Tara. *Reconstructing Dixie: Race, Gender, and Nostalgia in the Imagined South* (Durham: Duke University Press, 2003).

McRae, Elizabeth Gillespie. 'Caretakers of Southern Civilization: Georgia Women and the Anti-Suffrage Campaign, 1914–1920', *Georgia Historical Quarterly*, vol. 82, no. 4 (Winter 1998), pp. 801–828.

McVeigh, Rory. *The Rise of the Ku Klux Klan: Right-Wing Movements and National Politics* (Minneapolis: University of Minnesota Press, 2009).

Mendenhall, Marjorie. 'Southern Women of a "Lost Generation"', *South Atlantic Quarterly*, vol. 33 (1934), pp. 334–353.

Merritt, Keri Leigh. 'Race, Reconstruction, and Reparations', *Black Perspectives* (9 February 2016).

Merritt, Keri Leigh. *Masterless Men: Poor Whites and Slavery in the Antebellum South* (Cambridge: Cambridge University Press, 2017).

Merritt, Russell. 'Dixon, Griffith, and the Southern Legend', *Cinema Journal*, vol. 12, no. 1 (1972), pp. 26–45.

Messer, Chris M. *The 1921 Tulsa Race Massacre* (London: Palgrave Macmillan, 2021).

Meyers, Christopher C. '"Killing Them by the Wholesale": A Lynching Rampage in South Georgia', *Georgia Historical Quarterly*, vol. 90, no. 2 (2006), pp. 214–235.

Miller-Idriss, Cynthia. 'Women Are Increasingly Ditching Their Backstage Role in Right-wing Extremist Movements', MSNBC.com (8 January 2022).

Minervini, Amanda. 'Mussolini Speaks: History Reviewed', *Massachusetts Review*, vol. 60, no. 1 (Spring 2019), pp. 194–204.

Mitchell, Margaret. *Gone with the Wind*, revised edition (New York: Scribner, 2011).

Morgan, Edmund S. *American Slavery, American Freedom: The Ordeal of Colonial Virginia* (New York: W. W. Norton, 2003).

Morrison, Toni. *Playing in the Dark: Whiteness and the Literary Imagination* (Cambridge: Harvard University Press, 1992).

Moseley, Clement Charleton. 'Latent Klanism in Georgia, 1890–1915', *Georgia Historical Quarterly*, vol. 56, no. 3 (1972), pp. 365–368.

Moss, Carlton. 'An Open Letter to Mr. Selznick' in Richard Harwell (ed.), *Gone with the Wind as Book and Film* (Columbia: University of South Carolina Press, 1983), pp. 156–159.

Mott, Frank Luther. *Golden Multitudes: The Story of Bestsellers in the United States* (New York: Bowker, 1947).

Myers, Martha A. *Race, Labor, and Punishment in the New South* (Columbus: Ohio State University Press, 1998).

Nagourney, Adam. 'Reform Bid Said to Be a No-Go for Trump', *The New York Times* (14 February 2000).

Naylor, Brian. 'Read Trump's Jan. 6 Speech, A Key Part of Impeachment Trial', NPR (10 February 2021).

Naylor, Brian. 'Officers Give Harrowing Testimony on Their Experience Defending the Capitol On Jan. 6', NPR (27 July 2021).

Niven, William John. *Hitler and Film: The Führer's Hidden Passion* (New Haven: Yale University Press, 2018).

Nugent, Frank S. 'The Screen in Review', *New York Times* (20 December 1939).

Nuzzi, Olivia. 'Senior Trump Official: We Were Wrong, He's a "Fascist"', *New York Magazine* (8 January 2021)

O'Brien, Kenneth. 'Race, Romance, and the Southern Literary Tradition', in Darden A. Pyron (ed.), *Recasting: Gone with the Wind in American Culture* (Gainseville, University Press of Florida, 1984), pp. 153–166.

Ochiai, Akiko. 'The Port Royal Experiment Revisited: Northern Visions of Reconstruction and the Land Question', *New England Quarterly*, vol. 74, no. 1 (2001), pp. 94–117.

Okrent, Daniel. *The Guarded Gate: Bigotry, Eugenics and the Law That Kept Two Generations of Jews, Italians, and Other European Immigrants Out of America* (New York: Scribner, 2019).

Ortiz, Aimee. 'Nikki Haley's Confederate Flag Comments Spark Backlash', *New York Times* (7 December 2019).

Ortiz, Paul. *Emancipation Betrayed: The Hidden History of Black Organizing and White Violence in Florida from Reconstruction to the Bloody Election of 1920* (Berkeley: University of California Press, 2005).

Orwell, George. 'The Prevention of Literature', *Polemic*, no. 2 (January 1946).

Oshinsky, David M. *'Worse Than Slavery': Parchman Farm and the Ordeal of Jim Crow Justice* (New York: Free Press, 1996).

Osterweis, Roland G. *The Myth of the Lost Cause, 1865–1900* (Hamden: Archon Press, 1970).

Owley, Jessica and Jess Phelps. 'Understanding the Complicated Landscape of Civil War Monuments', *Indiana Law Journal*, vol. 93, no. 5 (2018), pp. 15–33.

Painter, Nell Irvin. *The History of White People* (New York: W. W. Norton, 2010).

Padover, S. K. 'How the Nazis Picture America', *Public Opinion Quarterly*, vol. 3, no. 4 (October 1939), pp. 663–669.

Parsons, Elaine Frantz. 'Klan Scepticism and Denial in Reconstruction-Era Public Discourse', *Journal of Southern History*, vol. 77, no. 1 (2011), pp. 53–90.

Parsons, Elaine Frantz. *Ku Klux: The Birth of the Klan During Reconstruction* (Chapel Hill: University of North Carolina Press, 2015).

Patterson, Orlando. *Slavery and Social Death: A Comparative Study* (Cambridge: Harvard University Press, 1982).

Paxton, Robert O. 'The Five Stages of Fascism', *Journal of Modern History*, vol. 70, no. 1 (1998), pp. 1–23.

Paxton, Robert O. *The Anatomy of Fascism* (New York: Alfred A. Knopf, 2005).

Paxton, Robert O. 'I've Hesitated to Call Donald Trump a Fascist. Until Now', *Newsweek* (11 January 2021).

Pegram, Thomas R. *One Hundred Percent American: The Rebirth and Decline of the Ku Klux Klan in the 1920s* (London: Ivan R. Dee, 2011).

Perelló, Carlos Amunátegui. 'Race and Nation: On Ius Sanguinis and the Origins of a Racist National Perspective', *Fundamina*, vol. 24, no. 2 (2018), pp. 1–20.

Perlstein, Rick. 'Exclusive: Lee Atwater's Infamous 1981 Interview on the Southern Strategy', *The Nation* (13 November 2012).

Perkins, Linda M. 'The Racial Integration of the Seven Sister Colleges', *Journal of Blacks in Higher Education*, no. 19 (Spring 1998), pp. 104–108.

Phillips, Gene D. '"Gone with the Wind": The Work of Many', *New York Times* (19 July 1998).

Pierpont, Claudia Roth. 'A Study in Scarlett', *The New Yorker* (31 August 1992).

Pollard, Edward A. *Southern History of the War* (New York: Charles B. Richardson, 1862).

Pollard, Edward A. *The Lost Cause: A New Southern History of the War of the Confederates* (New York: E. B. Treat, 1866).

Proctor, Bradley D., '"The K. K. Alphabet": Secret Communication and Coordination of the Reconstruction-Era Ku Klux Klan in the Carolinas', *Journal of the Civil War Era*, vol. 8, no. 3, University of North Carolina Press (2018), pp. 455–87.

Pugh, Tison. *Queer Chivalry: Medievalism and the Myth of White Masculinity in Southern Literature* (Baton Rouge: Louisiana State University Press, 2013).

Pyron, Darden Asbury, (ed.) *Recasting: Gone with the Wind in American Culture* (Gainesville: University of Florida Press, 1983).

Pyron, Darden Asbury. *Southern Daughter: The Life of Margaret Mitchell* (New York: Oxford University Press, 1991).

Quillen, Robert. 'Atlanta Should be Proud of Tribute to South', *Atlanta Constitution* (16 December 1939).

Rains, Sally Tippett. *Making of a Masterpiece: The True Story of Margaret Mitchell's Classic Novel Gone with the Wind* (London: Global Books Publishing, 2009).

Randall, Alice T. *The Wind Done Gone with Readers' Guide* (Boston: Houghton Mifflin, 2002).

Reddick, Lawrence D. 'Review of *Pro-Slavery Thought in the Old South* and *Gone with the Wind*', *Journal of Negro History*, vol. 22, no. 3 (1937), pp. 365–6.

Reeves, Jay, Lisa Mascaro, and Calvin Woodward, 'The Unfolding of "Home-Grown Fascism" in Capitol Assault', ABC News (11 January 2021).

Reidy, Joseph P. *From Slavery to Agrarian Capitalism in the Cotton Plantation South: Central Georgia, 1800–1880* (Chapel Hill: University of North Carolina Press, 1992).

Reynolds, Donald E. 'The New Orleans Riot of 1866, Reconsidered', *Louisiana History*, vol. 5, no. 1 (1964), pp. 5–27.

Richardson, Heather Cox. *How the South Won the Civil War: Oligarchy, Democracy, and the Continuing Fight for the Soul of America* (Oxford: Oxford University Press, 2020).

Richardson, Riché. 'Mammy's "Mules" and the Rules of Marriage in *Gone with the Wind*' in Deborah E. Barker and Kathryn McKee (eds), *American Cinema and the Southern Imaginary* (Athens: University of Georgia Press, 2011), pp. 52–78.

Richet, Isabelle. 'The "Irresponsibility of the Outsider"? American Expatriates and Italian Fascism', *Transatlantica*, vol. 1 (2014), pp. 1–23.

Rider, Jonathan. *Gospel of Freedom: Martin Luther King, Jr.'s Letter from Birmingham Jail and the Struggle that Changed a Nation* (London: Bloomsbury, 2014).

Robertson, Campbell and Katy Reckdahl. 'Stories of New Orleans: As Monuments Go Down, Family Histories Emerge', *The New York Times* (24 May 2017).

Rogin, Michael. '"The Sword Became a Flashing Vision": D. W. Griffith's *The Birth of a Nation*', *Representations*, vol. 9 (Winter 1985), p. 150–195.

Romey, Kristin. 'Decoding the Hate Symbols Seen at the Capitol

Insurrection', *National Geographic* (21 January 2021).

Roosevelt, Eleanor. 'My Day', *Oklahoma News* (22 August 1936).

Rosenberg, Jonathan. *How Far the Promised Land? World Affairs and the American Civil Rights Movement from the First World War to Vietnam* (Princeton: Princeton University Press, 2006).

Ruane, Michael E. '75 Years Ago, Charles Lindbergh Urged Congress to Stay Out of WWII', *Washington Post* (21 January 2016).

Sanders, Charles W., Jr. 'Jefferson Davis and the Hampton Roads Peace Conference: "To Secure Peace to the Two Countries"', *Journal of Southern History*, vol. 63, no. 4 (1997), pp. 803–826.

Scarborough, Ruth. *The Opposition to Slavery in Georgia Prior to 1860* (Nashville: George Peabody College for Teachers, 1933).

Schermerhorn, Calvin. *The Business of Slavery and the Rise of American Capitalism, 1815–1860* (New Haven, Yale University Press, 2015).

Schmich, Mary T. 'Atlanta Giddy Over Scarlett and Rhett's Return', *Chicago Tribune* (10 December 1989).

Schonbach, Morris. *Native American Fascism During the 1930s and 1940s: A Study of Its Roots, Its Growth, and Its Decline* (New York: Garland, 1985).

Schuyler, George. *Black No More* (London: Olympia Press [1931] 2007).

Scott, Anne Firor. *The Southern Lady: From Pedestal to Politics, 1830–1930*, anniversary edition (Charlottesville: University of Virginia Press, 1995)

Sealing, Keith E. 'Blood Will Tell: Scientific Racism and the Legal Prohibitions Against Miscegenation', *Michigan Journal of Race and Law*, vol. 5, no. 2 (2000), pp. 560–609.

Seidel, Kathryn Lee. *The Southern Belle in the American Novel* (Gainesville: University Press of Florida, 1985).

Sheley, Erin. '*Gone with the Wind* and the Trauma of Lost Sovereignty', *Southern Literary Journal*, vol. 45, no. 2 (2013), pp. 1–18.

Silber, Nina. *This War Ain't Over: Fighting the Civil War in New Deal America* (Chapel Hill: University of North Carolina Press, 2018).

Silver, Nate. 'The Most Diverse Cities Are Often the Most Segregated', FiveThirtyEight (1 May 2015).

Simkins, Francis B. 'Review of Stanley F. Horn, *Invisible Empire: The Story of the Ku Klux Klan, 1866–1871*', *Journal of American History*, vol. 26, no. 2 (September 1939), pp. 270–71.

Simpson, Brooks (ed.). *Reconstruction: Voices from America's First Great Struggle for Racial Equality* (New York: Library of America, 2018).

Sipperly, Emma. 'The Rubin Stacy Lynching: Reconstructing Justice', Civil Rights and Restorative Justice Clinic, pp. 1–29.

Smith, Lilian. 'One More Sigh for the Good Old South', *Pseudopodia*, vol. 1, no. 3 (1936), pp. 6 & 15.

Smith, John David. 'The Enduring Myth of "Forty Acres and a Mule"', *Chronicle of Higher Education* (21 February 2003).

Smith, Clint. 'The Whole Story in a Single Photo', *The Atlantic* (8 January 2021).

Sonmez, Felicia. 'McConnell says bill that would make Election Day a federal holiday is a "power grab" by Democrats', *Washington Post* (30 January 2019).

Spiro, Jonathan. *Defending the Master Race: Conservation, Eugenics, and the Legacy of Madison Grant* (Lebanon:

University Press of New England, 2009).

Staples, Brent. 'How the Suffrage Movement Betrayed Black Women', *The New York Times* (28 July 2018).

Stearns, Matt. 'Angry Supremacist Leaves Jury Selection', *Kansas City Star* (30 January 2001).

Steigmann-Gall, Richard. 'Star-Spangled Fascism: American Interwar Political Extremism in Comparative Perspective', *Social History*, vol. 42, no. 1 (2017), pp. 94–119.

Stephens, Alexander H. *A Constitutional View of the Late War Between the States*, vol. 1 (Philadelphia: National Publishing Co., 1868).

Stephens, Alexander H. *Recollections of Alexander H. Stephens: His Diary Kept When a Prisoner at Fort Warren, Boston Harbour, 1865*, Myrta Lockett Avary, (ed.). (New York: Da Capo Press, [1910] 1971).

Stephens, Alexander H. 'The Corner Stone Speech' (21 March 1861).

Stewart, Mart. 'Teaching *Gone with the Wind* in the Socialist Republic of Vietnam', *Southern Cultures*, vol. 11, no. 3 (Autumn 2005), pp. 9–34.

Stieb, Matt. 'Incoming GOP Senator Apparently Doesn't Know Basics of World War II', *New York Magazine* (12 November 2020).

Storace, Patricia. 'Look Away, Dixie Land', *New York Review of Books* (19 December 1991).

Summers, Mark Wahlgren. *A Dangerous Stir: Fear, Paranoia, and the Making of Reconstruction* (Chapel Hill: University of North Carolina Press, 2010).

Taifa, Nkechi. 'Race, Mass Incarceration, and the Disastrous War on Drugs', Brennan Center for Justice (10 May 2021).

Taylor, A. Elizabeth. 'The Origin of the Woman Suffrage Movement in Georgia', *Georgia Historical Quarterly*, vol. 28, no. 2 (1944), pp. 63–79.

Taylor, A. Elizabeth. 'The Last Phase of the Woman Suffrage Movement in Georgia', *Georgia Historical Quarterly*, vol. 43, no. 1 (March 1959), pp. 11–28.

Taylor, Helen. *Scarlett's Women: Gone with the Wind and Its Female Fans* (New Brunswick: Rutgers University Press, 1989).

Taylor, Helen. *Gone with the Wind: BFI Film Classics* (London: Bloomsbury Publishing, 2019).

Tetrault, Lisa. *The Myth of Seneca Falls: Memory and the Woman's Suffrage Movement, 1848–1898* (Chapel Hill: University of North Carolina Press, 2014).

Terborg-Penn, Rosalyn. *African American Women and the Struggle for the Vote, 1850–1920* (Bloomington: Indiana University Press, 1998).

Terrell, Mary Church. 'Lynching from a Negro's Point of View', *North American Review*, vol. 178, no. 571 (1904), pp. 853–868.

Thompson, H. Paul. *A Most Stirring and Significant Episode: Religion and the Rise and Fall of Prohibition in Black Atlanta, 1865–1887* (DeKalb: Northern Illinois University Press, 2013).

Thurner, Manuela. '"Better Citizens without the Ballot": American Anti-Suffrage Women and Their Rationale During the Progressive Era', *Journal of Women's History*, vol. 5, no. 1 (1993), pp. 33–60.

Tolnay, Stewart E. and E. M. Beck. *A Festival of Violence: An Analysis of Southern Lynchings, 1882–1930* (Champaign: University of Illinois Press, 1995).

Tracy, James F. 'Revisiting a Polysemic Text: The African American Press's Reception of *Gone with the Wind*', *Massachusetts Communication and Society*, vol. 4, no. 4 (2001), pp. 419–436.

Trelease, Allen W. *White Terror: The Ku Klux Klan Conspiracy and Southern Reconstruction* (Baton Rouge: Louisiana State University Press, 1995).

Tuttle, William M., Jr. *Race Riot: Chicago in the Red Summer of 1919* (Champaign: University of Illinois Press, 1996).

Waldrep, Christopher. *The Many Faces of Judge Lynch: Extralegal Violence and Punishment in America* (New York: Palgrave Macmillan, 2002).

Wallace, Max. *The American Axis: Henry Ford, Charles Lindbergh, and the Rise of the Third Reich* (New York: St. Martin's Press, 2003).

Wallace-Sanders, Kimberly. *Mammy: A Century of Race, Gender and Southern Memory* (Ann Arbor: University of Michigan Press, 2008).

Wallace-Wells, Benjamin. 'How a Conservative Activist Invented the Conflict Over Critical Race Theory', *The New Yorker* (18 June 2021).

Warren, Wendy Anne. '"The Cause of Her Grief": The Rape of a Slave in Early New England', *Journal of American History*, vol. 93, no. 4 (2007), pp. 1031–49.

Watkins, Floyd C. '*Gone with the Wind* as Vulgar Literature', *Southern Literary Journal*, vol. 2, no. 2 (1970), pp. 86–103.

Watson, Ritchie Devon, Jr. *Normans and Saxons: Southern Race Mythology and the Intellectual History of the American Civil War* (Baton Rouge: Louisiana State University Press, 2008).

Webster, Ryan. 'Fascism Most Searched Word on Merriam-Webster Election Night', *USA Today* (8 November 2016).

Wedlock, Lunabelle. 'The Reaction of Negro Publications and Organizations to German Anti-Semitism', The Howard University Studies in the Social Sciences, *Graduate School Publications*, vol. 4 (1942), pp. 7–208.

Weiner, Rachel. 'She Said She Wasn't Going to Jail for Jan. 6, Citing "Blonde Hair, White Skin"', *Washington Post* (4 November 2021).

West, Nathanael. *The Day of the Locust* (New York: Bantam Books [1939] 1975.)

West, Nathanael. 'Some Notes on Violence', in *Nathanael West: A Collection of Critical Essays*, Jay Martin, (ed.) (Englewood Cliffs, NJ: Prentice-Hall, 1971), pp. 50–1.

Whitman, James. *Hitler's American Model: The United States and the Making of Nazi Race Law* (Princeton: Princeton University Press, 2017).

Wheeler, Marjorie Sprull. *New Women of the New South: The Leaders of the Woman Suffrage Movement in the Southern States* (Oxford: Oxford University Press, 1994).

White, Walter. 'An Address by NAACP Executive Secretary Walter White over WNYC', New York Public Radio Archives and Preservation (20 February 1938).

Whites, LeeAnne. 'Rebecca Latimer Felton and the Wife's Farm: The Class and Racial Politics of Gender Reform', *Georgia Historical Quarterly*, vol. 76, no. 2 (1992), pp. 354–372.

Whites, LeeAnne. 'Love, Hate, Rape, Lynching: Rebecca Latimer Felton and the Gender Politics of Racial Violence' in David S. Cecelski and Timothy B. Tyson (eds), *Democracy*

Betrayed: The Wilmington Race Riot of 1898 and Its Legacy (Chapel Hill: University of North Carolina Press, 1998).

Wiley, John, Jr. *The Scarlett Letters: The Making of the Film Gone with the Wind* (Lanham: Taylor Trade Publishing, 2014).

Williams, Eric. *Capitalism and Slavery* (Chapel Hill: University of North Carolina Press, 1944).

Wilson, Charles. *Baptised in Blood: The Religion of the Lost Cause, 1865–1920*, second edition (Athens: University of Georgia Press, 2009).

Wilson, Steve. *The Making of Gone with the Wind* (Austin: University of Texas Press, 2014).

Wise, Tim. *Color Blind: The Rise of Post-racial Politics and the Retreat from Racial Equity* (San Francisco: City Light Books, 2010).

Wineapple, Brenda. *The Impeachers: The Trial of Andrew Johnson and the Dream of a Just Nation* (New York: Ballantine Books, 2019).

Woodward, Calvin Jay Reeves, and Lisa Mascaro. 'The Unfolding of "Home-Grown Fascism" in Capitol Assault', *Seattle Times*, (10 January 2021).

Woodward, C. Vann. *Origins of the New South, 1877–1913*, revised edition (Baton Rouge: Louisiana State University Press, 1971).

Woodward, C. Vann. *The Strange Career of Jim Crow*, commemorative edition (New York: Oxford University Press, 2002).

Worster, Donald. *Dust Bowl: The Southern Plains in the 1930s* (Oxford: Oxford University Press, 2004).

Wright, George C. *Racial Violence in Kentucky: Lynchings, Mob Rule, and 'Legal Lynchings'*, reprint edition (Baton Rouge: Louisiana State University Press, 1996).

Yang, Maya. 'Conservative Event Gives Rittenhouse a Standing Ovation a Month After Acquittal', *The Guardian* (21 December 2021).

Yarbrough, Fay A. 'Power, Perception, and Interracial Sex: Former Slaves Recall a Multiracial South', *The Journal of Southern History*, vol. 71, no. 3 (2005), pp. 559–588.

Zad, Martie. 'Hattie McDaniel Paved the Way', *The Washington Post* (5 August 2001).

Zeskin, Leonard. *Blood and Politic: The History of White Nationalist Movement from the Margins to the Mainstream* (New York: Farrar Straus & Giroux, 2009).

Zilinsky, Jan, Jonathan Nagler, and Joshua Tucker. 'Which Republicans Are Most Likely to Think the Election Was Stolen?', *The Washington Post* (19 January 2021).

Zuczek, Richard. 'The Federal Government's Attack on the Ku Klux Klan: A Reassessment', *South Carolina Historical Magazine*, vol. 97, no. 1 (1996), pp. 47–64.

Endnotes

Epigraph

1 James Baldwin, *No Name in the Street* (London: Michael Joseph, 1972), p. 166.

Prologue

1 Brian Naylor, 'Read Trump's Jan. 6 Speech, A Key Part of Impeachment Trial', NPR, 10 February 2021.

2 Elaine Godfrey, 'It Was Supposed to Be So Much Worse', *Atlantic Monthly*, 9 January 2021.

3 Spencer S. Hsu, Tom Jackman, and Devlin Barrett, 'Self-Styled Militia Members Planned on Storming the U.S. Capitol Days in Advance of Jan. 6 Attack', *The Washington Post*, 19 January 2021.

4 Carl Campanile and Yaron Steinbuch, 'Rioters Left Feces', *New York Daily News*, NY 8 January 2021.

5 See John Coski, *The Confederate Battle Flag: America's Most Embattled Emblem* (Cambridge: Harvard University Press, 2005).

6 Unlike most highly mythologized anecdotes, the gist of this one at least is likely accurate, as it was recorded by a delegate to the 1787 Constitutional Convention in his notes: 'A lady asked Dr. Franklin Well Doctor what have we got a republic or a monarchy. A republic replied the Doctor if you can keep it.' Quoted in Gillian Brockell, 'A Republic If You Can Keep It', *Washington Post*, 18 December 2019.

7 Brockell, 'A Republic If You Can Keep It'.

8 Quoted in Gary W. Gallagher, Myra MacPherson, and Alan T. Nolan, eds., Introduction, *The Myth of the Lost Cause and Civil War History* (Bloomington: Indiana University Press, 2010), p. 2.

9 An accurate, searchable full text of *Gone with the Wind* is available at https://gutenberg.net.au/ ebooks02/0200161h.html. Page numbers have been omitted here

413

because of the high number of quotations.

10 Quoted in Herbert Aptheker, *American Negro Slave Revolts* (New York: Columbia University Press 1943), p. 15.

11 Toni Morrison, *Playing in the Dark: Whiteness and the Literary Imagination* (Cambridge: Harvard University Press, 1992), p. 49.

12 James Baldwin, 'The White Man's Guilt' in Toni Morrison (ed.), *James Baldwin: Collected Essays* (New York: Literary Classics of the United States Inc., 1998), pp. 722–3.

13 Baldwin, *No Name in the Street*, p. 166.

A Note on Language and Violence

1 Nancy Coleman, 'Why We're Capitalizing Black', *New York Times*, NY, 5 July 2020.

2 In her study of lynching photos, the art historian Dora Apel makes the same argument: 'Despite the residue of sadistic voyeurism they carry, which may feed the appetite for sights of mutilation and degradation, they also powerfully evoke revulsion and outrage, which not only remind us of what horrors people are capable of visiting on each other, but of a specific history that must not be forgotten. Although the photos display the vulnerable black body and risk reproducing the prurient interest and humiliating effect of racist violence, we, as a nation, cannot afford to be innocent of these photos. The loss to historical understanding incurred by refusing to see them would only serve to whitewash the crimes of white supremacy.' See Dora Apel, *Imagery of Lynching: Black Men, White Women, and the Mob* (Rutgers University Press, 2004), p. 2.

Chapter 1

1 Tiffany Hsu, 'Tracking Viral Misinformation', *New York Times*, NY, 24 February 2022.

2 Lois Beckett and Vivian Ho, '"She Was Deep into It": Ashli Babbitt, Killed in Capitol Riot, Was Devoted Conspiracy Theorist', *Guardian*, 9 January 2021.

3 Calvin Woodward, Jay Reeves, and Lisa Mascaro, 'The Unfolding of "Home-Grown Fascism" in Capitol Assault', *Seattle Times, WA*, 10 January 2021.

4 Ryan Webster, 'Fascism Most Searched Word on Merriam-Webster Election Night', *USA Today*, 8 November 2016.

5 'Trending: "Insurrection"', Merriam-Webster Online, www.merriam-webster.com/news-trend-watch/insurrection-20210106

6 See, for example, Clint Smith, 'The Whole Story in a Single Photo', *Atlantic Monthly*, 8 January 2021.

7 Nathanael West, 'Some Notes on Violence', in *Nathanael West: A Collection of Critical Essays*, edited by Jay Martin (Englewood Cliffs, NJ: Prentice-Hall, 1971), p. 50.

8 John P. Diggins, 'Flirtation with Fascism: American Pragmatic Liberals and Mussolini's Italy', *American Historical Review*, vol. 71, no. 2 (Jan. 1966), p. 487.

9 Amanda Minervini, 'Mussolini Speaks: History Reviewed', *Massachusetts Review*, vol. 60, no. 1 (Spring 2019), p. 194.

10 *Brooklyn Daily Eagle*, NY, 13 March 1933.

11 Adam Edelman and Garrett Haake, 'Republican loyal to Trump claims Capitol riot looked more like "normal tourist visit"', NBC News, 12 May 2021.

12 Michael C. Bender, *Frankly, We Did Win This Election: The Inside Story of How Trump Lost* (New York: Twelve, 2021), p. 331.

13 George Orwell, 'The Prevention of Literature', *Polemic*, no. 2 (January 1946).

Chapter 2

1 James Baldwin, Preface to *Notes of a Native Son,* second edition (Boston: Beacon Press, 1984), p. xiv.

2 Ronan Farrow, 'A Pennsylvania Mother's Path to Insurrection', *The New Yorker*, 1 February 2021.

3 *New York Age*, NY, 6 January 1940.

4 Frank Luther Mott, *Golden Multitudes: The Story of Bestsellers in the United States* (New York: Bowker, 1947), p. 258.

5 *Des Moines Register,* IA, 20 February 1939.

6 Frank S. Nugent, 'The Screen in Review', *New York Times*, NY, 20 December 1939.

7 Martie Zad, 'Hattie McDaniel Paved the Way', *Washington Post*, 5 August 2001.

8 'Stepping Inside the Fox Hole: The Media Echo-Chamber of Fox News', *Navigator Research*, 21 March 2019.

9 Darden Asbury Pyron, *Southern Daughter: The Life of Margaret Mitchell* (New York: Oxford University Press 1991), p. 244.

10 *New York Age*, NY, 6 January 1940.

Chapter 3

1 Quoted in Pyron, *Southern Daughter* p. 258.

2 *Atlanta Constitution*, GA, 29 November 1936.

Chapter 4

1 'Blizzard of Black Sweeps Over Kansas', *Charleston Daily Mail,* WV, 17 April 1936.

2 Donald Worster, *Dust Bowl: The Southern Plains in the 1930s* (Oxford: Oxford University Press, 2004), p. 13.

3 *Pittsburgh Courier*, PA, 11 January 1936.

4 *Orlando Sentinel*, FL, 13 October 1936.

5 *Barre Daily Times*, VT, 13 October 1936.

6 *Gettysburg Times*, PA, 3 June 1936.

Chapter 5

1 Pyron, *Southern Daughter*, p. 240.

2 Quoted in Ibid., p. 244.

3 *New York Times*, NY, 30 June 1936.

4 *New Republic*, 16 September 1936, pp. 161–2.

5 *Salt Lake Tribune*, UT, 5 July 1936.

6 *Mail Tribune*, Medford, OR, 16 November 1936.

7 *Oakland Tribune*, CA, 19 July 1936.

8 Robert Quillen, 'Atlanta Should be Proud of Tribute to South', *Atlanta Constitution*, GA, 16 December 1939.

9 *Chattanooga Daily Times*, TN, 5 July 1936.

10 *New York Times*, NY, 30 June 1936.

11 Eleanor Roosevelt, 'My Day', *Oklahoma News*, OK, 22 August 1936.

12 Richard Harwell (ed.), *Margaret Mitchell's Gone with the Wind Letters, 1936–1939*, (London: Collier Macmillan, 1986), p. 162.

13 *Atlanta Constitution*, GA, 8 February 1936.

14 Pyron, *Southern Daughter*, p. 289.

15 Harwell, ed., *Margaret Mitchell's Gone with the Wind Letters*, p. 14.

16 *Daily Oklahoman*, Oklahoma City, 19 July 1936.

17 William Faulkner, 'An Introduction to *The Sound and the Fury*', *Mississippi Quarterly*, vol. 26 (Summer 1973), p. 412.; Malcolm Cowley, 'Going with the Wind', *New Republic*, 16 September 1936.

18 Alice T. Randall, *The Wind Done Gone* (Houghton Mifflin, 2002), Readers Guide.

19 *Chicago Defender*, IL, 13 March 1937.

20 'To a Virginia white woman, the blacks were acting "very independent and impudent", and like most whites she equated the two traits. To slave owners everywhere, the defections were difficult enough to understand but the ways in which some slaves chose to depart invariably provoked the most grievous charge of all – "ingratitude". Few stated it more succinctly than Emily C. Douglas, a resident of Natchez, who had earlier extolled the loyalty of her slaves: "They left without even a good-bye."' See Leon F. Litwack, *Been in the Storm So Long: The Aftermath of Slavery* (New York: Vintage, 1980), p. 144.

21 Litwack, *Been in the Storm So Long*, p. 154.

22 As Eric Foner notes, 'estimates – guesses really' put the total number of escaped slaves anywhere between 30,000 and 150,000 from 1830–1860 alone. See Eric Foner, *Gateway to Freedom: The Hidden History of America's Fugitive Slaves* (Oxford: Oxford University Press, 2015), p. 4.

23 Anderson, Melinda D. '"These are the Facts": Black Educators Silenced from Teaching America's Racist Past', *Guardian*, 14 September 2021.

24 Lillian Smith, 'One More Sigh for the Good Old South', *Pseudopodia*, vol. 1, no. 3 (1936), pp. 6, 15.

25 Ibid.

26 *Atlanta Constitution*, GA, 10 December 1939.

27 Ibid.

28 See, for example, Keri Leigh Merritt, *Masterless Men: Poor Whites and Slavery in the Antebellum South* (Cambridge: Cambridge University Press, 2017).

29 *Sunday News*, Lancaster, PA, 5 July 1936.

30 Hannah Arendt, 'Thinking and Moral Considerations: A Lecture'. *Social Research*, vol. 38, no. 3 (1971), p. 418.

31 *Oakland Tribune*, CA, 19 July 1936.

32 *Oakland Tribune*, CA, 18 May 1930.

33 Lawrence D. Reddick, Review of *Pro-Slavery Thought in the Old South and Gone with the Wind*, in *Journal of Negro History*, vol. 22, no. 3 (1937), p. 365.

34 Matt Stieb, 'Incoming GOP Senator Apparently Doesn't Know Basics of World War II', *New York Magazine*, 12 November 2020.

Chapter 6

1 Pyron, *Southern Daughter*, p. 312.
2 Ibid.
3 Carlton Moss, 'An Open Letter to Mr. Selznick' in Richard Harwell, (ed.), *Gone with the Wind as Book and Film* (Columbia: University of South Carolina Press, 1983), p. 159.
4 *Pittsburgh Courier*, PA, 27 February 1937.
5 *Pittsburgh Post-Gazette*, PA, 10 January 1939.
6 Malcolm Cowley, 'Going with the Wind', *New Republic*, 16 September 1936, p. 162.
7 *Courier-Post*, Camden, NJ, 23 March 1937.
8 *Star Press*, Muncie, IN, 18 July 1937.
9 Harwell, ed., *Margaret Mitchell's Gone with the Wind Letters*, pp. 273–4.
10 Ibid., p. 139.
11 Ibid., p. 273.
12 See Randall L. Kennedy, 'Who Can Say "Nxxxxr?" And Other Considerations', *Journal of Blacks in Higher Education*, no. 26 (1999), pp. 86–96.
13 'The captain was none other than his i--f---l runaway nxxxxr', *Times-Picayune*, New Orleans, LA, 14 February 1859. The debate over the Fugitive Slave law, which was the Civil War's proximate cause, routinely and casually appeared in Southern newspapers (as well as Northern) in terms of 'runaway nxxxxrs', and especially in Kansas,
where the issue came to a head: 'One runaway nxxxxr would bring down on us the whole army of the United States' (*Quindaro Chindowan*, Quindaro, KS, 14 November 1857); 'Missourians... come to Kansas and catch their runaway nxxxxrs' (*White Cloud Kansas Chief*, White Cloud, KS, 6 May 1858); 'Barnum has offered $500 to the runaway nxxxxr Burns' (*Knoxville Standard*, Knoxville, TN, 14 March 1855); 'as soon as the runaway nxxxxrs could be put out of the way' (*Mississippi Free Trader and Natchez Gazette* 27 November 1850), and on and on and on.
14 *Chicago Defender*, IL, 10 December 1938.
15 Ibid., 11 February 1939.
16 Ibid.
17 *Pittsburgh Courier*, PA, 4 February 1939.
18 Harwell (ed.), *Margaret Mitchell's Gone with the Wind Letters*, p. 273.
19 Leonard J. Leff, '*Gone with the Wind* and Hollywood's Racial Politics', *Atlantic Monthly*, 1 December 1999.
20 Quoted in Steve Wilson, *The Making of Gone with the Wind* (Austin: University of Texas Press, 2014), p. 319.
21 Ibid.
22 *New York Age*, NY, 12 February 1938.
23 *Santa Ana Register*, CA, 15 December 1939.

Chapter 7

1 F. Scott Fitzgerald, *A Life in Letters*, Matthew J. Bruccoli and Judith Baughman (eds) (NY: Charles Scribner's Sons, 1994), p. 430.

2 Steven Deyle, 'An "Abominable" New Trade: The Closing of the African Slave Trade and the Changing Patterns of U.S. Political Power, 1808-60'. *William and Mary Quarterly*, vol. 66, no. 4 (2009), p. 842.

3 For more n slavery and the development of American capitalism, see, for example, Sven Beckert and Seth *Slavery's Capitalism: A New History of American Economic Development* (Philadelphia: University of Pennsylvania Press, 2016); Calvin Schermerhorn, *The Business of Slavery and the Rise of American Capitalism, 1815–1860* (New Haven, CT: Yale University Press, 2015);

Edward E. Baptist, *The Half Has Never Been Told: Slavery and the Making of American Capitalism* (New York: Basic Books, 2014); Sven Beckert, *Empire of Cotton: A Global History* (New York: Knopf, 2014); Joshua D. Rothman, *Flush Times and Fever Dreams: A Story of Capitalism and Slavery in the Age of Jackson* (Athens: University of Georgia Press, 2012); and Joseph P. Reidy, *From Slavery to Agrarian Capitalism in the Cotton Plantation South: Central Georgia, 1800–1880* (Chapel Hill: University of North Carolina Press, 1992), among many others.

4 Reprinted in *Brooklyn Evening Star*, NY, 30 August 1862.

Chapter 8

1 Alexander H. Stephens, 'The Corner Stone Speech', 21 March 1861.

2 *Morning Herald*, St Joseph, MO, 6 May 1864.

3 *Daily Selma Reporter*, Selma, AL, 12 September 1863.

4 Abraham Lincoln, 'Second Inaugural Address', 4 March 1865.

5 'Confederate States of America; Georgia Secession', 29 January 1861.

6 This claim, which may still seem counter-intuitive, has been well established by historians of race and slavery. See for example Eric Williams, *Capitalism and Slavery* (Chapel Hill: University of North Carolina Press, 1944): 'slavery was not born of racism: rather, racism was the consequence of slavery'. Edmund S. Morgan discusses 'the social usefulness of racism' and the difficulty before 1660 of 'distinguish[ing] race prejudice from class prejudice' in slaveholding Virginia in *American Slavery,*

American Freedom: The Ordeal of Colonial Virginia (New York: W. W. Norton, 2003), pp. 327–8. W. E. B. Du Bois put it like this: 'The discovery of personal whiteness among the world's peoples is a very modern thing – a nineteenth and twentieth century matter... even up into the eighteenth century we were hammering our national manikins into one, great, Universal Man, with fine frenzy which ignored color and race even more than birth. Today we have changed all that': 'The Souls of White Folk', *Darkwater: Voices from Within the Veil* (Oxford: Oxford University Press [1920], 2007), p. 15. See also Nell Irvin Painter: 'It is still assumed, wrongly, that slavery anywhere in the world must rest on a foundation of racial difference... [whereas] slavery has helped construct concepts of white race', *The History of White People* (New York: W. W. Norton,

2010). Over the nineteenth century, Americans turned the pre-modern Anglo-Saxon peoples of Britain, themselves already a mongrel tribe who had proceeded to further mingle with peoples from all over the world over the next ten or so centuries, into a modern and entirely mythical American racial category. For an overview see Sarah Churchwell, 'White Lies Matter', *Prospect*, 10 July 2020.

7 Quoted in Gary W. Gallagher, *Lee and His Army in Confederate History* (Chapel Hill: University of North Carolina Press, 2001), p. 187.

8 Keith E. Sealing, 'Blood Will Tell: Scientific Racism and the Legal Prohibitions Against Miscegenation', *Michigan Journal of Race and Law*, vol. 5, no. 2 (2000), p. 560.

9 See Don H. Doyle, *The Cause of All Nations: An International History of the American Civil War* (New York: Basic Books 2014), pp. 8–12.

10 Ibid.

11 *New York Times*, NY, 17 November 1861.

12 Charles W. Sanders, Jr, 'Jefferson Davis and the Hampton Roads Peace Conference: "To Secure Peace to the Two Countries"', *Journal of Southern History*, vol. 63, no. 4 (1997), p. 825.

13 R. Jarrod Atchison, *A War of Words: The Rhetorical Leadership of Jefferson Davis* (Tuscaloosa, AL: University of Alabama Press, 2017), p. 92.

14 Stephens, 'The Corner Stone Speech'.

15 Alexander H. Stephens, *Recollections of Alexander H. Stephens: His Diary Kept When a Prisoner at Fort Warren, Boston Harbour, 1865*. Edited by Myrta Lockett Avary. 1910. (Reprint, New York: Da Capo Press, 1971), p. 171.

16 Alexander H. Stephens, *A Constitutional View of the Late War Between the States*, vol. 1 (Philadelphia: National Publishing Co., 1868), p. 10.

17 *Charleston Daily Courier*, SC, 29 October 1856.

18 *Richmond Dispatch*, VA, 21 September 1859.

19 *Philadelphia Inquirer*, PA, 24 March 1863; *Belmont Chronicle*, Saint Clairsville, OH, 5 March 1863.

20 Reprinted in *Wilmington Herald*, Wilmington, NC, 27 December 1865.

21 *Chicago Tribune*, IL, 27 December 1865.

22 *New York Times*, NY, 9 April 1866.

23 *Tarborough Southerner*, Tarboro, NC, 16 June 1866.

24 *Richmond Dispatch*, VA, 9 March 1866.

25 *Public Ledger*, Memphis, TN, 2 July 1866.

26 Edward Pollard, *Southern History of the War* (NY: Charles B. Richardson, 1862,) p. 202.

27 Ibid., original emphasis.

28 *Daily News*, London, UK, 13 January 1865.

29 Pollard, *The Lost Cause: A New Southern History of the War of the Confederates* (New York: E. B. Treat, 1866), p. 44.

30 See Eric Foner, *Reconstruction: America's Unfinished Revolution, 1863–1877*, updated edition (New York: Harper Trade, 2015), p. 269.

31 *Cincinnati Enquirer*, OH, 18 May 1865.

32 Pollard, *The Lost Cause*, p. 750.

Chapter 9

1 *New York Times*, NY, 6 July 1901.

2 Christina Katherine Adkins, 'Slavery and the Civil War in Cultural Memory', Harvard University PhD Dissertation (2014), p. 54.

3 *Chicago Evening Post*, IL, 24 August 1868.

4 C. Vann Woodward, *The Strange Career of Jim Crow* (New York: Oxford University Press, 2002 [1955]), p. 82. For more on how the North's acquiescence to the Lost Cause plot in the name of reconciliation has shaped American popular memory, see, for example, David W. Blight, *Race and Reunion: The Civil War in American Memory* (Cambridge: Harvard University Press, 2001) and Caroline E. Janney, *Remembering the Civil War: Reunion and the Limits of Reconciliation* (Chapel Hill: University of North Carolina Press, 2013).

5 W. E. B. Du Bois, *Black Reconstruction: An Essay Toward a History of the Part Which Black Folk Played in the Attempt to Reconstruct Democracy in America, 1860–1880*, reprint edition (New York: Athenaeum, 1935), pp. 713–14.

6 One widely syndicated review was openly sarcastic: 'Curiously enough, one might read hundreds of histories, even text books, and come out of them with the idea that the Negro had played no role whatever in those bitter times' of Reconstruction, 'or at the most that he was an inarticulate mass which exerted only the force of inertia upon events'. *Morning Chronicle*, Manhattan, KS, 14 June 1935. But this was precisely Du Bois's argument – all the hundreds of histories were biased.

Chapter 10

1 For 'negro politics', see, for example, *Courier-Journal*, Louisville, KY, 20 May 1867. For 'negro supremacy' see e.g. *Ouachita Telegraph*, Monroe, LA, 2 January 1868: 'The white man must rule America… upon every hill top the Conservative clans are building their watchfires'. 'Conservative clan' was an early variant of the Klan: see Bradley D. Proctor, '"The K. K. Alphabet": Secret Communication and Coordination of the Reconstruction-Era Ku Klux Klan in the Carolinas', *Journal of the Civil War Era*, vol. 8, no. 3 (September 2018), p. 468.

2 *Atlanta Constitution*, GA, 31 October 1868.

3 Charles Bethea, 'Georgia Betrays Its Voters Again', *The New Yorker*, 9 June 2020.

4 *New York Age*, NY, 28 May 1932; *Brooklyn Daily Eagle*, NY, 7 June 1932.

Chapter 11

1 See Jacquelyn Dowd Hall, 'The Long Civil Rights Movement and the Political Uses of the Past', *Journal of American History*, vol. 91, no. 4 (March 2005), p. 1242.

2 For more on how segregation shaped the New Deal, see Ira Katznelson, *Fear Itself: The New Deal and the Origins of Our Time* (New York: W. W. Norton, 2013).

3 David Chalmers, *Notes on Writing the History of the Ku Klux Klan* (Gainesville: University Press of Florida, 2013), p. 6.

4 *New York Age*, NY, 26 November 1927.

5 See for example *News Leader*, Staunton, VA, 19 August 1937 and *Corpus Christi Caller-Times*, TX, 25 January 1939.

6 For more on hypodescent, see Christine B. Hickman, 'The Devil and the One Drop Rule: Racial Categories, African Americans, and the U.S. Census', *Michigan Law Review* 95 (1997); Kristin A. Collins, 'Illegitimate Borders: Jus Sanguinis, Citizenship, and the Legal Construction of Race and Nation', *Yale Law Journal*, vol. 123 (2014), pp. 2134–2235; and Carlos Amunátegui Perelló, 'Race and Nation. On Ius Sanguinis and the Origins of a Racist National Perspective', *Fundamina*, vol. 24, no. 2 (2018).

7 Hickman, 'The Devil and the One Drop Rule', p. 1174.

8 Ibid., p. 1187.

9 Ibid.

10 Jones, Martha S. *Birthright Citizens: A History of Race and Rights in Antebellum America* (Cambridge: Cambridge University Press, 2018).

11 Edmund L. Drago, 'Georgia's First Black Voter Registrars during Reconstruction', *Georgia Historical Quarterly*, vol. 78, no. 4 (Winter 1994), p. 770.

12 Ibid, p. 760.

13 Drago, p. 787.

14 'Scholars have often failed to connect the practice of running blacks off their lands with lynching, but both were forms of oppression used by whites to keep blacks "in their place". George C. Wright, *Racial Violence in Kentucky: Lynchings, Mob Rule, and Legal Lynchings* (Baton Rouge: Louisiana State University Press, 1996), p. 10.

15 Mary Church Terrell, 'Lynching from a Negro's Point of View', *North American Review*, vol. 178, no. 571 (1904), p. 861.

16 *Caribou County Sun*, Soda Springs, ID, 8 June 1934.

17 Quoted in Foner, *Reconstruction*, p. 437.

18 Ibid., p. 551.

19 *Mineral Point Weekly Tribune*, WI, 1 October 1874.

20 Ibid.

21 *Chicago Inter-Ocean*, IL, 21 September 1874.

22 Ibid.

23 Ibid.

24 *Republic Magazine*, quoted in *Mineral Point Weekly Tribune*, WI, 1 October 1874.

25 Ibid.

26 See Wikimedia commons.

27 Campbell Robertson and Katy Reckdahl, 'Stories of New Orleans: As Monuments Go Down, Family Histories Emerge', *New York Times*, NY, 24 May 2017.

28 Sanford Levinson, 'They Whisper: Reflections on Flags, Monuments, and State Holidays, and the Construction of Social Meaning in a Multicultural Society', *Chicago-Kent Law Review*, vol. 70, no. 3 (1995), p. 1088.

29 Jessica Owley and Jess Phelps, 'Understanding the Complicated Landscape of Civil War Monuments', *Indiana Law Journal*, vol. 93, no. 5 (2018), p. 19.

Chapter 12

1 *Atlanta Constitution*, GA, 25 June 1892.
2 *Kenosha News*, WI, 11 November 1963. See Heather Cox Richardson, *How the South Won the Civil War:* *Oligarchy, Democracy, and the Continuing Fight for the Soul of America* (Oxford University Press, 2020).

Chapter 13

1 Proctor, '"The K. K. Alphabet", pp. 472–3.
2 Harwell, ed., *Margaret Mitchell's Gone with the Wind Letters*, p. 162.
3 Mya Fraser, 'Stop Using "Officer-Involved Shooting"', *Columbia Journalism Review*, 7 August 2020.
4 Jan Zilinsky, Jonathan Nagler, and Joshua Tucker, 'Which Republicans Are Most Likely to Think the Election Was Stolen? Those Who Dislike Democrats and Don't Mind White Nationalists', *Washington Post*, 19 January 2021.
5 The Trump campaign's allegations of rampant voter fraud have been comprehensively debunked. See, for example, Andrew C. Eggers, Haritz Garro, Justin Grimmer, 'No Evidence for Systematic Voter Fraud: A Guide to Statistical Claims About the 2020 Election', *Proceedings of the National Academy of Sciences*, vol. 118, no. 45 (2021), which assessed 'claims about Dominion voting machines switching votes from Trump to Biden, suspiciously high turnout in Democratic strongholds, and the supposedly inexplicable failure of Biden to win "bellwether counties"'. For an overview, see also the Brennan Center for Justice, 2020, 'The Myth of Voter Fraud': 'Politicians at all levels of government have repeatedly, and falsely, claimed the 2016, 2018, and 2020 elections were marred by large numbers of people voting illegally. However, extensive research reveals that fraud is very rare, voter impersonation is virtually nonexistent, and many instances of alleged fraud are, in fact, mistakes by voters or administrators. The same is true for mail ballots, which are secure and essential to holding a safe election amid the coronavirus pandemic.'
6 'Condition of Affairs in the Southern States', Reports of Committees: 30th Congress, first Session; 48th Congress, second Session, Klan Report, Georgia, vol. 1 (1871), p. 281.
7 *Harrisburg Telegraph*, PA, 11 August 1868.
8 Proctor, '"The K. K. Alphabet", p. 470.
9 *Weekly Standard*, Raleigh, SC, 27 July 1870.
10 A proposal to make election day a federal holiday was called a Democrat 'power grab' by then Senate Majority Leader Mitch McConnell in 2019: '"So this is the Democrats' plan to 'restore democracy,'" McConnell said, describing the legislation as "a political power grab,"' See Felicia Sonmez, 'McConnell says bill that would make Election Day a federal holiday is a "power grab" by Democrats', *Washington Post*, 30 January 2019.

11 Leon F. Litwack, *Been in the Storm So Long: The Aftermath of Slavery* (New York: Vintage, 1980), p. 277.
12 'Condition of Affairs in the Southern States', pp. 22–3.
13 *New National Era*, Washington, DC, 12 October 1871.
14 'Condition of Affairs in the Southern States', p. 1120
15 *New York Daily Herald*, NY, 29 May 1871.
16 W. Fitzhugh Brundage, *Lynchings in the New South: Georgia and Virginia, 1880–1930* (Urbana, IL: University of Illinois Press, 1993), p. 262.
17 Litwack, *Been in the Storm So Long*, p. 277.
18 'Condition of Affairs in the Southern States', p. 1120.
19 Ibid., p. 357.
20 Ibid., p. 431.
21 *Times-Argus*, Selma, AL, 27 September 1872.
22 *Chicago Tribune*, IL, 3 October 1937.
23 Equal Justice Initiative Report, 'Reconstruction in America: Racial Violence after the Civil War, 1865–1876.'
24 Kristofer Allerfeldt, 'The KKK is in Rapid Decline – But Its Symbols Remain Worryingly Potent', *The Conversation,* 1 March 2019.

Chapter 14

1 *Buffalo Commercial*, NY, 13 December 1847; *Buffalo Commercial*, NY, 25 September 1848.
2 *Muscatine Weekly Journal*, WI, 19 October 1860.
3 *M'Arthur Democrat*, McArthur, OH, 1 November 1860.
4 *National Republican*, Washington, DC, 9 August 1875.
5 *Brooklyn Times Union*, NY, 23 May 1870.
6 *Spirit of Jefferson*, Charles Town, WV, 31 May 1870.
7 Proctor, '"The K. K. Alphabet"', pp. 474–475.
8 Ritchie Devon Watson, Jr, *Normans and Saxons: Southern Race Mythology and the Intellectual History of the American Civil War* (Baton Rouge: Louisiana State university Press, 2008).
9 *Pall Mall Gazette*, London, UK, 5 July 1880.
10 *Brattleboro Reformer*, VT, 14 August 1936.
11 *Dothan Eagle*, AL, 24 August 1936.
12 Harwell, ed., *Margaret Mitchell's Gone with the Wind Letters*, p. 32.
13 Ibid., p. 93.
14 Morrison, *Playing in the Dark*, p. 68.
15 Mary T. Schmich, 'Atlanta Giddy Over Scarlett and Rhett's Return', *Chicago Tribune*, IL, 10 December 1989.
16 Ralph Ellison, 'Change the Joke and Slip the Yoke', in Ralph Ellison (ed.), *Shadow and Act*, reprint edition (London: Secker and Warburg, 1967), p. 50.
17 Frank Karimi and Doug Criss, 'Justin Trudeau Isn't the Only One. Here's a List of Politicians Who Got in Trouble Over Blackface', CNN, 20 September 2019.
18 'Negro Treads Kentucky Air', *Chillicothe Gazette*, OH, 10 April 1909; 'Two Negro Murderers Given Short Shrift by an Arkansas Mob', *Los Angeles Herald*, CA, 15 February 1892; 'Negro Murderer Given Short Shrift', *Boston Globe*, MA, 18 May

1900; 'Negro Murderer is Given Short Shrift', *Reading Times*, PA, 21 December 1912.

19 Raleigh *News and Observer*, NC, 20 August 1930.

Chapter 15

1 Ida B. Wells-Barnett, 'Lynching and the Excuse for It', *Independent*, vol. 53, 16 May 1901, pp. 1134.
2 *Daily State Sentinel*, Montgomery, AL, 25 March 1868.
3 *Pittsburgh Weekly Gazette*, PA, 4 September 1868.
4 See, for example, 'Mutilation is Laid to Klansmen: Five Suspects in Cargell Case After Year's Investigation of Florida Terrorism', *Hartford Courant*, CT, 10 April 1936.
5 *Chicago Defender*, IL, 6 January 1940.
6 See the Ku Klux Klan Act of 1871.
7 'State of the Union Interview with Presidential Candidate Donald Trump', CNN, February 28, 2016.
8 Adam Nagourney, 'Reform Bid Said to Be a No-Go for Trump', *New York Times*, NY, 14 February 2000.

Chapter 16

1 *New York Age*, NY, 6 January 1940.
2 Foner, *Reconstruction*, pp. 450–51.
3 Quoted in Foner, *Reconstruction*, p. 116.
4 In 1981, Republican strategist Lee Atwater infamously admitted that the Republicans had a 'Southern Strategy' to break the Democratic hold on the white South, which entailed consciously pandering to, while disavowing, racism. 'You start out in 1954 by saying, "Nxxxxr, nxxxxr, nxxxxr." By 1968 you can't say "nxxxxr" – that hurts you, backfires. So you say stuff like, uh, forced busing, states' rights, and all that stuff... Now, you're talking about cutting taxes... economic things, and a byproduct of them is, blacks get hurt worse than whites... "We want to cut this," is much more abstract than even the busing thing... and a hell of a lot more abstract than "Nxxxxr, nxxxxr."' See Rick Perlstein, 'Exclusive: Lee Atwater's Infamous 1981 Interview on the Southern Strategy', *The Nation*, 13 November 2012. A little over a decade later, Nixon's advisor John Ehrlichman similarly admitted that the 'war on drugs' and 'war on crime' were also racially and politically motivated. See Nkechi Taifa, 'Race, Mass Incarceration, and the Disastrous War on Drugs', Brennan Center for Justice, 10 May 2021. The 'war on poverty' was also racialized: 'much of the so-called war on poverty was... lambasted as a gigantic handout scheme for urban Blacks'. See Tim Wise, *Color Blind: The Rise of Post-Racial Politics and the Retreat from Racial Equity* (San Francisco, CA: City Lights Books, 2010), p. 29.
5 For more on the realignment of Democrats and Republicans over the twentieth century, see, for example, Timothy Galsworthy, 'Carpetbaggers, Confederates, and Richard Nixon: The 1960 Presidential Election, Historical Memory, and the Republican Southern Strategy', *Presidential Studies Quarterly* (2021).

Chapter 17

1 *Pittsburgh Courier*, PA, 27 February 1937.

2 In the 2019 TCM panel discussion ('The Complicated Legacy of *Gone with the Wind*') that HBO Max added to its streaming version of the film as part of its stated effort to correct the story's distortions of history, the chair Donald Bogle describes the incident inaccurately. He first says that in the novel 'it was the Klan that went out to get revenge' and lynch Scarlett's assailants, '*not* the noble Ashley and Frank Kennedy and the others', which is exactly backwards. Bogle strongly implies that Selznick eliminated the Klan entirely from the film, replacing them with Ashley and the others, instead of merely leaving implicit what the novel makes explicit. No one on the panel corrected him or recalled that in the novel the noble Ashley and Frank *are* the members of the Klan – Ashley is its leader – and they are indeed the ones who go to Shantytown on a lynching raid, which is how Frank dies.

All of this was left for an audience member to correctly point out during the Q&A, first without a microphone. When the audio picks her up, she is saying: 'Inferred in the movie is that those people *all* belong to the Klan… I read the book when I was very young, and I believe it's explicit in the book that they belong to the Klan… I read it when I was in elementary school, and I got that. And when I saw the movie: no question… I think there's a huge… I mean, I think we have to *admit* that.' The panellists agree that the novel makes Ashley and Frank's membership of the Klan explicit, but do not otherwise clarify the earlier mistake, or address the question about how to assess a story today in which the heroes are Klansmen. After observing that slavery is often euphemized today in the American heritage industry as 'unpaid labour', the audience member says to the panel: 'I'd like you to address that… Are we being too easy sometimes?' 'It's a good question,' Bogle responds, and then immediately invites 'Another question' from the audience, moving right past the request for direct consideration of the issue.

This rather extraordinary exchange makes the TCM panel yet another good-faith effort to reframe the history that fails to register how outrageous that history really is. This is popular memory in action – authorities who unconsciously reproduce mystifications despite their conscious intentions to the contrary, while the audience member trying valiantly to correct the record but being hurried past becomes emblematic of the cultural amnesia on display – and of the 'complicated legacy' under discussion.

3 See John Kellogg, 'Negro Urban Clusters in the Postbellum South', *Geographical Review*, vol. 67, no. 3 (July 1977), p. 315.

4 H. Paul Thompson, *A Most Stirring and Significant Episode: Religion and the Rise and Fall of Prohibition in Black Atlanta, 1865–1887* (DeKalb, IL: Northern Illinois University Press, 2013), p. 41.

5 Kellogg, 'Negro Urban Clusters', p. 316.

6 *Louisville Daily Courier*, KY, 26 June 1867.

7 Harwell, ed., *Margaret Mitchell's Gone with the Wind Letters*, p. 221.

8 *Indianapolis Star*, IN, 27 January 1936.

9 *New York Times*, NY, 27 August 2016.

10 The first was Chicago. See Nate Silver, 'The Most Diverse Cities Are Often the Most Segregated', FiveThirtyEight, 1 May 2015.

Chapter 18

1 Anne Edwards, *Road to Tara: The Life of Margaret Mitchell* (Lanham, MD: Taylor Trade Publishing, 2014, 1983), p. 53.

2 Karen L. Cox, *Dixie's Daughters: The United Daughters of the Confederacy and the Preservation of Confederate Culture* (Gainesville: University Press of Florida, 2019), p. 50.

3 'Whose Heritage? Public Symbols of the Confederacy', Southern Poverty Law Center, 1 February 2019.

4 'Trump Downplays Insurrection but Tells Supporters to "Go Home"', NPR, 6 January 2021.

5 Dart, Tom, 'Textbook Passage Referring to Slaves as "Workers" Prompts Outcry', *Guardian*, 6 October 2015.

6 Benjamin Wallace-Wells, 'How a Conservative Activist Invented the Conflict Over Critical Race Theory', *The New Yorker*, 18 June 2021.

7 'Florida Board of Education Passes Rule Banning Critical Race Theory in Classrooms', NBC News, 10 June 2021.

8 Anderson, Melinda D., '"These are the Facts"'.

9 'Texan Republican Cancel Culture Targets the Teachings of the Rev. Martin Luther King Jr.', *The Nation*, 21 July 2021.

10 'Trump Calls Critical Race Theory "un-American". Let's Review', *Washington Post*, 2 October 2020.

Chapter 19

1 Ralph Lowell Eckert, *John Brown Gordon: Soldier, Southerner, American* (Baton Rouge, LA: Louisiana State University Press, 1993), p. 13.

2 *Evening Star*, Independence, KS, 25 May 1907.

3 Quoted in Gaines M. Foster, 'A Respect for Confederate History' in Larry M. Logue and Michael Barton (eds), *The Civil War Veteran: A Historical Reader* (New York: New York University Press, 2007), p. 378.

4 Pyron, *Southern Daughter*, p. 10.

5 *Brooklyn Daily Eagle*, NY, 1 September 1906.

6 Pyron, *Southern Daughter*, pp. 31–2.

7 Aimee Ortiz, 'Nikki Haley's Confederate Flag Comments Spark Backlash', *New York Times*, 7 December 2019.

8 Joan E. Greve, 'Trump Would "Not Even Consider" Renaming Bases with Confederate Links', *Guardian*, 10 June 2020.

Chapter 20

1 Quoted in John Hope Franklin, "'Birth of a Nation": Propaganda as History', *Massachusetts Review*, vol. 20, no. 3 (Autumn 1979), p. 424.

2 Andrew Leiter, 'Thomas Dixon, Jr.: Conflicts in History and Literature', *Documenting the American South*, 2004.

3 Karen L. Cox, *Dreaming of Dixie: How the South was Created in American Popular Culture* (Chapel Hill, NC: University of North Carolina Press, 2011), p. 83.

4 Russell Merritt, 'Dixon, Griffith, and the Southern Legend', *Cinema Journal*, vol. 12, no. 1 (Autumn 1972), p. 26.

5 Counties were about five times more likely to experience a lynching or riot during the month in which the film premiered. See Desmond Ang, '*The Birth of a Nation*: Media and Racial Hate', working paper under revision.

6 *New York Tribune*, NY, 14 March 1915.

7 *Boston Globe*, MA, 9 April 1915.

8 *Atlanta Constitution*, GA, 12 December 1915.

9 See Mark E. Benbow, 'Birth of a Quotation: Woodrow Wilson and "Like Writing History with Lightning"', *Journal of the Gilded Age and Progressive Era*, vol. 9, no. 4 (October 2010).

10 Quoted in Michael Rogin, "'The Sword Became a Flashing Vision": D. W. Griffith's *The Birth of a Nation*', *Representations*, vol. 9 (Winter 1985), p. 175.

11 Benbow, 'Birth of a Quotation', p. 523.

12 *Knoxville Sentinel*, TN, 30 November 1915.

13 The chapter from Athens, Georgia, 'boasted two such veteran white supremacists'. Nancy MacLean, *Behind the Mask of Chivalry: The Making of the Second Ku Klux Klan* (Oxford: Oxford University Press, 1994), p. 130.

14 Quoted in Moseley, Charlton, 'Latent Klanism in Georgia, 1890–1915', *Georgia Historical Quarterly*, vol. 56, no. 3, Georgia Historical Society (1972), p. 365.

15 *New York Age*, 2 September 1915.

16 Ibid.

17 *Montgomery Advertiser*, AL, 18 August 1915.

18 *Chicago Tribune*, IL, 3 October 1937.

19 Quoted in Rudy Behlmer, ed., *Memo from David O. Selznick: The Creation of Gone with the Wind and Other Motion Picture Classics, As Revealed in the Producer's Private Letters, Telegrams, Memorandums, and Autobiographical Remarks* (New York: Viking, 1972), p. 162.

20 Thomas R. Pegram, *One Hundred Percent American: The Rebirth and Decline of the Ku Klux Klan in the 1920s* (London: Ivan R. Dee, 2011), p. 7.

Chapter 21

1 Harwell, ed., *Margaret Mitchell's Gone with the Wind Letters*, p. 263.

2 Ibid., p. 30.

3 Francis B. Simkins, 'Review of Stanley F. Horn, *Invisible Empire: The Story of the Ku Klux Klan, 1866–1871*', *Journal of American History*, vol. 26, no. 2 (September 1939), p. 270.

4 Frederick Lewis Allen, *Only Yesterday: An Informal History of the 1920s* (New York: Open Media Publishing, 1931, 2011), p. 65.

5 *New York Times*, NY, 23 April 1939.

6 Pyron, *Southern Daughter*, p. 36.

7 Edwards, *Road to Tara*, p. 78.

8 Moseley, 'Latent Klanism in Georgia', pp. 238–9.

9 *Boston Globe*, MA, 15 May 1921.

10 *St Paul Appeal*, MN, 9 December 1922.

11 *Brooklyn Daily Eagle*, NY, 4 May 1921.

12 *Tampa Times*, FL, 12 December 1922.

13 'Others spoke of it as "American Fascism",' according to Earl R. Beck, who cites an anonymous 1923 article in the Berlin magazine *Die Woche*: '*Amerikanischer Faschismus: Das "unsichtbare Kaiserreich vom Ku Klux Klan"*,' See Beck, 'German Views of Negro Life in the United States, 1919–1933', *Journal of Negro History*, vol. 48, no. 1 (January 1963), p. 23, n. 3.

14 David Chalmers, *Hooded Americanism: The History of the Ku Klux Klan* (Durham: Duke University Press Books, 1987), p. 113.

15 Pyron, *Southern Daughter*, pp. 142–3.

16 Moseley, 'Latent Klanism in Georgia', pp. 246–7.

17 Ibid., p. 247.

18 *Kansas City Sun*, KS, 10 August 1918.

19 *Atlanta Constitution*, GA, 20 May 1918.

20 Manfred Berg, *Popular Justice: A History of Lynching in America* (Lanham, MD: Rowman & Littlefield Publishers, 2015 [2011]), p. 111.

21 See Christopher C. Meyers, '"Killing Them by the Wholesale": A Lynching Rampage in South Georgia', *Georgia Historical Quarterly*, vol. 90, no. 2 (Summer 2006), p. 231.

22 *Chicago Chronicle*, IL, 15 October 1895.

23 *Knoxville Sentinel*, TN, 17 August 1901.

24 *Lawrence Daily Journal*, KS, 2 October 1905.

25 See, for example, *St. Louis Dispatch*, MO, 6 March 1892; *Cincinnati Enquirer*, OH, 29 November 1915; *Warren Times Mirror*, PA, 25 September 1930.

26 *Evening Mail*, Stockton, CA, 7 July 1893.

27 *Bangor Daily Whig and Courier*, ME, 21 June 1869.

28 See for example, Grace Elizabeth Hale, *Making Whiteness: The Culture of Segregation in the South, 1890–1940* (New York: Vintage Books, 1999), pp. 201–3.

29 See Erin Sheley, '"Gone with the Wind" and the Trauma of Lost Sovereignty', *Southern Literary Journal*, vol. 45, no. 2 (Spring 2013), p. 15.

30 *Sedalia Democrat*, MO, 12 July 1897.

31 *St. Louis Globe-Democrat*, MO, 12 July 1897. When Smith was finally captured the mob was held off by armed troops, who tried to transfer Smith to a jail. When the news got out, further lynch mobs formed along the route to 'intercept' Smith. He appears to have avoided being lynched, but contemporary reports were certain that the mobs would have found other victims to satisfy their blood lust. See, for example, *Buffalo Courier*, NY, 16 July 1897.

32 George Schuyler, *Black No More* (London: Olympia Press, [1931] 2007), p. 187.

33 *Clarksdale Press Register*, MS, 28 April 1936.

34 *Miami Herald*, FL, 30 September 1937.

35 Quoted in 'The Rubin Stacy Lynching: Reconstructing Justice', Civil Rights and Restorative Justice Clinic, pp. 15–16.

36 *Atlanta Constitution*, GA, 21 July 1935.

37 Apel, *Imagery of Lynching*, p. 41.

38 *Pittsburgh Courier*, PA, 10 August 1935.

39 Ibid.

40 For more on the complex trade-offs between the New Deal and segregationists, see Katznelson, *Fear Itself*, for example, pp. 14–16, 163–7, 267.

41 Charlotte Klein, 'Tucker Carlson Defends Kenosha Shooter for Just Trying to "Maintain Order"', *Vanity Fair*, 27 August 2020.

42 Walter White, 'An Address by NAACP Executive Secretary Walter White over WNYC', New York Public Radio Archives & Preservation, 20 February 1938.

43 Maya Yang, 'Conservative Event Gives Rittenhouse a Standing Ovation a Month After Acquittal', *Guardian*, 21 December 2021.

Chapter 22

1 Harwell, ed., *Gone with the Wind as Book and Film*, p. 75.

2 Linda M. Perkins, 'The Racial Integration of the Seven Sister Colleges', *Journal of Blacks in Higher Education*, no. 19 (Spring 1998) p. 104.

3 Pyron, *Southern Daughter*, p. 85.

4 Ibid., p. 84.

5 Personal correspondence with Nanci Young, Smith College Archivist: 'Miriam Courtney, Class of 1920; Eunice Hunton, Class of 1921, and Catherine Grigsby, Class of 1922 all took History 11, the course in which Margaret Mitchell was also a student.' Miriam Courtney would have been a junior when Mitchell enrolled, so would not have been in the seminar, although she also ended up in Atlanta, where by 1924 she was teaching psychology and calculus at Atlanta University. See *Smith Alumnae Quarterly*, Northampton, MA, November 1924.

6 *Montclair Times*, NJ, 21 November 1946.

7 For more on Carter, see Marilyn S. Greenwald and Yun Li, *Eunice Hunton Carter: A Lifelong Fight for Social Justice* (NY: Fordham University Press, 2021).

Chapter 23

1 Harwell, ed., *Margaret Mitchell's Gone with the Wind Letters*, p. 68.

2 Ibid, p. 112.

3 Tony Horwitz, *Confederates in the Attic: Dispatches from the Unfinished Civil War* (New York: Vintage, 1999), p. 300.

4 Mart Stewart, 'Teaching *Gone with the Wind* in the Socialist Republic of Vietnam', *Southern Cultures*, vol. 11, no. 3 (Autumn 2005), pp. 17–18.

5 Harwell, ed., *Gone with the Wind as Book and Film*, p. 137.

6 Mitchell's character Dilcey should not be confused with William Faulkner's Dilsey from *The Sound and the Fury* (1929), although readers would be forgiven for doing so.

7 Letter from Thomas Jefferson to John Wayles Eppes, 30 June 1820.

8 Fay A. Yarbrough, 'Power, Perception, and Interracial Sex: Former Slaves Recall a Multiracial South', *Journal of Southern History*, vol. 71, no. 3 (August 2005), pp. 564–5.

9 Bruce Burgett, *Sentimental Bodies: Sex, Gender, and Citizenship in the Early Republic* (Princeton: Princeton University Press, 1998), pp. 148–9.

10 Wendy Anne Warren, '"The Cause of Her Grief": The Rape of a Slave in Early New England', *Journal of American History*, vol. 93, no. 4 (2007), p. 1046.

11 Winthrop Jordan, *White over Black: American Attitudes toward the Negro, 1550–1812* (Chapel Hill: University of North Carolina Press, 1968), p. 155.

12 *Randolph Citizen*, Huntsville, MO, 12 July 1855.

13 'An outrageous rape and murder': *Nashville Union*, TN, 14 June 1854; 'A fiendish outrage': *Weekly Standard*, Raleigh, NC, 16 August 1854; 'Gross and unmentionable proposals': *Baltimore Sun*, MD, 26 August 1839.

14 Eugene Genovese, *Roll, Jordan, Roll: The World the Slaves Made* (New York: Pantheon, 1974), pp. 67–8.

15 See Kimberly Wallace-Sanders, *Mammy: A Century of Race, Gender and Southern Memory* (Ann Arbor: University of Michigan Press, 2008).

16 Molly Haskell says exactly this in the TCM 'Complicated Legacy' panel: 'The slave relationship… it echoed in a way, I mean, much worse, but the male–female, because the men owned the women in the South. They did. And they were terrified of anything, of any kind of women's rights. And I mean she [Scarlett] blasts through all of that.' The assumption that chattel slavery increased patriarchal control is based on famous accounts like that of enslaver Mary Boykin Chesnut, who wrote in 1861, 'there is no slave, after all, like a wife': 'all married women, all children and girls who live in their father's house, are slaves.' For a useful overview, see W. H. Foster, 'Women Slave Owners Face Their Historians: Versions of Maternalism in Atlantic World Slavery', *Patterns of Prejudice*, vol. 41, nos. 3 & 4 (2007), p. 30.

17 See Thavolia Glymph, *Out of the House of Bondage: The Transformation of the Plantation Household* (New York: Cambridge University Press, 2008); and Stephanie Jones-Rogers, *They Were Her Property: White Women as Slave Owners in the American South* (New Haven, CT: Yale University Press, 2020).

18 Jones-Rogers, *They Were Her Property*, pp. 155–6.

19 'White slaveowning women were propertied individuals who were economically invested in the institution of slavery… who had trouble accepting the new economic order of the South not simply because they despised performing labor they associated with slaves or because they yearned for the comforts that an enslaved labor force provided. White women

refused to embrace the new order of things in part because it robbed them of their primary source of wealth.' See Stephanie Jones-Rogers, "'Nobody Couldn't Sell 'em But Her": Slaveowning Women, Mastery, and the Gendered Politics of the Antebellum Slave Market', Rutgers University PhD Dissertation (2012).

Chapter 24

1 See Lisa Tetrault, *The Myth of Seneca Falls: Memory and the Woman's Suffrage Movement, 1848–1898* (Chapel Hill: University of North Carolina Press, 2014); and Rosalyn Terborg-Penn, *African American Women and the Struggle for the Vote, 1850–1920* (Bloomington: Indiana University Press, 1998).

2 See, for example, Chris M. Messer, *The 1921 Tulsa Race Massacre* (London: Palgrave Macmillan, 2021); and Randy Krehbiel, *Tulsa, 1921: Reporting a Massacre* (Norman: University of Oklahoma Press, 2019).

3 *Orlando Evening Reporter Star*, FL, 4 September 1920.

4 The Klan mustered at Ocoee when a dispute broke out after a prosperous African American businessman, who had been turned away from the polls, asserted his right to vote. But as the headline shows, they were organizing ahead of time and intimidating voters. Estimates of the number of victims varies, but for decades African Americans did not return to Ocoee. See Carlee Hoffmann and Claire Strom, 'A Perfect Storm: The Ocoee Riot of 1920', *Florida Historical Quarterly*, vol. 93, no. 1 (2014), pp. 25–43.

5 Henry B. Blackwell, 'What the South Can Do: How the Southern States Can Make Themselves Masters of the Situation' (1867), in Elizabeth Cady Stanton, et al. (eds), *History of Woman Suffrage*, vol. 2 (Rochester, NY: Charles Mann, 1887), pp. 929–30.

6 *Atlanta Constitution*, GA, 25 July 1919.

7 A. Elizabeth Taylor, 'The Last Phase of the Woman Suffrage Movement in Georgia', *The Georgia Historical Quarterly*, vol. 43, no. 1 (March 1959), p. 27.

8 Quoted in Kenneth R. Johnson, 'White Racial Attitudes as a Factor in the Arguments against the Nineteenth Amendment', *Phylon*, vol. 31, no. 1 (1970), p. 33.

9 *Atlanta Constitution*, GA, 25 July 1919.

10 *Tampa Tribune*, FL, 24 March 1918.

11 Taylor, 'Woman Suffrage', p. 18.

12 Johnson, 'White Racial Attitudes', p. 36.

13 Quoted in Elizabeth Gillespie McRae, 'Caretakers of Southern Civilization: Georgia Women and the Anti-Suffrage Campaign, 1914–1920', *Georgia Historical Quarterly*, vol. 82, no. 4 (Winter 1998), p. 812.

14 Taylor, 'Woman Suffrage', p. 25.

15 Ibid., p. 14.

16 Ibid., p. 20.

17 Glenda E. Gilmore, 'Gender and "Origins of the New South"', *Journal of Southern History*, vol. 67, no. 4 (November 2001), p. 776.

18 Patrick Allen (ed.), *Margaret Mitchell Reporter: Journalism by the Author of Gone with the Wind* (Charleston: University of South Carolina Press, 2000), pp. 238–40.

19 Josephine Bone Floyd, 'Rebecca Latimer Felton, Champion of Women's Rights', *Georgia Historical Quarterly*, vol. 30, no. 2 (June 1946), p. 83.
20 *Dayton Herald*, OH, 12 August 1897.

21 *Atlanta Constitution*, GA, 23 April 1899.
22 *Macon Telegraph*, GA, 24 April 1899.
23 Ibid.

Chapter 25

1 Mark Grimsley, *The Hard Hand of War: Union Military Policy Toward Southern Civilians, 1861–1865* (Cambridge: Cambridge University Press, 1995), p. 185.

2 James Baldwin, 'The Dangerous Road Before Martin Luther King', *Harper's Magazine*, February 1961.
3 *Statesville Record and Landmark*, NC, 10 January 1899.

Chapter 26

1 *Dayton Daily News*, OH, 2 March 1940.
2 For example, when in 1907 a New York mob nearly lynched a black man, who was only saved by police intervention, the *Chicago Tribune* found it worth headlining: 'Women Incite Mob to Action' (*Chicago Tribune*, IL, 5 August 1907). A few years later an Ohio paper was equally startled to find 'Women in the Mob' during a riot over anti-saloon laws that led to a detective being lynched (*Cincinnati Enquirer*, OH, 10 July 1910).
3 *Salina Daily Republican-Journal*, KS, 6 December 1899.
4 Church Terrell, 'Lynching from a Negro's Point of View', p. 861.
5 *New York Age*, NY, 5 June 1926.
6 'The Women Facing Charges for January 6, 2021', Anti-Defamation League, 6 April 2021.
7 Cynthia Miller-Idriss, 'Women Are Increasingly Ditching Their

Backstage Role In Right-wing Extremist Movements', MSNBC, 8 January 2022.
8 Paul Schwartzman and Josh Dawsey, 'How Ashli Babbitt went from Capitol Rioter to Trump-embraced "Martyr"', *Washington Post*, 30 July 2021.
9 Kenneth O'Brien, 'Race, Romance, and the Southern Literary Tradition', in *Recasting: Gone with the Wind in American Culture*, Darden A. Pyron (ed.), (Gainseville, University Press of Florida, 1984), p. 163.
10 Pyron, *Southern Daughter*, p. 248.
11 Ibid.
12 Rachel Weiner, 'She Said She Wasn't Going to Jail for Jan. 6, Citing "Blonde Hair, White Skin"', *Washington Post*, 4 November 2021.
13 Andrew McCormick, 'Madness on Capitol Hill', *The Nation*, 7 January 2021.

Chapter 27

1 *Greeley Daily Tribune*, CO, 20 February 1937.

Chapter 28

1 Pyron quotes Alexander Stephens Mitchell describing the whole family as reactionary: 'I don't mean a conservative. We are not conservative. She believed that there are certain principles we've always got to go back to. In any era, until the second coming of the Lord, there will be things that are bad. So you'd better go back and look for the things that were good in the past.' Such as, according to history as told by *Gone with the Wind*, chattel slavery. Pyron, *Southern Daughter*, p. 437.

2 Ibid., p. 441.

3 Ibid., p. 37.

4 Ibid., p. 40.

5 Taylor, Woman Suffrage, p. 18.

6 Pyron, *Southern Daughter*, p. 370; Harwell, ed., *Gone with the Wind Letters*, pp. 249–50.

7 Al Mackey, 'The Extent of Slave Ownership in the United States in 1860', Student of the American Civil War, 18 April 2017.

8 Foner, *Reconstruction*, pp. 512–15.

9 See John David Smith, 'The Enduring Myth of "Forty Acres and a Mule"', *Chronicle Review*, vol. 49, no. 24 (21 February 2003).

Chapter 30

1 *Kansas City Star*, MO, 21 October 1936.

2 *Chicago Defender*, IL, 13 March 1937.

3 Harwell, ed., *Margaret Mitchell's Gone with the Wind Letters*, pp. 25–6.

4 Nazi 'bigotism is contributive to an arrogant nationalism which is a menace to the world... German victory urged as a means of carrying out the biological law of the survival of the fittest': *The Courier*, Waterloo, IA, 12 July 1934. Hitler's attendance at Bayreuth was regularly reported: see, for example, *Hartford Courant*, CT, 5 August 1934. Rumours that Hitler intended to marry Winifred Wagner were circulated across the country, including in the *Atlanta Constitution*, GA, 9 October 1934.

Chapter 31

1 Matthew J. Mancini, 'Race, Economics, and the Abandonment of Convict Leasing', *Journal of Negro History*, vol. 63, no. 4 (October 1978), p. 339.

Chapter 32

1 Mancini, 'Race, Economics', pp. 339–52.

2 While there were clear economic disincentives against killing one's own human capital, it does not follow that killing slaves was rare in absolute terms. American law made a distinction between 'reasonable' and 'excessive' punishment of those in bondage and the legal record makes clear how frequently enslavers beat, mutilated, and tortured their slaves to death with impunity. See Andrew T. Fede,

Homicide Justified: The Legality of Killing Slaves in the United States and the Atlantic World (Athens: University of Georgia Press, 2017). Slave mortality also included suicide and rampant infectious disease.

3 David Oshinsky, *Worse Than Slavery: Parchman Farm and the Ordeal of Jim Crow Justice* (New York: Free Press, 1996), p. 63.

4 Ibid.

5 Sarah Haley, *No Mercy Here: Gender, Punishment, and the Making of Jim Crow Modernity* (Chapel Hill, NC: University of North Carolina Press, 2016), p. 166. See also Talitha LeFlouria, *Chained in Silence: Black Women and Convict Labor in the New South* (Chapel Hill, NC: University of North Carolina Press, 2016).

6 LeFlouria, *Chained in Silence*, pp. 77–8.

7 *Galveston Daily News*, TX, 23 May 1894.

8 Meyers, '"Killing Them by the Wholesale", p. 224.

9 *Baltimore Sun*, MD, 22 June 1937.

10 John Gramlich, 'Black Imprisonment Rate in the US', Pew Research, 6 May 2020.

11 E. Ann Carson, 'Prisoners in 2019', *Bureau of Justice Statistics*, US Department of Justice, October 2020.

12 The black person as 'national scapegoat' 'not only substantiates the audience's belief in the "blackness" of things black, but relieves it, with dreamlike efficiency, of its guilt by accepting the very profit motive that was involved in the designation of the Negro as national scapegoat in the first place'. Ellison, 'Change the Joke', p. 49.

Chapter 33

1 Originally a theological term pertaining to free will, the earliest example the *OED* offers of the American political usage of 'libertarian' is from 1945, and political scientists date the libertarian movement to the early 1950s. However, by the early 1930s it had already emerged as a way to describe both people whose politics were aggressively defined around ideological freedom, such that government limits on the exercise of liberty were said to have been 'denounced by the more extreme sort of libertarians as grossly hypocritical' (*Corsicana Semi-Weekly Light*, TX, 13 February 1931), while the term was used to describe 'a movement for economic freedom' as well as political (*Daily Herald*, Chicago, IL, 1 April 1932).

2 Morrison, *Playing in the Dark*, p. 57.

3 Smith, 'One More Sigh for the Good Old South', pp. 6, 15.

Chapter 34

1 Foner, *Reconstruction*, p. 683.

2 'Trump's Touting of "Racehorse Theory" Tied to Eugenics and Nazis Alarms Jewish Leaders', *Los Angeles Times*, CA, 5 October 2020.

Chapter 35

1 Gavin Lambert, 'The Making of *Gone with the Wind*', *Atlantic Monthly*, February 1973.

2 *Medford Mail Tribune*, OR, 16 November 1936.

3 'She could not desert Tara; she belonged to the red acres far more than they could ever belong to her. Her roots went deep into the blood-colored soil and sucked up life, as did the cotton… [Her ancestors] had not been broken by the crash of empires, the machetes of revolting slaves, war, rebellion, proscription, confiscation… All of those shadowy folks whose blood flowed in her veins seemed to move quietly in the moonlit room.'

4 *Philadelphia Inquirer*, PA, 13 January 1936.

5 *Dayton Daily News*, OH, 15 December 1933.

6 *Miami Herald*, FL, 4 March 1939.

7 Behlmer, ed., *Memo from David O. Selznick*, p. 147.

8 Federico Finchelstein, 'On Fascist Ideology', *Constellations*, vol. 15, no. 3 (September 2008), p. 323.

9 Robert O. Paxton, 'The Five Stages of Fascism', *Journal of Modern History*, vol. 70, no. 1 (1998), p. 5.

10 *Chicago Defender*, IL, 13 March 1937.

11 Quoted by Taulby H. Edmondson, 'The Wind Goes On: *Gone with the Wind* and the Imagined Geographies of the American South', Virginia Polytechnic Institute and State University PhD Dissertation, 2018, p. 49.

12 Quoted in Steve Wilson, *The Making of Gone with the Wind* (Austin: University of Texas Press, 2014), p. 18.

13 Quoted in Helen Taylor, *Gone with the Wind: BFI Film Classics* (London: Bloomsbury Publishing, 2019), p. 81.

14 F. Scott Fitzgerald, *The Letters of F. Scott Fitzgerald*, Andrew Turnbull (ed.), (New York: Penguin Books, 1963), p. 289.

15 Harwell, ed., *Margaret Mitchell's Gone with the Wind Letters*, p. 66; Pyron, *Southern Daughter*, p. 312.

16 Harwell (ed.), *Margaret Mitchell's Gone with the Wind Letters*, p. 233.

17 See Sarah Churchwell, *Behold America, A History of America First and the American Dream* (Bloomsbury, 2018), pp. 235–7.

18 Sarah Churchwell, 'American Fascism: It Has Happened Here', *New York Review of Books*, 22 June 2020.

19 Clare Boothe, 'Introduction to *Kiss the Boys Goodbye*', in Harwell (ed.), *Gone with the Wind as Book and Film* pp. 92–3, original emphasis.

20 Boothe, p. 93, original emphasis.

21 *Miami Herald*, FL, 4 March 1939.

22 Paxton, 'The Five Stages of Fascism', p. 12. See also Richard Steigmann-Gall, 'Star-spangled Fascism: American Interwar Political Extremism in Comparative Perspective', *Social History*, vol. 42, no. 1 (2017), pp. 94–119.

23 Grant, Madison, *The Passing of the Great Race: Or, the Racial Basis of European History* (New York: Charles Scribner's Sons, [1916] 1921), pp. 87, xxxi.

24 For more on Grant, eugenics, and immigration law, see Daniel Okrent, *The Guarded Gate: Bigotry, Eugenics and the Law That Kept Two Generations of Jews, Italians, and Other European Immigrants Out of*

America (New York: Scribner, 2019); and Jonathan Spiro, *Defending the Master Race: Conservation, Eugenics, and the Legacy of Madison Grant* (Lebanon: University Press of New England, 2009).

25 Spiro, *Defending the Master Race,* p. 213.

26 Max Wallace, *The American Axis: Henry Ford, Charles Lindbergh, and the Rise of the Third Reich* (New York: St Martin's, 2003), pp. 2, 68.

27 Hitler sent Madison Grant a letter thanking him for writing *The Passing of the Great Race* and telling him that 'the book is my Bible', while '*Mein Kampf* is riddled with passages that seem directly inspired by *The Passing of the Great Race,* in particular the chapters entitled "Race and People" and "The State", which encapsulate all the aspects of Grant's writings': Spiro, *Defending the Master Race,* p. 357. See also James Whitman, *Hitler's American Model: The United States and the Making of Nazi Race Law*

(Princeton: Princeton University Press, 2017) and Stefan Kühl, *The Nazi Connection: Eugenics, American Racism, and German National Socialism* (Oxford: Oxford University Press, 1994).

28 See Klaus P. Fischer, *Hitler and America* (Philadelphia: University of Pennsylvania Press, 2011), pp. 9, 27–9.

29 Geoff Eley, 'What Is Fascism and Where Does it Come From?', *History Workshop Journal,* vol. 91, no. 1 (Spring 2021), pp. 15–16.

30 Robert O. Paxton, *The Anatomy of Fascism* (New York: Alfred A. Knopf, 2005), p. 218.

31 See Federico Finchelstein, *Fascist Mythologies: The History and Politics of Unreason in Borges, Freud, and Schmitt* (New York: Columbia University Press, 2022).

32 *Pittsburgh Courier,* PA, 12 August 1933.

33 *New York Age,* NY, 29 July 1933.

34 Ibid., 14 October 1933.

Chapter 36

1 Doyle, *The Cause of All Nations,* pp. 8–9.

2 Ibid., p. 301.

3 Isabelle Richet, 'The "Irresponsibility of the Outsider"? American Expatriates and Italian Fascism', *Transatlantica,* vol. 1 (August 2014), p. 3.

4 Richet, 'The "Irresponsibility of the Outsider"?', p. 4.

5 *Richmond Times-Dispatch,* VA, 25 November 1934.

6 *Capital Journal,* Salem, OR, 30 July 1934

7 *Decatur Herald,* IL, 31 December 1933.

8 *Kansas City Star,* MO, 25 February 1934.

9 'Blackshirts v. Blackmen', *Time,* 8 September 1930, np.

10 *Chattanooga News,* TN, 21 August 1930.

11 *Sunday Record,* Columbia SC, 19 October 1930.

12 Lunabelle Wedlock, 'The Reaction of Negro Publications and Organizations to German Anti-Semitism', The Howard University Studies in the Social Sciences, *Graduate School Publications,* vol. 4 (1942), p. 50.

13 *Pittsburgh Courier,* PA, 5 August 1933.

14 Ibid., 24 October 1936.

15 *Napa Journal*, CA, 5 October 1937.

16 S. K. Padover, 'How the Nazis Picture America', *Public Opinion Quarterly*, vol. 3, no. 4 (October 1939), p. 665.

17 Matt Stearns, 'Angry Supremacist Leaves Jury Selection', *Kansas City Star*, MO, 30 January 2001.

18 *Burlington Free Press*, VT, 9 June 1936.

19 *Record*, Hackensack, NJ, 29 January 1936.

20 Langston Hughes, 'Soldiers from Many Lands United in Spanish Fight', *The Afro-American*, December 1937, in *The Collected Works of Langston Hughes, Volume 9: Essays on Art, Race, Politics, and World Affairs*, Christopher De Santis (ed.), (Columbia: University of Missouri Press, 2002), p. 181.

21 *Pittsburgh Sun-Telegraph*, PA, 21 June 1936.

22 Thomas Eliot, 'Review of *The Coming American Fascism* by Lawrence Dennis', *Social Forces*, vol. 16, no. 2 (December 1937), p. 299.

23 *Indianapolis Star*, IN, 3 June 1941.

24 *Time*, 30 September 1940.

25 Quoted in Gerald Horne, *The Color of Fascism: Lawrence Dennis, Racial Passing, and the Rise of Right-wing Extremism in the United States* (New York: New York University Press, 2009), pp. vii, ix.

26 Ibid., p. 90.

27 *New York Times*, NY, 14 July 1936.

28 *Pittsburgh Courier*, PA, 22 July 1933.

29 *New York Times*, 14 July 1936.

30 Quoted in Johnpeter Horst Grill and Robert L. Jenkins, 'The Nazis and the American South in the 1930s: A Mirror Image?', *The Journal of Southern History*, vol. 58, no. 4 (November 1992), p. 685.

31 See Stetson Kennedy, *Southern Exposure: Making the South Safe for Democracy* (New York: Doubleday, 1946), pp. 170–1.

32 *Birmingham News*, AL, 13 October 1933.

33 *News and Observer*, Raleigh, NC, 24 November 1938.

34 Quoted in Grill and Jenkins, 'The Nazis and the American South', p. 686.

35 *Chattanooga News*, TN, 6 December 1938.

36 Quoted in Grill and Jenkins, 'The Nazis and the American South', p. 676.

37 *Saturday Evening Post*, 27 May 1939, pp. 70, 6.

38 *Leader-Telegram*, Eau Claire, WI, 8 June 1939.

39 *Pittsburgh Courier*, PA, 14 October 1939.

40 *Atlanta Constitution*, GA, 14 August 1938.

41 Harwell, ed., *Margaret Mitchell's Gone with the Wind Letters*, p. 221.

42 Ibid., p. 162.

43 *Atlanta Constitution*, GA, 21 August 1936.

44 Quoted in Charles Bullock, Scott Buchanan, and Ronald Keith Gaddie, *The Three Governors Controversy: Skullduggery, Machinations, and the Decline of Georgia's Progressive Politics* (Athens: University of Georgia Press, 2015), pp. 85–6.

Chapter 37

1 *Chicago Defender*, IL, 13 January 1940.
2 *Argus-Leader*, Sioux Falls, SD, 26 November 1939.
3 *Pittsburgh Courier*, PA, 4 February 1939.
4 *New York Age*, NY, 6 January 1940.
5 Quoted in Steve Wilson, *The Making of Gone with the Wind* (Austin: University of Texas Press, 2014), p. 116.
6 *Taylor Daily Press*, TX, 26 January 1940.
7 *Daily Chronicle*, DeKalb, IL, 26 January 1940.
8 Thomas Cripps, *Making Movies Black: The Hollywood Message Movie from World War II to the Civil Rights Era* (New York: Oxford University Press, 1993), p. 23.
9 *Chicago Defender*, IL, 13 January 1940.
10 Ibid., 6 January 1940.
11 *Tampa Times*, FL, 2 September 1940.
12 Peter A. Fritzsche, *An Iron Wind: Europe Under Hitler* (New York: Basic Books, 2016), p. 63.
13 Bruce Clayton, 'Dixie's Daughter: Margaret Mitchell Reconsidered', *Georgia Historical Quarterly*, vol. 76, no. 2, Georgia Historical Society (1992), p. 393.
14 *Daily Oklahoman*, Oklahoma City, OK, 2 September 1941.
15 John Haag, 'Gone with the Wind in Nazi Germany', *Georgia Historical Quarterly*, vol. 73, no. 2 (Summer 1989), p. 282.

16 Ibid., p. 286, his translation and paraphrase.
17 Ibid.
18 Claudia Roth Pierpont, 'A Study in Scarlett', *The New Yorker*, 31 August 1992, p. 101.
19 *Tampa Bay Times*, St Petersburg, FL, 21 September 1941.
20 Haag, 'Gone with the Wind in Nazi Germany', p. 286, his translation and paraphrase.
21 Quoted in William John Niven, *Hitler and Film: The Führer's Hidden Passion* (New Haven: Yale University Press, 2018), p. 151.
22 Quoted in Haag, 'Gone with the Wind in Nazi Germany', pp. 296–7.
23 Ibid., p. 98.
24 *Owensboro Messenger*, KY, 10 December 1944.
25 *Santa Cruz Evening News*, CA, 29 October 1941.
26 Mark Glancy, 'Going to the Pictures: British Cinema and the Second World War', *Past and Future: The Magazine of the Institute of Historical Research*, Issue 8 (October 2010), p. 9.
27 Clark, George R., 'G.W.T.W.', *Harper's Magazine*, vol. 198, no. 1185 (February 1949), pp. 97–8.
28 Harwell, ed., *Margaret Mitchell's Gone with the Wind Letters*, p. 385.
29 *New York Times*, NY, 26 January 1941.
30 *Richmond Times-Dispatch*, VA, 4 May 1941.

Chapter 38

1 *Salinas Index-Journal*, CA, 6 August 1934.
2 Ibid.
3 Erin Blakemore, 'The Story Behind the Famous Little Rock Nine "Scream Image"', History.com, 1 September 2017.

4 Harwell, ed., *Margaret Mitchell's Gone with the Wind Letters*, p. 162.

5 One of the few who did was Morris Schonbach, who treats the plot's failure as contingent rather than pre-ordained in his *Native American Fascism During the 1930s and 1940s: A Study of Its Roots, Its Growth, and Its Decline* (New York: Garland, 1985), pp. 234–6. More recent historians have recognized the similarity of the 'Business Plot' to the Trumpist coalition of business and finance interests with white nationalist politics. See, for example, Bradley Hart, *Hitler's American Friends: The Third Reich's Supporters in the United States* (New York: St. Martin's Press, 2018), pp. 118–20.

6 Robert O. Paxton, 'I've Hesitated to Call Donald Trump a Fascist. Until Now', *Newsweek*, 11 January 2021.

7 Olivia Nuzzi, 'Senior Trump Official: "We Were Wrong, He's a 'Fascist'", *New York Magazine*, 8 January 2021.

8 Donna Cassata and Michael Scherer, 'Trump Drops His Support for Rep. Mo Brooks', *Washington Post*, 23 March 2022.

9 Damon Linker, 'The Intellectual Right Contemplates an "American Caesar"', *The Week*, 28 July 2021.

Chapter 39

1 Godfrey, Mollie. "'They Ain't Human": John Steinbeck, Proletarian Fiction, and the Racial Politics of "The People"', *Modern Fiction Studies*, vol. 59, no. 1, (2013), p. 108.

2 Whittaker Chambers, 'The New Pictures: "The Grapes of Wrath"', *Time*, 12 February 1940, reprinted in Whittaker Chambers, *Ghosts on the Roof: Selected Essays*, Terry Teachout (ed.), (New York: Transaction Publishers, 1996), p. 58.

3 Nathanael West, *The Day of the Locust* (New York: Bantam Books, 1975, 1939), p. 66.

4 Brian Naylor, 'Officers Give Harrowing Testimony on Their Experience Defending the Capitol on Jan. 6', NPR, 27 July 2021.

5 Tucker Carlson, 'Democrats Pushing Unity Through Domination of Their Opponents', Fox News, 15 January 2021.

6 Michael C. Bender, *Frankly, We Did Win This Election: The Inside Story of How Trump Lost* (New York: Twelve, 2021), p. 331.

7 Holmes Lybrand, Hannah Rabinowitz, and Katelyn Polantz, 'Oath Keeper Pleads Guilty to Seditious Conspiracy and Will Cooperate with Justice Department', CNN, 3 March 2022.

Picture Credits

1. Andrew Lichtenstein / Getty Images
2. Nur Photo / Getty Images
3. Saul Loeb / Getty Images
4. Wikimedia Commons
5. Photo Twelve / Getty Images
6. John Kobal Foundation / Getty Images
7. Everett Collection Inc / Alamy Stock Photo
8. New York Public Library
9. Wikimedia Commons
10. John Kobal Foundation / Getty Images
11. Hulton Archive / Getty Images
12. John Kobal Foundation / Getty Images
13. Library of Congress
14. Smith Collection / Gado / Getty Images
15. Courtesy, Georgia Archives, Vanishing Georgia Collection, image number cob831–82
16. Chicago Tribune photos
17. Bettmann / Getty Images
18. Wikimedia Commons
19. Courtesy, Georgia Archives, Vanishing Georgia Collection, image number ful0391
20. LMPC / Getty Images

Index